GREEK HISTORY

GREEK HISTORY

Advisory Editor:

W. R. CONNOR

CHAIRMAN, DEPARTMENT OF CLASSICS
PROFESSOR OF GREEK
PRINCETON UNIVERSITY

Studies in

LAND AND CREDIT
IN ANCIENT ATHENS,

500–200 B.C.

The *Horos*-Inscriptions

Moses I. Finley

NYT

ARNO PRESS
A New York Times Company
New York / 1973

333.3
F513a

Reprint Edition 1973 by Arno Press Inc.

Reprinted from a copy in
  The Wesleyan University Library

Greek History
ISBN for complete set: 0-405-04775-4
See last pages of this volume for titles.

Manufactured in the United States of America

回回回

Library of Congress Cataloging in Publication Data

Finley, Moses I
    Studies in land and credit in ancient Athens,
500-200 B.C.

    (Greek history) *74-8882*
    Reprint of the 1952 ed., which was originally
presented as the author's thesis, Columbia University.
    Bibliography: p.
    1. Real property--Athens. 2. Credit--Athens.
I. Title.
HD134.F5 1973   333.3'3   72-7890
ISBN 0-405-04786-X

Studies in

LAND AND CREDIT IN ANCIENT ATHENS
500—200 B.C.

Studies in

LAND AND CREDIT
IN ANCIENT ATHENS,

500–200 B.C.

The *Horos*-Inscriptions

Moses I. Finley

RUTGERS UNIVERSITY PRESS

New Brunswick · New Jersey

PRINTED IN GERMANY AT J. J. AUGUSTIN, GLÜCKSTADT

To

MY FATHER AND MOTHER

PREFACE

While working on problems of money and credit, planned as the opening section of a book on business practices in the Greek cities, I soon felt the lack of a systematic modern account of the guaranty aspects of credit, apart from purely juristic studies (chiefly German) of the law of security. Since security is the external link between land, the basic form of wealth in the Greek economy, and credit, a full examination of this bond appeared essential as a prelude to the larger work on business practices. The social and economic aspects of land-credit relationships, in particular, seemed to require consideration alongside the juristic. Ultimately, I found it necessary, for reasons of substance as well as the limitations of space, to narrow the field once again, this time to the city of Athens.

This book is intended as the first of several volumes which will eventually embrace the whole of the city-state world and which will examine many questions that have been excluded or merely skimmed in the present volume. The most important subject left for later consideration in detail is the law of creditors' rights. That delimitation of the field, in turn, has prevented my attempting a final synthesis of the social, economic, and juristic aspects of security obligations. Otherwise, I have tried to be as thorough as I could. The outward forms of the transactions, the legal instruments, the kinds of real property customarily used to guarantee debts, and the parties engaging in these transactions, both individuals and groups, have been studied as fully as the sources permit. The guiding methodological principle is a dual one: concentration on the basic patterns of economic behavior, rather than on the exceptional instances, and consideration of the whole range of literary and epigraphical documents, of the "negative" evidence as well as the "positive."

Although I have not hesitated to turn to non-Athenian materials on occasion for clues and analogies, I have rigidly followed the rule of drawing no conclusions from any but Athenian sources. I have done so out of a growing conviction that the generally accepted notion that there was one legal system common to all the Greek cities is a working hypothesis at best. Only by a precise analysis of single institutions in individual cities can the hypothesis be tested properly. If I am able to follow this volume with similar studies, necessarily smaller in scale because of the more limited sources, of other important Greek communities, perhaps a firm basis can be laid for a decisive examination of the unity (or disunity) of Greek law in the field of security.

Above all, I have deliberately avoided Ptolemaic and Seleucid materials, in which the institutions of Greece and the ancient Orient are amalgamated. Since the publication of Ludwig Mitteis' *Reichsrecht und Volksrecht* in 1891, it has been assumed with increasing frequency and assurance that one may draw upon any document written in Greek, regardless of time or place, in a study of "Greek" institutions. Little attention seems to have been given to Mitteis' own warning, written in 1909: "Indeed, there is also the danger that we may carry too much over from the papyri to ancient Greek law, that is to say, that we date back to ancient Greek law phenomena from the papyri of the imperial era, which are the products of a later development. Further, in using such later sources, we must always reckon with the possibility of local or temporary legal variations." I should prefer an even sharper statement of the danger. And nowhere is the need for careful distinction more acute than in the field of land economics, the touchstone of the royal economies of the Ptolemies and the Seleucids. The land regimes and the political structures of Egypt, Ptolemaic and Roman, and of Athens (and the Greek cities generally) being as different as they were in their very essence, land-credit relationships in the one cannot be studied directly from the documents of the other, even though the Greek conquest unquestionably influenced and molded the institutions of Egypt to a substantial degree.

In point of time, no attempt will be made to penetrate the age before the earliest written Athenian texts. For all practical purposes, the starting point is 500 or even 450 B.C. The question of where to end is more difficult, for again we are face to face with a broad generalization commonly accepted by historians, namely, the existence of a qualitative difference in economy between the classical and the Hellenistic Greek cities. It is my belief that city-state economic practices were scarcely touched by the political struggles, wars, and machinations set into motion by and against Philip of Macedon. Athens may have had its ups and downs, Alexander's looting of the Persian gold stocks may have driven the price of gold downward, and the rule of the *demos* may have given way to King's agents and adventurers, but the basic ways of economic life did not change in essentials. This study, then, goes down to 200 B.C., in round numbers, when Rome and the Romans moved into the Greek world.

It is pleasant to acknowledge the help I have received from various sources. Professor John Day of Columbia University was unsparing of his time, to my great advantage, in discussing many questions that arose in the course of the work and in reading and rereading the manuscript. Dr. Adolph Berger of the École Libre des Hautes Études of New York was most helpful whenever juristic problems needed clarification. Professor Edward Rosen of The City College of New York has been an able critic. A fellowship from the American Council of Learned Societies gave me much needed leisure for the preliminary research. The Research Council of Rutgers University has been very generous in its assistance, especially in making possible publication of the volume. The resources of the Columbia University Library have been invaluable, the courtesy of its staff unfailing.

Above all, I owe a debt to Professor William Linn Westermann of Columbia, who long ago introduced me to the study of the ancient world and who has remained a source of inspiration and wisdom; and to Professor A. Arthur Schiller of the Columbia School of Law, who gave me my first realization of the proper place of legal studies in the field of history and who has been a rare guide and mentor ever since.

August, 1951   m.i.f.

TABLE OF CONTENTS

STUDIES IN LAND AND CREDIT IN
ANCIENT ATHENS, 500—200 B.C.

CHAPTER I

INTRODUCTION

THE FORTY-SECOND ORATION IN the Demosthenic corpus was prepared for a plaintiff whose name we do not know, in a case growing out of the *antidosis* procedure. This was a formal judicial proceeding available to an Athenian seeking exemption from a liturgy on the ground that someone else had greater wealth and ought to assume the quasi-tax instead. To bring about an evaluation of the respective property holdings, the man who wished to pass the burden to another challenged the latter either to take over the liturgy or to accept an exchange of property, hence the term *antidosis*. If the latter refused, a formal adjudication took place.[1] The basic requirement was then an accurate inventory showing the value and legal condition of the holdings of the two contesting parties. Since each one naturally tried to undervalue his own wealth and overvalue his opponent's, the first thing the plaintiff did, he tells us, was to visit the estate of the defendant Phainippos on the border of Attica, in the company of some friends.

"Making the circuit of the farm," he continues, "which was more than 40 stades around (perhaps 1,000 acres), I showed them and asked them to bear witness, in the presence of Phainippos, that there was not a single *horos* on the estate. I instructed Phainippos, if he said there were any, to speak up and show them, so that later no debt should turn up there."[2]

When the issue was subsequently joined, Phainippos claimed that he had several outstanding debts and he sought to have them deducted in order to arrive at the actual value of his property. The plaintiff insisted they were fictitious. In the course of his demonstration, he turned to the defendant with the rhetorical question: "How is it, Phainippos, that when I asked you in the presence of witnesses if you owed anything on the farm and instructed you to show any *horos* that was on it," you did not reveal any of these debts?[3]

The basic meaning of the word *horos* in Greek is "limit," "boundary," "definition." By an easy figure of speech the same word was applied to the object that marked a boundary. These markers are known to us from all periods and all regions of the ancient Greek world: slabs of marble, limestone, volcanic rock, or other available stone driven into the ground at appropriate spots. They were used for private estates, city limits, state boundaries, temple and cult properties, and graves. The visible half might be entirely blank; but most often it was engraved either with the single word *horos* or with an additional word or phrase naming the god of a temple or giving some equally distinctive bit of information. The quality of the stone used, the extent to which it was dressed, and the accuracy and artistry of the stonecutting ranged from an obviously amateurish job done by some peasant to professional work comparable with the best of the Greek steles.

Several hundreds of these boundary-stones have been found, singly, in pairs and even triplets. A glance at the indices of the *Inscriptiones Graecae* reveals their widespread and continuous use from the fifth century B.C. to late in the Roman Empire. Frequent reference is also made to them in contemporary legal and adminis-trative texts.[4] In a Chian decree of the late fifth century B.C., for example, orders are given that a certain area, the site of properties confiscated by the state, is to be marked off by 75 *horoi*. The decree goes on to levy the severe penalty of a 100-stater fine and loss of civil rights against anyone who removes or displaces one of the stones. Responsibility for supervision is placed in the hands of special officials called, in the Ionic dialect, *ourophylakes* (guardians of the *horoi*).[5]

At some point, the Athenians found a second use for the *horoi*. It is this kind of *horos* that the plaintiff was looking for on Phainippos' estate, a stone serving to make public the fact that a particular piece of property was legally encumbered and hence in a certain sense not fully at the disposal of the proprietor. Here it was economic and legal status that was important, not geography, and therefore not the location of the stone but the text inscribed on its face. In very simple form, we have the following from a block of Hymettian marble (no. 7) found within the city: "*Horos* of a workshop hypothe-cated, 750 (drachmas)" — in the Greek, just three words and a numeral.[6] And rarely do the inscriptions become much wordier or very much more complex. A fair sample of the "average" *horos* would be this one (no. 6) from Eleusis, set up in 291/0 B.C.: "In the archonship of Aristonymos. *Horos* of the house hypothecated to Nausistratos of Eleusis, 200 (drachmas), according to the agreement deposited with Theodoros of Oinoe."

In the case of land, there was nothing to prevent the same stone from serving both purposes at once, to mark boundaries as well as legal encumbrance. When Phainippos' adversary underscored the 40-stade hike he and his friends took around the farm, he was saying to the jurors: What an enormous estate that was! His rhetoric would have been pointless, however, if the familiar legal *horoi* were never to be found on the boundaries of the property but only at the entrance to the house. In the literary sources, the word *horoi* regularly appears in the plural. The Phainippos oration presents an exception, and again it is the speaker's seeking after the proper effect on the jury that provides the explanation. I found *not a single horos*, he says with unmistakable emphasis.

The *horos*-stones themselves invariably open with the word *horos* in the singular, even in the not infrequent cases in which they mark the encumbrance of more than one piece of property.[7] Probably the same stones were sometimes used to mark boundaries and a legal charge simultaneously, in which event there would be several on the property, and at other times *horoi* were used for one or the other purpose alone.[8] For houses, of course, the single *horos* would suffice, whether driven into the ground or placed in a wall.[9]

Legal encumbrance, it must be remembered, was not the only reason for using boundary-stones for explicit public notice. Thus, the following text was found identically worded on each of a pair of boundary-stones from a rural district of Attica: "*Horos* of the land of the fraternity of the Eikadeis. No one is to make any loan whatsoever on this land."[10]

The important point is that, whether the legal *horoi* were merged with the boundary-stones in any given case or not, the two functions of the stone were quite distinct. Whenever a Greek referred to a stone of either type, he said simply *horos*, without any qualifying adjective (or he used the related verb, *horizo*), because there could be no confusion between the two in context, just as there was no confusion between *horos* as "boundary" and *horos* as "boundary-stone."[11]

Many modern editors and commentators have unfortunately clung to the name and external appearance, divorced from content and purpose, and have persisted in combining both types into the one category of boundary-stones.[12] It is not difficult to reject the translation of *horos* as "boundary-stone" but it is not easy to find an adequate and reasonably simple English substitute. "Hypothecation-stone" is cumbersome and not particularly clear. Since precise clarification of the legal situation is involved in the translation, I shall continue to write *horos* (always to be understood as the stone marking legal encumbrance unless otherwise indicated).[13]

The total number of texts thus far published as *horoi* is 182,[14] but 28 are so doubtful in character or content that I have excluded them from the analysis except in special instances.[15] Of the 154 that remain as the working base of the present study, six were found in Amorgos, nine in Lemnos, two in Naxos, one in Skyros, and the remainder in Attica. That archaeologists have not found a single *horos* of the type with which we are concerned, or a reference to one, anywhere else in the Greek world can no longer be considered mere accident. The *horoi* were a specifically Athenian phenomenon, as Harpocration and Suidas say explicitly.[16] From Athens they spread only to some of the Aegean islands, over all but one of which Athens held direct administrative control at certain periods. How systematically this use of *horoi* was extended within the Athenian sphere and whether it was imposed more or less forcibly by the Athenians are interesting problems for the history of Greek law and interstate relations. One significant clue appears in the Lemnian *horoi*, where the parties specified almost always have Athenian demotics. Here at least it was clearly the cleruchs who introduced the use of *horoi*. But the relatively large number of such stones from Amorgos must have some other explanation, since there is no evidence of the existence of an Athenian colony on that island at any time.[17]

There was presumably strong resistance to the *horoi*, for not all the communities influenced by Athens, not even all those which had received cleruchies, seem to have adopted the institution. Not a single *horos* has been found in Euboea, or in Delos or Samos, for example, where fourth-century Athenian rule was of particularly long duration. Nor are any known from Priene, though that city was very much under Athenian legal and constitutional influence in the last third of the fourth century B.C., precisely when the *horoi* seem to have been most common.[18] Hypothecation of land and houses was of course universal in Greece; only the *horos*-technique of public notice remained strictly localized. Why that should have happened is, I think, not answerable today. Nor is it too important; legal security is basic, the *horoi* merely a device. Other cities had other methods of achieving the same limited purpose of giving publicity to the fact that a farm or a house had charges against it.

Only nineteen of the published Attic *horoi* are dated.[19] The earliest date we can fix is 363/2 B.C., the latest between 267 and

259 B.C. For the rest, the dating problem is most difficult. Many of the stones are rough-picked and even the surface prepared for the writing is not always well smoothed off. The spelling is poor, stone-cutting errors frequent and form inconsistent; the terminology, on the other hand, is uncommonly rigid in its consistency. As a result, the various tests that enable epigraphists to date many Greek inscriptions within twenty or thirty years, and on occasion even more closely, are here not as reliable as usual. It seems agreed that no extant Attic *horos* can be placed with any certainty before the beginning of the fourth century B.C.[20]

The earliest firm reference in a classical Greek author appears in a speech by Isaeus written in 365/3 B.C.[21] A lost oration of Lysias, prepared in a case against the Socratic philosopher Aeschines, seems also to have dealt with *horoi*,[22] but then we must go back nearly two centuries for another reference, to the famous and endlessly disputed lines of Solon, "dark earth, whose *horoi* affixed in many places I once removed; once she was a slave, now free."[23] None of this is conclusive proof that the use of *horoi* began in Athens (or was resumed) around 400 B.C. and not earlier. All that we can say is that we have indisputable documentation of their existence from about 400 to about 250 B.C.[24] Within that period of a century and a half, neither a distribution curve nor a correlated analysis of content and chronology seems at all possible.

A different and somewhat perplexing picture is revealed by the eighteen *horoi* from the Aegean islands. Eight are certainly dated and one other probably, though the condition of that stone leaves some margin for doubt. No. 9 adds the name of the month, a practice unparalleled in Athens.[25] With two exceptions, all are fixed by their editors, by the usual epigraphic tests, as either at the end of the fourth century B.C. or in the third, chiefly in the first half. This is a narrow time span and indicates a relatively late date of introduction. Two Lemnian *horoi* recently published are dated by the editor in the fifth century B.C. If this dating is correct, we must assume the absence of any fifth-century Athenian *horoi* to be the result either of chance or of the fallibility of epigraphical analysis, as already indicated.[26]

Though the *horoi* have been known to historians and given some consideration at least since Augustus Boeckh early in the nineteenth century, they have been treated casually and incidentally. The approach has always been to start with the literary sources, especially the orators, and to spice the discussion with an occasional comment or argument drawn from one of the longer and more detailed *horoi*. The justification given for this method has been that no *horos* offers substantial information.[27] But the irony is that the few *horoi* that do say a little more than the average confuse more than they illumine. After all, the function of the *horoi* was to give public notice of the legal condition of a piece of property, and they served their purpose completely by the proper choice of two or three key words that made the situation fully intelligible to the Athenians. Unfortunately, in the imperfect state of our knowledge of Greek law and even of many social and economic institutions, these same two or three words raise more problems for us than they solve. It is no wonder, then, that the longer *horoi* have found almost as many interpretations as interpreters.

It would be absurd to deny that taken individually the uncomplicated *horoi* are not very helpful. What I propose to do is to take them in a body, to treat them as a statistical series, so to speak, rather than emphasize the individual texts. Approached in that way, the *horoi* offer clues and insights not available from any other source.

Three distinct terms for security appear on the *horoi*: *hypotheke*, *prasis epi lysei*, and *apotimema*. The last-named, in turn, falls into two categories which I shall designate, for purposes of convenience, as the dotal type (in which the property serves to guarantee the return of a dowry) and the pupillary type (in which the property acts as security for the return of the estate of an orphan given out on lease for the duration of the child's minority). It is a reasonable hypothesis that the Athenians had some purpose in maintaining this terminological distinction, and I have therefore clung to it throughout. At the same time, I should indicate that I am by no means convinced that the distinctions were very sharp in the fourth and third centuries B.C. I find in the sources definite indications that the three types (that is, the uses of the three basic terms) tended to merge into each other, that the Greeks here, as throughout their legal activity, lacked the juristic formalism and dogmatism, and the professional jurists, necessary to refine and preserve the subtle lines of distinction and classification, the *elegantia iuris*, characteristic of Roman and modern law.[28] Here and there in the present volume, some of these indications will be noted. But since the conception I have indicated is still a rather tentative one, I shall retain the distinction among the three terms quite rigorously throughout the book.

The translation of *hypotheke*, *prasis epi lysei*, and *apotimema*, of course, depends on the interpretation of the institutions they name.

Further, it requires the assumption of the existence in another society of closely comparable if not identical institutions. In modern jurisprudence, various forms of real security are distinguished according to the nature and extent of the rights granted the creditor under the agreement.[29] Repeated attempts have been made to apply similar categories, even though somewhat modified, to the forms of security in the Greek cities. In my judgment, the effort is foredoomed to failure first because the total juristic situation in the two worlds is not comparable, second because such a procedure almost inevitably destroys important differences in shading and emphasis, and third because we simply do not know enough about creditors' rights in Greek security to achieve valid results. I shall therefore retain the Greek wording, though when the context does not require precise differentiation, "security," "encumbrance," and even "hypothecation" (though it is frankly jargon in English) will serve as generic words for the forms of security represented by all three Greek terms.[30]

Above all, the word "mortgage" is to be avoided. In its long historical development, and even to a substantial degree in our own day, the mortgage is a peculiarly Anglo-American instrument, inseparable from the basic notions of equity, and particularly the equitable estate and the trust. To identify the mortgage with ancient Greek institutions, whatever similarities there may be, is to confuse and ignore essential differences in legal thinking and economic context and to evoke by association totally erroneous notions of what happened in Athens when one man borrowed from another and offered his house or land as security.[31]

CHAPTER II

THE FUNCTION OF THE *HOROI*

I. POSSESSION OF THE PROPERTY

WITH BUT FOUR EXCEPTIONS, the *horoi* give no explicit indication of the current possessor of the encumbered property, that is, whether the debtor or the creditor occupies the land or house during the term of the obligation. The stones offer powerful implicit evidence, however, fully supported by the literary sources, that the setting up of *horoi* was a regular practice precisely because the owner-debtor remained in physical possession of his holding while it served as guaranty of a debt.[1]

Of the Attic *horoi*, the majority name the creditor or creditors, not one names the owner-debtor.[2] Such a contrast is intelligible only if the person named is not the occupant. So long as the owner remains in possession, it is unnecessary to inform his neighbors that the property is his; it is sufficient, for reasons to be discussed, to publicize the fact that there is a charge against it. Usually the claimant was identified, though not always. If the creditor were to move in, the fact of his possession would be known soon enough; the stone would then have to indicate that the new possessor was there only as creditor, and who the actual owner was.

In the *apotimema* type of obligation, retention of possession on the part of the debtor is inherent in the very nature of the transaction.[3] Yet there is absolutely no distinction to be noted in the language of the *horoi* to separate the *apotimema*, in this respect, from the *hypotheke* or the *prasis epi lysei*. Since in the two latter types transfer of possession to the creditor cannot be excluded a priori, the identity in language offers another argument that where there were *horoi*, the owner-debtors remained in occupancy.

The Amorgian *horoi* read quite differently. Five of the six name the debtor as well as the creditor and the sixth (no. 155) is not properly an exception because it is a hybrid, half-*horos* and half-dedication. It should not therefore be concluded, however, that in

10

Amorgos possession was treated differently from Athens in fact or in law. Of the other island *horoi*, only no. 105, a fifth-century Lemnian stone, names the debtor. Now Amorgos alone of the islands on which *horoi* have been found was never the site of Athenian cleruchies. Whereas the use of *horoi* in Lemnos, Skyros, and Naxos can be attributed to Athenian settlers, in Amorgos it was a "borrowed" institution. We find in the Amorgian *horoi* a tendency to spell out the transaction in some detail, as if to make up by greater explicitness for the lack of familiarity with an "alien" institution. The addition of the debtor's name to the inscription on the *horoi* seems to me to be nothing more than that.[4]

The literary evidence serves to underscore the implications of the *horoi* beyond any reasonable doubt. It is hardly necessary to continue beyond the Phainippos case. His opponent toured Phainippos' estate, in the company of witnesses, to search for *horoi* indicating charges against the land. That Phainippos was in possession is clear. Had his adversary found *horoi*, they would either have named no one or have given the name of a creditor, not of Phainippos himself, as we know from the extant stones. If occupancy by the creditor were customary, then the whole expedition, not to mention the impassioned rhetoric before the jury, would have been absurd. Phainippos' mere presence on his own estate would have established the absence of any charges on the land.[5] Then there is the Spudias case, the heart of which is the plaintiff's contention that he was being denied access to a house which was his, by right of ownership, in lieu of 1,000 drachmas (the unpaid portion of his wife's dowry). *Horoi* had been affixed to the house by his father-in-law as a sign that the house would serve to guarantee the obligation by *apotimema*. Yet not only did he not have or claim possession before, he could not even gain it after the debt fell due.[6]

While Demosthenes was embroiled in his efforts to recover some of the fortune embezzled by his guardians, he was trapped, he claims, in an *antidosis* challenge which, had he accepted it, would have deprived him of the right to sue Aphobos and the others. He escaped the trap by accepting the trierarchy despite his slender means and he borrowed 2,000 drachmas for the purpose on the security of his property (a house primarily). This house he continued to inhabit.[7] A few years later Pasion's son Apollodoros hypothecated a farm to meet trierarchy expenses (this is but one of the security obligations involved in the case) and he too retained

possession, for he complains that the farm was not productive that
year because of a drought.[8]

Finally, there is the accusation Apollodoros makes against
Timotheos. His property being fully burdened with charges, says
Apollodoros, the general sought to defraud his creditors by removing
the *horoi*.[9] Whether he did or not and how effective a technique that
may have been are questions that need not concern us here. Obviously it would have been useless to remove *horoi* from property
which the creditors were already occupying. That is the one conclusion that can be drawn with certainty from Apollodoros' statement.[10]

The prevailing practice in Athens, then, the rule in fact, was
retention of possession by the debtor in all types of hypothecation
until the debt was paid or until the creditor was able to take over the
property because of default. (This rule applies only to real property;
movables were normally transferred to the creditor for the term of
the obligation.) For a variety of reasons there might be an exception
from time to time by agreement of the parties. Three *horoi*, nos. 1
and 2 from Attica and no. 10 from Lemnos, contain the phrase, on
condition that "the creditor have and have power" (sometimes
translated, erroneously, "possess and own").[11] All three, furthermore, read immediately following, "according to the agreement
deposited with" an individual who is named. Reference to a written
agreement appears on but fourteen of the *horoi* altogether. That all
three with which we are now dealing fall within that group is strong
confirmation of the view, which must follow from the "have and
have power" clause in any event, that these *horoi* marked exceptional instances. For reasons we cannot possibly discover, the parties
agreed, when the contract was drawn up fixing security for an
obligation, that the creditor would occupy the premises until the
debt was liquidated.[12] Isocrates tells us that when a certain Nikias
was threatened by the Thirty Tyrants, he sent his slaves out of the
country, deposited his personal belongings and money with friends,
hypothecated his house, and went to live on his farm. Clearly this
transaction, if true, involved transfer of possession, but under
circumstances so atypical as to render the whole incident of no
general evidentiary value.[13]

In the final analysis, the question of possession is a matter of
economic considerations. To Isocrates' client, who had a country
residence and land to which to withdraw, the menace to his life and
property was paramount. Since a house, unlike money and slaves,

cannot be deposited with someone for safekeeping, he resorted to the legal device of hypothecation, obviously fictitious in fact if not in form. But in the usual case, the need of money was the motive, not protection from political tyranny. If a man derived his livelihood, in whole or in substantial part, from his land, surrender of the use and products of the land would be ruinous. Such a procedure is well known in the early history of many societies; its abandonment has been called a substantial victory for the debtor class.[14] In Athens in the period under investigation, whatever the earlier practice, the men on whose property the *horoi* stood retained possession, together with the rights to the profits and fruits, for the life of the obligation. Whether or not this fact may be interpreted as a parallel to the development in England, for example, depends on whether the owners of the land may properly be categorized as a "debtor class" in the customary sense of that term. An examination of the people involved seems to require a negative answer.[15]

2. PUBLIC NOTICE

In all types of society, land (and to a lesser extent realty generally) is a category apart from all other forms of property. By its very nature, above all its permanence, land has attributes and gives rise to considerations not shared by slaves or money or chattels. One result is the special importance attached to proper public records and public knowledge of the legal and economic condition of the land at any given moment. Publicity has a dual aspect here, from the standpoint of the community and from the standpoint of its individual members. The state's interest is fiscal and, wherever there are property qualifications for officeholding or military service or any other public activity, it is also political and administrative. Indirectly every citizen shares these interests, insofar as he is concerned with the maintenance of political inequalities or with the effective and equitable (however the given community conceives that notion) collection of taxes. Beyond that, he has a juristic concern. Once the alienability of land is recognized, he wishes to know who is the actual owner of a given parcel, servitudes and other rights that may be attached to it, and the presence or absence of special charges (hypothecation).

The character of public land records and the forms of public notice are a valuable index of the size and complexity of a community and of the level of its economy and its law. The range is a

wide one, from primitive reliance upon the knowledge of the
neighbors, kept up-to-date by various requirements of public ritual
whenever land was conveyed, to the elaborate network of title and
deed registers in the modern world.[16] With rare exceptions, the
Greek city-states stood much nearer the primitive than the modern.
Public record-keeping in Greece was generally spasmodic, imper-
manent, and unreliable.[17] Land records were no exception, in
marked contrast to the practice of the Hellenistic empires of the
Ptolemies and Seleucids or of the Romans.

Athens, it must be added at once, was quite typical of the Greek
cities in this respect. The roster of citizens was kept separately in
each deme and occasional purges were necessary to correct the
records and remove men who had entered the ranks of the citizens
illegally.[18] Of a roster of landed properties there is not a trace.[19]
The *eisphora* and the liturgies were paid on the basis of the individual's own declaration, the *timema*.[20] The controls exercised on him
to make a full and honest declaration did not come from government officials or documents. In part there were the social pressures
of a relatively small community in which ownership of landed
property could not easily be concealed, in part the coercive force of
a criminal indictment brought by an individual citizen or of the
antidosis. The *antidosis*, in fact, is wholly unintelligible as an institution except in the absence of other ways of determining a man's
wealth. When such a challenge is made, furthermore, the decision
rests on whatever witnesses each party can muster.[21] Surely if there
had been some form of public archive in Athens, Phainippos' opponent would not have resorted to the uncertain and tiring device of
walking about a farm of 750 or 1,000 acres in search of *horoi*. When the
demes were required to report property owners subject to the so-
called *proeisphora*, Apollodoros tells us, "my name was reported in
three demes because my property was visible," that is to say, it was
in land and hence generally known, an absurd explanation except
for the lack of formal records.[22]

In the brief fragment on the law of sale, respecting realty, which
is virtually all that remains of a treatise of Theophrastus on the
laws of the Greek cities, fully half is devoted to an annotated
enumeration of various legal requirements of public notice.[23] Among
them are announcement by herald, consummation of the sale before
a magistrate, payment of a token to three neighbors, or public
sacrifice and an oath. In Athens, he says, the law demanded posting
of the proposed sale at the magistrate's headquarters for not less

than 60 days, "so that it be possible, for anyone who wished, to contest (the sale) and to bring witnesses against it,"[24] whereas Cyzicus required announcement by herald on five successive days not only to validate sales but also for hypothecation. That no such requirement existed for Athenian security transactions is clear.

Heralds and bulletin boards may have some use in protecting the rights of various parties at the moment. They have none a month or a year later. "By and large," says Theophrastus, "they are employed in the absence of another law. For wherever there is a record of properties and of transactions, it is easy to learn from them whether (the property) is free and unencumbered and whether (the vendor) is selling his property legally. For the magistrate immediately inscribes the purchaser's name in his place."[25] Unfortunately, Theophrastus names no cities that kept such records. Whether to interpret his statement as an indication of common Greek practice or of an exceptionally high level attained by a few communities is a matter of subjective judgment. Other evidence is scarce, possibly because the records were kept on wood or other destructible materials, or perhaps because there were but few.[26]

Because no formal method of public notice and official recording of hypothecation existed in Athens (and in Amorgos, Lemnos, Naxos, and Skyros), the poor alternative of the *horoi* came into use. They are in no way properly comparable with any of the techniques enumerated by Theophrastus because they represented a purely private action, without participation of an official of the state and without binding effect on anyone. But they did serve the important purpose of informing all interested parties that there was a charge on a particular piece of property. *Horoi* were inscribed and placed on the encumbered land or house, says the fullest definition to be found among the Greek lexicographers, "so that no one enter into a transaction regarding the (property) already held."[27] In other words, the *horoi* were to prevent third parties from acting with respect to the property, and, though their force was neither imperative nor binding in law, their effect should not be underestimated. A potential lender or purchaser would certainly hesitate long in the presence of a *horos*, for the stone promises legal entanglements if he goes ahead with the proposed transaction.[28] The creditor who placed the *horos* thus protected himself against further disputes with third parties. That, of course, was his objective, not a humanitarian desire to protect others.

The fact of encumbrance, then, and not the details, constituted the essential purpose of the *horoi*. It was necessary to indicate what property was encumbered, whether land alone or a house or both, and, apparently, whether the form of the security was *hypotheke*, *prasis epi lysei*, or *apotimema*. The name of the creditor or creditors, the amount of the obligation, and, above all, the date may have been matters of interest. They were not necessary, however, and they were not infrequently omitted.[29]

The *horoi* served still another purpose, for they were open evidence of the existence of an obligation on the part of the owner-debtor to a creditor, named or unnamed. No source informs us directly whether the placing of *horoi* was mandatory or not. That there was no statutory requirement is certain, I think, first because Athenian law allowed wide latitude to the parties in any agreement, and second because there is no trace of a special body of legislation dealing with security transactions anyway.[30]

Had *horoi* nevertheless become more or less obligatory in practice, at least by the middle of the fourth century B.C.? The evidence is difficult to evaluate because so much of it is reduced to the argument from silence. When the deme Myrrhinus instructed temple officials to obtain real security for loans and to place *horoi* on the encumbered property, with penalties for failure to do the latter, one may argue either (1) that the explicitness of the decree demonstrates that, without the threat, the officials might as a matter of ordinary practice have omitted *horoi*, or (2) that *horoi* had become the customary proof of the existence of a debt, so that their absence would seriously prejudice the deme's claim should a legal dispute arise.[31] Against the first interpretation one may adduce the tendency of deme decrees to go into minute detail; against the alternative view the failure to specify *horoi* in the land-lease provisions requiring the tenant to provide security.[32] Other epigraphical evidence is lacking.

Evaluation of the few pertinent passages in the orations is still more difficult. It is worth recalling that we always have but one side of the story,[33] that the testimony presented in court is no longer available, and that, though the speakers (more properly, the speechwriters) would not be likely to lie baldly about facts (when the opponents could easily refute them by testimony), they were masters of the art of twisting an interpretation of the law or an analysis of motive to suit their clients' needs.[34] That is precisely why an Isaeus or a Demosthenes was hired. Thus, when Apollodoros says that Timotheos sought to defraud his creditors by removing the *horoi* from his property, how seriously is he to be taken?[35] The charge is totally irrelevant in the case at issue. Apollodoros dragged it in solely to prejudice the jurors against Timotheos. It seems incredible that the mere act of digging up the stones could have served to destroy the creditors' claims, yet it is also hard to believe that Apollodoros would have been stupid enough to raise so irrelevant an accusation if it sounded as absurd to an Athenian audience as it may to us. For whatever it is worth, the fact should be added that Apollodoros apparently won the case.[36]

After Demosthenes was declared victor in his suit against his guardian Aphobos, he was compelled to go to court against the latter's brother-in-law Onetor. The two had conspired, according to the orator, to conceal Aphobos' holdings by claiming that he had divorced his wife, thereby giving Onetor prior right over Aphobos' house and farm in restitution of the dowry. As proof, they pointed to *horoi* affixed to the property. Demosthenes was thus prevented from collecting his judgment against Aphobos and he brought suit against Onetor. Both of his speeches in the case are preserved. His claim rested on a matter of fact rather than of law: Aphobos had received no dowry and the divorce was a pure fiction. Much of the second speech is devoted to an elaborate demonstration that the *horoi* lied, that they were the stigmata of the conspiracy.[37] Obviously Onetor had scored heavily with the jurors because of the *horoi*. (There is no mention of the *horoi* in the first oration, perhaps because Demosthenes wished to hear Onetor's original presentation before selecting the arguments he would need to break down the very tangible evidence of the stones.)

In the Phainippos case the issue was the evaluation of each party's wealth. Phainippos deducted various outstanding debts from the value of his real property and cash holdings. But, says his opponent, I searched for *horoi* and found none; therefore all the debts Phainippos now alleges are fictitious.[38] In part, at least, this is dishonest reasoning and it is possible to imagine Phainippos' defense, along some such lines as the following: "The debts I owe were not secured by my farm and were therefore not marked by *horoi*. One of them is my widowed mother's dowry. Much as you may deny my right to deduct that sum, you could hardly have expected to find the proof one way or another by hunting for *horoi*.[39] As for the other three debts, here is the proof — read the deposition of the witnesses who were present when I borrowed these sums and who testify that they were all unsecured loans, still outstanding."[40] In the opponent's speech, the one we have, it is particularly significant that a deposition was read in court proving that one of the three debts had been repaid by Phainippos, while a careful silence was maintained about the other two.[41]

Obviously the presence or absence of *horoi* was a powerful argument. In turn, that can only mean that creditors normally set up the stones whenever the debt due them was backed by a guaranty in real property. And that is why the Athenians sometimes used the verb, "to place *horoi*" (*horizo*), as a synonym for "to lend on real security," and the phrase, "unmarked land," for "unencumbered land."[42]

The road from evidence to proof is a long and difficult one. Demosthenes said "Lie!" when faced with the *horoi* on Aphobos' property just as Apollodoros cried "Forgery!" when faced with Pasion's will.[43] For a *horos*, like a will, could be forged or it could be fraudulently destroyed or removed.[44] Athenian court practice never recognized documents as decisive evidence because, in the absence of official registers of private deeds and of reliable private accounting procedures, frauds could not easily be uncovered through an examination of papers and records. Phainippos' opponent was therefore careful to inform the jurors that he had not only searched for *horoi* but had also, still in the presence of witnesses, asked Phainippos point blank to indicate his outstanding debts.[45] In the final analysis, personal testimony was decisive in court along with the persuasiveness of the oration. The presence or absence of *horoi* could have been embarrassing, even very difficult, but it was no more impervious to argumentation than any document, a contract, for example, or a will.[46]

Properly to evaluate the significance of the *horoi*, we must get away from the atmosphere of disputation that pervades the literary sources. Though court action is the ultimate test of a legal institution, only a fraction of the legal transactions in any given society find their way into court. The normal procedure in Athens, I have no doubt, was the creation of an obligation by mutual agreement, the affixing of *horoi* in the presence of witnesses, eventually the payment of the debt on the agreed date and the removal of the *horoi*, again before witnesses, all without undue fuss or fear.[47] When a dispute arose between the two parties or with others, then and only then did the problem of acceptable, reliable evidence become an issue. The *horoi* as such could give no real protection against fraud, hence the unconcern for dates and other details.[48] A dishonest debtor or creditor could forge a date, a name, or an amount on a stone even more easily than he could remove the stone itself.[49]

Whatever information the stones did give had to be accurate and up-to-date if the function of public notice were to be properly served. The use of stone as a medium was a nuisance, which the Greeks overcame by making necessary corrections with a chisel whenever possible, not merely on such crude things as the *horoi* but even on so weighty a public document as the decree announcing the establishment of the second Athenian League in 378/7 B.C.[50] A variety of changes is to be noted on the extant *horoi*. On two (nos. 28 and 154) some of the numerals were removed, indicating a partial reduction of the debt and implying, furthermore, that the same property remained as security even though the obligation had become much smaller, by one-half in one instance and by two-thirds in the other.[51] The significance of that implication for the problems of the value-factor and the extent of the creditor's claim in Greek hypothecation is noteworthy. In no. 63, the words *epi lysei* were eliminated, so that the stone then read: "*Horos* of land sold."[52] Presumably the debtor had defaulted, whereupon the security transaction became a true sale and the creditor, now the owner, took possession. For reasons we can only surmise, the new owner wished to make it a matter of public knowledge that the property had changed hands. The easiest, cheapest, and most effective way to accomplish that was to allow the *horos* to remain standing, with the decisive words *epi lysei* removed.

The name of the creditor was also tinkered with; in no. 33 it was replaced by another, in no. 78 it was simply cut out. Since no amount is given in no. 33, it is impossible to determine whether the same property (land and a house) served as security on two different occasions, or whether someone took a conveniently discarded stone, replaced the name with his own, and set the revamped *horos* on his debtor's holding. No. 78 marked a house and carries the figure, 400 drachmas. Though that stone, too, may have been moved from one house to another, the greater likelihood is that the owner, having settled one debt, took on another in the same amount and again offered his house as security.[53] The creditor's name was also removed from no. 27, without replacement, but no explanation suggests itself since the stone retains the year, the creditor's demotic, and the name of the person holding the agreement, all unchanged.

Horos no. 71 marked the *prasis epi lysei* of a house in 309/8 B. C. The following year the writing was deleted, though it can still be

2*

read, and a new *horos* (no. 152) was inscribed immediately below, this time marking a dotal *apotimema*. No. 22 may have undergone similar treatment. Nos. 19 and 20 reveal a lazier technique. The discarded *horos* was simply turned upside down and a new one inscribed on the blank part of the surface, the writing going in the opposite direction. In no. 19, incidentally, the creditors are Aristophon of Teithras and Autokles of Anaphlystos and the amount is 1,100 drachmas; in no. 20, we have Autokles the sole creditor for 2,200 drachmas.[54] Nos. 36 and 37 appear on reverse sides of the same stone and were possibly parallel to nos. 19 and 20, but they are in too fragmentary a condition to be analyzed.

Three other pairs present serious difficulties. Nos. 4 and 5 were inscribed on a stone built into the wall of a modern house in the district between the Pnyx and the Areopagus, where they could still be seen at the end of the nineteenth century. No. 4 begins, "*Horos* of a house hypothecated," followed by the figure, 1,000 (drachmas), subsequently deleted, then by another line that was removed, and then "to Periandros of Cholargos." No. 5, which was never changed, reads simply: "*Horos* of a house hypothecated to the demesmen of Halai, 200 (drachmas)." No. 80, a fieldstone of unknown provenience, reads: "*Horos* of a house put up as security (*prasis epi lysei*) to Menophilos of Ikaria, 270 (drachmas)." No. 81 follows immediately on the stone, though in a different hand: "*Horos* of a house (*oikema*) put up as security (*prasis epi lysei*) to Phaylles of Ikaria, 200 (drachmas)."[55] No. 107, a late fourth-century Lemnian stone, reads: "In the archonship of Nikodoros. *Horos* of land and a house put up as security (*prasis epi lysei*), 1,000 (drachmas), to the *orgeones* of Herakles in Kome, according to the orgeonic record-book." The final three letters appear on the eighth line of the stone, followed without a break by no. 108, which is identical word for word, except that the archon is Archias and the numeral, most of which is lost, cannot be 1,000.

It is tempting to see in these three pairs of *horoi* direct evidence of separate transactions on the security of the same piece of property. That interpretation, however, creates some difficulties. What is the meaning of the deletion of the sum in no. 4? Why should the regular word for house appear in no. 80 and the rare *oikema* in no. 81? Most serious of all, what is the significance of nos. 107/8, indicating that the same piece of property guaranteed two different debts, necessarily by the same man, to the same group of *orgeones*, dated in different years? A possible answer is that, just as there were cases in which the debt was reduced while the amount of property put up as security was not reduced correspondingly, here we have the reverse, an increase in the amount of the debt backed up by the same farm and house. But then why was the change not indicated simply by a correction in the numeral? I have no answer to any of these questions, but they are probably not too serious in any event.[56]

3. WRITTEN AGREEMENTS

Should a dispute arise between the parties over the date when repayment was due or the rate of interest, the *horoi* would be worthless as evidence because they did not carry the pertinent information. Reference would have to be made to the original agreement. Fourteen of the stones, ten from Attica and two each from Amorgos and Lemnos, include the phrase, "according to the contract deposited with," followed by a name. This item takes about as much space on the stone as all the other details together, and, since it is not indispensable (certainly no more so, it would seem, than the date), historians have commonly assumed that its presence or absence was largely a matter of whim, that, in other words, a written contract always existed whether the *horos* said so or not.[57] The question merits closer study, however, for it is part of the broader question of the extent to which written documents had become an integral part of Athenian practice by the fourth century B.C. even despite the absence of any legal requirement.[58]

In the early orators, Lysias and even more notably Isaeus, references to a written agreement are very infrequent apart from wills. The absence of such references is all the more significant because the cases at issue so often turned on a question of fact, a marriage, an adoption, a loan or its repayment, where the failure of both sides to speak of a contract can only mean that none was in existence. As we approach and then pass the middle of the fourth century B.C., written agreements become increasingly evident, particularly in the later speeches incorrectly attributed to Demosthenes. But this statistical observation must be qualified according to the substance of the agreement. In the Spudias case, for example, in which the husband and his father-in-law had agreed to a long postponement in the payment of 1,000 drachmas to complete the dowry, everything was arranged verbally.[59] A 1,000-drachma dowry obligation was no small matter and in this case, as not infrequently, it led to a court action. The fact is noteworthy that the obligation was entered into on a purely verbal basis despite its somewhat complex character, and there is evidence enough to show that the procedure was by no means exceptional.[60]

After Pasion died, his son Apollodoros brought a series of lawsuits to collect debts he claimed were due his father's estate. In one action, he charged Timotheos with attempting to deny the existence of four debts he had incurred at different times, totaling 4,438 drachmas and 2 obols. The issue was strictly one of fact. Before launching into his proofs, Apollodoros made the following revealing remark to the jurors: "None of you should wonder if I am very exact. For the bankers are accustomed to write memoranda (*hypomnemata*) of the moneys they give out and the purpose, and of the sums which someone pays, so that the receipts and the payments may be known to them for their reckoning."[61] Both the character of the explanation and the very fact that Apollodoros felt called upon to make it are intelligible only if written agreements were not the rule.

It was in the commercial field, more narrowly in the speculative world of maritime loans, that the written contract became more or less universal. This world lacked permanence and stability both in its personnel and in its property. Neither a farm nor a citizen-landowner could disappear easily; an alien shipowner or merchant could, along with his ship and its cargo. Furthermore, the marked expansion of maritime activity and bottomry loans in the fourth century B.C. was accompanied by some growth in the complexity and variety of the transactions undertaken. Verbal agreements therefore became less and less satisfactory and there was a strong stimulus for putting the provisions in writing. Wills are analogous. The testator's death removes from the scene the principal party to the transaction and the provisions are likely to be rather numerous and complicated. But, under ordinary conditions in Athens, security transactions involving land and houses, marriage contracts, and even the sale and lease of property tended to retain their traditional content. In those areas, not a part of the commercial world in any real sense, the need for writing as a control over variations from standard practice was far from compelling.[62] Here as elsewhere, the fact that landed property and money were to a considerable degree separate and unrelated spheres in the economy — the persistent denial of the right of land ownership to non-citizens is the most salient illustration — had as a consequence a certain dichotomy in the law as in politics.[63]

I suggest, therefore, that in the field of real security a written agreement was the exception rather than the rule. Its appearance was usually an indication that there were special conditions, though there was nothing to prevent any creditor or debtor from insisting on a contract in an unexceptional case if he were so moved. A study of the *horoi* reveals enough of a pattern of consistency to warrant this conclusion, provided it is not held too rigidly.

Not a single *horos* marking a pupillary *apotimema* mentions a written contract, presumably because the entire proceedings were conducted under the direct supervision of the archon under fixed rules. Only one dotal *apotimema* was concluded by a written instrument, according to the texts of the *horoi*, and that one, no. 154, unquestionably departed from the norm in some way.[64] All three stones (nos. 1, 2, and 10) that announce the rare condition whereby the creditor took possession of the property during the life of the obligation specifically indicate that this was done "according to the contract deposited with" somebody. The evidence of these three *horoi* seems nearly decisive. The rule was retention of possession by the debtor. When the parties agreed to depart from the rule, we are told quite explicitly in the *horoi* which served as public notice, a written instrument was drawn up. Then there is the word order of no. 32: "*Horos* of land and a house put up as security (*prasis epi lysei*) to Hieromnemon of Halai, 500 (drachmas), according to the contract deposited with Lysistratos, and to the Dekadistai, 130 (drachmas), and an *apotimema* to the eranists, those with[65] Theopeithos of Ikaria." The position of the key phrase indicates that the agreement with Hieromnemon was in writing, those with the Dekadistai and the eranists not. No *horos* in which a group is named, whether a subdivision of the state, a cult body, or an *eranos*, mentions a contract. In one instance, the Lemnian pair nos. 107/8, there is an essentially different clause, "according to the orgeonic record-book" (*kata to grammateion to orgeionikon*), which suggests that the only writing was a notation in the group's own records, like the memoranda kept by Pasion.[66]

The decree of the deme Myrrhinus, in which the priests were carefully instructed, on pain of severe penalty, to mark with *horoi* all realty they accepted as security for loans, says nothing about drawing up a written agreement.[67] It is noteworthy that this decree is dated after 340 B.C., in other words, precisely in the period in which we have the most abundant evidence of commercial contracts. In view of the known penchant of public and quasi-public bodies for engraving all kinds of information on stone at this time, there seems to be significance in the marked contrast between the leases, available in some number and revealing a not inconsiderable variation in terms, and the absence of any comparable testimony on stone in the field of security. Either public and quasi-public groups rarely participated in hypothecation, it would seem, or if they did, they followed the usual rules and therefore did not trouble to engrave the pertinent decrees. It probably is more likely that both together make up the correct explanation.[68]

Finally, the *horoi* reveal an interesting statistical distinction. Five of the ten stones marking *hypotheke* obligations mention a contract, but only 8 out of 102 in the *prasis epi lysei* group refer to such an instrument. The disproportion is too great to be rejected as mere chance. One could suggest as the explanation the fact that the *hypotheke* was somehow more flexible than the *prasis epi lysei* and lent itself more readily to special terms and conditions, hence the more frequent need to commit the agreement to writing. A full analysis of the law, however, would be necessary to determine whether this explanation is valid or not.[69]

The literary evidence is not helpful in the attempt to distinguish among the types of hypothecation in this respect because, by implication at least, it more often than not points to transactions made orally. Timotheos' alleged removal of the *horoi* from his property would have been doubly senseless if his creditors could promptly have come foreward with well-authenticated contracts. Having failed in his search for *horoi*, Phainippos' opponent would have requested him not to speak up if he claimed any debts but to produce the documents. Demosthenes would have had much less difficulty proving his claim against his guardians if he had written agreements to exhibit, including one defining the terms under which his father possessed the twenty pledged slaves;[70] he would also have been spared the elaborate argument over Onetor's alleged right to Aphobos' property by *apotimema*.

The complex dispute between Nikobulos and Pantainetos that arose out of a *prasis epi lysei* agreement is in a different class. The amount involved was a huge one, 10,500 drachmas. The parties, including the two co-creditors, were not well acquainted. The contract was in writing; it covered the duration of the obligation, the rate of interest, and "other things" which are left unspecified in the oration, perhaps deliberately so.[71] Here certainly we are dealing with an agreement in which there were special clauses and conditions, so much so that when it was dissolved, the creditors demanded and obtained a formal release from their ex-debtor, an action as mysterious as it is unprecedented.[72] In one of his lawsuits, Apollodoros describes how he had hypothecated his farm to raise money for his trierarchy and how, in his absence, his creditors made certain demands "according to the contract." Just what the demands were is unclear, but it would not be difficult to argue from the language that the terms were unusual. We need not stress the point, however, and may leave the case as an exceptional instance in which the parties simply desired documentary validation of their transaction.[73]

Finally, note must be taken of a peroration in the first oration against Aristogeiton, the authorship of which is still disputed. "I think it is necessary for you," the speaker tells the jurors, "to examine the defendant and the justice of the case in the same way you would examine a private debt. Now suppose someone claimed someone owed him money and the other denied it. If the agreement according to which the loan was made was manifestly in place (*i.e.*, with the person with whom deposited) and the *horoi* placed were standing, you would hold that the one who denied was clearly shameless; but if these things had been destroyed, the claimant (was to be blamed). That is natural. Now the articles of agreement regarding what Aristogeiton owes to the *polis* are the laws according to which all (public) debtors are inscribed, the *horos* is the wooden tablet (containing the names of the debtors) deposited with the goddess."[74] At first glance, this rather poor rhetoric would seem to imply that both written agreements and *horoi* were unfailing proof of the existence of an obligation and that they were prepared whenever a debt was incurred. But we need look no further than the orations of Demosthenes to find ample proof that debts based solely on a verbal understanding were by no means infrequent. Further, *horoi* might prove the existence of a secured debt; they could hardly be called upon as evidence, one way or the other, of an unsecured debt or of one backed by personal suretyship or pledge of movables. Actually, the speaker himself reveals the weakness of his analogy. "If these things had been destroyed," he says at the end, not "if they did not exist." In other words, once *horoi* were placed — and only then — their subsequent removal would undermine a claim for repayment of a debt. That qualification renders the passage of little probative value, like so many similar appeals to the court scattered among the orations.

Whenever the existence of a contract is indicated in the *horoi* (and often in the literature as well), the name of the individual with whom it was deposited for safekeeping is given. In the absence of public registration or other forms of governmental control, only the repute of this man (and the supporting testimony of the men who witnessed the agreement) can guarantee the accuracy and authenticity of the documents should a dispute arise.[75] In his manual for professional speech-writers, Aristotle placed particular stress on the credibility of the holder of the document. Attack it or defend it vigorously, he advised, depending on which side of the case you are arguing.[76] Occasionally further protection was sought by preparing more than one copy, each deposited with a different person.

One *horos*, no. 17, an undated stone found in Laureion, differs from all the others in that the contract is deposited with the thesmothetes, not with a private individual. Only two Athenian parallels are known. In a speech of Isaeus that cannot be dated precisely, the entire case hinges on a document, which was either a will or a *donatio mortis causa*, that was deposited with state officials, probably the *astynomoi*.[77] A century or so later, the philosopher Epicurus filed a *donatio mortis causa* in the Metroon.[78] An analogous situation is revealed by the Amorgian *horos*, no. 155, which can be dated about 300 B.C.:[79] "*Horos* of houses and gardens, those adjoining the houses, put up as security (*apotimema*) to Nikesarete for her dowry,[80] consecrated and dedicated to Aphrodite Urania in Aspis by Nikesarete, wife of Naukrates, and her *kyrios* Naukrates, and according to the testaments deposited in the temple of Aphrodite and with Eunomides the archon and with the thesmothete Ktesiphon." Here we have a triple safeguard, two deposited with officials and the third in the temple. The reference to the thesmothete is as unique in Amorgos as is *horos* no. 17 in Athens.[81]

Deposit in the temple and with two different public officials of a deed devising property to the goddess Aphrodite is readily understandable, whether the law required such action or not. Neither Epicurus nor Isaeus' client made dedications to a goddess, but there is a possible link with Nikesarete, namely the confirmation by will of a prior *donatio mortis causa*. The legal implications need not concern us. Only the fact that all three actions were more than ordinarily complex explains the unusual action of depositing the definitive documents with officials rather than with private persons. The motive was more effective safekeeping, not official approval and registration, for, in the Isaeus speech, difficult as it is to interpret, one fact stands out with certainty — the testator did not require approval of the official who was guardian of his document in order to change it as he pleased.[82] I have no idea what special circumstances may have been involved in the transaction marked by *horos* no. 17. Like all the Attic stones, it tells us nothing about the background of the obligation, but there can be little doubt that some unusual feature existed which prompted the decision to deposit the contract with the thesmothetes.[83]

Ultimately, the important point is that in the decisive period, 400—200 B.C., precisely three instances of governmental caretaking of documents are known from Athens.[84] Furthermore, they are too well spaced in time to permit any suggestion of a trend, as some historians have suggested, among other reasons, in order to explain the cessation in the use of *horoi* about the middle of the third century B.C. It is reasonable to assume that some other device of public notice replaced the *horoi*. But what it was does not seem to be ascertainable in the available sources.[85]

"The family and the neighbors who know everything," Wilamowitz once wrote in concluding a brief summary of Athenian record-keeping, "that is to say, rustic village relationships and the economy of the peasant lay at the foundation of Attic law, and among the peasants is the large landowner, the noble *Herr*."[86] The world of the *horoi*, we shall see in later chapters, is not the world of the money market and overseas trade. Verbal agreements and the "neighbors who know everything" needed no better form of public notice than the often crude markers driven into the ground or scratched on a house-wall.

CHAPTER III

HYPOTHEKE AND *PRASIS EPI LYSEI*

It was a universally recognized principle of archaic Greek law that, should the need arise, a creditor could obtain satisfaction on both the person and the property of his debtor if he had the ability to carry out execution. In Athens after Solon — and in some other Greek communities, though by no means all — the person of the debtor was no longer subject to seizure for a private obligation. But his property always remained subject to execution. Throughout Greek history, furthermore, though the law developed and procedures were changed, with the state playing an increasingly important role, the element of self-help never disappeared.[1]

A significant variant came into being when two parties agreed in advance that a designated piece of property (or a third person in communities in which personal execution survived) would serve as the means of satisfying the creditor should the debtor fail to make payment or perform whatever action the obligation required. This new type of understanding, also archaic in origin, introduced the institution of security into the law. The link between security, execution, and self-help was never fully destroyed in Greek law, as the dual use of the word *enechyron* shows (much like the German word *Pfand* today).[2] Nevertheless, the difference between execution in general and execution on property predesignated for that purpose is clear-cut, with practical consequences of the greatest import in economics and law. Our discussion will be limited entirely to the latter, to security in the form of real property.

In this and the next chapter, we shall be concerned only with what may be called the external aspects of the transactions. We shall consider such questions as the relative frequency of *hypotheke*, *prasis epi lysei*, and *apotimema*, the kinds of obligations with which they were employed, or the arrangements made. We shall not enter into a systematic analysis of creditor's rights, foreclosures, or related questions. And, as already indicated, the three terms will be assumed to indicate three distinct forms of security and they will be treated separately. Whether or not the distinction among them was

28

rather shadowy by the fourth century B.C. can be determined only after a full discussion of all aspects of the problem, and above all the legal.[3]

I. HYPOTHEKE

Two terms were used almost universally in the Greek world to express the idea of legal security. As the generic word for the thing put up as security, we find *enechyron* (often used in the plural form for a singular object), derived from *echyros*, "strong," "secure." The usual verb is *tithemi*, "to place," most often in the form, *hypotithemi*, "to place under," "to put down" (in the passive, *hypokeimai*, "to lie under").[4] *Enechyron* also appears commonly in two specialized, more limited senses. It was used regularly for the pawn, the pledged object that passed into the creditor's possession for the duration of the obligation, in contrast to hypothecated property that remained with the debtor. For the latter, *hypotheke*, "the object put down" (it is the noun from *hypotithemi*), was the standard expression.[5] Ultimately this word entered the vocabulary of Roman law and from there came into modern legal systems. (The other specialized meaning of *enechyron* is the object seized by a creditor in execution proceedings following default, with or without a court-judgment, where there has been no security agreement, no prior designation of the substitute for the debt. The related verb, *enechyrazo*, was used solely in this latter context.)[6]

Though deviations from these norms are infrequent (with the outstanding exception of the *horoi*), they appear often enough to bedevil the historian who is trying to understand a particular transaction mentioned briefly, often casually, in a play by Aristophanes or an oration by Isaeus.[7] The exceptional situation in the *horoi* is notable. Out of 154 stones, only 10 indicate a *hypotheke*, if their wording is to be accepted as precise.[8] The remaining stones introduce completely different terms, with different linguistic roots — *prasis epi lysei* in 102 and *apotimema* in 42.[9] One explanation that comes to mind immediately is that Athenian practice was somehow quite different from that of the rest of the Greeks, for both *prasis epi lysei* and *apotimema* are virtually unknown in non-Attic texts, as we shall see. There are serious difficulties in this interpretation, however. In Athenian literature and inscriptions, the *apotimema* transaction is mentioned a few times but the phrase *prasis epi lysei* is unknown (as a technical term in this precise combination of three common Greek words).[10] Were it not for the *horoi*, therefore, we would be unaware of the importance, almost of the existence, of *prasis epi lysei* and we would know hardly anything of the *apotimema*.[11] Now the *horoi* were an Athenian idea. Other communities had their own devices of public notice, no longer in existence. Is it unreasonable to assume, at least as a possibility, that were the Rhodian or Milesian or Corinthian equivalents of the *horoi* to come to light, we should find either the same variation known for Athens from the *horoi* or still other departures from the almost unfailing use of *hypotheke* in the literary sources? Or was Athenian terminology (and presumably therefore also its practice) somehow unique, despite the failure of its literature to reveal any singularity? These questions cannot be answered without a full juristic analysis of the material, and perhaps not even then, in view of the information at our disposal.

Although ten *horoi* constitute too small a number for decisive analysis, certain differentiating tendencies seem evident. Five of the fourteen *horoi* that specifically announce the existence of a written agreement are in this *hypotheke* group, as are all three *horoi* (nos. 1, 2, and 10) that contain the exceptional clause, "on condition that the creditor have and have power."[12] The amount of the debt is relatively low, ranging from 90 to 2,000 drachmas with the median at 525 drachmas. In the *horoi* marking *prasis epi lysei* obligations, the range is 150 to 7,000, the median 1,050; in the dotal *apotimema* texts, 300 to 8,000 and a median of 1,900. Assuming that these figures represent more than mere accident — and we must lend them some credence — we may explain the tendency of the last-named group to run into substantially larger sums of money as suggesting that only the wealthier Athenians, those who gave very large dowries, ordinarily requested guaranties in the form of real security for the return of the dowry in case the marriage should later be dissolved.[13] But at present no explanation can be offered for the several special characteristics that seem to set the *hypotheke* transactions apart from the *prasis epi lysei* obligations, other than the suggestion made in the previous chapter that the *hypotheke* was the more flexible of the two and hence was more commonly used when the parties to an agreement wished to depart from the usual conditions of Athenian hypothecation in one way or another. Having said that, however, I am promptly brought back to the point that a similar distinction cannot be drawn in the literary material because of the absence of the term *prasis epi lysei*. And surely we cannot assume that, by some remarkable coincidence, all the available literary references to security fall into one category, while the transactions marked by *horoi* fall largely into another (excluding *apotimema* for the moment).[14]

2. *PRASIS EPI LYSEI*

The language of buying and selling was extraordinarily complex among the ancient Greeks. There was no basic single verb meaning "to sell," but three (perhaps four) distributed more or less rigidly among the different moods and tenses. Behind this peculiar linguistic phenomenon lies the whole evolution of exchange transactions in early Greek society, and in part an attempt to differentiate between offering for sale and completing a sale.[15] Nor does the complexity end there. Verbally at least, the leasing of mines and of tax-collecting rights (tax farming) was conceived as the sale of the ore and the tax-money, respectively, and the lessees were called "buyers."

In *prasis epi lysei* we find still another application of the language of sale, this time in the field of security. Literally, the phrase may be translated "sale on condition of release"; more fully, it means "sale on condition that the seller may release the property from the buyer's claim on it."[16] (*Lysis* is the ordinary Greek word for release from an obligation or condition, from a debt, for example, or captivity.) As a technical term in Athenian sources, it is known only from the *horoi* and from one recently discovered inscription; it is never used in the extant literary sources.[17] Elsewhere it appears only in a fragmentary and almost unintelligible silver tablet from Sicily, perhaps of the first century B.C.,[18] and in a Greek parchment from Syria, also badly torn and obscure, dated in 195 B.C.[19]

The paradoxical situation created by the Greek terminology has already been indicated.[20] Outside the Athenian sphere, the existence of *prasis epi lysei* can be demonstrated for third-century Tenos and possibly for Sardis and for Olynthus just prior to its destruction in 348 B.C.[21] Otherwise the documents speak solely of *enechyron* and *hypotheke* (or use the verb *tithemi* in some form). Whether this means that *prasis epi lysei* was relatively unknown outside of Athens and its sphere of juristic influence or that the terminology is inconclusive or that no significant distinction had been retained between *prasis epi lysei* and *hypotheke* cannot be determined until the institutions are fully explained juristically.[22]

Of the 102 *horoi* marking *prasis epi lysei* obligations, only one, no. 102, a stone found several miles east of Arkesine on Amorgos, that can be dated about 300 B.C., departs sufficiently from the ordinary terseness of the *horoi* to provide some insight into the character of the institution. (This stone, it should be noted, lacks the word *horos* and is actually a hybrid text.) It reads: "The gods. In the archonship of Phanokrates, month of Anthesterion, Nikeratos and Hegekrate and her *kyrios* Telenikos put up as security (*prasis epi lysei*) to Ktesiphon son of Pythippos the lands, the house, and the roof, all of which Nikeratos has having divided with his brother Anthines, and the lands which Nikeratos bought from Ischyrion, in full, and the lands which Nikeratos has as pledgee from Exakestos, in full — for 5,000 drachmas in silver. Nikeratos will pay Ktesiphon as rent for each year 500 drachmas in silver, clear."[23]

For an understanding of this transaction (ignoring such problems as the role of the wife and her *kyrios*), we turn to the speech prepared by Demosthenes for Nikobulos, defendant in a suit against Pantainetos, probably in 346/5 B.C.[24] The pertinent facts, according to Nikobulos, are these: Pantainetos had purchased an ore-crushing mill and thirty slaves from Telemachos for an unnamed price. Presumably to pay for his purchase, he borrowed 10,500 drachmas, 6,000 from Mnesikles and 4,500 from Phileas and Pleistor. The mill and slaves were to serve as security for the loan and this was accomplished by having Telemachos, the original owner, "sell" directly to Mnesikles, the principal creditor. Subsequently Pantainetos wished or was compelled to satisfy his creditors. He thereupon arranged to borrow 10,500 drachmas again, 4,500 from Nikobulos, the defendant in the present action, and 6,000 from Euergos.[25] This money was turned over to the first group of creditors in satisfaction of the original loan. The mill and slaves continued to serve as security. Mnesikles now "sold" them to Euergos and Nikobulos because, the latter goes on to explain, "he (Mnesikles) bought them for him (Pantainetos) from Telemachos, the former owner."[26] A contract was drawn up between Pantainetos and the new "owners" whereby the former agreed to rent the property at 12 per cent interest, and to redeem it "in a given period" not defined further in the speech. Nikobulos makes frequent reference to other clauses of the contract but he carefully and deliberately refrains from indicating what they were, nor does he submit the text of the agreement in evidence.[27] (Whatever the outcome may have been for Nikobulos, his evasiveness is most unfortunate for us, since citation of the complete agreement would have removed many of the obscurities about *prasis epi lysei*.)

Upon completion of the deal, Nikobulos left Athens on business. While he was away, Pantainetos defaulted on his rent-interest and Euergos took possession of the property. Then followed a series of complex machinations (that need not concern us), as a result of which Nikobulos worked out an arrangement whereby he could dispose of the mill and slaves and recover in cash his 4,500 drachmas and Euergos' 6,000. This was accomplished by finding a new "purchaser," again acting on behalf of Pantainetos. The way Nikobulos describes the negotiations is most significant:

"When the project had reached this point and it was time for us to receive the money, the parties who had previously made that offer said that they would not pay the money unless we would be the sellers of the properties to them.... When the matter stood in this way, and they whom he (*i.e.*, Pantainetos) had introduced would not turn over the money, and it was manifest that we were rightfully in control of what we had bought, he begged, prayed, and entreated us to be the sellers....(I agreed but) I requested that if I withdrew and became the seller for this property... I receive a full release. This having been agreed to, he gave me a full discharge of everything and I became the seller of the properties, as he requested, just as I myself had bought (them) from Mnesikles."[28]

Nikobulos' troubles were by no means over, but we may take leave of him except for some additional quotations. Turning to Pantainetos at one point, he says: "For, what we had bought for 10,500 drachmas you later sold for 3 talents and 2,600 drachmas (*i.e.*, 20,600 drachmas). But who in the world would have given you a single drachma, having you for the seller outright?"[29]

No summary can begin to give the flavor of this speech, and certainly not a summary in translation. Seller and lender, rent and interest, your property and my property — the words tumble after each other and in place of each other with complete impartiality. Yet there is no real difficulty in grasping the situation. Referring to the 12 per cent in the original contract between Pantainetos and Nikobulos and Euergos, Libanios of Antioch (fourth century after Christ), in the Argument of the speech, put his finger on the key: "In reality this was interest, but in appearance rent."[30] Essentially, then, the speech deals with a series of manoeuvers and deals in the field of security, not genuine sale. Though conveyance of the property occurs and recurs over his head, so to speak, Pantainetos remains in continuous possession and control so long as he meets the interest payments and the mysterious unidentified terms of the agreement.[31] When he defaults, the creditors take the security as forfeit; this they would have done whether the transaction was called *prasis epi lysei* or *hypotheke* or *apotimema*. (The legal aspect of the seizure, the procedure required, and the question whether or not title was transferred at that time need not concern us in this discussion.)

Nikobulos emphasizes the fact that legally Pantainetos himself could have served as buyer and seller. "Afterwards," he says, "we sold (the property) to others in the same way, on the same terms on which we ourselves had bought (them), he (Panatinetos) not only having told but implored (us to do so); for no one was willing to accept him as seller."[32] That Pantainetos did not himself act as seller, his opponent suggests, was the result of his poor reputation, not a disability inherent in the nature of the transaction. The "buyers" (both those who were lending 10,500 drachmas and those who eventually purchased the mill and slaves outright for 20,600) were seeking adequate warranty. For this purpose they insisted that someone else, not Pantainetos, function as vendor, allegedly because he was not a trustworthy warrantor.[33]

The emphasis on warranty probably is to be explained by the fact that Athenian law did not have the institution of the third-party warrantor.[34] The buyer had to depend on the seller himself to protect title should a dispute arise.[35] The various Pantainetos transactions were in a sense conditional sales. Should the creditors be compelled to accept the property, the question of title would become important. Therefore they wanted someone other than Pantainetos to be in a position to warrant it, whether because of his poor standing, as Nikobulos says, or for some other reason is immaterial. Warranty may also be the clue to the creditor-buyer's demanding a release from the debtor-seller, as Nikobulos did, an otherwise most peculiar procedure. And when Pantainetos eventually sold the mill and slaves outright, the question of who would be the vendor, and hence the warrantor, was again a serious one.

It was Pantainetos and no one else who brought an end to the whole series of manipulations by selling the property off once and for all. "On property on which you were never able to borrow more than 100 minas and which you sold outright for three talents and 2,000 drachmas...," Nikobulos says, addressing him directly.[36] Pantainetos "borrowed" on the property. There lies the essence of the "sales." And the so-called rent was simply an interest payment, calculated on the amount of the loan, not on the value of the property or its yield. Here it was 12 per cent, in the Amorgian *horos* no. 102, it was 10 per cent.[37]

Yet, the fact remains that the transaction was called a sale. To differentiate between the *prasis epi lysei* and genuine sale, Nikobulos adds the word "outright" to "sell" when he is referring to the final disposal of the property for 20,600 drachmas.[38] The problem of proper classification is most difficult. Clearly *prasis epi lysei* was not a genuine, complete sale; it is significant that the literal meaning of the term is "sale on condition of release," not "sale with the right (or option) to re-buy" as in the French *vente à réméré*. Nor can it be described as a fictitious sale or a fiduciary sale, as some historians have suggested. Only a hybrid category will fit, such as "security in the form of conditional sale." The reasons for the creation of such a mixed institution, and incidentally for the elliptical name given to it, will be found historically in the rise of security transactions in the period when free alienability of landed property was difficult and socially as well as legally restricted, juristically in the problems of execution after default and in the need for a device that would strengthen the creditor's right to evict the debtor and that would protect the new owner's claim to the property.

The outward form, then, is sale, the essence hypothecation.[39] One is reminded of Maitland's famous dictum on the mortgage deed: "it is one long *suppressio veri* and *suggestio falsi*."[40] As a security transaction, *prasis epi lysei* was given publicity by way of the *horoi*, and, if the statistics of the *horoi* have validity, it was the characteristic form of Athenian security. Both the *horoi* and the Pantainetos case show that on the vital matter of possession, the debtor as a rule retained his property in *prasis epi lysei* as in other types of security. However one may interpret the complicated manoeuvers that constituted the background of the case against Apaturios, about 340 B.C. or a little later, there, too, Apaturios retained possession of a ship and slaves which served as security for a loan of 4,000 drachmas. As in the Pantainetos case, several parties took the role of creditor in turn, but only the final transaction can be considered a *prasis epi lysei* with any certainty. Like Pantainetos, too, Apaturios was the active party in making the arrangements, and he retained his property while the debt passed from hand to hand.[41] Eventually the property was sold outright, but Apaturios was not as fortunate as Pantainetos in this respect, for the sale produced only 4,000 drachmas, the precise amount of his debt.[42]

3*

Then there is the matter of the house owned by a certain Theosebes, confiscated by the state and sold by the *poletai* in 367/6 B.C.
for 575 drachmas.[43] When the state took over the house, there were
four charges on it, a *hypotheke* for 150 drachmas, two *praseis epi
lysei*, one for 100 drachmas and the other for 24, and an unlabeled
charge (perhaps comparable to the modern lien) of 30 drachmas to
the man who had paid the funeral costs for Theosebes' father and
mother. There can be no question of the fact that Theosebes' father,
who had incurred the debts, and then Theosebes himself remained
in continuous possession up to the moment of confiscation. The
reason for state intervention, it may be added, was a charge of
sacrilege and had nothing whatever to do with the debts or the
status of the house. Nor can there be any question of the fact that
prasis epi lysei was an encumbrance rather than a sale.[44] Otherwise
it would be difficult, if not impossible, to understand how there
could be two "sales" of the same property, already previously
encumbered to boot, and how it could be "sold" for as little as 24
drachmas.[45] When the state seized the house, the "buyers" did not
contest on the ground of prior ownership through purchase. They
merely claimed the amount of their debt by a regular procedure set
up for this purpose.

The discussion in the previous chapter of the possibility of exceptional agreements, written or unwritten, need not be repeated here.
In both the Pantainetos and Apaturios cases there were written
contracts, necessarily so because of the complications. Only eight of
the 102 *horoi* involving *prasis epi lysei* make specific reference to a
written agreement. For the rest, the *horoi* provide little significant
information. Nos. 33 and 78 reveal changes in the creditor, thereby
suggesting a transfer of the obligation from one creditor to another,
as in the Pantainetos case.[46] No. 71 was set up in 309/8 B.C. and
removed by the end of the year, implying a one-year term for the
obligation. Otherwise, no information is available about the duration of *prasis epi lysei* obligations and there is nothing to indicate
that they were of longer term or less definite in their time limits than
any other security transaction.[47]

Specific evidence of possession passing immediately to the
creditor in *prasis epi lysei* is both scarce and uncertain. When
Euktemon of Kephisia died in 365/4 B.C. at the age of 96, a squabble
over the inheritance ended in court. The claimant, whose speech we
have, based part of his case on the charge that the old man had
fallen into the hands of adventurers. In their conspiracy to steal

Euktemon's wealth, they allegedly persuaded him to convert his holdings into cash, which was "invisible" and could be readily made away with. In a very short time, says the speaker, "he sold his farm in Athmonon to Antiphanes for 75 minas, the bath-house in the Serangeion to Aristolochos for 3,000 drachmas; the house in the city hypothecated for 44 minas he released to the hierophant," and so forth. "The whole which was hurriedly sold after Philoktemon's death (brought in) over three talents."[48] If the original transaction with the hierophant was a *prasis epi lysei*, and there is no proof other than the language of this one passage, the probability is that here we have one case in which the creditor-buyer held possession.[49] Then there is the transaction, mentioned in a speech incorrectly attributed to Lysias, in which a horse given in pledge for a 1,200-drachma loan died while in the creditor's possession, thus wiping out his claim for the return of the money. That the transaction was a *prasis epi lysei* is most uncertain, and in any event the fact that the pledged object was a horse renders it of little value in our discussion.[50] That exhausts the evidence. Even if another illustration or two were to be uncovered, the conclusion would remain unshaken that possession normally remained with the debtor in all forms of real security.[51]

Whatever the juristic aspect of *prasis epi lysei*, one should underscore the fact that, economically, it was usually not a sale transaction at all. In the modern chattel mortgage and conditional sale, it is the buyer who is the debtor, the seller the creditor. In the Greek *prasis epi lysei*, the situation is reversed. The "seller" is the debtor, the "buyer" the creditor. The reasons for entering into the obligation may have been sale, as in the first Pantainetos transaction, but they need not be. And from everything we know about the economic life of the time, they rarely were.[52] The *horoi*, of course, give no more indication of the source of a *prasis epi lysei* obligation than they do of any other. Nos. 49, 82, 82A, and perhaps 93 indicate that guarantee of a dowry was the purpose; they will be discussed in the next chapter. The others give no information.

We are equally ill-informed on the question of interest. Pantainetos paid interest, Apaturios did not. One and maybe a second *horos* indicate interest, and the rest are silent. Again we must turn to our knowledge of the general practice to decide whether interest payments were the rule in this type of security transaction or not. Nothing in the nature of the transaction warrants the assumption, as a matter of course, that the rent-interest arrangement of the Pantainetos case and of *horos* no. 102 was the rule.[53]

CHAPTER IV

APOTIMEMA

THE WORD *apotimema* INTRODUCES a third and totally different notion into the field of legal security. Whereas in *hypotheke* the root-idea is "to set" or "to place" and in *prasis epi lysei* "to sell," *apotimema* comes from the verb *timao*, with a basic meaning of "to evaluate." The verb *timao* and the nouns *time* and *timema* were applied by the Greeks to a wide variety of activities involving some kind of measurement or evaluation. In some, as in the use of *time* for honor, the idea of evaluation can be found only in early Greek thought, largely lost in the classical period. But in other uses, as in *timema* as the monetary fine imposed by a court or as a property rating, the root-concept retains·its full strength. It is this idea of evaluation that distinguishes *apotimema* from the other words meaning legal security and that explains its introduction into Athenian legal terminology.[1]

I. PUPILLARY *APOTIMEMA*

Horos no. 130, a late fourth-century text from Arkesine in Amorgos, reads as follows: "*Horos* of the *apotimema* of Simone (and) Demodike, daughters of Simon, in the (properties) of Dexibios. Lessee: Dexibios. Aristotimos son of Xanthiades set the evaluation at one third, having been sent for the purpose by the archons Xanthippides son of Xanthippides, Praxikles son of Theognotos..." (the stone breaks at that point).[2] For an understanding of this *horos*, we turn to a brief statement in Aristotle and to a somewhat expanded definition in the lexicon of the Attic orators prepared by the Alexandrian grammarian, Valerius Harpocration, some time during the second century after Christ. In defining the authority of the Athenian archon in matters of family law, Aristotle writes: "He also leases out the estates of orphans and *epikleroi*, (the latter) until they become fourteen years of age, and he receives the *apotimemata*."[3] Harpocration defines *apotimema* as follows: "Those who leased the estates of orphans from the archon (*i.e.*, acting in a supervisory

38

capacity, not as owner) provided securities for the lease. It was necessary for the archon to send out persons to evaluate the securities. Therefore the evaluated securities were called *apotimemata*, those sent for the evaluation *apotimetai*, and the procedure *apotiman*."[4]

This device (technically called *misthosis oikou*), whereby the administration of an orphan's estate during his minority was transferred from his guardian to a lessee, is attested in the sources for Athens, for Amorgos and Naxos by *horoi*, and nowhere else in the Greek cities.[5] The nature of the sources does not warrant the conclusion, however, that *misthosis oikou* was a peculiarly Athenian institution. It is known solely from the *horoi*, Aristotle's *Constitution of the Athenians*, and the forensic speeches of the Attic orators (together with the lexica based on them). No sources of these types are known elsewhere. Other types of literature and the inscriptions (apart from the *horoi*) are as silent about *misthosis oikou* in Athens as everywhere else.[6]

The decision whether the guardian was to administer the estate himself or was to have it leased through the archon could be predetermined by the father's will. In the lawsuit between Demosthenes and his guardians, for example, he accused the latter of having failed to carry out such a provision of the will. They replied, in turn, that the will made quite the opposite request, that in fact it left instructions that the estate should not be leased out.[7] Such a testamentary provision was no doubt as binding as any other and the suspicion is inescapable, confirmed by the whole tone of the argument adopted by Demosthenes (who admittedly saw no will), that the truth lay either with the guardians or somewhere between the two contentions (*i.e.*, the will was silent on the subject).[8]

If the father left no instructions or died intestate, *misthosis oikou* followed if the guardian so chose or if a third party brought a successful action to compel rental. Thus, in the final decade of the fifth century B.C., a plaintiff suing a guardian for alleged dissipation of a huge estate, running into many talents, says: "Furthermore, if he had wanted to be just with regard to the children, it was permissible for him to act in accordance with the laws regarding orphans, which have to do with both incapable and capable (*i.e.*, of administering the property) guardians; he might have leased the estate, thereby getting rid of a great many difficulties, or have bought land and supported the children from the income. (In either case), they would have been no less rich than any other Athenian."[9]

Clearly the law was permissive, not mandatory, and the guardian's decision to retain the administration in his own hands constituted a matter for reproach in case of loss, not grounds for prosecution.[10] During the period of guardianship, however, it was apparently possible for a third party to intervene, charge the guardian with mismanagement, and by court action compel the leasing of the estate.[11] We have no information as to who could take such action or under what circumstances.

Since the *horoi* indicate the nature of the lessee's property that has been put up as security but not the nature of the orphan-lessor's estate, and since the literary references to *misthosis oikou* are all buried in a swamp of allegations, charges, and counterclaims, it is virtually impossible to discover a pattern or line of reasoning that determined when a guardian chose to administer the estate himself and when he preferred to give it out on lease. Superficially considered, the evidence might seem to suggest that a guardian was likely to retain landed property and rent out liquid or "business" holdings. Thus, Demosthenes' inheritance certainly fell into the latter category and he speaks bitterly of the failure of his guardians to lease it. But is it Demosthenes' complaint or the guardians' actions that typified the usual practice? In other words, one may argue equally well from this case that it was "business property" that tempted guardians to retain control, rather than the reverse. Furthermore, the law provided machinery not merely for *misthosis oikou* but also for the purchase of land on behalf of the orphan.[12] A guardian presumably had free choice among these possibilities, and we know of one case in which a guardian, when taken to court over failure to rent out an estate that consisted largely of loans receivable, obtained permission from the court to remain in control and eventually bought land and multiple-dwellings with the money, property that his wards received upon attaining their majority.[13] In the final analysis, the determining factors were probably to be found in the temperament and circumstances of the guardian rather than in a rigidly drawn rule based on the character of the holding.

What was leased was always the estate as a whole. This is shown not only by the absence of a single source revealing rental of a part but even more convincingly by the almost unfailing use of the word *oikos*. Literally, *oikos* means "household" and it takes us back to an earlier stage in society, when household meant family members *and* goods, like the Latin *familia*. Though it was commonly employed in the fourth century B.C. for an estate, it was by no means the only word. What sets it apart from other terms, *ousia* for example, is its archaic flavor in the emphasis on the *familia* and its unequivocal implication of totality, of the whole estate.[14] A guardian who remained in control could of course lease a part of the property, a house for example, but that would be an ordinary private rental, not a formal *misthosis oikou* arranged under public supervision.

The actual leasing in *misthosis oikou* took place under the archon's supervision and, like all such publicly conducted transactions in Athens, was accomplished by auction, the lessee being the highest bidder. It was permissable for two or more men to take the lease jointly.[15] The guardian himself could bid. Presumably that was rare and perhaps not even socially acceptable. A guardian's reasons for bidding can only be surmised; a plausible explanation is failure on the part of the deceased to make adequate arrangement to repay the guardian for his efforts, so that the latter decided to lease the estate, thereby retaining control and at the same time obtaining an income.[16]

The archon was the responsible official. He conducted the auction, chose the assessors of the *apotimema* (who undoubtedly had the right to decide that the highest bidder was not possessed of sufficient property to guarantee his obligation, thus canceling the bid), and "received" the security, in Aristotle's language. The extent of his authority and his discretionary power is revealed in an oration of Isaeus dated in 364 B.C. The inheritance is being contested on the ground that the deceased Euktemon, a very wealthy man who lived to be 96, had for some years been in the clutches of two collateral relatives, Androkles and Antidoros, who had contrived to make away with half of the estate by one trick or another, and to persuade the old man to enroll as his own, two sons of a prostitute named Alke and a freedman named Dion.[17] When Euktemon showed signs of approaching death, according to the speaker, Euktemon's grandson Chairestratos, the plotters concocted "the most outrageous scheme of all" so that they could have control of the estate after Euktemon was gone. He describes their plan as follows:

"They registered these two boys with the archon as the adopted children of the deceased sons of Euktemon, inscribing themselves as the guardians, and they instructed the archon to lease the estates as (the estates) of orphans. (They did this) so that some of the property would be leased in the children's names and some put up as *apo-*

timema and *horoi* affixed while Euktemon was still alive, while they
themselves, becoming lessees, would receive the income. On the
first day that the courts met, the archon put up (the property) at
auction and they sought to rent it. Some people who were present,
however, notified the relatives of the plot, and the latter came and
informed the dicasts of the state of affairs. As a result, the dicasts
voted that the estate should not be leased.... Please call as witnesses those who were present."[18]

The nature of the plot that was foiled is beyond understanding
and need not detain us.[19] But the character of the procedure before
the archon is clear and very revealing. A *misthosis oikou* was ini-
tiated by a formal application in writing. The archon made no
investigation, but conducted the auction at a regular court sitting.[20]
At that point, interested parties had an opportunity to contest the
proposed lease. Their opposition was submitted to the court, which
then made the final decision whether to proceed with the auction or
not.[21] All in all, the archon and the dicasts, representing the government, played a passive role. They would receive complaints and
adjudicate them; they made no independent investigation and took
no initiative. Such an approach is fully consonant with the self-help
procedures that still permeated Greek law and with the primitive
methods of public notice and the absence of a genuine public
register discussed in a previous chapter. And the perfect ending is
the affixing of the rude *horoi*, a simple private means of making
known what had been achieved under the supervision of the archon
and the courts.

Both this Isaeus text and the one-sentence statement by Aristotle
quoted in the beginning imply that guarantee by *apotimema* was a
regular feature of the *misthosis oikou*, and the former also suggests
that *horoi* were regularly placed once the security had been fixed by
the official evaluators. Though another passage in Isaeus, also incomprehensible in large part, seems to indicate at least one instance
in which an orphan's estate was rented out without any formal
guaranties, there is little doubt that if the text were clarified it
would prove to be no genuine exception and that an *apotimema* was
required by law.[22] Otherwise, the whole procedure loses its point.
Since the archon's role was largely a passive one, only the brief
opportunity given to interested individuals to intervene at the
moment of auction and the *apotimema*, checked by official evaluators, protected the orphan against fraud. Without that security,
official supervision would have been a meaningless mockery. The

law might then better have left the matter entirely in the hands of the guardian, the orphan retaining the protection afforded him by the kind of action for mismanagement of which Demosthenes availed himself when he came of age.

Whether the law further required that the security be in the form of real property is probable though not completely demonstrable.[23] That this was the usual practice, whether mandatory or not, is certain. Not one instance of an *apotimema* in any form other than real property (with or without household goods) is known. This in turn means that the non-citizens who played such an important part in Athenian money transactions, and who, as a group, were not permitted by law to own realty, were automatically barred from this type of economic activity.[24]

Though *horoi* nos. 130 and 131 are the only ones that go into sufficient detail to reveal the underlying *misthosis oikou*, there can be no doubt that fourteen others, all of which link *apotimema* and children, also marked pupillary *apotimemata*. As a group, these sixteen stones differ from the other *horoi* in two significant respects. In the first place, not one makes reference to a written agreement. The reason, I suggest, is that the agreements were always identical, apart from the amount of the rent-interest which was determined by bidding at auction, and fixed by the law regarding *misthosis oikou*. Hence there was no need to draw up a special written instrument to be deposited with a third party for safekeeping.[25] In the second place, only two of the stones indicate the amount of money being guarantied. *Horos* no. 131, a recently discovered Naxian text, reads: "*Horos* of the lands and house and roof put up as security (*apotimema*) to the children of Epiphron. For the principal, 3,500 (drachmas), and the annual rentals, 400 drachmas, (beginning) in (the archonship) of —etos; of this land, every part was evaluated (*i.e.*, as necessary to cover the value of the leased property and the rental), both the (property) in Elaious and the (property) in Melas." *Horos* no. 127, an early fourth-century Attic stone, gives the amount as 800 drachmas, without distinguishing the principal from the rental.[26]

The pupillary *apotimema* differed from other security transactions in that it guarantied not only a sum of money (the annual rent-interest) but also the return of the leased property.[27] If the orphan's estate consisted entirely of money, whether cash on hand or loans receivable, that sum together with the interest-total could be inscribed on the *horos* placed on the property tendered by the lessee as security. If, however, the estate was in realty, whether in whole or in part, only a fictitious sum could be inscribed. Such a procedure would be pointless, since it was the orphan's property that was to be restored to him when he became of age, not its price. The proportion of fourteen to two, therefore, is an indication, though perhaps not entirely exact, of the ratio of realty to liquid holdings in the sixteen cases of pupillary *apotimema* available on the *horoi*. Nor did the official evaluators operate in monetary terms. Aristotimos of Amorgos, named in *horos* no. 130, designated one third of Dexibios' property as adequate security. The anonymous assessor of no. 131 selected the lessee's entire holding in two different places on the island of Naxos.[28]

2. DOTAL *APOTIMEMA*

State intervention through the archon occurred in a *misthosis oikou* because orphans were involved, not because of the security transaction that completed the proceedings. The term *apotimema* as a designation for security was not restricted to this one use, however, and though Aristotle did not go on to consider its other applications, since he was concerned only with the functions of the archon, the lexicographers, seeking an understanding of the then obsolete word, *apotimema*, did go further. After completing his account of *misthosis oikou*, Harpocration continues: "They of that time were also accustomed, if the relatives gave a dowry to a woman on her marriage, to demand from the husband some security equal in value to the dowry, such as a house or land."[29] The purpose of the security, what I have called a dotal *apotimema*, was to assure return of the dowry in case of divorce, decease of the wife without issue, or other circumstances in which the law required the husband to pay it back.[30]

The transaction was a purely private agreement between the two parties, the dowry-giver and the husband, without state intervention in any form. Furthermore, it was a voluntary action though there are indications that it was customary whenever large dowries were at stake.[31] That the law did not require a dotal *apotimema*, although it did require return of the dowry in specified instances, is suggested by Harpocration's phrase, "they were accustomed." Confirmation comes from several orations in which the issue turns on proof that a dowry had been paid at the time of marriage. In these cases, failure to call upon the existence of an *apotimema* as proof of the dowry must mean that there was no *apotimema*, for had there been such security, the entire development of the argument would have been quite different.[32] And finally there is the law which fixes at 18 per cent the interest to be paid by a man who does not return a dowry when required.[33] Were security mandatory, this law would have been unnecessary, for the recourse against a man who did not repay the sum would have been seizure of the *apotimema*. We might add the obvious point that, if a guaranty in the form of real property were demanded of all men receiving dowries along with their wives, a very large number of Athenian males would have been prevented from marrying altogether, or at least would have been driven into the arms of dowryless women.

The dotal *apotimema* differed from the pupillary in two respects. Dowries were usually sums of money, and even when they were not, a monetary evaluation was customarily placed on them. The dotal *apotimema* therefore guaranteed the return of a fixed sum, which could be indicated on the *horos* like any other monetary debt. The available *horoi* reveal a few in which no amount appears, but the proportion of such omissions is no greater than in the *horoi* marking *hypotheke* or *prasis epi lysei* obligations. A second distinction is that whereas in the pupillary *apotimema* an obligation exists in actuality, for the lessee has agreed to pay an annual rent and to return the estate when the orphan attains his majority, in the case of the dotal *apotimema* the obligation is only contingent. Should there be no divorce, for example, the husband would not be obliged to return the dowry.

Before considering the similarities, which far outweigh these differences, we must note still another context in which the security was called *apotimema*. Harpocration completes his definition with one additional sentence: "The same word (is used) also in the case of other debts."[34] In the rules laid down by the deme Peiraieus for the leasing of its sacred enclosures (inscribed on stone in 321/0 B.C.), tenants whose annual rental exceded ten drachmas were required to "put up an *apotimema* sufficient in value for the rental."[35] About 400 B.C. the deme Plotheia instructed its officials to lend available funds either on the security of an *apotimema* or on personal suretyship.[36] Two Attic *horoi* use the word *apotimema* where neither *misthosis oikou* nor a dowry could have been involved. No. 163 reads: "*Horos* of land put up as security (*apotimema*) to Dionysos according to the agreement, 750 (drachmas)." No. 32 marks several security obligations, one of which is an "*apotimema* to the eranists." No further explanation is given but it is almost inconceivable that either a dowry or the estate of an orphan could have been the occasion for the *apotimema*.[37]

There are two common elements that tie together the different uses of *apotimema*. The first and perhaps more significant is rooted in the word itself, the evaluation. In one type of transaction establishing a security obligation, the property comes first and the money second, so to speak. If X sells Y a piece of land and Y, unable to pay all or part of the price, uses the land to guarantee that he will eventually pay the price in full, the land-debt relationship is fixed beforehand. There is nothing to evaluate; that had been done when X and Y agreed on the sale price, prior to any consideration of hypothecation. Similarly, if Y needs a loan for whatever reason and offers his house as security, the potential lender will fix the size of the loan he is willing to make by his estimate of the value of the house. Again it is the property which is the fixed amount, the prior item. Stated differently, it is the value which is adjusted to the given property, not the amount of property that is measured against a fixed amount of money.

In the *apotimema* the situation is reversed. X marries off his daughter with a 2,000-drachma dowry. Then he demands of the husband adequate security against the eventuality that the dowry becomes returnable. The 2,000 drachmas are fixed, so the problem becomes one of evaluating the husband's land to determine what proportion is an acceptable equivalent. In the pupillary *apotimema* we begin with a fixed property holding, the orphan's *oikos*, and a fixed amount of money, the annual rent to be paid by the lessee as determined through the mechanism of the auction. Then comes the evaluation, the measuring off of a proportionate share of the successful lessee's holdings, proportionate to an amount of money and property that has been fixed beforehand.

This distinction between two different relationships, property = money and money = evaluated-portion-of-property, was sufficiently important in Athenian economic and legal practice for them to have invented a new security-word, *apotimema*. The necessity for this invention rests in the problem of the "surplus." In all legal systems, a central question in the field of security is the following: If the debtor defaults, does the creditor have a right to the whole of the property offered in security, regardless of whether it is greater in value, less, or equal to the amount of the obligation? In other words, is the encumbered property automatically deemed the equivalent of, and therefore a substitute for, the debt, or is it merely a way of guaranteeing that the debt itself will be paid, no more and no less ? The answer, as I shall indicate later, is that the fundamental Greek conception of real ·security was one of substitution.[38] In certain kinds of transactions, therefore, a decision was made at the very beginning of the relationship as to just what property would be accepted as a substitute for the debt. This *apotimema*, this measured-off portion, being fixed, subsequent disputes were avoided.[39]

The second common element among the various uses of *apotimema* is the time factor. The practice in moneylending was one of short-term loans, in bottomry for as little as a few months.[40] In the leasing of the estates of orphans, however, the agreement was for the duration of the child's minority, in the case of *epikleroi* to the age of fourteen, of boys to eighteen. Ordinary land leases ran for ten or more years. The term of a dotal *apotimema* was uncertain, since the obligation was contingent and might never materialize, but a considerable number of years was a probability to be reckoned with. The longer the time that elapsed between the original agreement and the dissolution of the obligation, the greater was the possibility of dispute over the value of the property offered in security, that is, in substitution for the debt. This danger was intensified by the fact that the value of realty is difficult to determine in any economy, all the more so in the absence of either a real-estate market or an official property-assessment register for tax purposes.[41]

It so happens that the overwhelming majority of cases in which the *apotimema* was used falls in the area of the family — dowry and the estates of orphans. Interesting and significant as that fact may be for an understanding of certain aspects of Greek life, it is fundamentally irrelevant in the present context. That is to say, whatever distinction existed between *apotimema* on the one hand and *hypotheke* and *prasis epi lysei* on the other arose from the need for evaluation. In practice, the application was largely limited to two kinds of transactions but not *because* they were family matters. The late Greek and Byzantine lexicographers were struck by the coincidence and failed to probe further. Modern scholars have too often followed their lead, thereby introducing a discordant and confusing element into the analysis of the law and practice of security.[42]

Harpocration and the other lexicographers agree, with absolute unanimity, that the dotal *apotimema* was employed solely to guarantee the return of the dowry. Most legal historians have disputed this. The *apotimema*, they say, could be used either way, to guarantee later delivery of the dowry in the event, not infrequent in Athens, that the father was unable to complete payment at the time of marriage, as well as to guarantee its return by the husband if that should prove necessary.[43] There is some logic in this view, because a delayed dowry-payment falls within the category of transactions in which the sum of money was fixed, the security then evaluated in proportion. But the sources argue for acceptance of Harpocration. Only twice in the extant Greek literature is there a clear reference to an *apotimema* securing a dowry.[44] In Demosthenes' lawsuit against Onetor, the issue centers on a factual dispute over an *apotimema* guaranteeing the return of the dowry the latter had provided for his sister, the wife of Aphobos.[45] There can be no question that the transaction between Aphobos and Onetor, honest or not, fits precisely Harpocration's definition.

The second case requires more detailed consideration. It appears in the lawsuit against Spudias by a plaintiff whose name we do not know. Demosthenes' brief for the latter is the forty-first of his extant orations. The plaintiff had married the elder daughter of an Athenian, Polyeuktos of Teithras.[46] The marriage contract specified that his dowry was to be 4,000 drachmas, 3,000 payable in cash at once, the remainder after the death of Polyeuktos. The unpaid portion was guaranteed not by an *apotimema* or other form of real security but by the personal guarantee of Leokrates, Polyeuktos' adopted son and husband of the younger daughter. Some time later — the speech gives no dates — the father and adopted son had a bitter quarrel which resulted in Leokrates' divorce from his wife and withdrawal from the family. Polyeuktos then gave his daughter in marriage, along with the dowry returned by Leokrates, to the defendant Spudias. That left the plaintiff without any form of security for the 1,000 drachmas still coming to him. To correct the defect, five days before dying Polyeuktos put up a house as security by *apotimema* and in a will left instructions for *horoi* to be placed on the building as acknowledgement of the debt.[47]

Polyeuktos died without male issue and his two daughters therefore inherited the estate jointly. The lawsuit arose over the division of the inheritance. The sons-in-law, acting as *kyrioi* of their respective wives, disagreed over the inventory of the estate, for each claimed the right to withdraw certain sums prior to the division. Our one concern is with the plaintiff's insistence that he was entitled to withdraw 1,000 drachmas in satisfaction of the outstanding dowry-obligation, attested by Polyeuktos' deathbed act and the *horoi.* Apparently Spudias did not contest these facts but made the usual counterclaim that the deathbed action and will were invalid because executed under undue influence by the plaintiff and his wife, and that there were other reasons why the plaintiff's claim should be judged extinguished.

How shall we interpret Polyeuktos' action in giving security on his deathbed and including the provision about *horoi* in his will? To prevent his heirs from defaulting on the 1,000-drachma obligation seems to be the only possible answer.[48] The marriage contract provided that this sum was to be paid after Polyeuktos' death, that is, by the heirs. Polyeuktos himself never denied the obligation, or so the speaker says.[49] But the heirs might; that is why he wanted security, originally the suretyship of Leokrates, then the death-bed hypothecation by *apotimema.*

It is significant that until Polyeuktos was at death's door, there was no *apotimema* for the unpaid portion of the dowry (after Leokrates' withdrawal from the family, no guaranty of any kind).[50] When *horoi* were affixed at the last moment, a security transaction was created for the first time. And yet this situation does not seem to warrant the generalization that the dotal *apotimema* was given by the father for an unpaid dowry as a matter of regular, or even occasional, practice. As in every other instance of an unpaid marriage-portion known from the literature, here too there was no *apotimema* until one was created at the last moment because of special circumstances. The dowry was irrelevant and accidental in this case, so to speak. What was decisive and justified the use of the word *apotimema* was the notion of measuring off a piece of property to match a predetermined sum, 1,000 drachmas. The 1,000 drachmas happened to be due because of a dowry-promise; they could just as well have been owed for a dozen other reasons with the same result. Assuming that the plaintiff was speaking the complete truth, we can translate what happened in this way: When Polyeuktos realized he was dying, he wished to protect the husband of his elder daughter from any possible deprivation of the unpaid 1,000 drachmas. He therefore set aside, from his total estate, one house as the equivalent. Should the plaintiff subsequently not receive 1,000 drachmas in cash, he could take the house in satisfaction through the regular legal machinery available for execution in a security obligation. This, incidentally, is in part the interpretation of Libanios, who writes in his Argument that the dying Polyeuktos "took the house out from the rest of his property and gave it for the debt."[51] I think

Libanios was wrong in interpreting the act as a conveyance, but quite right in emphasizing the literal connotation of *apotimao*.

Interestingly enough, the plaintiff says that Polyeuktos gave him the *apotimema*,[52] whereas in the *horoi* it is invariably the name of the woman that appears as the recipient (her name is given in the dative case). This distinction should not be pressed too far, but it is a suggestion, as we shall see in a moment, that all the *horoi* mark *apotimemata* given by the husband to the dowry-giver. In a sense, the wife "owned" the dowry. But she never administered or controlled it in Athens; she administered no property. Every Greek understood the situation and they were always careless in their language in this respect, so that among the orators, for example, we find dowries given to the wife and dowries given to the husband, more or less indiscriminately.[53] Yet the rigid consistency in language in the *horoi* has a point. Wherever the stone marked security put up by the husband against the eventual return of the dowry, naming the wife was the one sensible procedure, for, since the latent obligation was of uncertain duration, no one could know the man to whom the dowry would have to be repaid should such a contingency arise. To name the father on the *horos*, without lengthy explanation, would be to invite legal difficulties in the event of his death. Naming the woman was completely safe, for should the security become payable, it would automatically go to her *kyrios* whoever he might be at that moment.[54]

Thirteen of the *horoi* further identify the woman by adding her father's name and eleven of these also give his demotic. We have already seen that the *horoi* systematically avoid naming the person on whose property they stood.[55] It follows that in these instances the father was not the man who put up the property as security. The husband therefore must have been. This is confirmed by the one *horos* in which the husband is actually named, a third-century Amorgian stone (no. 154), which reads: "*Horos* of house(s) —— (2 or 3 words lost) put up as security (*apotimema*) in the archonship of Kritobulos by Exakestos to Kleinokrate daughter of Timagoras (a line follows that was deleted) for a share of the dowry for 3,000 (numerals representing 2,000 of the 3,000 were deleted) drachmas (followed by another deleted line) according to the agreement (deposited) with Aristonikos."[56] In view of the missing lines, this text is not fully intelligible. Conceivably Exakestos could have been a relative, acting after the father's death or in lieu of the father for another reason, who promised a dowry after some delay. Such an interpretation is most unlikely from the language, especially from the absence of the word *kyrios*. The natural explanation is that Exakestos was the husband and that by special agreement — this is the only *horos* marking a dotal *apotimema* that mentions the existence of a written agreement — he had arranged to repay the dowry in installments. He had repaid 2,000 drachmas, and the appropriate numerals were therefore deleted.[57]

Horos no. 156, a Naxian stone that can be dated about 300 B.C., reads as follows: "*Horos* of a house, including the roof and the furnishings in the house, put up in full as security (*apotimema*) to —— (name lost) for the dowry, in the archonship of Timagoras, 1,500 (drachmas), 1,000 the house and 500 all the furnishings." This text can be taken either way, that it was the dowry-giver who was the debtor or that it was the husband who had put up the security. The absence of the father's name removes the argument that the husband was necessarily the "debtor."[58] *Horoi* nos. 49, 82, 82A, and perhaps 93 mark guaranties provided for dowries by *prasis epi lysei*. The first does not name the father; nos. 82 and 93 do; no. 82 A is an incomplete fragment. In principle, *prasis epi lysei* was certainly available to both the dowry-giver and the husband. It is not inconceivable that other *horoi* indicating a *prasis epi lysei* without stating the underlying reason for the security transaction also stemmed from arrangements regarding the marriage-portion, though the fact that men are named as the creditors makes that most unlikely.[59]

In sum, the predominance of family matters in *apotimema* transactions rested on the need for special evaluation of the security, not on some special link between *apotimema* and intra-family arrangements. The literary evidence reveals two types of transaction in which the *apotimema* was used regularly, *misthosis oikou* and guarantee of the return of the dowry. (The insistence of the lexicographers on this point shows that the now lost orations, which were still available to them, confirmed the evidence of the extant texts.) Occasionally, *apotimema* was also used for other purposes, when evaluation was the important idea. Among these other purposes might have been payment of an overdue dowry, but the emphasis sometimes placed on that use stems from a false link between *apotimema* and family affairs.

In reality, the *apotimema* represents a combination of two separate elements: evaluation and hypothecation. Once the evaluation has been made, that is to say, once a particular piece of property or a particular share has been decided upon as the proper equivalent

4*

for the debt, then the *apotimema* becomes nothing more than an ordinary security obligation. What has occurred is a kind of redefinition of the property. Where there had been one unit there were now two, one unencumbered and one encumbered. On the latter the charge was called *apotimema* but the name is no longer relevant. In other words, the distinction between *apotimema* and *hypotheke* was not one of juristic substance at all, but one of practical procedure, made necessary in certain types of transaction by the fundamental principle of Greek law that security was substitutive in character. By *apotimema* a more or less precise determination was made at the time the agreement was reached, fixing the property that would be accepted as the substitute for the debt, should that become necessary in the future (usually in the relatively distant future).[60]

This conception of the *apotimema* alone, I think, leads to an explanation of the law which, according to the plaintiff in the Spudias case, orders that whatever was hypothecated by *apotimema* may not be disputed in a court action. He does not quote the law and no other reference to it is known.[61] There can be little doubt that the law did not bar third parties but applied only to the two parties to the agreement, and that even they retained the right to contest the fact of hypothecation. Beyond that there has been little agreement among scholars. The prevailing view sees in this law a general rule applying to all security transactions.[62] There are two objections, however, which seem unanswerable. First, all the evidence we have points unmistakably to the absence of special legislation on security. Second, Demosthenes' choice of the verb *apotimao* in preference to *hypotithemi* in his paraphrase of the law cannot be brushed aside without powerful proof, and there is no proof.

The key to the correct explanation, it seems to me, is to be found in another law, which holds that there can be no action for the return of a dowry in case of divorce unless the dowry has been evaluated in monetary terms at the time it was agreed upon.[63] Here the implication is unmistakable. To avoid later disputes over the worth of property (land, clothing, furniture, jewelry) that had been conveyed, the law required that the parties mutually decide upon the monetary equivalent from the very first. The problem was no less serious in the case of security by *apotimema*. There too the law held that the evaluation could not later be disputed. In my opinion, that is all it meant. Whatever legal actions might arise from security transactions remained applicable, but there could be no action about the worth of the property.

CHAPTER V

THE PROPERTY

I. INTRODUCTION

IN THE SECOND BOOK OF THE *Politics*, Aristotle considered at length various expedients that had been tried or proposed in order to prevent civil disorder by checking the over-concentration of wealth. Phaleas of Chalcedon, for example, had suggested the equalizing device of having the rich give dowries but not receive them, the poor receive but not give. Aristotle objected. Phaleas erred, he said, "because he creates equality only with respect to land, and there is wealth in slaves and livestock and money and there is much holding in what are called furnishings."[1]

Closer scrutiny shows that Aristotle's breakdown of the kinds of wealth can actually be reduced to three categories, land, money, and slaves, insofar as fundamental economic considerations are concerned. Furnishings are wealth as objects of use and display, not in the productive sense of capital goods.[2] The elevation of livestock to an independent category is only an oblique way of dividing land into arable and pastoral. There were regions of the Greek world in which even in the fourth century B.C. pasturage was an important, sometimes the basic, source of wealth. But the leasing of livestock, well known in the Ptolemaic and Seleucid economies, played a minor role in the city-states, and then only in the form of draft animals hired cut for the transportation of construction materials, not the rental of farm animals.[3]

Of the three kinds of wealth — land, money, and slaves — it was land that was still, in Aristotle's day, the one stable, satisfactory, socially and politically necessary form. Not a few states maintained landowning qualifications for the full exercise of the rights of citizenship.[4] That was the characteristic mark of oligarchy, to be sure, but even in the democracies the possession of land gave the owner added status, intangible perhaps but none the less important. And re-distribution of the land was at the heart of every "revolutionary" program.[5] All states limited the right to own land to their citizens; non-citizens could acquire the right only by special enactment and there is ample evidence that such privileges were not easily obtained in normal times.[6] So close was the link between property and land that Aristotle himself used the phrase "lands and houses" (*choria* and *oikiai*, precisely the words that constantly recur in the *horoi*) to mean "property" generally when he was summarizing the functions of the *poletai*, the Athenian officials responsible for the adjudication and sale of confiscated properties.[7] The *poletai* sold everything and anything, slaves for example.[8] Yet in Aristotle's mind, and in the minds of his readers, his expression was no error but simply a linguistic reflection of the fact that confiscated property was made up predominantly of land and houses.

Such usage also reflects the fact that there was no word in the Greek language meaning "real property"; further, that the common modern distinction between real and personal property was not important enough in the Greek world, legally or administratively, to compel the formulation either of a typology or of a fixed terminology. The lexica are filled with words which, in certain contexts (and at certain times or in specific localities), may best be rendered in English as "real property." It is the context alone that fixes such a rendition, however, and it is not possible to single out one of the words as the usual or characteristic Greek term for real property. Not even within the works of a single author is there a vocabulary of property terms that is in any way classificatory. This is as true of the orators, who might be assumed to be more "technical" in their language, as of the poets or historians.[9]

Of course, there were obvious, and sometimes important, factual distinctions between real property and other kinds, and the Greeks could not have been unaware of them. The significant point is that it was always concrete factual considerations, not juristic principles or broad economic categories, that determined the distinctions drawn and the language used in a given situation. That is why the Greeks could so frequently talk of "visible" and "invisible" property, a distinction that was very fluid and by no means always equivalent to real property and personal property or to frozen and liquid assets.[10] "Visible" and "invisible" are to be understood quite literally. The most common context, in Athens at least, was the assessment of liturgies. Thus, in the catalogue of crimes and misdeeds that the orator Aeschines drew up against Timarchos, one, charged to his opponent's father, was that he had deliberately sold some of his holdings, thereby rendering that portion of his wealth invisible and escaping liturgies.[11] With variations, this accusation appears over and over in the orators, and there is good reason to believe that it was not always mere libel.

A second context was the division of an inheritance, an operation that could become highly complicated when there were conflicting claims. In one of Isaeus' cases, the speaker remarks: "I say nothing about the other things which were left but which they (my opponents) do not reveal; I include only the things that were visible and admitted by them."[12] Among the "visible" items were several landed estates and houses, sheep, goats, furnishings, crops, 4,000 drachmas in loans receivable (at interest), and some 1,000 drachmas in collectible, but not interest-bearing, friendly loans (*eranoi*).

Still a third context was restitution of property, either to political exiles who were readmitted to their native city or to individuals who had suffered losses at the hands of freebooters. Here we must turn to non-Athenian sources for illustration. Each time a group of exiles left a city or returned, almost a daily event in the Greek world of the fourth and third centuries B.C., disposal of their property became an important question. One way to handle restitution was the method proposed in Phlius about 385 B.C., which was to have the state buy the visible properties back from those who had acquired them at the time of confiscation and return them intact to their original owners.[13] Very probably the reference was to real property.[14] But in the decree of the Aetolian League in 201 B.C. granting the city of Teos in Asia Minor inviolability against seizures of any kind, neither land nor houses could have been involved. Should anyone, in violation of the decree, "carry off either them (*i.e.*, persons) or things from the city and land, the *strategos* and the *synedroi* in office at the time shall recover the visible, and those who made the seizure shall be liable to legal action for the invisible."[15]

One situation in which the factual distinction between real and personal property takes on clear significance is legal security. Roughly stated, the rule is that personal possessions are pawned, realty hypothecated in a transaction involving no transfer of possession. In part, this difference in method may be explained by the differences in magnitude involved; but only in part, for there were cases involving sums running into the thousands of drachmas in which the creditor took over the hypothecated property, and there were other cases in which realty was offered as security for relatively small sums and remained in the debtor's possession. More basic than size of the transaction, probably, is the qualitative difference, economically, socially, even politically, between land and other forms of wealth. A man who surrenders possession of his farm will find it virtually impossible to repay his debt, but he can pawn his pots and pans and his wife's jewelry without destroying his ability to repay.

Two kinds of wealth stand in the middle, as it were, and endlessly complicate the rough rule. Slaves make up one type and there is no fixed pattern for their use as security for loans.[16] The other type appears in maritime loans, for which the ship, the cargo, or both were normally, perhaps always, hypothecated.[17] From the very nature of bottomry, however, it is not possible to generalize from its practices to security in general. An elementary distinction becomes immediately apparent from the Dionysodoros case. The plaintiffs lent money for a voyage to Egypt and back. Instead, they say, the defendant "took his ship to Rhodes, unloaded the cargo there and sold it in violation of the agreement and of your laws. From Rhodes he again sent the ship to Egypt and from there to Rhodes, and to this day he has neither repaid the money to us, the lenders at Athens, nor produced the security."[18] In a sense, the parallel between slaves and ships, their mobility, sets them apart from other forms of security, and above all from security in real property. The law necessarily took cognizance of this factual distinction and we must do so, too, by restricting our discussion to realty.[19]

2. LAND

In the Greek world, realty was above all agricultural land (understood in its broadest possible sense, including vineyards, pastureland, and so on). Aristotle, it will be remembered, did not even bother to mention houses in his enumeration of the forms of wealth, and urban land values are a relatively modern phonomenon in any serious sense. But when we try to get at the proportion of the population that owned land — the citizen population only, of course — we find almost no source material.

For Athens there is one figure. Dionysius of Halicarnassus, writing in the time of Augustus, says that in 403 B.C., a certain Phormisios proposed limiting political rights to those who owned land and that 5,000 citizens would have been disfranchised by the measure if it had been carried.[20] That would mean that perhaps 20 or 25 per cent were landless at the end of the Peloponnesian War, if Dionysius is to be believed.[21] The figure is difficult to control, however, and the objections and emendations that have been offered by historians diverge widely.[22] One argument brought forward against Dionysius is the large number of cleruchs — the total figure for the fifth century B.C. has been placed as high as 20,000[23] — driven out of their holdings during and immediately after the Peloponnesian War, many of whom certainly had not acquired or re-acquired land in Attica.[24] But this argument is nothing but one guess piled on another. The cleruchy estimates are highly speculative; there are no figures of the number returning to Athens or of the proportion who found their way back to the land in one fashion or another. In any event, many citizens did leave Athens in the fifth century B.C. to accept land as military colonists elsewhere, and that fact demonstrates the tremendous hold that the possession of land had on the Athenians.

For the fourth century B.C. the evidence comes from the orators, chiefly Isaeus and Demosthenes. It is not evidence that lends itself to statistical analysis, for more often than not the speaker refers to individual holdings without listing all the property of his opponent or himself. What may have been included in the depositions is of course not available to us. Yet the conclusion from the speeches is unmistakable. The citizens who were involved in these cases — and they were the wealthier ones, the property owners — owned land much more often than not. Demosthenes himself is a notable exception. The inheritance for which he sued his guardians, apparently one of the largest fortunes in Athens at the time, was made up of slaves used in manufacture, raw materials (copper and ivory), two houses, and a considerable quantity of cash, some on hand, the rest out on loan. There are other exceptions, too, but the typical citizens were such men as the leading general Timotheos, whose holdings in the year 373/2 B.C. included a farm "in the plain,"[25] Apollodoros, son of the banker Pasion, who held land in three different demes,[26] or the family line founded by Buselos of the deme Oion, which can be traced through the fifth and fourth centuries and included a considerable number of men of some prominence in the military and political affairs of Athens.[27] The property of the Buselos line was involved in numerous legal disputes, all over inheritance rights, from about 395 B.C. through the middle of the century. Two of the extant orations were written for cases in this series of lawsuits and they reveal extensive holdings, including farms in Eleusis and Thria (the values are given at 2 and 2½ talents, respectively, the two most highly rated estates in the whole of Athenian literature), another in

Oinoe, several houses, and miscellaneous goods.[28] As usual, there is no sure indication of the total wealth held by various members of the family.

For the fifth and fourth centuries B.C., it seems more than probable that a majority, perhaps as high as three fourths, of the citizens of Athens owned some workable land, with or without additional properties. Of those who did not, a considerable number were altogether propertyless, depending on their work as craftsmen, on petty trade, and on governmental assistance for their livelihood. Only a small minority had their wealth exclusively in money or in slaves who produced income by work in the mines or in handicraft production. The numerous private societies such as *orgeones* and the public bodies (such as demes and phratries) were owners of land above all else, if they were big enough and rich enough to own anything.[29]

It then becomes a matter of simple arithmetic to discover that so widespread a distribution of the relatively small Attic territory meant that nearly all the parcels were small.[30] Figures are simply unavailable. I know of exactly five in Athenian literary sources, none from the inscriptions. We have already noted the farm of Phainippos, for which the speaker gives a linear measure; the acreage could be anywhere from 700 to 1,000, depending on the contour of the farm.[31] Then there is the estate of Aristophanes son of Nikophemos, confiscated in 390 B.C. when he was condemned to death because of a military disaster. It measured over 300 *plethra*, about 70 acres, the same as Alcibiades' patrimonial estate.[32] The fourth figure is the 200 *plethra* in Euboea (about 45 acres), half arable and half orchard, given to Aristeides' son Lysimachos by the Athenian state in the latter part of the fifth century B.C.[33] Finally, there is a 60-*plethra* (about 14 acres) figure in an oration dated about 389 B.C.[34] In three of the instances the dimensions are stated by the speaker because he wishes to emphasize that these were large holdings; the last-named, the 60-*plethra* farm, was specified as a sign of its small size. If 45 and 70-acre holdings were not unusual, they were clearly above average, and Phainippos' farm must have been quite exceptional even if the common statement that it is the largest known is almost meaningless when we know the size of only five.

Calculations have been made of the landholdings needed for each rating in the Solonic classification.[35] One estimate would require for the highest rating, the *pentakosiomedimnoi*, 75—145 acres if the land were only grain-producing, or 20—25 acres of vineyards and olive orchards, or 50—75 acres if the holding were mixed; for the knights, 45—75, 12—15, or 30—45, respectively; and for the zeugites, 30—50, 7½—10, or 25.[36] Whatever value these estimates have, and their tenuousness is acknowledged, they are as applicable to the fourth century B.C. as to Solon's time.[37] There had been no significant technological improvement beyond the low level attained some three or four centuries earlier, and the trend to olive and grape culture made smaller holdings all the more feasible and profitable.[38] The estimates seem clearly to confirm the fact of small holdings, even for the wealthier citizens.

Every part of Attica was farmed. It is generally stated that not more than 18 or 20 per cent of the soil was suitable for grain, concentrated in four plains, and that olive and grape culture rendered perhaps another 5 or 10 per cent productive.[39] Horoi have been found all over the district. Although an analysis of the horoi which would reveal the ratio of rural to urban holdings and the relative frequency in the various demes and districts would have been desirable, such a study has proved to be impossible for several reasons. An intensive excavation such as the American School has been conducting in the Agora creates an artificial imbalance between horoi found in the city and those found in rural districts. Then, it is well known that Greek inscriptions had a way of moving about, so that the place of discovery might be at a considerable distance from the original home.[40] Though the percentage of such wandering stones may be small and there are horoi which can be linked textually with the area of discovery, the number of those which have been found in the wall of a modern house or in a cistern in the Agora is large enough to invalidate any attempt at a statistical distribution. When the horoi are divided among the demes in which they were found, the number for all but four demes ranges from one to three, obviously too few for statistical analysis. It goes without saying that the horoi themselves, placed directly on the property to which they referred, gave no geographical indications except when necessary to prevent confusion. Altogether there are only three such documents from Athens, one from Amorgos, and one from Naxos.[41]

Nor do the horoi give a functional (economic or architectural) description of the property hypothecated. Except for one reference each to a furnace (in the mining region), a stoneworking establishment, an outhouse or dung-pit, an oikema (a difficult word to translate in the absence of any context), and building lots, all lands, houses, and workshops are always choria, oikiai, and ergasteria, respectively. Nor is the number of units indicated if more than one is involved. Yet, in the case of land at least, the Greek language is relatively rich in descriptive terminology and even the most routine administrative texts often distinguish wooded from arable land or farmland from vineyards.[42] That a considerable variety of holdings lies concealed beneath the monotonous terminology is more than probable. Thus, three of the *horoi* from the Peiraieus deal with a *chorion* without a house; two (nos. 58 and 144) unfortunately give no monetary figure, but the third (no. 55) has the exceptionally low sum of 150 drachmas. It is conceivable that the land involved was farmland in the plain between Athens and the Peiraieus,[43] but it is much more likely that it was urban realty. The 150-drachma figure probably refers to a building lot.[44] (The technical word for a lot, *oikopedon*, is found on only one *horos*, no. 143, a stone discovered in the ancient residential district at the foot of the Acropolis.) Though building site is not the normal sense of *chorion*, it is by no means unprecedented.[45] In the final analysis, there seems no way to determine with any precision what types of land were given in security in the bulk of the *horoi*.

3. HOUSES

With regard to buildings, some measure of precision is possible. The legal and administrative texts, with rare exceptions, use language that indicates specifically whether the reference is to a piece of land, a house, or both. Decrees by the hundreds have been found in excavations all over the Greek world (though very few, significantly enough, in Athens), granting non-citizens the special privilege of owning real property. The formula is regularly "the right to own land and a house," so regularly that, when there are variations, we must assume that the departure from the norm was intentional and was to be understood quite literally. When Athens, for example, gave Theogenes of Naukratis the right to own a house in 348 B.C., the privilege was a limited one and did not extend to farmland, precisely in the spirit in which Xenophon proposed that the state make vacant house lots available to "worthy" metics who were prepared to build homes.[46] In an interesting variation, eight Athenian decrees are known, ranging in date from the middle of the third century to 166/5 B.C., which set a monetary limit on the value of the property the individual receiving this special privilege might acquire. Each decree not only distinguished between land and house but fixed separate maxima, in most cases 3,000 drachmas for a house, 6,000 for land.[47]

It may be difficult to assume that in the reverse situation, decrees granting the right to own land without mention of a house, the recipient is prohibited from building on his land. Such cases are extremely rare, in any event. In another type of document, lists of confiscated property sold by the *poletai* in Athens, the distinction between farms with and farms without houses on them seems to be drawn with unfailing regularity.[48] The summaries inscribed on stone were copied directly, in abbreviated form, from the temporary records kept by the *poletai*, which would have to be quite exact in the interest of possible claimants and prospective purchasers.[49]

The *horoi*, too, had to be exact on this point. Their function was to make known publicly the existence of a legal encumbrance on the property. To do this properly, they also had to indicate, no matter how briefly, just what property was encumbered. We may therefore accept literally the variations which we find, the absence or presence of the word "house," the use of the singular or plural, the occasional inclusion of a garden, a well, or a watercourse. (The possibility must be reckoned with, of course, that there has been an omission by the stonecutter in any given instance.) Urban building sites alone constitute an exception; while they are vacant, they are treated as land, but once a house is placed on one, the land seems to disappear and the single word "house" to suffice. The significance of this exception is obviously a reflection of the fact that under ordinary circumstances urban real estate had little, if any, monetary value.[50] Modern American practice, significantly enough, is exactly the reverse. We speak of "land with improvements" when we mean land plus a building, despite the fact that it is usually the building which bears the larger share of the price.

For the present discussion, it will be best to eliminate those *horoi* that mark *apotimemata*, for that type of security transaction involved an evaluating procedure which could lead to artificial divisions of property.[51] In the remainder, those summarized in Tables A and B, the figures for all Attic *horoi* on which the identification of the property has been fully retained on the stone in its present state show the following ratio (ignoring, for purposes of simplification, the presence or absence of gardens and excluding all properties listed in the plural): land alone, 29; land and house, 26; house alone, 23.[52] The last figure represents chiefly city homes, but not entirely, for two of these *horoi* were found in Eleusis where wealthier citizens had begun to build residences in the fourth century B.C. in order to be near the scene of the most important of the religious festivals.[53]

The similarity in the two figures, land alone and land and house, is subject to certain qualification, particularly because some of the first-named group mark urban holdings. Yet the equation provides clear substantiation for two important points in Athenian history. One is the infrequency of substantial buildings on the farms — "By the gods and goddesses, men of the jury," exclaims Phainippos' opponent, "there were two threshing-floors there."[54] The other is the trend, beginning in the fifth century B.C. and becoming marked in the fourth, towards urban residence.[55]

Movement to the city does not necessarily mean movement away from the land economically.[56] Under certain conditions, it may mean a change in residence, with consequent social and political implications of great significance but without fundamental economic shifts. In large parts of central and eastern Europe, farmers have lived in communities and traveled miles to their fields in antiquity as in modern times.[57] "The majority of the wealthy among the Naxians," wrote Aristotle, "lived in the city, while the others were scattered among the villages."[58] In 385 B.C., Sparta laid down as a peace condition for defeated Mantinea that the city be razed and the people return to the villages in which they had once lived. Xenophon goes on to comment: "At first they were discontent because it was necessary to demolish the houses they had and to build new ones. But when the property owners were living nearer the lands they had around the villages, and they had an aristocracy, and they were rid of the burdensome demagogues, they were pleased with the state of affairs."[59] One of the series of land-lease inscriptions from Boeotian Thespis, of the second half of the third century B.C., mentions tenants who do not live on the farms they have leased; another deals with the rental of twenty-two lots which had earlier been leased as a single unit and only one of the twenty-two has a farmhouse as far as we can tell.[60] When a Greek colony was established about 385 B.C. on the Adriatic island called Kerkyra Melaina by the Greeks, the agreement with the native Illyrians provided that each settler should receive a building lot in what was to become the city and land in the rural district.[61]

With the exception of Naxos, the examples I have given were taken from purely rural communities in different areas of the Greek world. Clearly the social and psychological pressure towards residence in the city would be even greater on Athenians, provided they could afford the added cost. What the high proportion of *horoi* marking land without houses tends to demonstrate, and quite strongly, is that the movement into Athens was a shift in *residence* from the outlying villages to the city proper, not a fundamental shift in property relations.

Full and decisive proof is not available. The information provided by the orators is too fragmentary and much too tendentious. A list of the individuals they name who are known to own both a farm and a house or two in the city could be matched by another list of men whose holding seems to be limited to one or the other kind, but there is no way of evaluating the validity of the proportion. In many cases, it should be noted, those whose stated property seems to be no more than a house have no visible means of support, unless it be pandering.[62] I do not know of a single instance in which we can trace the actual wealth of an Athenian family through two generations, and certainly not the fate of specific land parcels, individually or in a group.[63] Though the fourth century B.C. was clearly a time of increasing poverty for many Greeks, it does not seem to have been a period of increasing wealth at the other end of the scale. Individual fortunes of which we are told actually run into higher figures in the fifth century B.C. than in the fourth, at least in Athens.[64] Nor is there evidence of significant concentration of land ownership, either in the form of direct statement or indirectly through indications of changes in the technique, agronomic or economic, of the exploitation of land. Fourth-century population was smaller than in the preceding hundred-year period, and that suggests the possibility of some concentration of ownership. There is the further possibility that though the individual parcels of land did not increase noticeably in either average or maximum value — and for our purposes that is most important — wealthy citizens may have acquired more and more such separate holdings. But the essential pattern is one of considerable fluctuation in wealth around a fixed level. The reason behind the *antidosis* as an institution, says the speaker in the Phainippos case, is that the number of citizens who enjoy unbroken prosperity is small.[65]

None of this is to deny that there were Athenians of wealth who voluntarily abandoned their land for other forms of economic activity. Speaking of Timarchos, Aeschines says: "But perhaps someone may say that, after selling his paternal house he acquired another one somewhere in the city, and that in place of the farm at the borders and the land in Alopeke and the craftsmen and the other things, he set himself up in the mines, like his father before him. But nothing remains to him, not a house, not a multiple-dwelling (*synoikia*), not land, not slaves, not a loan (receivable), not a thing by which men who are not evildoers live."[66]

The banker Pasion apparently left two multiple-dwellings at his death in 370/69. One was included in the dowry he provided for his widow by will and was evaluated by his son Apollodoros at 10,000 drachmas, while the other was inherited by Apollodoros. No value is indicated for the latter but not long after his father's death Apollodoros put it up as security for a loan of 1,600 drachmas at 16 per cent interest.[67] A contemporary, Euktemon of Kephisia, had two multiple-dwellings, one in the Peiraieus and the other in the Kerameikos.[68] And a third, Kiron, owned in addition to a farm in Phlya, two houses, one near the sanctuary of Dionysos in the Marshes, worth 2,000 drachmas and leased out, and the other in which he lived, worth 1,300 drachmas.[69]

House rental was surely a considerable operation in Athens. There may have been as many as 30,000 non-citizens permanently residing there at the outbreak of the Peloponnesian War and nearly half as many again a century later.[70] Except for the very few who had received the privilege of acquiring real property, they were compelled to lease their living quarters. Multiple-dwellings must have been rather numerous, and the oblique indications in the literature would indicate that they were as flimsy as most of the homes in which citizens lived. They were concentrated in the Peiraieus and they inevitably acquired the reputation that always accompanies lodgings in harbor towns.[71] In the *Poroi*, Xenophon not only proposed a more generous extension of the right to own houses to "worthy" metics but he made the additional suggestion, with a vagueness on the economics of the idea that is characteristic, that the state build lodging houses for ship captains near the harbors.[72] Citizens also rented dwelling space, to be sure, even among the wealthy, but it would seem that the great bulk of this activity was rental to non-citizens.[73]

It is noteworthy that the word *synoikia* does not appear on a single *horos*. A decree of the deme Myrrhinus authorized the priests to lend temple funds "on land or a house or a *synoikia*" and to affix a *horos* to the property to be received as security.[74] Other texts are available to suggest that *synoikia* was something of a technical word in legal and administrative documents.[75] We could therefore attribute the absence of a single *horos* marking a multiple-dwelling to the accident of excavation. And yet it is tempting to find the explanation in another direction. "Where several men," writes Aeschines, "having leased one residence, occupy it, dividing it among themselves, we call it a *synoikia*, but where one lives, a house."[76] This is a purely functional and, so to speak, non-architectural conception of a house, precisely the approach we have already found in the language of the *horoi*, where all forms of landed property, from urban building lots to more extensive farms, receive the identical designation, *chorion*. It seems not improbable that behind the uniform *oikia* of the *horoi* lie similar variations, that some of the buildings hypothecated were in fact multiple-dwellings.

The amounts, it may be added, offer no clue. The numbers inscribed on the *horoi* represent the debt, not the value of the property. We have a great variety of house-value figures, with a considerable range, but not nearly enough information from which to draw any conclusions. But since Apollodoros hypothecated a multiple-dwelling for 1,600 drachmas, the three *horoi* from the Peiraieus that mark houses alone, at sums of 1,000, 1,800, and 3,000 drachmas respectively, could easily, on that score, refer to multiple-dwellings.[77] I am not suggesting that ordinary residences of single families were not normally subject to hypothecation nor even that they would be less likely to be offered as security than multiple-dwellings operated for profit. On the contrary, an analysis of the economics of real security will show that, in all likelihood, it is the personal residence that is usually meant by the word "house" in the *horoi*.[78]

4. WORKSHOPS

Immediately following his definition of a *synoikia*, Aeschines continues in the same vein: "And if perchance a physician settles in one of these shops (*ergasteria*) along the streets, it is called a doctor's office. But if he moves out and a smith settles in the same shop, it is called a smithy; if a laundryman, a laundry; if a carpenter, a carpenter's shop; and if a pimp and harlots, from the work itself it is called a brothel."[79] And the scholiast adds the following comment: "that the appellations are not from the shops to the men but from the men to the places." In the latter part of the fourth century B.C., then, *ergasterion* still retained its original denotation of a place where work was done, any kind of work and not necessarily manufacture (the usual sense of the English word "workshop").[80]

If we consider the Athenian workshop only in its character as property, stripped of all considerations of the economics of manufacture, three questions arise. To what extent were there separate and distinct buildings that could be called workshops and nothing else? How did they compare in value with houses? What characteristics, in a property sense, did a workshop have that set it apart from any other building?

In their enumeration of the forms of wealth, neither Aeschines nor Aristotle mentioned *ergasteria*.[81] In the case of Aristotle this omission takes on added significance when we remember how often he, like Plato, discussed handicraft labor as a form of economic activity. Aeschines made an oblique reference, however, when he said that Timarchos had not even "set himself up in the mines, like his father before him," for earlier in the same speech the orator had spoken of two *ergasteria* that his opponent's father had owned in Laureion.[82] In the Attic mining regions, the existence of numerous workshops — mills for crushing and washing the ore and smelters — is well attested archaeologically and epigraphically.[83] In fact, the prevalence of small-scale operations on short-term leases served to multiply considerably the number of *ergasteria* in Laureion. In the same category, though of less significance, would be the stone working establishments at or near the quarries.

The eight *horoi* that specify *ergasteria* are all from Attica. Three (nos. 88, 89, 92) were found in the mining district (one actually in the remains of an ancient mine) and a fourth (no. 87), found near the Dipylon Gate, mentions a stoneworking establishment.[84] A fifth (no. 90) was discovered near the modern village of Markopoulo, which is outside the mine area but only a short distance away.[85] Two others (nos. 7 and 161) were found in the city.[86] I have been unable to trace the provenience of the eight (no. 91).[87] Eight out of a total of 154 is a small proportion and the ratio shrinks even further when the mining and quarrying operations are eliminated. Analysis of the available leases and *poletai* sale records would reveal a comparably small, if not identical, percentage.

Again we face the possibility that the rigid terminology of the *horoi* is misleading. In this case, however, the situation is complicated by the indisputable evidence of a considerable amount of production going on in the residence of the producer, even with a sizable number of slaves. Here, for example, is how Kallistratos, the speaker in the case against Olympiodoros, describes their agreement to divide up the inheritance of Komon (to which they were admittedly not entitled): "When we had sworn mutual oaths and the agreement was deposited with Androkleides, I divided the property into two shares, men of the jury. One share was made up of the house in which Komon himself lived and the slaves, sailmakers; the other share was another house and the slaves, color grinders.... I gave the defendant Olympiodoros the choice to take which of the shares he wished and he chose the color grinders and the little house. I took the sailmakers and the other house."[88]

Demosthenes' two speeches in his suit to recover his patrimony from his guardians are even more instructive.[89] Early in the first speech, Demosthenes says his father left "two *ergasteria*" in which 52 or 53 slaves worked, making cutlery and furniture.[90] Though he makes repeated reference to these *ergasteria* and though he goes into great, if hopelessly confusing, detail about the slaves, the raw material, the cash, and the jewelry which his guardians embezzled in ten years, he has not a word to say about any workshop in a physical sense. Upon attaining his majority, he received from the guardians in real property only a house worth 3,000 drachmas. But a workshop cannot disappear into thin air.[91] Obviously the house in which the family lived was also the workshop.[92] This conclusion is confirmed textually when Demosthenes speaks on two occasions of the slaves having been left "at home" and in two other places of the raw material "in the house."[93]

Similarly, there is Xenophon's account of the colloquy between Socrates and Aristarchos. It begins with the latter's bemoaning his distressed economic condition following the political upheavals during and immediately after the Peloponnesian War. The land cannot be worked; there has been such a flight to the Peiraieus that Aristarchos finds himself with all his female relatives on his hands, "so that there are fourteen free persons in the house." The discussion ends with Socrates' persuading Aristarchos to put the women to work. He thereupon borrows money and purchases wool, and his sisters, nieces, and cousins work happily and profitably at home, even at mealtime.[94] That this story may be purely apocryphal is unimportant. It was credible to Xenophon and his readers.

In Greek literary sources, then, the appearance of the word *ergasterion* does not necessarily indicate the existence of a workshop as a distinct building. It may mean a group of slaves employed in one place in the production of goods. Demosthenes says "two *ergasteria*" because his father had two distinct sets of slaves, cutlers

5*

and cabinetmakers.[95] He uses the same equation several times in arguing his case. In one place, for example, he accuses his guardians of having "made the *ergasterion* disappear" and in another he writes, "he has made the men (slaves) disappear."[96] Elsewhere in the speech, he makes the following calculation. The guardians, he says, sold half the cutlers in order to raise 3,000 drachmas in cash towards the dowry Aphobos was to receive for marrying the orator's widowed mother. Demosthenes therefore reduces his claim for the income the cutlers should have produced from 3,000 to 1,500 drachmas a year — half as many slaves, half as much production, half as much income.[97] So close is the identification, as Max Weber noted, "One could arbitrarily divide such an *ergasterion* like a lump of lead, by the sale of a portion of the slaves."[98]

In a world in which non-citizens, who could own no real property, played a major role in business, the technological fact that special structures were fundamentally unnecessary for production is of basic significance. The perfumer Athenogenes, defendant in a case between 328 and 323 B.C. in which Hypereides prepared the speech for the plaintiff, owned three shops (whether simultaneously or in succession is not clear), called interchangeably *ergasterion* and *myropolion* (place for the sale of perfume).[99] Athenogenes was being sued by a young Athenian landowner who had fallen in love with a slave boy belonging to the perfumer and was manoeuvered, he says, into buying the boy's father and brother as well, at a price of 4,000 drachmas. Having agreed to the purchase of all three slaves, the ardent young man found himself owner of the perfumery itself, for he signed a contract to take over the stock (some unguents and utensils) and debts of the business.[100] He had not the slightest interest in the perfumery nor any intention to operate it. He agreed to the deal only because, in his lack of experience, he was tricked into believing that unless he rushed to complete the transaction, Athenogenes might change his mind and refuse to sell the slaves.

The price originally agreed upon for the three slaves, 4,000 drachmas, remained the price after the transaction was extended, Athenogenes having indicated that the debts were small and would be balanced by the supplies on hand. Within three months, the purchaser found himself overwhelmed by creditors of whose existence he did not know and he then brought suit for fraud. That he had very uncertain legal ground on which to stand is obvious from the oration as a whole. The one juristic argument he brings forth — the rest of the speech is devoted to a recital of the case and to moral-

istic accusations — is the law which nullifies the sale of a slave if
the seller conceals a physical defect.[101] "But an epileptic slave," he
reasons, "does not involve in ruin the property of the purchaser,
whereas Midas, whom you sold to me, has ruined both my friends'
and mine." We need not examine the validity of the legal position
taken. It is enough to stress that the case for the cancellation of a
contract involving the sale of a perfumery is argued from a law
dealing with the sale of slaves.

Now Athenogenes was not a citizen of Athens. Therefore he could
not have owned the building, whatever its nature, in which he conducted his perfume business. (That he was not among the privileged
few who had been granted the right to own realty is reasonably
certain.) Nowhere does the plaintiff make any reference to the
building and it is clear that it was not involved in any way in the
transaction. Two alternatives present themselves. Either Athenogenes' perfumery was his home, which he rented and in which the
purchaser of the slaves and supplies would not be interested (as
Demosthenes' father was not interested in the previous place of
work of the slaves whom he received as security for a loan). Or it was
no more than a reed booth in the market-place, of negligible value
and not considered a house coming under the ban against non-
citizens' owning land and houses.[102] If a perfumery is not a fair
test, since it required no more equipment or material than can be
found in any apothecary's shop today, surely an establishment for
cutlerymaking, one of the more advanced and more complex kinds
of technological operation, could be expected to involve the largest
and most complicated equipment. Yet fundamentally there is no
difference in this respect between the perfumery of Athenogenes and
the "workshop" of Demosthenes senior.[103]

In a *horos*, however, whenever reference is made to an *ergasterion*
it can mean nothing but a building, with or without slaves in
addition, as the case may be. The relative infrequency of such references has already been indicated. It now remains to examine the
added insights offered by the value figures inscribed on the stones.
Only four of the eight *horoi* marking *ergasteria* state the amount of
the debt involved: (no. 7) an *ergasterion* hypothecated for a debt of
750 drachmas, (no. 90) an ergasterion and slaves, 700, (no. 88) an
ergasterion and slaves (in the mining district), 6,000, and (no. 87)
a house, a stoneworking establishment, and at least two *ergasteria*,
together 6,000. The number of slaves is not indicated on the *horoi*
where they are included in the encumbered property. Four figures

should not be overstressed, but they are suggestive. Tables A and B show that the median value in *horoi* marking houses alone is 700 drachmas and that we have cases running as high as 3,000. Skilled individual slaves sold in this period at a price level that tended to fluctuate around 200 drachmas and that not infrequently went to 300 and over.[104] Yet we have a record of an *ergasterion* that was hypothecated with two or more slaves for only 700 drachmas. All in all, the conclusion seems reasonable that there were relatively few buildings so closely identified with production that they were labeled *ergasteria*, not simply "houses." Furthermore, they were apparently no more, or hardly more, valuable to a creditor as security because they were *ergasteria*.[105]

Whatever other epigraphical evidence is available is extremely thin but it points in the same direction. A fragment of the sale record of the *poletai*, probably for the year 342/1 B.C., lists two *ergasteria* sold as a unit, part of the confiscated wealth of Philokrates, son of Pythodoros. The sale price was 1,500 drachmas.[106] Single houses worth that much and considerably more are mentioned repeatedly in the orations, and the range in the *horoi*, reaching 3,000, indicates a substantially higher value, since we must assume that property was normally worth well above the amount for which it was hypothecated. The one pertinent lease, a mid-fourth century B.C. rental of an *ergasterion* together with an adjoining house and a "little house" in the Peiraieus, specifies an annual fee of 54 drachmas.[107] The term of the agreement is in perpetuity, so that perhaps it ought not to be compared with leases for fixed terms. But we do have the lease, probably two or three decades later, of the sanctuary of Hypodektes and adjoining land, also rented in perpetuity at an annual figure of 50 drachmas.[108]

The exceptional *ergasteria* of high value would probably all be in the mining district. In fact, I know of but one, the crushing mill that was the subject of a lawsuit between Nikobulos and Pantainetos in or about 346/5 B.C.[109] The dispute began with a loan by Nikobulos and Euergos to Pantainetos of 10,500 drachmas, secured (*prasis epi lysei*) by the mill and thirty slaves.[110] This transaction is identical with those lying behind the *horoi* marking a *prasis epi lysei* on a mining *ergasterion* and slaves. The amount, 10,500 drachmas, is 30 per cent higher than the largest figure given in any known *horos*, of whatever type. This is the sole example in any source of an Athenian debt secured by real property in an amount greater than the largest figures appearing on the *horoi*. The story of how Timotheos borrowed seven minas from each of the sixty trierarchs to pay the crews during a campaign, and hypothecated his property in Athens as security, even if true, reports a clearly political action which is not germane to the present discussion.[111]

5. MISCELLANEOUS

Towards the middle of the third century B.C., the *gene* of the Salaminioi, once merely two groups within a single *genos* but now two independent bodies, called in mediators to settle a long-standing dispute between them over the rights to the sacred precinct of Herakles at Porthmos in Sunion. The mediators decided that they should hold the precinct in common (reversing a settlement of 363/2 B.C. dividing the land into two equal parts), that each should have its own threshing-floor, that the two buildings should be owned separately, "that the gardens and half the well shall belong to each *genos*, that the Hale (salt-pans) and the agora in Koile shall be common to both *gene*."[112]

Community property was not uncommon in the Greek world, even in Athens in the classical period. Realty, in particular, might be retained undivided after ownership passed from the father to two or more sons.[113] The mediators for the Salaminioi introduce us to an interesting variation. They distinguish between property that remains undivided and is held in common (the land) and property that cannot be divided and yet is held separately, half by one and half by the other (the well). Just how such "fractional" ownership worked out in practice and in law is not readily determined from the scanty evidence available, and the question need not detain us.[114] It is sufficient merely to note that the owner of a fraction could, in law, use it as security like any other holding. One could likewise offer a portion of one's holding as security. Should the creditor ultimately seize the security, he would in turn become owner of a fraction. Such a procedure is inherent in the *apotimema* and it is specifically indicated in the Amorgian *horos*, no. 130, which states that the official assessor had designated one third of the lessee's property as the appropriate security in a *misthosis oikou*.[115] The new acquirer could of course avoid difficulties by arranging to eliminate fractional ownership through sale, and probably he would; the fact remains, however, that he need not do so. *Horos* no. 130 is unique and the language of the others, especially of those marking *apotimema* obli-

gations, indicates that the introduction of fractions into such transactions was rare and exceptional.

Easements constitute a somewhat different category. In the *horoi*,
they are limited to water rights. Two Attic stones (nos. 116 and 159)
specifically include a watercourse as part of the property put up as
security, and a third (no. 2), also Athenian, specifies a well.[116] There
is no proof that it is an easement, not outright ownership of a thing,
that is meant. The precise specification makes the former probable,
both in the *horoi* and in the two land-lease agreements that explicitly
grant the tenant water rights.[117]

Three *horoi*, one from Amorgos (no. 102) and two from Naxos (nos.
131 and 156), indicate the hypothecation of *keramos* along with a
house. The basic meaning of *keramos* is "clay," but it was soon
extended to anything made of clay. In the agreement whereby the
shrine of Egretes in Athens was leased in 306/5 B.C. for a term of ten
years, one clause authorized the tenant, at the expiration of the
lease, to take with him the woodwork, *keramos*, and doors (together
with the door-frames). These items were to be forfeited, however, if
the tenant failed to live up to the terms of the agreement.[118]
Keramos certainly meant the roof here and, there is little doubt, in
the three *horoi* as well.[119] No generalizations can be drawn from
these three texts. Greek buildings tended to be flimsy, farm buildings especially so. Just as tenants were sometimes required to provide the woodwork and roofs themselves and at other times not, so
the *horoi* mention roofs in three cases, the other times not. Presumably failure to specify roofs implied that they were a fixed part of the
building, although in any given instance the possibility cannot be
excluded that the roof (and woodwork) was classed with the furnishings and exempted from the encumbrance.[120]

Household furnishings and other movables are listed in but two
horoi, the Naxian stone, no. 156, which states that the house secures
1,000 drachmas of the dowry, the furnishings the remaining 500,[121]
and no. 8, from Amorgos, which includes among the property the
incomprehensible phrase, "recorded pledges."[122] Except for three
stones that mention slaves, the *horoi* otherwise speak only of realty.
Obviously, movable goods, from their very nature, are not suscep-
tible to the kind of treatment suitable for land and houses. A creditor
who accepts furniture as security for a debt would normally insist on
immediate possession. Otherwise, his security may turn out to be
non-existent when he seeks to take it in substitution for the money
owed to him.[123]

In this respect, slaves too would be pawned as the usual procedure when they were offered as security. Nevertheless, slaves are mentioned (without indication of the number) in three Attic *horoi* (nos. 88—90).[124] The significant point about these stones is that all three mark the hypothecation of *ergasteria* and slaves (the other five *horoi* mentioning *ergasteria* do not include slaves as well). Slaves never appear on the *horoi* in conjunction with agricultural property. Though only three texts are involved, I find in this distinction a clear reflection of the fact that slavery in Athens played its chief role in mining and handicrafts, not in agriculture, a branch of the economy in which it was relatively unimportant.[125]

CHAPTER VI

THE PARTIES — INDIVIDUALS

I. LEGAL CAPACITY

SHORTLY BEFORE HIS DEATH in 370/69 B.C., Athens' leading banker, Pasion, leased his bank and workshop to his ex-slave Phormio. The agreement was to terminate in 361 B.C., when Pasion's younger son Pasikles attained his majority. In that year Phormio returned the property and received a release. Some time later, Pasion's elder son Apollodoros sued Phormio for certain sums and won an arbitrator's award of 5,000 drachmas. Then, in 350 or 349, Apollodoros brought still another suit, this time charging Phormio with having held back eleven talents of the bank's money when he restored the property in 361. Phormio's defense, prepared for him by Demosthenes, rested on two grounds: the fact that he had received a full release, and the operation of the statute of limitations, so many years having elapsed before Apollodoros brought suit. This defense required no explanation of the eleven-talent debt, but, in the fashion usual in Athenian cases, Demosthenes went on to tell the jury that the debt was in fact fictitious:

"When therefore he leased the income of the bank and the deposits, seeing that, since he had not yet obtained citizenship with you, he would not be able to recover what Pasion had lent on land and multiple-dwellings, he preferred to have Pasion as his debtor for these moneys rather than the other debtors to whom he had made loans. That is why Pasion was inscribed in the lease as owing eleven talents, as has been deposed before you."[1]

Fortunately, it is not the accuracy of Phormio's explanation that concerns us but the nature of his reasoning. He won the suit; in fact, Apollodoros failed to receive one fifth of the jury votes and was condemned to a fine of three talents and twenty minas. Apollodoros promptly returned to the struggle by suing one of Phormio's witnesses, Stephanos, for perjury. In an address filled with venomous invective, Apollodoros argued, long but not well, that the clause in the lease which read merely, so he claimed, "Pasion owes eleven talents on the deposits," was a pure forgery committed by Phormio in order to steal eleven talents from his predecessor's heirs. At no point in the harangue does Apollodoros refer to Phormio's explanation of the debt or attempt to refute it.[2] From the two speeches and what we know of the characters of the two men, Apollodoros and Phormio, it would not be difficult to decide where the truth lay. But the decision need not be made, for, even if the eleven-talent debt were a pure invention, Phormio's explanation remains unchallenged. A non-citizen would find it bad business to accept real property as security because, should the debtor default — and the word Phormio used for "recover," *eisprattein*, means to "compel repayment" — the creditor would find himself without the normal legal recourse, the right to seize the security in satisfaction of his claim.[3]

Phormio does not suggest that it was the law which prohibited him from taking over the debts secured by land and houses, merely good sense. I doubt if there was a separate legislative enactment on the subject, for none was needed. Firm possession of property is defined by Aristotle to mean the right of alienability, and alienability in turn as "giving and sale."[4] His failure to add hypothecation seems to be nothing more than the application of simple logic: The right to sell subsumes the right to borrow on one's property and to risk forfeit; conversely, only one who has the right to acquire title to a piece of property will accept that property as security for a debt, for his security is worthless if he does not have the coercive threat of seizure and assumption of ownership.

This logic was so consistently applied in Athens that almost the only texts which specifically include hypothecation in a general context of the right to alienate are a few with a marked political purpose. The decree establishing the second Athenian League in 378/7 B.C., for example, expressly provides that neither the Athenian state nor any of its citizens shall be permitted "to acquire either a house or land in the territories of the allies, whether by purchase or by hypothecation or by any other means whatsoever."[5] In view of the record of the Delian League, the Athenians had ample political reason to indulge in a bit of excess phraseology. Where sufficient reason did not exist, hypothecation is usually not mentioned.[6] One illustration will suffice. The law prohibited an outgoing official who was awaiting the audit of his year in office from leaving the city, from consecrating or dedicating his property to a divinity, from adopting an heir, or from disposing of his property by will — the enumeration given by the orator Aeschines in 330 B.C. stops there, with the addition of an *etcetera*.[7]

If Pasion and Phormio were able to overcome this handicap resulting from the latter's lack of citizenship, how many other non-citizens were able to do likewise? The answer must be very few. In the first place, no parallel case is known in the sources. Second, the relationship between Pasion and Phormio was unusually close, to the point that the dying banker not only arranged to have his freed-man take charge of his extensive affairs for a decade but also provided in his will that his widow marry Phormio and take with her a dowry worth several talents. Apollodoros called the will a forgery, to be sure, but his argument is transparently fragile.[8] Third, Pasion's willingness to enter the land-secured debts to his own account was beneficial to his heirs, the owners of the bank, more than to Phormio, the lessee. In sum, the whole transaction seems unusual. That it was not unique is possible, but the more important point is that everything we know about the life and work of the metics suggests that what Pasion did was not in conformity with the usual pattern of behavior.

In his dealings with the state, in court proceedings for example, the non-citizen required a *proxenos*, a citizen-sponsor or guarantor. And this procedure was the normal one in private transactions, as well. Whether as lender or as borrower, as debtor or as creditor, the non-citizen gave or obtained security in the form of suretyship, personal guaranty, whenever security was required. Thus, after the perfumer Athenogenes had persuaded the gullible young Athenian to take over the debts of the perfumery along with the slaves and supplies, he asked for surety against the possibility that the young man might refuse to honor the debts.[9]

Of course, if a non-citizen received the privilege of owning real property, then the situation changed. In respect to hypothecation, his status was then basically no different from that of any citizen. Grants of this privilege were rare in Athens, however, at least until Roman times. Nor were they always intended as practical gifts; as Wilamowitz once pointed out in connection with the awarding of honorary citizenship, "The danger that the Athenian citizens, Sadokos of Thrace or Leukon of Bosporus, would be called upon to be trierarchs or *choregoi* was therefore an illusory one, just as the grant of *ateleia* or *isopoliteia* in most of the proxeny decrees is an empty phrase. Sophistical orators naturally twisted the facts as it suited them."[10]

The generalization that non-citizens are basically to be excluded from all discussion of legal security on real property therefore needs no substantial qualification.[11] The evidence of the *horoi* offers additional proof. There are 99 identifiable names of parties on the available Attic stones. Of these, 87 have demotics and are therefore citizens, 11 have neither patronymic nor demotic, and one (in no. 116) is labeled an *isoteles*.[12] The grant of *isoteleia*, equality with citizens for tax purposes, does not automatically subsume the right to own realty, but it is an obvious assumption that in this case Charias, whose orphaned sons are the recipients of a pupillary *apotimema* on lands and a house, had also received that right. The absence of a demotic in eleven cases is no indication of status. The *horoi* were not official documents and were subject to no rules, so that brevity alone can explain the omission of a demotic just as it explains the omission of the creditor's name entirely in many cases. Possibly some of the eleven men were non-citizens, but, even so, the total number makes up a negligible fraction of all the names we have. Since the names of the debtors, the actual property owners, are not given, the *horoi* offer no clue as to their political status. The literary evidence, fragmentary as it is, indicates that the proportion of non-citizens was equally negligible on that side of the transaction.[13]

Few Greek cities — perhaps only Rhodes and Delos — matched Athens in the number and importance of its permanent non-citizen inhabitants. Twenty or thirty thousand metics and an incalculable number of transients played a leading role in the economic life of Athens, and particularly in financial dealings. Their contribution was welcomed, even sought after.[14] In the fourth century B.C., important changes in legal procedure were introduced to facilitate and expedite the settlement of legal disputes in which they may have become involved and to make their participation in commercial and financial dealings simpler and therefore more attractive.[15] Yet a legal wall was erected and maintained between them and the economic base of the society, its landed property. They could reach over the barrier to lease farmland, houses, or mines — but only with the cooperation of a citizen suretor. Except for a Pasion or, eventually, a Phormio, they could not transcend the barrier in the field of property ownership, and hence not in the field of credit relations. However one may explain the jealous insistence upon the citizen's monopoly of real property, the fact remains that in large measure land and money remained two separate spheres. A citizen could mediate between them, a non-citizen could not. Throughout the period of Greek independence, the economy did not demand that the wall be torn down. Even Xenophon's bold proposal was restricted to the liberalization of grants of housing privileges to worthy metics; in no way did he touch upon the basic economic cleavage.[16] The economic history of Athens might well be written with this as the point of departure.[17]

The term "citizens" must be defined to mean adult males of sound mind.[18] Athenian women and children were permitted to make legally valid agreements only to the value of one *medimnos* (about a bushel and a half) of barley, at least in the fourth century B.C.[19] In all larger transactions, their *kyrios* (guardian)[20] acted on their behalf.

Behind the rigid legal insistence on the *kyrios*, there was nevertheless considerable room for variation in the degree of actual participation of women in the property regime. The large number of women involved in the transactions listed in the so-called Tenos land-register of the middle of the third century B.C., for example, suggests that Hellenistic Greece saw a loosening of the severe restrictions under which women were placed in the classical period, though the legal requirement of the *kyrios* remained unchanged.[21]

Three of the Amorgian *horoi* name women in contexts other than that of a dotal *apotimema*, all from the third century B.C. or the very end of the fourth. In one (no. 9), a woman is the creditor in a small *hypotheke* of 90 drachmas; in another (no. 102), a man and woman together make over by *prasis epi lysei* extensive holdings, possession of which the former retains by paying rent (that is, interest) at 10 per cent, though there is no indication of the reasons, legal or otherwise, why the woman's participation in the transaction was needed; and in the third (no. 8), a wife "agrees" to her husband's hypothecating land as security to an *eranos*, and the *horos* indicates that both the head of the *eranos* and the latter's wife were somehow legally implicated in the arrangement.[22] (In every instance but that of the wife of the *eranos*-chief, the woman's *kyrios* is named on the *horos*.) The interesting point is that these three are the only *horoi* from Amorgos that mark security obligations other than *apotimemata* (in which women's names would necessarily appear whenever dowries were involved). Quite the opposite picture is revealed by the texts from the other islands and from Athens: not a single *horos* names a woman in any context other than dowry.[23] Too much stress should not be placed on this seemingly sharp distinction, however, for the Attic stones (and the Lemnian which deal largely, if not entirely, with Athenian cleruchs) do not give the background information available in the Amorgian *horoi*. It is idle to speculate on the legal complications, including property rights of women, that may be concealed behind the terse texts.

2. ECONOMIC AND SOCIAL LEVEL

The next question to be raised with regard to both the people and the property involved in hypothecation is the economic and social level represented. Taken collectively, do the *horoi* reflect the activities of the poorer, middle, or wealthier strata of the Athenian citizen body? And since the *horoi* constitute a fair sampling over a period of about two centuries of Athenian transactions in which debts were secured by real property, the answer to that question is also the answer to a still broader one: Among which sections of the population did the hypothecation of land and houses play a significant role?

The most decisive material comes from the *horoi* marking dotal *apotimema* obligations. In this group of documents we are dealing with a fixed value, the amount of a dowry. Seventeen of the stones as preserved give figures. The range is from 300 to 8,000 drachmas, with the median 1,900 and the average 2,650.[24] If, as some scholars have argued, one or two of the *horoi* represent security for unpaid portions of dowries, rather than for the whole amount, then the average dowry reflected in this group of texts would be even higher than 2,650 drachmas.

There was no legal obligation on the part of the father to dower his daughter.[25] Economic and social pressures were virtually as strong as law, however, and they not only made dowries more or less mandatory in fact but they also tended to fix the amount appropriate for a given social position. Roughly, 3,000—6,000 drachmas seems to have been the accepted standard for the wealthiest people.[26] A dowry of more than 6,000 drachmas could be grounds for gossip, even suspicion; it was a sign of the nouveau riche when Phormio, the ex-slave, gave his daughter 10,000,[27] and the story of the twenty talents (120,000 drachmas) allegedly promised to Alcibiades, ten at the marriage and ten at the birth of a first child, went the rounds of the Greek world for centuries.[28] Authenticated dowries exceeding 6,000 drachmas are in fact so rare that we may set that figure as the normal maximum.[29]

In one of his orations, Isaeus has his client make the following argument: "Stratokles and I had a patrimony such as to be enough (to live on) but not worth enough for liturgies. Proof is that each of us received a dowry of twenty minas (2,000 drachmas) with his wife and such a small dowry would not be given to someone if there were substantial property."[30] This may be a rather strained argument — and the speaker, Theopompos, is very careful throughout the oration to avoid giving an accurate inventory of his inheritance — but it is not unintelligible. Isaeus was obviously counting on the jurors' recognition of 2,000 drachmas as a sum below the socially acceptable minimum for families in the upper bracket, those who were liable for liturgies. That is consistent with the tradition that when the Athenian people came to the rescue of the impoverished children of Aristeides, they not only gave his son Lysimachos 200 plethra of land, admittedly a generous grant, but they dowered each of his daughters with 3,000 drachmas.[31]

The *horoi* marking dotal *apotimemata* therefore take us into the world of the wealthier, even of the wealthiest, Athenian citizens. Only three are for sums under 1,000 drachmas — one of 300 and two of 500 — and even they indicate dowries far beyond the reach of the poorer section of the population. A mid-fourth-century oration quotes a law, worth citing here though its authenticity is by no means certain, which reads: "With regard to *epikleroi* who are rated as thetes, if the nearest relative does not wish to marry one (himself), let him give her in marriage with a dowry of 500 drachmas if he is a *pentakosiomedimnos*, a knight 300, a zeugite 150, in addition to what is her own."[32] These figures point up the magnitude of the dowries reflected in the *horoi*. So do the provisions in the wills of the third-century philosophers, Straton and Lykon, designating bequests of 500 drachmas as adequate to maintain a decent life, on the social level of the freedman.[33] Finally there is the evidence of the two orations, both by Demosthenes, specifically mentioning *horoi* in connection with dotal *apotimemata*. In the Spudias case the dowry was 4,000 drachmas and in the Onetor case either 6,000 or 8,000.[34]

An evaluation of the social and economic level reflected by the other *horoi* is more difficult. A sum of money allocated against an undefined parcel of land is not easily compared with other sums. Nor is there a ready formula by which to establish the ratio between the amount of the debt and the value of the property hypothecated for it. For the present, it will suffice to note that the mill and slaves on which Pantainetos borrowed 10,500 drachmas were sold for over

20,000; that a confiscated house on which there were four charges totaling 304 drachmas brought 575 at public auction.[35] All the debts included in Tables A and B, taken together, show a median of 1,000 drachmas and a range up to 7,000. These are large debts. In 322 B.C., Antipater imposed a 2,000-drachma property qualification on the right to vote and hold office in Athens, thereby disfranchising a majority, perhaps 70 per cent, of the citizen body.[36] This evidence leads to the same conclusion, then, that we have just drawn from dowry figures.[37]

As significant as the sums involved, perhaps even more so, is the purpose of the original transactions leading to hypothecation. The *horoi* cannot provide the necessary information; in fact, they offer hardly any clues at all. A detailed examination of this problem would entail a study of all the pertinent literary and epigraphical material on credit in ancient Athens. Such a study is beyond the scope of the present work. Nevertheless, some tentative suggestions and an indication of some of the material may be useful in completing the analysis of the social and economic level represented by the people who were the debtors and creditors of the *horoi*.

Under modern economic conditions, hypothecation occurs most often in conjunction with the purchase of real property, the property being encumbered for the unpaid part of the purchase price, or as a way of financing the cost of building and improvements. Hypothecation is thus intimately linked with the conditions of the real estate market and the money market, with rising or falling land values and interest rates.[38] The mere statement of these facts brings us face to face with the fundamental, qualitative differences to be found in the Greek institution, differences rooted in the profoundly un-modern character of the city-state economy.

Among the Greeks, sales were cash sales. This rule found few exceptions, notably few when real property was the object of sale.[39] A striking illustration is found in the institution of the *arrhabon* (or *arrha*), earnest-money, binder, deposit, or option, as the situation may be. In the more than one thousand years from Homer to the later Roman Empire, Greek sources of every type (apart from the papyri) reveal less than a dozen references to the *arrhabon*. The earliest is a difficult passage in Isaeus about a deposit paid down on some funerary equipment.[40] Then comes Aristotle's well-known, and possibly apocryphal, story of how Thales, to silence someone who scoffed at the usefulness of his knowledge, obtained a monopoly of the oil-presses by leasing them through deposits made well in advance of the harvest.[41] A somewhat longer, more generalized though often obscure, account of the institution appears in a fragment of Theophrastus.[42] And finally there are such miscellaneous references as those in Plautus, presumably based on Greek practice, or a somewhat corrupt and nearly unintelligible reference in Harpocration.[43] Quantitatively and qualitatively, this list is convincingly unimpressive. The uses of the *arrhabon* known to us — in fact, the word itself, borrowed from a Semitic tongue despite the large number of Greek terms available for the idea of "deposit" — highlight the Greek practice, whereby a sale was usually, almost invariably, a transfer of property against a payment of the full purchase price.[44]

Such a practice of necessity eliminates the purchase of realty as a significant source of security obligations. One *horos* alone, no. 3, explicitly indicates such a source. It reads: "In the archonship of Theophrastos (340/39 or 313/2 B.C.), *horos* of land (hypothecated) for the price owed on it to Phanostratos of Paiania, 2,000 (drachmas)."[45] In the Pantainetos case, to which we have returned frequently, the whole series of transactions revolved around a loan of 10,500 drachmas with which to purchase a crushing-mill and slaves, the property serving as security for the purchase-money. I know of no third instance in which purchase of property clearly lay at the root of hypothecation.[46]

As for loans for building and improvement, the second major category in modern practice, the negative picture in the Greek world is even more absolute. "Improvement" as the word is used in technical real-estate parlance simply does not enter into consideration. The lease agreements regarding lands owned by demes and various cult bodies make this quite clear. Among the clauses to be found in one or another of these documents are provisions requiring the tenant to restore the property, at the end of the rental period, with the identical number of trees and vines, to repair the buildings, to cut the olive-trees in such a way that their regrowth was assured, to pursue the fallow system, and the like. Only once is there a reference to improvements in the proper sense of the term, despite the length of time involved (ten years at the least).[47] All in all, there are not a dozen references in Greek literature to increasing the value of a farm or urban holding; and the scattered few that there are speak of the results of zeal, hard work, temperance, or some other moral quality rather than of a substantial outlay of funds to bring about a change, an improvement, in the economic quality and potentiality of the property.[48] Not a single text indicates the encumbrance of property growing out of a loan for building or improvements.

In a few cases, hypothecation served to guarantee the rental payment in land leases.[49] Far more significant as the basis of the transaction was family property. Thirty of the *horoi* were set up to secure dowries, twenty-six by *apotimema* and four by *prasis epi lysei*. Another sixteen involved security for the return of the property of orphans leased out by their guardians. If the latter group is unquestionably one important area in which hypothecation was linked with a "business" activity,[50] the former, dotal hypothecation, is as surely an indication of the considerable role — in fact, the preponderant part, as we shall see in a moment — of non-productive activities in the entire field. What the relatively large proportion of *horoi* marking dowered property serves to reaffirm is the extent to which property was the base of the classical Greek family. If there were no legitimate sons, Isaeus tells us, not even the father himself could dispose of an orphaned daughter, an *epikleros*, in his will without disposing of his property along with her.[51]

For the rest, loans must be assumed to be the reason for hypothecation. Legally it may be sufficient to probe no further, but socially and economically the important point is the nature of the loan itself, whether it was a friendly loan or a professional interest-bearing loan, whether it was made for productive purposes or for non-productive. The texts of the *horoi* offer little evidence. In one marking a dotal *apotimema* for 3,000 drachmas (no. 135), the woman's father is called a physician. No. 39 states that the written agreement was deposited with "the banker Eukles."[52] No other *horos* characterizes the people named. A substantial number of names can be identified, with considerable probability, with men known from trierarchic inscriptions, list of arbitrators, and similar sources.[53] Such evidence suggests rather strongly that we are dealing with leading figures of the community in many instances, with men who were not "professionally" engaged in moneylending.[54] This suggestion is of course effectively supported by the major role played by metics in banking and moneylending operations, that is, by men who could not lend on the security of real property. The whole field of overseas trade is also ruled out, partly by the prominence of non-citizens, partly by the fact that the large loans needed for commercial operations were usually bottomry loans secured by ship and cargo, not by land and houses.

What about the borrowers and their motivation? Again non-citizens may be ruled out because they ordinarily possessed no realty

6*

that they could offer in security. The *horoi* provide no information at all, but the orators do, and what they indicate is quite decisive. Wherever a substantial sum is borrowed and a real guarantee is given, in the cases now extant, the purpose is not a productive one. This is not to say that productive loans were absolutely unknown, but that they were neither the more common kind nor the significant kind.[55] As a general rule, the Athenian property owner borrowed sizable sums not to improve or increase his holdings or his "business" interests but to pay taxes, fulfill liturgies, or meet a financial demand of equally unproductive character.[56] Two cases may be considered in some detail.

Pasion's son Apollodoros became embroiled in a complex series of legal manoeuvers, probably in the period 368—365 B.C., with a certain Nikostratos and the latter's brother.[57] Nikostratos had been captured in war and subsequently ransomed. He had succeeded in repaying 1,000 drachmas of the ransom-money but could not return the balance and was being threatened with enslavement, in accordance with Athenian law on the subject. In this emergency, he appealed to his old friend Apollodoros for help. The latter summarizes what transpired in the following way.

"'Nikostratos,' I said, 'I was your true friend until the present moment and I have now assisted you in your misfortune as far as I was able. Since at the present time you cannot find the entire sum of money, nor have I any cash any more than yourself, I will lend you as much of my property as you wish and you shall hypothecate it for as much money as is lacking; you may have the use of the money for one year without interest and pay off the strangers. When you have collected the *eranos* (*i.e.*, a friendly loan Nikostratos intends to raise to meet the debt),[58] as you yourself say, release my property.' Hearing this, he thanked me and urged me to act as quickly as possible, before the days should go by in which, he said, he had to pay off the ransom. I therefore hypothecated the multiple-dwelling to Arkesas of Pambotadai, whom this man himself recommended to me, for 16 minas (1,600 drachmas) at interest of 8 obols per mina per month (16 per cent)."[59]

At about the same time, Apollodoros brought a successful suit against the famous Athenian general Timotheos to recover 4,438 drachmas and 2 obols that Pasion had lent the latter in a series of transactions in 373/2 B.C.[60] According to the plaintiff, Timotheos was in a hopeless financial position, his real property fully encumbered to 60 trierarchs, among others, and marked by *horoi*, when Pasion, out of friendship, lent him various sums with which to meet obligations he had incurred in his political and military activities. The loans were made without witnesses or documents, they were unsecured, and bore no interest. Pasion having died, the general denied the existence of the obligations, hence the suit by Pasion's son.[61]

It is not difficult to see a political motive in Pasion's "friendly" gesture.[62] The fact remains, however, that here, as in the Nikostratos case, the debtor's interests had nothing to do with economic activity. Furthermore, both Timotheos and Nikostratos sought financial assistance on a friendly basis, the former successfully, the latter unsuccessfully only to the extent that Apollodoros was not in a position to help him with a direct cash loan. "Where a loan is involved," wrote the Peripatetic author of the book of *Problems* attributed to Aristotle, "there is no friend; for if a man is a friend he does not lend but gives."[63] Birmingham and Manchester may laugh at this queer ethical principle, to borrow Sir Alfred Zimmern's phrase, but the philosopher was doing no more than generalizing from a common practice of his day. The *eranos*-loan which Nikostratos proposed to collect among a group of his friends is an excellent example, and that form of loan was widely common on all social levels.[64] Nikostratos planned to repay the money with which he had been ransomed. Athenogenes' opponent obtained such a loan in order to complete the purchase of the slave-boy with whom he had fallen in love; that he acquired a perfumery in the process was incidental, irrelevant, and most inconvenient.[65] Neither goal was economically productive.

Eranos-loans were by their very nature interest-free. Loans obtained from individuals were also often without interest, even when the lender was the banker Pasion, as in the Timotheos story. There was no rule here, but simply a matter of agreement in each individual case. Nor was there a rule regarding the absence or presence of interest when a loan was secured by realty. We shall see that even *eranos*-loans were not infrequently backed up by hypothecation. Interest-free individual loans might also be. Hence it is incorrect to assume that all the obligations indicated on the *horoi* were necessarily interest-bearing. The pupillary *apotimemata* of course were, in a sense, for the very nature of the transaction was the lease of property at an annual rental. One recently discovered *horos* (no. 131), from the island of Naxos, states explicitly that the lands, house, and roof had been put up as security to cover both the 3,500-drachma valuation placed on the estate of the orphaned children of a certain Epiphron and the annual rental of 300 drachmas. Contrariwise, whenever a dotal *apotimema* was given by the husband to his wife's *kyrios* there was no interest, since the obligation was only contingent.

One other *horos*, no. 162 from Amorgos, mentions interest. It marks a *prasis epi lysei* in the amount of 5,000 drachmas; the annual interest was 500 drachmas. An Attic stone (no. 26) suggests that a low interest was involved, also in a *prasis epi lysei*.[66] Otherwise the *horoi* are completely silent on the matter and there is no way for us to break the silence. Obviously there was no reason why the stones should give information about interest or other conditions of the loan.

The life-term of the obligation, too, is never stated on the *horoi*, not even on the fuller island stones. Thus no. 131 gives the rate of interest but no indication of the number of years during which it was to be paid. A pupillary *apotimema* necessarily had a fixed term, ending when the orphan attained his majority. Dotal *apotimemata* had no term. While the marriage continued, there was no obligation; the moment the marriage ended, the husband was obliged to return the dowry. Of all the other cases, we know the facts just once, thanks to an imperfect erasure. The text of a *horos* (no. 71) marking a *prasis epi lysei* had been deleted so that the stone could be re-used for a dotal *apotimema* (no. 152), but it can still be read. By further good fortune, both *horoi* were dated, no. 71 in 309/8 B.C., no. 152 in 308/7. The first obligation thus came to an end within a year, either because the debtor paid up or because the creditor foreclosed on the property. What we cannot tell is whether the action taken came at the end of the term specified in the agreement or at a still earlier date.[67]

In the orators, for all the endless detail they provide, the evidence regarding the duration of secured loans (or unsecured, for that matter) is remarkably skimpy. For reasons to be sought in the nature of their cases and of the tactics they elected to pursue in court, they made it a practice to avoid indicating specific time-limits on loans. The loan to Pantainetos, we are told, for example, was to be repaid "in a fixed period."[68] What that period was is never divulged. The incidental information that the orators do give, however, indicates that the predominant practice was one of short-term loans, as in the one year suggested by Apollodoros to Niko-stratos.[69]

Short-term loans at high rates of interest must of necessity be non-productive, from the viewpoint of the debtor. The burden is too great to justify, or even to permit, their use as a device for the securing of funds with which to purchase or improve income-producing property. (Bottomry loans are the exception, to be explained in part by the insurance element they contain, in part by the unusual rates of profit from maritime ventures in compensation for the extraordinary risks.) People resorted to these loans, and offered their property as security, chiefly because they needed immediate cash with which to meet a non-business obligation, in situations in which they had no choice.[70] Psychologically, their approach was one of grief and despair, the atmosphere that is associated with "mortgaging the old homestead." To be compelled to hypothecate one's property was a calamity to be rectified as quickly as possible. Today, in complete contrast, the objective of the owner of income-producing property is, under ordinary circumstances, to encumber it as much as he can because the interest he will have to pay will be less than the interest he can obtain by re-investing the borrowed money.[71]

In sum, when we study land and credit in Athens, the normal link between the two all through the classical period, hypothecation, is an institution limited largely to men of property acting in non-economic capacities, so to speak. To a large section of the population — the small farmers, the landless laborers, the tradesmen and craftsmen, and virtually all non-citizens — this form of security and this type of credit relationship were unavailable. For them, the picture is the one given by Aristophánes, writing in 392 or 391 B.C. When Chremes, in the *Ecclesiazusae*, decides to take inventory of his stock, which he plans to bring to the common pool being established under Praxagora's scheme, he drags out a sieve, a mirror, pots and pans, a rooster, a tripod, and the like. A citizen, who has been watching this performance from a distance, finally walks up to Chremes and asks him: "Friend, what is the meaning of these utensils? Have you carried them out because you are moving or are you carrying them to place in pawn?"[72] A century later Theophrastus exemplified the miser as one who goes to your house before the end of the month to demand repayment of his half-obol.[73]

CHAPTER VII

THE PARTIES — GROUPS

I. INTRODUCTION

"But all *koinoniai* are parts, as it were, of the political," writes Aristotle. "Thus, travelers associate together for some advantage and to provide some of the necessities. And the political *koinonia*, too, it seems, was originally formed and continues to be maintained for the sake of advantage.... The other *koinoniai*, therefore, aim at advantage in proportion; for example, sailors at what is advantageous on a voyage for the income from goods or the like, fellow-soldiers for what is advantageous in warfare, whether money or victory over the enemy or the capture of a city; and likewise the members of a tribe or deme. And some *koinoniai* seem to be formed for the sake of pleasure, for example *thiasotai* and *eranoi*, which are organized for sacrifice and social intercourse. All these seem to be subordinate to the political, for the political aims not at a temporary advantage, but at one for the whole of life."[1]

The word *koinonia* is usually translated as "association" or "community" and the concrete noun, *koinon*, as "association" or "society" (in German, most often *Verein*). The problem of translation is one of basic conception. Aristotle's inclusion of every kind of grouping, permanent and temporary, voluntary and involuntary, under the one name is fully confirmed by the literature. *Koinon* is the standard Greek word for all types, for the *polis* itself and for leagues of cities (Boeotian League, for example, or the League of the Hellenes established by Philip of Macedon), for subdivisions of the state, for religious associations, and for temporary partnerships.[2] Greek failure to distinguish sharply among the possible varieties of groups is well illustrated by the old Athenian law, attributed to Solon and preserved in a fragment of the Roman jurist Gaius in Justinian's Digest, which read: "If a deme or members of a phratry or *orgeones* of heroes or members of a *genos* or messmates or funerary associates or *thiasotai* or those away for booty or for trade make arrangements in these matters among themselves, they shall be valid unless forbidden by the laws."[3]

In economic and legal contexts, unfortunately, the English words "association" and "society," not to mention "guild" or "corporation," take on specific connotations of corporate existence, of juristic personality.[4] The extent to which such a conception was known to Greek law is a debatable point, requiring detailed investigation. In this study, we may avoid the problem altogether. The issue which concerns us is the extent to which groups are named on the *horoi* and seem to participate in transactions involving hypothecation, not the legal question of the ways in which property rights were held or transmitted by them. Whether these groups were endowed by law with legal personality or whether, as I believe, the modern institution of the juristic person was largely unknown in the Greek cities, cannot be determined by the relative frequency or infrequency of group holdings of real property or of group participation in the taking and giving of land as security.[5]

One aspect of the legal problem must be considered. Before the end of the fifth century B.C. groups of foreigners began to receive permission to set up cult associations of their own. By the end of the fourth century, if not sooner, groups with mixed membership, citizen and non-citizen, became common.[6] What was their status with regard to the ownership of real property? For the purely foreign groups the answer is unequivocal. A decree of 333/2 B.C. granted the merchants of Kition in Cyprus "the right to acquire land in which to set up a sanctuary of Aphrodite, as the Egyptians, too, have set up a sanctuary of Isis."[7] A private decree, dated in 261/0 B.C., of the Thracian society associated with the cult of Bendis, says with some exaggeration, "Since, the *demos* of the Athenians having given the Thracians alone of the nationality groups (*ethne*) the right to own real property and to establish a sanctuary...."[8] Clearly an explicit grant of the privilege of land ownership was necessary. How the law treated groups whose membership was mixed, citizens and non-citizens, is not revealed directly by any text. The fact that virtually every group did hold some property, no matter how small, indicates that there was an easy solution. Possibly the answer lay in the practice, continuing through the Hellenistic period, of leaving most of the official posts in Athenian hands.[9]

Twenty *horoi* name a total of twenty-six groups of one type or another as creditors.[10] In all instances but one, the group is identified not by its name but by that of the members collectively. That is to say, the property is put up as security to the Phlyasians, not to the deme Phlya; to the Glaukidai or Lykomidai; to the eranists, not to an *eranos*. The one exception is the Amorgian stone, no. 8, which speaks of an *eranos*; and even there reference is made to the "law of the eranists." Similar usage appears normally in other inscriptions, land leases for example, though not with the same unfailing regularity as in the *horoi*. For demes, tribes, and *gene* the collective proper noun (*e.g.*, the Phlyasians) was considered sufficient identification as a rule.[11] Where groups within a tribe or phratry were involved, however, or *eranoi*, precision was achieved by adding the words, "those with," followed by the name of an individual.[12] This practice, too, was standard for all kinds of legal documents.[13]

2. THE STATE AND ITS SUBDIVISIONS

The state itself was never mentioned in the *horoi*. Involvement as debtor was virtually impossible, for public loans were the exception throughout Greek history and completely unknown in Athens.[14] When neither the regular income nor the reserves sufficed to meet a necessary expenditure, the Athenian state resorted either to a special tax, most notably the *eisphora*, or to the collection of "voluntary" contributions, the *epidosis*. It was never in a position in which it had to offer security. Other states occasionally were, but only the case of the city of Arkesine on the island of Amorgos is relevant to the present discussion. At the very end of the fourth century B.C. or the beginning of the third, Arkesine (as well as other cities on the island) was compelled to borrow large sums of money, running into several talents at the least. The funds were obtained from various individuals, perhaps all citizens of neighboring islands in the Cyclades; formal contracts were drawn up and inscribed on stone.[15] In the best preserved inscription, the city hypothecated to the creditor "all the common (property) of the *polis* and the private property, here and overseas, of the Arkesinians and of those living in Arkesine." Another, more lengthy, clause guaranteed him full freedom of execution on both public property and private holdings in case of default.[16]

Amorgos was one of the communities which had adopted the Athenian device of the *horoi*. Despite the use of hypothecation in these loans, the situation was not one in which the creditor could have indicated his claim by placing *horoi* on all the real property in the city, both public and private. Nor was it the type of situation from which generalizations may safely be drawn either as to the frequency with which Greek states used the property of their residents as security for public loans or as to the alienability of public property in general.[17] The hypothecation of a specific piece of realty by a state is not firmly attested by any source.[18]

Still another clause of the Arkesine agreements held the city treasurers personally responsible for any default on the interest, as distinct from the over-all security offered for repayment of the principal. Should the city fail to make an interest payment, the creditors were empowered to carry out execution on the property of the treasurers for the interest due and a 50 per cent penalty.[19] Such unmitigated liability for acts performed on behalf of the state was a general feature of Greek government.[20] It was inherent in the liturgy-system, for example. In the conduct of their assigned tasks, individuals might find themselves financially embarrassed, as often happened to the generals and trierarchs in the fourth century, and forced to resort to borrowing. The loans would be strictly private and the security they offered a matter of private law, of agreements between one individual and another. The fact that the debt arose out of the performance of a public duty was irrelevant in the eyes of the law. It is highly probable that a substantial number of the *horoi* were set up to mark precisely such obligations. But we cannot be certain, and the question is pointless in any event within the present context.[21]

If the Athenian state never appears as a debtor, it is continually in evidence as a creditor. As creditor, it could conceivably have asked for land as security, as other Greek states are known to have done on occasion. The evidence, however, is entirely in the negative, for reasons inherent in the character of Athenian public finance. In the first place, the law rendered a defaulting public debtor subject to confiscation of his entire property, if necessary to pay off his obligation.[22] In a sense, then, the whole of a man's wealth was the security whenever he entered into dealings with the state. Whether the legal condition is to be construed as a lien in the Anglo-American sense or as the *Generalhypothek* of modern continental law or as neither, is a complicated question of legal rights with which we need not here be concerned. The fact of the state's right to confiscate and the frequency with which it exercised that right in Athens are sufficiently attested to require no extended discussion. In the second place, the acceptance of realty as security would have been most inefficient and uneconomical, since the Athenian state had no administrative machinery with which to deal readily with land or houses and it invariably sold at public auction whatever it confiscated.

The form of security used by the Athenian state as creditor was always personal suretyship. The suretor assumed a responsibility equal to that of the original debtor. In case of default, his property too was subject to confiscation in full and the state thereby obtained a double opportunity to obtain satisfaction by way of real execution. Legally, the state's claim over the property of the suretor, both before and after the obligation had fallen due, was identical with its claim on the principal debtor. When the latter was a non-citizen and the former a citizen, suretyship offered the further advantage of making real property available for seizure; the non-citizen's property would of necessity have been liquid and hence easily rendered "invisible."

How the institution of suretyship worked in Athens is nicely illustrated by the incomplete record of the sales conducted by the *poletai* in 342/1 B.C. or thereabouts. One section reads as follows: "Euthykles son of Euthymenides of Myrrhinus denounced a multiple-dwelling in the Peiraieus... belonging to Meixidemos of Myrrhinus, who owes to the public treasury of the Athenians the surety which he guaranteed for Philistides son of Philistides of Aixone who shared in collecting the metic tax in the archonship of Pythodoros (343/2): the sixth and seventh and eighth and ninth payments, these four, each of 100 drachmas; and another surety on the mines for the five-drachma tax: the sixth and seventh and eighth payments, these three, each of 125 drachmas; and another surety which he guaranteed for Telemachos son of Hermolochos, dwelling in the Peiraieus (*i. e.*, a metic), who joined in collecting the five-drachma tax for Theseus: the fourth and fifth and sixth and seventh and eighth and ninth and tenth payments, these seven, each of 100 drachmas; and another surety for a quarry in the Peiraieus: the fourth and fifth payments, these two, each of 115½ drachmas; and another surety which he guaranteed for Kallikrates son of Kallikrates, dwelling in Besa (*i.e.*, a metic), who joined in collecting the one-drachma tax for Asklepios: the seventh and eighth and ninth and tenth payments, these four, each of 36 2/3 drachmas; these sums having been doubled since neither Philistides nor Telemachos nor Kallikrates paid to the city the price of their tax-farming nor did Meixidemos pay the sureties which he had guaranteed to the city...."[24]

Suretyship does not preclude hypothecation. That is to say, it is conceivable that, under certain conditions, a creditor may demand and obtain property security from the suretor, a pledge of movables or the hypothecation of realty, either in lieu of or in addition to security put up by the principal debtor. Two *horoi* make explicit reference to suretors, no. 8 in conjunction with an *eranos*-loan and no. 18 in a puzzling fashion ("Hagnodemos and the co-suretors" are the creditors in a *prasis epi lysei*). Once again, the terseness of the *horoi* prevents us from knowing how many of the debtors may have been obligated in the capacity of suretors. The probability is that the number was very small. Legally the question is of no moment, furthermore, since in hypothecation as in all other respects the suretor acted as a substitute for the original debtor. That no such combination of suretyship and hypothecation is known where the Athenian state was the creditor follows necessarily from our discussion.[25]

Unlike the state itself, all subdivisions of the state were subject to private law. Land owned by the demes was taxable like privately owned land; the incidence of the *eisphora* was a matter of agreement whenever a deme leased out some of its holdings.[26] The most dramatic illustration of the private-law character of the acts of subdivisions of the state is offered by a transaction involving not a deme but a tribe. The *poletai* inscription already cited to exemplify suretyship reports at length on the sale of a parcel of land confiscated from one Nikodemos son of Aristomenes, of the deme Oinoe.

The property was seized, says the text, "Nikodemos owing to the public treasury 1,000 drachmas and being inscribed on the Acropolis as having incurred a penalty because, having become steward of the tribe Aiantis and having collected the sacred money of the tribe, he has not paid it back, and being inscribed on the Acropolis as also owing to Ajax 666 2/3 drachmas, and this sum having been doubled for him in the archonship of Archias (346/5 B.C.)....

"Claim: The stewards of the tribe Aiantis (names follow)... claimed on behalf of the tribe Aiantis that there was owing to the tribe Aiantis on the land of Nikodemos...666 2/3 (drachmas), Nikodemos not having paid back this money to the tribe Aiantis when he had become steward and had collected the sacred money of Ajax, and having incurred the penalty — even after losing all his possessions if he should not pay back the money according to the laws of the tribe Aiantis — of owing in addition a fine of 666 2/3 (drachmas) to the public treasury. It was decided that the claim of the tribe was (valid).

"Purchaser: Nikokrates son of Xenokrates of Rhamnus, 680 (drachmas); this amount paid in full all at once."[27]

Nikodemos' entanglements began with his misappropriation of 666 drachmas and 4 obols of the tribe's money, an action which created in the first instance a private debt, from him to the tribe, in that amount. By the rules of the tribe, the embezzlement also entailed a penalty, payable to the state (the tribe was a public body, after all), equal to the sum misappropriated. This penalty, the tribal rules insisted, could not be waived even on a plea of poverty. Nikodemos failed to make good either on the 666 2/3 drachmas due the tribe or on the penalty due the state. His failure automatically placed him in the category of a public debtor; his name was inscribed on the Acropolis in the list of defaulters and the penalty (not the private-law debt to the tribe) was doubled. (In addition, he seems also to have been in default to the state for another 1,000 drachmas; this sum too was now owed with a 100 per cent penalty.)

Once he was formally entered as a public debtor, Nikodemos' property was subject to confiscation *in toto*. Any citizen in full possession of his civil rights was empowered to bring an action in condemnation against whatever holdings Nikodemos may have had, charging that the property "belonged to the state."[28] Three members of the deme Aphidna did so in the Nikodemos case, thereby initiating the legal steps of which the *poletai* have left us a relatively detailed record.

Following formal denunciation before the Eleven, the person whose property was at stake had the opportunity to defend it by regular court proceedings, with the responsibility resting upon the complainant to prove the state's right to the property.[29] If the property owner lost or if he did not contest, the property was turned over to the *poletai* for sale by public auction. But first publicity was given by herald to the forthcoming sale, so that other claimants could come forward. They too received a formal hearing and a verdict was rendered in court on the validity or falsity of their claims. That phase of the proceedings the Athenians called *enepiskemma*. Successful claimants received priority over the state's interest and were paid from the proceeds of the sale of the property. The decisive point for us is that the tribe Aiantis, the original creditor, was compelled to resort to the *enepiskemma*, just like any individual, in order to collect its 666 drachmas and 4 obols.[30]

It is interesting to note, too, that the property brought only 680 drachmas at the sale, a trifling sum in proportion to the debts and penalties that Nikodemos had piled up. It was sufficient to cover his debt to the tribe, but whether they actually received their money

or not must remain an open question. Under Athenian law, the three
men who brought the original denunciation were entitled to three
fourths of the sale proceeds. Whether claims established by *enepiskemma* were paid first and the three fourths calculated on the remainder or vice versa is not determinable from the sources.[31]

Because of their different legal position and their different status
generally, demes and other subdivisions, unlike the city-state itself,
did ask for guarantees in the form of real property on occasion. The
evidence of the *horoi* points to the rarity of such occasions. *Horos*
no. 5, found in the city between the Pnyx and the Areopagus,
indicates the hypothecation of a house for 200 drachmas to the deme
Halai Aixonides, a coastal deme situated south and west of Mt.
Hymettos.[32] No. 146 marks a dotal *apotimema* for 6,000 drachmas
and the hypothecation of the surplus of the land to a tribe, a *genos*,
and the demesmen of Phlya, where the stone was found. (This stone,
incidentally, is the sole *horos* naming a tribe, Kekropis, more
correctly, the tribesmen.) Then there is the decree of the deme
Myrrhinus, dated after 340 B.C., authorizing the priests, if money is
needed, to lend temple funds "on land or a house or a multiple-
dwelling and to set up a *horos*," indicating to which god the loaned
money belongs.[33] The so-called temple funds were deme funds, of
course, and the administrative technique, common in Athens and
elsewhere, of handling such moneys through the temple had no
special significance, legally or otherwise.[34]

The explanation for the unmistakable infrequency with which
demes entered into transactions involving *horoi* lies in two closely
interrelated developments revealed by the land leases. Like the
polis itself, its subdivisions show a tendency to seek security in the
form of personal suretyship.[35] At times, they seem not to have
required any form of special security at all but to have contented
themselves with a penalty clause authorizing execution against a
defaulting tenant's property.[36]

It may be argued that leases are not comparable with loans,
especially because their considerable duration — 10, 20, or 40 years,
or in perpetuity — virtually precludes the hypothecation of realty,
which would tie up the property of a tenant or his suretor for years.
And what of the landless tenant, precisely the kind of person who
would normally seek to rent a plot, if guarantees of land or houses
were the usual practice? Yet there is incontrovertible evidence in
the general rules inscribed on stone by the deme Peiraieus in 321/0
B.C. for the leasing of its sacred precincts, whereby tenants whose

annual rental exceeded ten drachmas were required to put up "an *apotimema* sufficient in value for the rental," those leasing for sums under ten drachmas to supply a suretor.[37] The term was to be ten years. For whatever reason, the demesmen were not satisfied with personal guarantees for sums over ten drachmas — the ridiculously low amount selected as the dividing line is noteworthy — and requested security in property.

The use of the word *apotimema* is the key, I think, and brings us to the second aspect of the explanation of the rarity of *horoi* naming demes and other public bodies. In a formal, legal text like the Peiraieus inscription the choice of *apotimema* must be presumed to have been deliberate. The one notion that the word implies that cannot be equally well supplied by *hypotheke*, the word we should have expected, is "measuring off." In view of the small sum at stake, the deme as lessor requests a proportionate, and comparably small, guaranty. That could take the form either of 20 or 30 or 40 drachmas' worth of land, that is to say, of a grant to the deme of the right to levy execution on the tenant's property up to the amount fixed, and no more, or of an evaluated amount of personal or movable goods. It seems to me that we are not compelled to assume real property in every case in which the words *apotimema* or *hypotheke* appear, although it is a necessary assumption in most instances.[38] If movables were in fact accepted, whether as pledge with the transfer of possession or as hypothecation with possession by the debtor, there would of course be no *horoi*. But even if immovables were offered, I suggest, the affixing of *horoi* did not follow. *Horoi* marking debts below 100 drachmas have not been found in Athens. The deme's regulations, which are very detailed, fail to instruct the appropriate officials to place *horoi*, and this silence cannot be ignored. Furthermore, it was not the presence or absence of such markers that determined the existence of hypothecation but the agreement itself. Where small sums were at stake, publicity could well seem quite unnecessary.

But what about loans made by demes? Though no doubt all demes owned "temple" land and rented it out, the income from that source was certainly small — 134 drachmas and 2½ obols in the one figure we have, from the small deme of Plotheia;[39] probably never more than several hundred drachmas in any case.[40] The bulk of the income of the demes, normally no great sum, presumably came from taxes, fines, and liturgies.[41] Interest on loans was a third source, but we are singularly uninformed about the magnitude, frequency, or conditions of moneylending by the demes. About 400 B.C. Plotheia instructed its officials to make loans either on the security of an *apotimema* or on suretyship. The language implies that the choice rested with the official and was not determined by the size of the loan.[42] That text together with the decree of Myrrhinus already cited, insisting on the use of *horoi* where the deme's money was loaned out, virtually exhausts the source material. The conclusion seems inescapable that loans by the deme were not numerous, were made in relatively small amounts, and were generally not backed by hypothecation publicized through the medium of the *horoi*.[43]

3. RELIGIOUS (CULT) BODIES

Though "there was no true community among the Greeks which was not at the same time a cult-community," whether family, *genos*, tribe, or the state itself,[44] it is perfectly legitimate in the context of the present discussion to separate cult associations from other bodies. On the other hand, since all groupings apart from the *polis* proper were subject to private law in matters of property and finance, no distinction need be drawn between such groups as *gene*, that could be created only by action of the state, and the strictly private organizations like the *orgeones*.[45]

Attica was dotted with altars, sacred precincts, and temples of gods and heroes, all but a few the private property of one or another group. A relative handful were substantial in size and productivity; the great majority were hardly more than a few sticks and stones in a grove. Yet whatever their nature and extent, these holdings were freely negotiable according to the desires of the group owning them. That is the sense of the old law attributed to Solon that we have considered earlier in this chapter. Presumably alienation of cult property was rare for it would be tantamount to dissolution of the group in most cases, but that does not alter the legal situation. One third-century inscription, unfortunately fragmentary, reports on the decision of an arbitration board called in to settle an internal dispute within a body of *orgeones*. The arbitrators decided that the land belonging to the group could not be hypothecated and, if the generally accepted restorations of the text are correct, could not be alienated. Neither the nature of the dispute nor the ground for the decision is known, but the implication seems unmistakable that the negative ruling was based on a disagreement in policy among the members, not on a prohibition laid down by the law of the state.[46]

7 Finley

The following text was found identically worded on each of a pair of boundary-stones from Markopulo and Koropi, in northern Attica immediately adjoining the buffer district of Oropos separating Athens from Boeotia: "*Horos* of the land of the fraternity of the Eikadeis. Let no one make any loan whatsoever on this land."[47] The Eikadeis were a small cult group who assembled on the twentieth day of the month (hence their name) to worship Apollo. Why they felt it necessary to add to their boundary-stones a prohibition against loans is of course unknown but it is easy to speculate that, like the unnamed *orgeones* who went to arbitration, the brothers had a dispute about their land and decided to warn possible lenders that the group was unwilling to hypothecate its property for any purpose. The obvious way to publicize such a warning was through the medium of the stones marking the boundaries of their land. This suggestion may be supported by another inscription, a decree of the Eikadeis in 324/3 B.C., found in the same region as the boundary-stones, honoring a member for his work on behalf of the fraternity in a legal dispute, the nature of which is not indicated.[48]

Two skimpy texts are not much evidence. Yet we may properly conclude first that cult bodies did not often engage in legal transactions with their property, apart from rental, and second that this infrequency may be attributed to the character of these groups and, more generally, to the property regime of the time, rather than to any legal prohibition. In the absence of the legal institution of the trust or foundation, only explicit legislation in some form could have rendered cult property absolutely inalienable. I know of no trace of such legislation or of other indications of inalienability.[49]

It is a reasonable presumption that none of the unnamed debtors of the *horoi* is a cult body. As creditors, the *gene* of the Glaukidai and Epikleidai appear on *horos* no. 41, owed 600 and 150 drachmas respectively, the Lykomidai in no. 146, and the Gephyraioi in 147. *Thiasotai* appear twice in no. 41 and once in no. 43.[50] The Dekadistai, a group whose holy day was the tenth of the month, is creditor for 130 drachmas in *horos* no. 32. This list includes all the cult bodies found in the Attic *horoi*. Ironically, the only mention of *orgeones*, the most peculiarly Athenian of all the groups, is in three Lemnian texts, nos. 107—9. None of the other island *horoi* names a religious body.

What is particularly striking about this group of *horoi* is that in all but no. 43 and the three from Lemnos, more than one claim on the property is indicated as existing simultaneously. No. 41 has five creditors, an individual, two *gene*, and two *thiasotai*; no. 32 has three, an individual, the Dekadistai, and an *eranos*; no. 147 has at least two, though part of the stone is illegible. No. 146 is perhaps the most revealing of all, for it marks property offered as security in a dotal *apotimema* for 6,000 drachmas and then goes on to say that the balance, whatever is worth more than 6,000, is hypothecated to the tribe Kekropis, the *genos* of the Glaukidai, and the demesmen of Phlya, with no sum of money indicated for any of the three groups.[51]

There is no need to repeat what has already been said about the rarity of sale and improvements as the transactions leading to hypothecation. Infrequent as they were in the case of individuals, they must have been very much more scarce in the case of religious bodies.[52] That leaves loans as the seemingly logical source of the obligations noted on the *horoi*, and this is the generally accepted explanation.[53] Yet there are serious difficulties. Direct references to moneylending by Athenian religious bodies are strikingly. rare. The implication, further, is that the amounts involved are small. Thus, in an early third-century B.C. fragment of a decree of a society of *orgeones*, found on the Areopagos, a decision is recorded to draw up a list of debtors, the amounts owed, and the interest. The list is unfortunately lost, but the decree reveals that the group had to consider the possibility that its funds might not be enough to purchase one ox. And this was a small society whose members were, in Ferguson's words, "respectable, fairly well-to-do families."[54] Financial difficulties are a recurrent theme in the inscriptions emanating from the groups. There are honors voted officials for contributing their own money for the sacrifices, decrees calling upon the members to make small voluntary contributions for building repair and maintenance, and the like. All in all, the picture is one of dealings on a very small scale and of the nearly total absence of cash reserves of any size, in other words, of the lack of money that could have been lent out in small amounts, let alone sums in the hundreds of drachmas.[55]

If we return to *horos* no. 146, is it plausible to assume that the wealthy husband of Hippokleia first put up 6,000 drachmas' worth of his land as the *apotimema* for his dowry, and then borrowed un-named sums from a deme, a tribe, and a *genos* on the remainder? Is it not peculiar that, on the Attic *horoi*, associations seem hardly ever to be sole creditors, but are joined by others in four of the five cases? The answer that suggests itself is that what we have here is

7*

not a record of loans at all — in most instances, at least — but some other form of transaction under the legal fiction of hypothecation. In the absence of the juristic notion of trust or foundation, such a fiction might serve to secure for an owner, threatened in some fashion, continued or future enjoyment of his property under divine protection.[56]

4. ERANOI

In ten of the *horoi*, one Lemnian, one Amorgian, and the rest Attic, the creditor is an *eranos*, or, to follow the terminology of the stones more precisely, the property is put up as security to eranists.[57] The usual formula is "to the eranists, those with" followed by a proper name (nos. 30—32, 42, 70, and 110). Twice the stones say merely "to the eranists" without attaching an individual's name (nos. 44 and 71); whether this was due to an oversight by the stone-cutter or to the general trend towards terseness characteristic of the *horoi* is immaterial. Only nos. 8 and 40 depart radically from the regular practice, and we shall return to them shortly. Unlike the *horoi* naming religious bodies, furthermore, these stones name but one creditor in each case, the *eranos*. The sole exception is no. 32 and there the exception is only apparent, for the guaranty given the eranists is in the form of an *apotimema*, which means that the balance of the property was as free and unencumbered as if no *apotimema* existed.[58]

Now the word *eranos* had three distinct, technical meanings in Greek. Its earliest use, found in Homer and persisting into the classical period, was for a common dinner or picnic. By the fifth century B.C., if not earlier, it also came to mean a friendly loan made by an *ad hoc* group of individuals (or the loan-making group itself). As a general rule, the *eranos*-loan was sharply differentiated from the ordinary loan by several characteristics: the funds were supplied by a group (more precisely, a plurality) of people, without interest, and with an arrangement for repayment over a period of years in regular installments. Such loans were sought for a variety of purposes, though personal emergency was the theme in most cases: ransom, tax or liturgy payments, manumission of a slave, and the like. Frequently the man in need collected the *eranos* himself, but not always.

The third meaning of *eranos*, and the latest to put in its appearance, is that of a certain kind of club, found chiefly in Athens and

Rhodes.[59] The important question for us is which meaning is to be
assigned to the eranists of the *horoi*. Have we a reflection here of
economic activity on the part of permanently organized groups, in
substantially greater number than was true of the *orgeones* and other
traditional cult bodies, or merely examples of real security offered
for a specific kind of loan? The answer will have implications of
some significance for the general evaluation of hypothecation in the
Greek world.

From the outset, the available evidence argues in favor of the
eranos-loan. In Greek literature, *eranos* almost invariably means
loan (or the lending group) and not club; the earliest use that may
be rendered "club" or "society" is in the passage in Aristotle's
Nicomachean Ethics quoted at the beginning of this chapter. The
earliest epigraphical documents of *eranos*-associations date in the
middle of the third century B.C.[60] The one dated *horos* mentioning
eranists, in contrast, is no. 71 of the year 309/8 B.C. Furthermore,
all indications point to 250 B.C. as more or less the terminal date for
the *horoi* generally, as we have seen. Those who would argue that the
eranoi of the *horoi* are clubs must therefore bear the burden of explaining why ten *horoi*, some if not all dating from the fourth
century B.C., have been found referring to *eranoi*, when not a
single epigraphical text of another type has been found from the
years before 250 B.C. and when the literary references are almost
non-existent. They must explain further why cult bodies are rare in
the *horoi* but frequent in other epigraphical texts, while *eranoi* are
proportionately much more common in the *horoi*. They must explain finally how the *eranos*-societies differed so radically in purpose,
constitution, and, above all, financial position, as to be able to make
loans ranging as high as 6,000 drachmas, when phratries, *orgeones*,
and the rest, could do so rarely, if ever.

The internal evidence of the *horoi* is largely inferential, but it
supports the loan interpretation. *Horos* no. 40 from Eleusis reads as
follows: "*Horos* of the land put up as security (*prasis epi lysei*) to
Leochares the *plerotes* and to the fellow-eranists, 3,000 (drachmas)."
Plerotes is a technical word for a contributor to an *eranos*-loan.[61]
Leochares, we may safely assume, was the "head" of the group of
men who made the loan, in the same position as the individuals
usually named in the formula, "to the eranists, those with." There
can be no question of a club in this instance.

Horos no. 8, an unusually lengthy third-century B.C. Amorgian
text, presents difficulties that no one seems to have been able fully

to resolve. I suggest the following translation: *"Horos* of the lands in —— and of the house and gardens of Xenokles located in Phylincheia and of the recorded pledges, hypothecated, with the agreement of his wife Eratokrate and her *kyrios* Brukion, to the *eranos* and to Aristagoras the *eranos*-head and to his wife Echenike, for the surety for which he inscribed Xenokles in the matter of (for) the *eranos*, which Aristagoras had collected according to the law regarding eranists."[62]

Several of the complications may be ignored, specifically the participation of the wives of Xenokles and Aristagoras, the right of Xenokles to hypothecate things he had apparently received in pledge, and the suretyship arrangements. What remains can be interpreted as follows. Aristagoras assumed the responsibility of collecting an *eranos*-loan, in accordance with the law of the city of Arkesine on the subject. As the man who took the initiative, he became "head" of the group of lenders, like Leochares in no. 40 and the individuals named, though by another formula, in the other *horoi* involving eranists.[63] Xenokles was committed somehow to a suretyship agreement and he hypothecated various holdings, both real and personal, to the eranists, that is, in the formula customary when a group of any kind is involved, to the group and at the same time to its head or representative. If this interpretation is correct, *horos* no. 8 uses the word *eranos* only in the loan sense, once as the *ad hoc* group who lent the money, and the other time as the loan itself, not as an *eranos*-club. True, it contains the collective noun *eranos* rather than the word "eranists," whereas all the other *horoi* use the latter. This fact does not seem to me to be of paramount importance in the light of the inconsistency in usage already indicated.[64]

That exhausts the clues to be found in individual *horoi*. As a group, however, the ten *horoi* reveal two peculiarities that differentiate them from the stones naming indubitable associations. One has already been indicated, namely, the fact that *eranoi* always stand alone as the creditors whereas the associations more often than not appear in combination. The second peculiarity is that not a single one of the ten *horoi* refers to a written instrument or contract. That fact may be no more than a statistical accident but the more probable explanation is that it reflects the friendly character of the transaction, the underlying philanthropic ethic.[65]

Admittedly the evidence for taking all references to *eranoi* in the *horoi* to signify loans is not decisive. But there is no genuine evidence of any kind for the alternative view that they are societies, and that fact is decisive to my mind. The question may then be raised: If *eranoi* were by definition friendly loans, how can that notion be reconciled with the demand for security? In the absence of detailed information, only a generalized, hypothetical answer is possible, that in the thousands upon thousands of *eranos*-loans made and received in the fourth and third centuries, it is not difficult to conceive of special circumstances that would occasionally induce the man in need of a large sum of cash to offer some realty as a guaranty, especially if he were a man of substantial property. Not only would such an offer facilitate the collection of the *eranos*, it would also be a mark of good faith on his part commensurate with the act of friendship he was requesting. Occasional suretyship in the *eranoi* is attested, and suretyship is no less a weakening of the purely friendly loan than hypothecation.[66] *Horos* no. 8, no matter how it is interpreted, documents one case of real security in an *eranos*-loan. Ten further illustrations scarcely make an overwhelming number; nor do they destroy the general pattern, which remains one of unsecured, non-interest-bearing loans.[67] The failure of the literary sources, particularly the orators, to make any mention of security for *eranoi* has no testimonial value. An examination of the contexts will show that in nearly every instance there was no occasion to indicate the presence or absence of guarantees. In similar fashion, though we know the bare fact of the existence of a special procedural action for *eranoi* in Attic law, we do not have a single literary text about it.

But what of the four *horoi* (nos. 112—5), three Attic and one Lemnian and all undated, which say "sold" and not "sold with the right of redemption" (*prasis* without the *epi lysei* added)? In each of the three from Athens, the "purchaser" is an *eranos*. If the word "sold" is to be interpreted literally, the *eranos* must be a club, since sale of land to a loan-group seems impossible. For various reasons, however, it seems preferable to assume nothing more than an "abbreviation" for *prasis epi lysei*. Other illustrations of the use of "sell" to mean "put up as security" are very rare, but they do exist.[68] Then there are such stones as no. 146, in which the word *apotimema* is missing, no. 129 in which the property is not specified, or no. 3 in which there is no verb for "putting up as security." Further, I know of no evidence, literary or epigraphical, that the Athenians used stone markers to indicate that a piece of property had changed ownership through sale. In principle there was nothing to prevent this from being done sometimes, even if it were not the practice. But then one must explain the remarkable coincidence that all three such stones from Attica deal with *eranoi*, a coincidence that becomes absolutely incredible when we remember that the only known case in which a Greek society of any type purchased land dates from Roman times.[69] Once again we are reminded that the *horoi* were a commonplace to the Athenians. Short-cut formulations that are difficult, even unintelligible, for us gave them no problems and require no subtle, complicated explanations. If the *horoi* regularly indicated hypothecation, an occasional omission of a word. or phrase would have gone almost unnoticed.[70]

It may be illuminating to digress briefly and consider another group of documents in which the type of *eranos* has been hotly debated. They are the so-called "freedmen's bowls," 100-drachma silver bowls paid over to the city of Athens by manumitted slaves following their victory in a special legal procedure known as the *dike apostasiou*. Lists of these payments were recorded on stone and the fragments discovered so far, all dated on epigraphical grounds in about the year 330 B.C., include well over 200 entries.[71] Most of the entries give the name, occupation, and residence (by deme) of the freedman or freedwoman and the name and demotic of the ex-owner (manumittor). In seventeen entries an *eranos* appears, usually in the form, "Nikodemos of Leukonoe and *koinon* of eranists."[72]

Some historians have interpreted these seventeen entries to be cases in which the freedman had been a slave in the possession of a society, hence the society was the manumittor and the opponent in the suit.[73] The addition of an individual's name, they say, is nothing but the usual form indicating the head of the *eranos*. Three objections seem to render this view entirely untenable. The first is one already raised in connection with the *horoi*, the fact that the lists of freedmen's bowls are three quarters of a century or more earlier than the first inscriptions of *eranos*-clubs. The second may be phrased as a question: What kind of Athenian society had reason to own midwives, incense sellers, or ring engravers (occupations enumerated in precisely these seventeen entries)? In the whole of Greek literature I know of no answer or precedent.

The third and most decisive objection stems from formal considerations. Thirteen of the seventeen entries follow the form, "Nikodemos and *koinon* of eranists." Two others are too fragmentary for judgment. But the remaining two are significantly different, one reading "Chairippos son of Chairedemos of Halai and *koinon* of eranists, those with Chairippos of Halai," and the other, "Philokrates son of Epikrates of Eleusis and *koinon* of eranists, those with Theophrastos son of Bathyllos of Cholargos."[74]

The clue to the explanation will be found in an almost contemporaneous document, the speech in the case of Pasion's son Apollodoros and the latter's brother-in-law Theomnestos against the prostitute Neaira, between 343 and 340 B.C.[75] Neaira had been a slave. At one point in her career, says the speaker, Eukrates of Leukas and Timanoridas of Corinth bought her, in the latter's native city, for 3,000 drachmas. When the two men were about to marry, they offered Neaira her freedom upon payment of 2,000 drachmas. She raised some of the money from various ex-lovers, contributed some herself, and persuaded Phrynion, a relative of Demosthenes', to take these sums, add the remainder out of his own pocket, and purchase her freedom from Eukrates and Timanoridas.[76]

What Neaira did, says the orator, was to "collect an *eranos* for freedom."[77] It is a procedure known from many parts of the Greek world, whereby a slave is permitted to purchase his freedom through sums borrowed, in an *eranos*-loan, from an *ad hoc* group. Prior to his emancipation a slave lacks legal personality, hence some one else must collect the *eranos*, in law if not in fact. Neaira obviously did her own collecting but for the completion of the legal act of purchasing her freedom a free man, Phrynion, must intervene. Under the law, he was the collector of the *eranos*, the person who would appear in a document in the formula, "the eranists, those with." (That Neaira did not "borrow" the money in the sense that she did not promise to repay in cash is clear but totally irrelevant in establishing the pattern.) Usually it was the owner himself who collected the *eranos*, but at times, as in Neaira's case, someone else took on the responsibility. Legally that was a matter of complete indifference.[78]

This is the procedure reflected in the lists of freedmen's bowls. In the thirteen "normal" entries (*e.g.*, "Nikodemos and *koinon* of eranists"), as in the entry which needlessly repeats the name of Chairippos ("Chairippos...of Halai and *koinon* of eranists, those with Chairippos of Halai"), the owner himself arranged the *eranos*-loan. In the summary of the lawsuit, therefore, his name only appears along with the *eranos*. But in one manumission a third party collected the funds, hence we have the name of the owner and then an *eranos* with the name of this third person. This view, that the *eranos* was an *ad hoc* loan group, makes the double name perfectly intelligible; the *eranos*-society interpretation, apart from the other objections, cannot explain the two names.

We have now completed the rather lengthy process of eliminating any form of permanent or continuing group as a significant factor in the field of hypothecation, and even in the field of moneylending generally, in Athens before the Roman era. A word remains to be said about the moral and social aspects of the *eranoi*. In one of the practise speeches that have come down to us in the name of Antiphon, we read: "As for me, from my past actions you will know that I am not one to plot (against another) nor one of those to reach out for another's (property). Quite the contrary, I am one of those who have paid numerous and high *eisphora* taxes, have often been trierarch, executed the choregy brilliantly, participated in many *eranoi*, paid out large sureties for many...."[79] Proud inclusion of *eranoi* as evidence of civic virtue and social conscience is perfectly consonant with the Peripatetic's "if a man is a friend, he does not lend but gives"[80] and with Plato's recommendation that *eranos*-loans not be actionable at law.[81] In his own fashion, Theophrastus reflected the same notion when his braggart ran up the sum of 10 talents in paid-out *eranoi* on an abacus.[82]

The *eranoi* have brought us back to the world with which we dealt in the previous chapter, of wealthy men and non-productive loans. Of the six sums of money given on the *horoi* involving *eranoi*, five are above the median figure for all *prasis epi lysei* texts.[83] In a fundamental sense, the distinction between the individual friendly loan, like Pasion's to Timotheos, and the group friendly loan is meaningless insofar as the economic and social aspects of hypothecation are concerned, and not too meaningful from a legal point of view. Ordinarily the friendly loan was unsecured, occasionally it was guaranteed by real property. The same kinds of people participated in both, as borrowers and lenders, and their motives were the same.

Here too the *horoi* do not take us into the world of the poor, of the small farmer and the petty trader or the craftsman. Not that *eranoi* were not common enough in those circles, but they lacked the property to put up as security. Theophrastus' miser quickly makes a detour when he sees a friend approaching for a contribution to an *eranos*.[84] That is the other side of the civic-virtue picture, the begging quality as a man of no means seeks the assistance of others in an emergency.[85]

CHAPTER VIII

MULTIPLE CREDITORS

THOUGH THE *horoi* DID NOT as a rule reveal the legal status of the property prior to its having been encumbered, whether it was owned by a minor, for example, or was part of an undivided inheritance, they did customarily give some indication when special complications followed hypothecation. A priori, three legally distinct types of transaction were possible apart from the simple one in which X hypothecates his land to Y; he may offer the property as security (1) to two or more creditors jointly, or (2) to two or more creditors severally in a single agreement, or (3) to two or more creditors (jointly or severally) in successive acts. Examples of all three might seem to be available:

1) No. 19 — "*Horos* of land and a house put up as security (*prasis epi lysei*) to Aristophon of Teithras, to Autokles of Anaphlystos, 1,100 (drachmas)."

2) No. 46 — "*Horos* of land put up as security (*prasis epi lysei*) to Autodikos of Oion, 500 (drachmas), to Ergophilos of Atene, to Ergochares of Atene, 2,300 (drachmas)." (Actually, this *horos* might seem to be a combination of types 1 and 2.)

3) No. 146 — "*Horos* of land (put up as security) for the dowry of Hippokleia daughter of Demochares of Leukonoe, one talent; by whatever it is worth more, it is hypothecated to the Kekropidai and to the Lykomidai and to the demesmen of Phlya."

Upon further examination, it becomes clear that the texts themselves do not in fact tell us whether the transactions fall into any one of the three types. All the key words are missing; not even the punctuation marks are on the stones. What is there *in the language* of no. 46, for instance, to prevent the following interpretation, that the land was first put up as security for a loan of 500 drachmas made by Autodikos and later, in a transaction analogous to the modern second mortgage, used to guarantee an additional loan received from Ergophilos and Ergochares? Or how are we to know whether in no. 146 the husband of Hippokleia, daughter of Demochares, hypothecated the balance of his land, after the amount deemed adequate security for one talent had been determined, at one time or on three different occasions? and whether the three groups acted jointly or independently? If there are answers to these questions, they must come from sources other than the texts of individual *horoi*.

Two *horoi*, nos. 146 and 147, start with an *apotimema* and end with a *hypotheke*, the two transactions being linked by the technical term, "by whatever it is worth more."[1] A third, no. 32, marks a *prasis epi lysei* to an individual for 500 drachmas and to the society of the Dekadistai for 130, followed by an *apotimema* to an *eranos*, with no indication of time, sequence, value relationship, or priority.[2] And a fourth, no. 13, ends with an unintelligible tag-end phrase, "and to another," followed by a numeral. For the rest, ten *horoi* list more than one creditor — two creditors five times (nos. 11, 19, 22, 35, and 97), and an uncertain number in one, *horos* no. 105, a Lemnian stone and the only non-Attic text in this entire group.[3] In three of the texts only one amount is given (as in no. 19 previously quoted); separate amounts appear in three others (as in no. 46); and the remaining four are unclear.

That the existence of multiple creditors in hypothecation was not rare is therefore a safe conclusion. That it was the exception rather than the rule seems equally true. To clothe these bare statements, supported by the literary evidence, so as to create a full picture of the way in which such transactions worked would take us far beyond the scope of this study, however, into the whole area of creditors' rights in Greek law, into the problems of correality and solidarity, real and personal rights, foreclosure and execution. For the present, a few suggestions and cautions must suffice.

Neither in the literature nor in the epigraphical texts did the Athenians consistently show "proper" concern for precision of language in matters of multiple creditors. The following passage from the oration against Phainippos is a fair sample of what may be found scattered through the extant speeches:

"You hear, men of the jury. He says that he owes one talent jointly to Pamphilos and Pheidoles of Rhamnus and 4,000 drachmas to Aiantides of Phlya and 14 minas to Aristomenes of Anagyrus.... That you lie, Phainippos, and that you have come before these gentlemen perjuriously, I shall straightway show clearly. Clerk, take the deposition of Aiantides and Theoteles, to whom the defendant has declared himself to be in debt for 4,000 drachmas. He lies, for he repaid it long ago, not willingly but after court judgment. Read."[4]

The opening seems clear enough. Phainippos claimed three debts payable, one to two creditors jointly and two others to single individuals. But a few sentences later the speaker has a deposition read from which we discover that one of the latter debts also involved two creditors. The discrepancy provokes no explanation, nor does the speaker feel the need for one.[5] Similarly, the lease of land owned by the deme Aixone in 346/5 B.C. is made for a forty-year term to Autokles and his son Anteas, but in a rider appended to the lease the word "lessee" appears in both the plural and the singular, and the problem is completely ignored in the penalty clause.[6]

In each instance the precise legal relationship between debtor and creditors and between one creditor and another was no doubt clearly fixed among the parties themselves. The point here is that this relationship usually remains undefined in the documents available to us. Occasionally we are able to discover the legal situation, but only from sources other than, or at least in addition to, the language of the particular text. The more compressed the text, of course, the greater the confusion. And no text can be compressed beyond the brevity of the *horoi*. Hence, we may categorically reject any attempt to define the legal picture suggested by a particular *horos* from such criteria as the sequence of names or the number of creditors listed.

In the passage just quoted from the oration against Phainippos, the sentences were omitted in which the speaker asks, rhetorically, why there were no *horoi* on the estate to indicate the debts Phainippos was claiming. Such a stone would perhaps read: *"Horos* of land hypothecated to Pamphilos of Rhamnus, Pheidoles of Rhamnus, one talent, to Aiantides of Phlya, 4,000 (drachmas), to Aristomenes of Anagyrus, 1,400 (drachmas)." In another case, the one involving Pantainetos, there is no reference to *horoi*, but one may very well have been affixed to the mill, reading *"Horos* of a workshop and slaves put up as security (*prasis epi lysei*) to Euergos, 6,000 (drachmas), to Nikobulos, 4,500 (drachmas)." In the former it is clear from the oration that the three debts were quite unrelated but that the debt of one talent was due to Pamphilos and Pheidoles jointly; in the latter, on the other hand, there was a connection between the two debts, difficult as it may be for us to pin it down precisely. But when the facts are reduced to the language of the *horoi*, the distinctions disappear. The *horoi* cited are imaginary, to be sure, but not a single *horos* known reveals a formula that would retain the legal distinctions.[7] The function of the *horoi*, it must be said once again, rendered further detail and clarity unnecessary.

Horos no. 41 reads: "*Horos* of land put up as security (*prasis epi lysei*) to Kephisodoros of Leukonoe, 1,500 (drachmas), and to the brothers (*i.e.*, members of a phratry), those with Eratostratos of Anaphlystos, 200 (drachmas), and to the Glaukidai, 600 (drachmas), and to the Epikleidai, 150 (drachmas), and to the brothers, those with Nikon of Anaphlystos, 100 (drachmas)." With some hesitation, the Corpus reading of 200 drachmas for the amount of the second debt has been adopted rather than the original editor's 1,200. The latter makes a neat and tempting picture, five debts placed in a row from the largest to the smallest in a descending scale. Several commentators have seized upon the sequence to see here a record of five successive transactions, each taking a bite out of what was left of the property, a first, second, third, fourth, and fifth "mortgage."

There are at least three objections to that interpretation: (1) It is based on a general picture of moneylending and "investing" activities on the part of Greek phratries and tribes that, as we have seen, cannot be supported from the available evidence. (2) Such a series of transactions would require a procedure of foreclosure and compulsory sale in order that the debts could be realized in case of default, whereas the essence of Athenian hypothecation was seizure of the property as a substitute for the debt, with rare exceptions, and there was no provision for adjustment in case of surplus or deficit. Hence there was no place for secondary obligations and creditors.[8] (3) In *horos* no. 46, where the reading is undisputed, a 500-drachma debt appears on the stone first, followed by one of 2,300. In such a case, the notion of successive transactions is most unlikely in my judgment, and, if they did exist, then the value-sequence on the stones is surely irrelevant.

Much the simpler explanation of *horos* no. 41 is to assume one debt, shared in unequal ratios by five creditors. Should the debtor default, the problem of obtaining compensation would become one to be solved upon their taking over the land jointly, not as a matter of ranking claims.[9] There is no basis for assuming that the sequence of names on the *horos* has any legal significance, just as it is wrong to assume some organic connection among the four groups just because they each had an equity in the same piece of property.[10] The orators provide ample evidence of loans made by two or more persons who were brought together, by a mutual acquaintance and sometimes even by chance, for one transaction, and who had no other dealings with each other, before or after the one joint action.[11]

The extent to which the Greek world knew, and its law permitted, the practice of using the same property as security for two debts, incurred separately and involving priority in the creditors' claims, is one of the most interesting questions in the whole field of credit relations. It is also one of the knottiest. The answer entails a full analysis of the rights of the creditor in hypothecation during the term of the obligation as well as in case of default. Legal historians are neither agreed nor very certain in their views, and we cannot undertake an extensive discussion here.[12]

An inscription published in 1941 is so germane to the whole problem that the pertinent section is quoted in full (except for some names of officials and the lengthy boundary descriptions). It is the public record of the Athenian *poletai* for the year 367/6 B.C. The second portion deals with the leasing of mines but the first thirty-nine lines cover the sale of a single confiscated house:[13]

"In the archonship of Polyzelos, the *poletai* ... sold the following, having received it from the Eleven.... On the tenth (day) of Munichion, Theomnestos son of Deisitheos of Ionidai denounced for confiscation[14] a house in Alopeke ... of Theosebes son of Theophilos of Xypete — (the latter) having been charged with sacrilege and not having remained for the trial — by whatever it is worth more than it was hypothecated to Smikythos of Teithras for 150 drachmas....[15]

"Kichonides son of Diogeiton of Gargettos and the *koinon* of the brothers of the Medontidai claimed that 100 drachmas were owed to him and to the brothers on the house in Alopeke which Theomnestos of Ionidai denounced as the property of Theosebes of Xypete..., 'Theophilos of Xypete, the father of Theosebes, having put up this house as security (*prasis epi lysei*)[16] to me and to the brothers.' It was decided that (the debt) was owed.

"Isarchos son of Philon of Xypete contends that 30 drachmas are owed to him on the house in Alopeke which Theomnestos son of Deisitheos of Ionidai denounced, 'I having buried Theophilos, whose house this was, and the wife of Theophilos.' It was decided that (the debt) was owed.

"Aischines of Melite and the *koinon* of the *orgeones* claimed that 24 drachmas were owed to them on the house which Theomnestos of Ionidai denounced, 'we having taken this house as security (*prasis epi lysei*) from Theophilos for this money.' It was decided that (the debt) was owed.

"Purchaser: Lysanias son of Palathion of Lakiadai, 575 (drachmas). The city has one fifth of this as payment on account and the

sales tax and the herald's fee and Smikythos of Teithras (has) the
one hundred and fifty (drachmas), (paid) all at once in accordance
with the denunciation."

This inscription offers much new material and the problems it
raises cannot all be discussed here. The insights it gives into the law
and practice of legal security must be sharply qualified by the
special factor of state intervention through confiscation. When the
state stepped in, prior claims on the property were recognized and
formally adjudicated. But what would have happened to those
claims if there had been no confiscation and if Theosebes had defaulted on one or more of the obligations? The text gives no answer,
of course, and it would be improper to assume that, in a purely
private matter, the procedure would necessarily have been parallel
to the one summarized in the inscription.

Several points, it seems to me, can nevertheless be established
tentatively on the basis of this text. (1) It was possible, by agreement of the parties, to offer real property as security for a debt and
to limit the guaranty to the amount of the debt, the property-
owner retaining his full rights in the property beyond that amount.
A step in that direction had been taken when the *apotimema* was
developed, but no unequivocal Athenian text had been known
revealing the practice in case of a *hypotheke*.[17] (It is assumed that
the use of the verb *hypokeitai* in the inscription is precise.)

(2) When only a portion of a man's realty was encumbered, he
was free to treat the remainder as he would any unencumbered
holding and hence to put it up as security for further debts if he
chose. That again was a characteristic of the *apotimema*. In the
present instance, the house served to secure two additional obligations,[18] each by *prasis epi lysei*, significantly enough, and each, we
may assume from the small amounts involved, encumbering the
house only to the value of the debt.

(3) When property was encumbered by several obligations and the
agreements so specified, there may have been priority in rank among
the creditors, but there need not have been. If the language of this
inscription is a reliable guide, Smikythos' claim outranked the
others. That is demonstrated in the final paragraph, which states
that Smikythos was paid immediately upon completion of the sale
by the *poletai* and implies that the other claimants had to wait for
satisfaction. This section is taken to mean that it was a condition of
the sale that the buyer pay at once not only the one fifth that the
law required when confiscated houses were sold,[19] together with the

sales taxes, but also Smikythos' debt, which was privileged. As for the other claims, they held inferior status. There is no suggestion, however, that there was inequality in rank among them on that lower level, though again we must remember that state intervention may have altered the normal private-law relationships.

In a sense, it would be proper to say that what Theomnestos had denounced, and what was therefore put up for public auction, was a house less 150 drachmas. Smikythos' claim, unlike the others, did not have to be adjudicated as part of the condemnation proceedings because Theomnestos had from the outset denounced the property only "by whatever it is worth more" than 150 drachmas. The parallel with *horoi* nos. 146 and 147 is obvious and very striking. And in both this inscription and the two *horoi*, cult groups are the creditors on the remainder of the property. Though one should not draw an inflexible generalization from that fact, it does suggest a rather peculiar specialized application of the right further to encumber one's land or house after a part had been marked off, so to speak, to cover an obligation. In the two *horoi* the original security transaction is called *apotimema*, here *hypotheke*. That variation suggests that it was not so much the term that was decisive as the more basic question whether or not the parties had reached a prior agreement.

Only a complete re-examination of the available evidence will show the tenability of these propositions and the extent to which they need further correction and qualification. But a certain over-all approach can be formulated. I am convinced that neither the law nor the practice of Athenian hypothecation was set by legislative enactment, at least in the fourth century B.C. from which most of the material comes.[20] Nevertheless, a pattern had developed in the course of the years that was dominant in the actual practice of the fourth and third centuries B.C. It is this pattern that ought to occupy the central point in the discussion, not the rare or exceptional practice. The pattern was controlled by the concept of substitution (as opposed to collateral) and hence precluded the use of property once encumbered as security for a second or third debt, as security of inferior or secondary rank and right, except on the most infrequent occasons.[21]

In the area of hypothecation, Athenian citizens operated under the law that whatever was agreed upon between parties was binding.[22] From time to time, when circumstances warranted, variations from the pattern were introduced in particular transactions, such as the occasional transfer of possession to the creditor for the duration of the obligation, or the use of *apotimema* for other than dotal or pupillary purposes, or the use of the same property as security for two or more unrelated debts.[23] The variations are interesting and worthy of analysis. To try to argue them away or to fit them into a neat pattern by casuistic subtleties is as wrong as to generalize from any single document that seems to mark an exceptional procedure. What is significant above all is that those variations which show a more advanced institution remained exceptional; they failed to displace the traditional, more primitive pattern, at least to the end of Greek independence.

At no point, perhaps, is there a more immediate link, historically and conceptually, between the economics and the law of security than in the character of the forfeit. In its elemental, primitive form, security is simple substitution. X owes Y something, an object, money, or performance, which he is unable or unwilling to render, and Y accepts a substitute object in full satisfaction of X's obligation to him. A later, and in the end essentially different, conception is that of collateral. X turns over to Y, or sets aside in reserve, some of his property in order to give Y tangible assurance that he will render whatever it is that he owes. Should X then default, Y may accept the collateral in lieu of the original obligation; the collateral is then transformed into a substitute. But Y may be unwilling to take a substitute and may insist on the specific performance originally promised by X (or the law may so compel). In that event, the collateral must be converted into a form identical with the original obligation and Y then receives precisely what he had been promised, no more and no less. Thereby collateral has become something different in essence from a substitutive guarantee.

Concretely, suppose X borrows $ 5,000 from Y and offers his house as security. If X defaults and Y receives the house instead of the $ 5,000, a simple substitution has taken place. But if the house is sold at Y's behest and brings $ 7,500 on the market, from which sum Y takes his $ 5,000 and X receives the balance, we have collateral security in the true sense. In the first illustration, there has been an exchange of house for money, irrespective of the disparate monetary values. In the second case, Y received exactly what was due him, $ 5,000 in cash, the house having served merely as the medium through which the payment was accomplished.

Between substitution and collateral there lies a profound economic transformation, akin to the shift from barter to the commodity market. "We are not to seek in the law of pledge itself for the reasons of the change," writes Wigmore. "The change came about as soon as the community recognized credit widely and developed varieties of obligation and forms of action for them...."[24]

The transformation cannot be expressed merely as the introduction of money and simple credit relations into the economy, though it is self-evident that without money substitution alone is possible. For the collateral idea to dominate, a relatively fluid credit economy is required, in which everything is readily translated into money; in which, in other words, all goods and commodities may have an immediate market value and are so conceived by the society. Our creditor, Y, must from the outset think of X's house not as a house which he will possess if X fails to pay him $ 5,000, but as $ 5,000 temporarily concealed in the form of a house. That notion is what the seventeenth-century English Chancellor, Lord Nottingham, the "father of equity," revealed when he held: "The principal right of the mortgagee is to the money, and his right to the land is only as security for the money."[25]

As credit relations became more and more complex, collateral security underwent two more important extensions. One was full negotiability. The other was the development of the second hypothec (or second mortgage) as a regular practice. In the modern world, the profound distinction between the first and second hypothec is immediately revealed not only by the considerable difference in the amounts of money involved but also by the character of the lenders. The first hypothec is above all the province of the financial institution, the second hypothec a favorite investment or speculation for the individual of relatively moderate means.[26]

As already stated, the conclusion seems inescapable that Athenian security was normally substitutive in character. The creditor took the property in case of default and that was the end of the matter as far as the debtor was concerned. How the new owner then dealt with the property was a matter of his free volition unhampered by the law of hypothecation. In the Pantainetos case, the creditors wanted no part of the mill and did everything to re-convert it into cash as quickly as possible.[27] Fourth-century Athenian bankers, with their extensive pawnbroking operations, came into possession of a wide variety of things, gold plate, raw materials, sometimes even farms. Usually they resold, but not always, and never under compulsion.

Without compulsory sale of the property, there can be no genuine development of the collateral idea. Only by sale on the market can the property be converted into money, and only by conversion into money can the creditor receive the actual debt due him rather than a substitute in a non-monetary form. It is therefore impossible to overstate the significance of the fact that there was no compulsory sale by law in the Greek cities.[28] The state regularly sold confiscated goods, to be sure, but that is quite a different matter from the practice of private parties; nor does it have any connection with hypothecation.

The way in which Demosthenes tells the court his version of the facts about the slaves taken over by his father in lieu of a debt throws light on the thinking of the Greeks in such matters. (For our present discussion, the fact that slaves were involved, not realty, and that ownership of the slaves apparently remained with the debtor despite transfer of possession, is irrelevant.) "My father, members of the jury," said the orator, "left two 'workshops,' in each of which there was no small manufacture.[29] One consisted of thirty-two or thirty-three cutlers at five or six minas each; none was worth less than three minas. From them he received an annual income of thirty minas clear. The other consisted of bedmakers to the number of twenty hypothecated (to my father) for forty minas; they brought him twelve minas clear."[30]

The facts presented by Demosthenes in this speech are confusing, to say the least, and the arithmetic hopelessly inaccurate. I have nevertheless quoted the passage at length because the formulation remains decisive regardless of the accuracy of the numbers. For the slaves who made cutlery, Demosthenes indicates, in a rough way, a market price. It is uncertain whether this was the price his father had actually paid or what the slaves would have brought if they had been sold at the time the elder Demosthenes died, but it is a genuine price in either event. For the twenty bedmakers, however, he gives the size of the debt which they secured, and this figure is correlated with the actual price of the other group of slaves. That the bedmakers were worth more on the market than the amount of the debt is obvious.[31] Yet Demosthenes, who is seeking to show the magnitude of his inheritance and hence the great wealth of which he has been robbed by Aphobos, does not think of re-calculating the value of the twenty slaves in market terms. His father had received them against a loan of forty minas, and forty minas was to be their figure forevermore. The idea of hypothecation, like the reality, was purely substitutive.[32]

It would be absurd to suggest that the value of the debt on the one

hand and of the encumbered property on the other bore no relationship whatever. Certainly an Athenian had a pretty good idea of the
value of the security he was offered before he agreed to make a loan.
But what he would look for in value would be something different
from what his modern counterpart would seek. If the property
serves as collateral, the test of acceptability is basically whether or
not it will bring enough on the market to repay the loan, plus interest and other charges, in case of default. There is no incentive to
drive a hard bargain if the creditor can, in the end, come out of the
transaction with no more than the original loan terms assured him.
The Athenian creditor, however, must ask himself whether he will
be satisfied to take the property instead of the promised money,
better than that, whether he will not be a substantial winner if the
debtor defaults and leaves him with property worth far more than
his loan. This schematic formulation admittedly ignores the numerous complexities and combinations in security practice, and yet it
seems correctly to differentiate the essential core of the two systems
of hypothecation.

One must deny that there is an integral tie, historically and
functionally, between hypothecation and money and credit if one is
not willing to draw the necessary economic conclusions from the
legal situation. In Athens, the very idea of collateral is to all intents
and purposes unknown even in the fourth and third centuries B.C.[33]
To explain this fact, as the lawyers have done, by the weakness of
the law of hypothecation is inadequate.[34] Weak law can be corrected.
First the society must perceive that it is weak, however. This
Athens, unlike Stuart England, did not do, because their law of
hypothecation was fully adequate to the prevailing practice, the latter
in turn geared to the level of money and credit of the era.[35]

APPENDIX I

THE TEXTS OF THE *HOROI*

The arrangement of the texts follows, first of all, the Greek terminology: *hypotheke*, *prasis epi lysei*, and *apotimema* (pupillary and dotal). Within each of these basic categories, further subdivision by city is obvious. Chronological arrangement would also have been desirable but since only a handful of the *horoi* can be dated with any precision, I have abandoned chronology altogether. Instead, I have arranged the texts within each basic category according to the nature of the property and the amount of the obligation, in a descending scale as indicated in the four tables at the end. Too many of the stones are incomplete or fragmentary, so that a perfect scheme is impossible. I have therefore taken the liberty of departing on occasion from the property-value sequence in order to group several *horoi* that offer a common peculiarity of special significance, although never if such grouping necessitates disregard of the fundamental separation according to terminology. When a *horos* marked two or more obligations in combination, *apotimema* and *prasis epi lysei* for example, I have placed it under the type that appears first on the stone.

I have entirely ignored the order in which the texts are published in IG II², for the principle of arrangement there is neither coherent nor consistently maintained. Kirchner followed the editors of IJ, with some modification. He has seven subdivisions: (a) *hypothecae a tutore pupillis collocatae*, 2542—58; (b) *hypothecae pro dote uxoris*, 2659—83; (c) πρᾶσις ἐπὶ λύσει, 2684—2757; (d) *antichreseos institutum*, 2758—59; (e) *res hypothecae nomine obligatae*, 2760—62; (f) *termini fundis emptis appositi*, 2763—66; (g) *incerta*, 2767—70. This arrangement offers an excellent illustration of the impossibility of classifying this material according to the content of the obligation. A system which has three categories of 17, 25, and 73 units, respectively, and three others of 2, 3, and 4 units (the *incerta* may be ignored) is necessarily faulty in conception.

My copies of the texts are based on printed editions exclusively, for I have examined neither stones nor squeezes. In reproducing the texts, I have tried to be very precise in indicating lacunae and doubtful letters. All uncertain restorations have been removed but noted in the comments. I have made one minor exception to this rule. Where a break in the stone makes it impossible to tell whether the property-word ("land" or "house") appeared in the singular or plural, and the grammar (the number of the verb) does not provide the answer, I have always used the singular. This practice can be justified on statistical grounds. It leaves a margin for error, to be sure, but a slight one.

I. *HYPOTHEKE*

A. ATHENS

1. IG II² 2758 (II 1139 — *Syll.* 1192 — M 1378 — IJ I viii, no. 62)
    Athens, marble

    ὅρος χωρίου καὶ οἰκίας
    ὑποκειμένων ⲅΗΗΗ
    δραχ(μῶν) : ὥστε ἔχειν καὶ κρα
    τεῖν [τ]ὸν θέμενον κατὰ
    συνθήκας τὰς κειμένας
    παρὰ Δεινίαι Εὐωνυμεῖ.

2. IG II² 2759 (II 1140 — IJ I viii, no. 63)
    At the Illisus, marble

    ...ΙΟ? — —
    ... Λ[— — χω]ρίο κ[αὶ κή]
    [π]ου καὶ τῆς προσούσης [κρήνη]
    ς τῶι κηπιδίωι ὑποκειμ[έ]
    νων δραχμῶν ΗΗΗ ἐφ᾽ ὧ[ι]
    τε ἔχειν καὶ κρατ[εῖν τὸν]
    ὑποθέμενον [κατὰ συνθή]
    κας τὰς κειμ[ένας παρὰ Σ]
    είμαλον — —

    — —

In line 2, IG gives Ziebarth's restoration, ἐργαστη]ρίο κ[αὶ], but neither the place of discovery nor the link with a garden and well nor the relative infrequency of ἐργαστήριον in the *horoi* warrants that reading. I have therefore inserted the much more obvious χω]ρίο.

3. IG II² 2762 (II 1134 — *Syll.* 1194 — M 1377 — IJ I viii, no. 61)
   Acharnai

   ἐπὶ Θεοφράστου
   ἄρχοντος· [ὅ]ρος
   χωρίου τιμῆς
   ἐνοφειλομέν
   ης Φανοστράτωι
   Παιαν(ιεῖ) ΧΧ.

There were two fourth-century archons named Theophrastos, in 340/39 and 313/2 B.C. The stone itself leaves little basis for choice; see Dow and Travis, "Demetrios of Phaleron" 163.

4. IG II² 2761A (II 5,1116b — *Syll.* 1195A — M 1379A — IJ I viii, no. 69)
   Between the Pnyx and the Areopagus

   ὅρος οἰκίας ὑπο
   κειμένης ⟦Χ⟧
   0.12 rasura
   Περιάνδρωι
   Χολαρ(γεῖ).

No. 5 followed immediately after on the stone in slightly larger letters.

5. IG II² 2761B (II 5,1116c — *Syll.* 1195B — M 1379B — IJ I viii, no. 70)
   Between the Pnyx and the Areopagus

   ὅρος οἰκίας
   ὑποκειμένης
   ῾Αλαιεῦσι: ΗΗ.

No. 4 came immediately before on the stone in slightly smaller letters.

6. Δελτ. 14 (1931/2) παρ. 31, no. 4
Eleusis, local stone, 291/0 B. C.

ἐπ' 'Αριστωνύμου
ἄρχοντος· ὅρος οἰκίας
ὑπ[οκ]ειμένης Ναυσιστρ
άτωι 'Ελευσινίωι
ΗΗ κατὰ τὰς συν
θήκας τὰς κειμένας
παρὰ Θεοδώ
ρωι Οἰν[αίωι].

7. IG II² 2760
In the city, marble

ὅρος
ἐργαστηρ[ί]
ο ὑποκειμέ
νο
ⲚΗΗⲚ.

B. AMORGOS

8. IG XII 7,58 (Syll. 1198 — M 1380 — IJ I viii, no. 64)
Arkesine, 3rd cent. B. C.

ὅρος χωρίων [τῶν ἐν......]
ρει καὶ οἰκίας καὶ κ[ήπων]
τῶν Ξενοκλέος τῶ[ν κει]
μένων ἐμ Φυλινχείαι καὶ τῶν
5   ἐπικυρβίων ἐνεχύρων ὑποκει
μένων, συνεπιχωρούσης τ[ῆ]ς
γυναικὸς 'Ερατοκράτης καὶ τοῦ
κυρίου Βρουκίωνος, τῶ[ι] ἐράν[ωι]
καὶ 'Αρισταγόραι τῶι ἀρχεράνωι
10   καὶ τῆι γυναικὶ αὐ[τοῦ] 'Εχε[νίκηι]
πρὸς τὴν ἐγγύαν ἣν ἐγ[ράψα]
το Ξενοκλῆν τοῦ ἐρά[νου ὂν]
συνέλεξεν 'Αρισταγόρα[ς]
[κα]τὰ τὸν νόμον τῶν [ἐρα]
[νισ]τῶν.

L. 2 — the restoration of the plural is probable, at best.
L. 10 — the wife's name is restored in *Syll.*, not in IG.

9. IG XII 7,412 (*Syll.* 1190 — SGDI 5372 — IJ I viii, no. 65)
Aigiale, rough bluish marble, 3rd cent. B. C.

[ἐ]π' ἄρχοντος Λεοντέως,
μηνὸς 'Απατοριῶνος· ὅρ[ος]
[ο]ἰκιῶν [κ]αὶ κήπου ὧν κατέθηκεν 'Αν[τή]
[ν]ωρ Κλευδίκου Πασαρίστηι
[Ε]ὑαγόρου μετὰ κυρίου Σάμω
[νο]ς ἀργυρίου δραχμῶν
ἐνενήκοντα κατὰ συ[ν]θήκας
τὰς κειμένας παρὰ
[Ε]ὑάκει Κριτολάου.

In line 3, the words καὶ κήπου had originally been omitted
by the stonecutter and then added above the line in smaller
letters.

C. LEMNOS

10. *Annuario* 15/16 (1932/3, publ. 1942) 298, no. 6 (reprinted
REG 62 [1949] 42)
Provenience unknown, dark stone, script not later than 3rd
çent. B. C.

ἐπὶ Μεναίχμου [ἄρχοντος· ὅρος]
οἰκήματος ὑποκ[ειμένου — —]
ηι μετὰ κυρίου Α[— — 'Οτρ]
υνέως δραχμῶν [— —, ὥστε ἔχ]
ειν καὶ κρατεῖν [κατὰ τὰς συν]
θήκας τὰς κειμ[ένας]
παρὰ Καλλιστ[ράτωι]
Λαμπτρεῖ.

II. `PRASIS EPI LYSEI

A. ATHENS

11. IG II² 2725
Spata, marble, 315/4 B. C.

ἐπὶ Πραξιβού(λου) ἄρχ(οντος).
ὅρος χωρί
ων καὶ οἶκι
ῶν πεπραμένων ἐ
[πὶ] λύσει Θεοδώρωι Δε
[κελεεῖ, Λ]αμπύτωι Κη
[φισιεῖ κ]ατὰ σ[υνθήκας]

— — —

12. IG II² 2718 (II 5,1141b — IJ I viii, no. 31)
Dionyso, marble

ὅρος χωρίων ἐν
᾽Ανθρείωι καὶ κή
πων καὶ οἰκίας πε
πραμένων ἐπὶ λύ
σει Λυσιστράτωι
Κεφαλῆθεν.

13. IG II² 2724
Koropi, marble

[ἐπὶ ἄρχοντος —
...]οδώρου· ὅρος
[χωρί]ου καὶ οἰ[κί]ας καὶ
[κήπο]υ πεπρα[μ]ένων
[ἐπὶ λ]ύσει Εὐθυκλεῖ
[᾽Αγγ]ελῆθεν ⋤ κατὰ
[τὰ]ς συνθήκας τὰς
[κει]μένας παρὰ Γνι
[φ]ωνίδει Σουνιεῖ
[κ]αὶ ἑτέρω⟨ι⟩ ⋤ ⟦.Δ.⟧ ΗΗ.

Kirchner in IG gives the archon as [᾽Απ/ολλ]οδώρου, but
Dow and Travis, "Demetrios of Phaleron" 162–63, propose
[Νικ]οδώρου. The latter had no squeeze available and offer
rather fanciful reasons to justify their suggestion, apart from
a desire to shift the date from 319/8 B.C. to 314/3 and thus
bring the text into line with "Ferguson's law," on which see
Appendix II.

In the final line, the erasure and the addition of the two
H's were probably done sometime after the original inscription.

14. AJP 69 (1948) 203, no. 3
Vari, blue marble with traces of red paint in letters, 315/4 B.C.

ἐπὶ Πρα
ξιβούλου
ἄρχοντος·
ὅρος οἰκία
5   ς καὶ χωρίου
καὶ οἰκίας τῆς
ἐν ἄστει πεπ
ραμένων ἐπὶ
λύσει Χ Χ Χ
10   Μνήσωνι ʿΑλ
αεῖ, Μνησιβο
ύλωι ʿΑλαῖ,
Χαρίνοι ʿΑλ
αιεῖ.

15. IG II² 2687
Patissiai, marble

ὅρος οἰκίας,
χωρίου πεπ
ραμένου ἐπὶ
λύσει: ⟦ℙ Χ Χ⟧
ʾΑλκίαι ʾΑφιδναίωι.

16. IG II² 2694
White marble

ὅρος χωρί[ο]
καὶ οἰκίας πε
πραμένων
ἐπὶ λύσει
Χ Χ Χ Χ.

17. Ἑλληνικά 8 (1935) 223, no. 3
Laureion, limestone

> ὅρος χωρίου
> καὶ οἰκίας πεπ[ρ]
> αμένων ἐπὶ λ
> [ύ]σει Αἰσχύλωι
> Διφιλίδου Πρ
> οσπαλτίωι: ΧΧ
> ΧΗΗΔΔΔΔ: κ
> ατὰ συνθήκα[ς τ]
> [ὰ]ς κειμένας πα
> ρὰ τοῖς θεσμο[θ]
> έταις.

18. *Athen. Mitt.* 59 (1934) 42, no. 4
Iraklion, brown limestone

> ὅρος χωρίου
> καὶ οἰκίας
> πεπραμέν[ω]
> ν ἐπὶ λύσ[ει]
> Ἁγνοδήμ[ω]
> ι καὶ συνεν
> γυηταῖς
> ΧΧΧ.

19. 20. IG II² 2693 — the two *horoi* appear on the same side of
the stone, written in opposite directions
Keratea, tufa

> 19 — [ὅρος χωρίου καὶ οἰκίας]
> [πεπρ]αμ[έν]ων
> [ἐπὶ] λύ[σ]ει Ἀρισ[τοφῶν?]
> [τ]ι Τ[ει]θρασίωι,
> Αὐτοκλεῖ Ἀν[αφ]
> λυστίωι ΧΗ.

The restorations in line 1 are based on no. 20. The assumption that the same property was involved in both is by no means certain; see Chap. II at note 54.

20 — [ὅρος χωρίου]
[κ]αὶ οἰκίας πε
[π]ραμένων
[ἐ]πὶ λύσει Αὐτ
οκλεῖ ᾿Αναφλυ
στίωι ΧΧΗΗ.

21. IG II² 2696
Marble

ὅρος [χωρίου]
καὶ ο[ἰκίας πεπρα]
μένω[ν ἐπὶ λύσει]
ΧΧ —

22. *Hesperia* 13 (1944) 19
Supposedly from Marusi, marble

ὅρος χωρίο
πεπραμέν
ο ἐπὶ λύσε⟨ι⟩
καὶ οἰκίας
ΧΧ Φιλοκτή
μονι ᾿Αθμο
νεῖ, Θεοκλε
[ῖ] ᾿Αθμονεῖ.

The editor, D. M. Robinson, writes: "The inscribed surface
was only roughly dressed and is considerably lower below the
third line, as if the stone had been reused, which might account
for the peculiar order of words" and for lines 4–8 beginning
one letter further to the left.

23. *Kerameikos* 19 *(Arch. Anz.* [1940] 330—31, reprinted REG
54 [1941] 245, no. 48)
Bluish limestone, carefully cut

ὅρος χωρ
ίου καὶ οἰκί
ας πεπραμένων ἐ
πὶ λύσει
ΧΧ.

24. AJP 69 (1948) 201, no. 1
Near Sunion, rough, badly cut

> ὅρος χωρίο
> καὶ οἰκίας πεπρ
> αμένων ἐπὶ λ
> ύσει Φιλοθέ
> ωι Φρεαρρί
> ωι Χℙ.

25. IG II² 2688 (II 5,1114c — IJ I viii, no. 32)
Dionyso

> [ὅρ]ος χωρίο
> [καὶ] οἰκίας
> [πεπ]ραμένων
> [ἐπὶ λ]ύσει : Χℙ
> — — σίαι —

26. IG II² 2685 (II 1130 — IJ I viii, no. 47)
Kallirhoe, marble

> [ὅ]ρος χωρίου
> [κ]αὶ οἰκίας πε
> πραμένων
> ἐπὶ λύσει
> Ἀριστωνύ
> μωι Θριασ[ί]
> ωι ΧΗΔΔΔ.

27. IG II² 2726 (M 1739)
Marble, 315/4 B. C.

> ἐπὶ Πραξιβούλου·
> ὅρος χωρίου κα[ὶ]
> οἰκίας πεπραμ
> ένων ἐπὶ λύσει
> ⟦Νικογένει⟧ Αἰξω(νεῖ)
> ΗΗΗΗΔΔ κατὰ συνθή
> κας τὰς κειμένας
> παρὰ Χαιρεδήμωι
> Ῥαμν(ουσίωι).

Between lines 6 and 7, the numerals ΔΔΓΗΗ̣ΙΙΙ⟨ were incised in smaller letters.

28. IG II² 2686 (II 1144 — I J I viii, no. 53)
Menidi, rough stone

ὅρος

vac 0.04

ὅρος χωρ
ίου καὶ οἰκίας
πεπραμένων
ἐπὶ λύσει ῾Ηφαιστί
ωνι ῾Αλ̣αιεῖ
ΗΗ ⟦ΗΗ⟧.

The final two H's were deleted from the stone at a later time.

29. IG II² 2684 (II 1136 — I J I viii, no. 44)
Bluish stone

ὅρος χωρίου [κα]
ὶ οἰκίας πεπ[ρ]
αμένων [ἐπ]
ὶ λύσει Εὐθ[υμί?]
δαι Μυρρινου[σί]
ωι ΗΗΗ.

30. IG II² 2699 (II 1148 — I J I viii, no. 58)
Spata, marble

ὅρος χω[ρί]
ου καὶ οἰκία
ς πεπραμέ
νων ἐπὶ λύσ
ει ἐρανισταῖς
τοῖς μετὰ
᾿Αριστοφῶν
τος Εἰρεσ
ίδου Τ.

31. IG II² 2700 (II 5,1140 b — IJ I viii, no. 58 bis)
Temple of Daphnios, limestone

[ὅρος χω]ρίο[υ]
[κα]ὶ οἰκίας πε
[π]ραμένων ἐπ
ὶ λύσει ἐρανισ
ταῖς τοῖς με
τὰ Φίλωνος
ΧΧ.

32. IG II² 2701 (II 5,1139b — *Syll.* 1196 — M 1374 — IJ I viii, no. 50)
Spata, marble

ὅρος χωρίου καὶ οἰκ
ίας πεπραμένου ἐπ
ὶ λύσει ῾Ιερομν
ἤμονι ῾Αλαεῖ
5   Ͱ κατὰ τὰς συνθ
ἤκας τὰς παρὰ Λυσι
στράτωι κειμένα[ς]
καὶ δεκαδισταῖς Η
ΔΔΔ καὶ ἀποτίμημ
10 α ἐρανισταῖς τοῖ[ς]
μετὰ Θεοπείθους
᾿Ικαριῶς.

33. IG II² 2689 (II 1112 — IJ I viii, no. 30)
Athens, marble

ὅρος χωρί
ο καὶ οἰκία
ς πεπραμέ
νων ἐπὶ λύσ
ει Χαρίαι
Φα[ληρεῖ —]

The name of the original creditor in line 5 had been deleted. Χαρίαι is carved in larger, cruder letters than the rest of the text.

34. IG II² 2690
Marble

> ὅρος χωρίο κ
> [α]ὶ οἰκίας πε[π]
> [ραμ]ένων ἐπὶ λ
> [ύσει...]ρατοι
> — — οψ

35. IG II² 2691 (II 1118 — IJ I viii, no. 37)
Acropolis, bluish marble

> [ὅ]ρος χωρίο
> [καὶ] οἰκίας πε
> [πρα]μένων ἐπὶ
> [λύσ]ει Δημοχά[ρ]
> [ει κ]αὶ Θεν —

The restoration of the last line has no parallel among the *horoi*, but I have been unable to discover an alternative.

36. 37. IG II² 2697
Foot of the Pnyx, rough marble

Front

36. ὅρος χω[ρίου καὶ]
   οἰκίας π[επραμ]
   ένων ἐ[πὶ λύσει]

— — —

Back

37. [— π]επρα[μέν..]
   [ἐπὶ] λύσει —

38. IG II² 2698
Marble

> ὅρος χωρίο
> καὶ οἰκίας
> [π]επρα⟨μ⟩έ⟨ν⟩
> ων ἐπὶ ⟨λύ⟩σει

— —

39. IG II² 2741
Marble, stoichedon

ὅρος οἰκίας πε[πραμένης]
καὶ τῶν Μελησ[ίου χωρίων?]
ἐπὶ λύσει Λυσ[....... 'Ε]
πιτέλους Φαλ[ηρεῖ κατὰ σ]
υνθήκας τὰς κ[ειμένας πα]
[ρ]ὰ Εὐκλεῖ τρα[πεζίτηι].

Ziebarth's proposed restoration of line 2 requires the naming of the debtor, otherwise unprecedented on Athenian *horoi*. No alternative seems satisfactory, however

40. IG II² 2721

Eleusis

[ὅρ]ος χωρίο πε
[π]ραμένου {ι} ἐπὶ λύσει
Λεωχάρει πληρωτεῖ
[κ]αὶ συνερανισταῖς
ΧΧΧ.

41. IG II² 2723 (*Syll.* 1197 — M 1738)
White marble

ὅρος χωρίου
πεπραμένου
ἐπὶ λύσει Κηφι
σοδώρωι Λευκον(οεῖ)
5 ΧΓ καὶ φράτερ
σι τοῖς μετὰ 'Ερα
τοστράτο 'Ανα
φλυ(στίωι) ΗΗ καὶ Γλ[α]
υκίδαις Γ Η κ[αὶ]
10 'Επικλείδαις
ΗΓ καὶ φράτερ
σι τοῖς μετὰ Νί[κ]
ωνος 'Αναφλ(ύστιος) Η.

In line 8 I have retained the Corpus reading originally proposed by Premerstein "Phratern-Verbände." The original

editor, D. M. Robinson, in AJP 28 (1907) 430, no. 4, read
ΦΛΧΗΗ, giving a figure of 1,200 drachmas for the debt to the
brothers with Eratostratos, instead of 200. Robinson has
since reiterated his reading, in *Hesperia* 13 (1944) 18, note 13.
He argues that his version leads to the same abbreviation for
the demotic, Anaphlystios, which appears in line 13 and that
it provides a descending sequence in value of the five debts.
The first argument cannot be given much stress in view of the
notorious inconsistency of the *horoi* in all matters of orthography; the second argument has been analyzed at length in
Chap. VIII. The excellent photograph published by Premerstein seems clearly to substantiate his reading of the disputed
letter as Υ, not Χ. In any event, my discussion shows that the
issue is not one of great moment.

42. IG II² 2719 (II 1147 — IJ I viii, no. 57)
Dekelea, rough stone

> ὅρος χωρίο[υ]
> πεπραμένου
> ἐπὶ λύσει ἐραν[ι]
> σταῖς τοῖς μετὰ
> Δημύλου Λαμ(πτρέως)
> ΧΗΗ.

43. IG II² 2720 (II 1111 — II 5,1111 — IJ I viii, no. 29)
Parthenon, marble

> ὅρος χωρίο
> πεπραμένο ἐπὶ λ
> ύσει θιασώταις ΙΣ
> ΔΗΜΟΤΟ Η.

Poland, building on a suggestion of Hiller's, would read at
the end ᾽Ισ⟨ο⟩δήμο το⟨ῦ⟩ ᾽Η — —

44. IG II² 2722
White marble

> [ὅρ]ο[ς χωρίο]
> [πεπρ]αμένο
> [ἐρα]νιϲταῖς

[ἐπὶ] λύσε[ι]
|ˡ.

45. IG II² 2713 (II 1108 — I J I viii, no. 28)
Limestone

ὅρος χωρίο
πεπραμένο
ἐπὶ λύσει Τ.

46. IG II² 2705
White marble

ὅρος χωρίο πεπρ
αμένο ἐπὶ λύσει
Αὐ⟨τ⟩οδίκωι ἐξ Οἴο Ⱶ,
'Εργοφίλωι 'Ατηνε[ῖ],
'Εργοχάρ⟨ει⟩ 'Ατηνε[ῖ]
ΧΧΗΗΗ.

47. IG II² 2703
Blue marble

[ὅρ]ος χω
ρίου πε
πραμένου
ἐπὶ λύσει
Φιλοκλεῖ Λα
[μ]πτρεῖ ΧΧ.

48. *Hesperia* 10 (1941) 53, no. 16
Marble

[ὅ]ρ[ος χωρί]
[ο] πε[πραμ]
[έ]νο ἐπ[ὶ λύ]
[σ]ει : ΧΗ — —
— — —

49. IG II² 2681 (II 1105 — I J I viii, no. 27)
Hymettos

[h]όρος χωρίο πε
πραμένο ἐπὶ λύ

[σ]ει Εὐθυδίκει
προ[ι]κὸς ΧⲢ.

50. IG II² 2702
Black stone

ὅρος χω
ρίο πεπρα
μένο : ἐπὶ λ
ύσει Αἰσχυ
λίωνι : ἐξ
Οἴο Χ.

51. IG II² 2712 (II 1103 — M 1371 — IJ I viii, no. 25)
Markopulo

ℎόρος χωρίο
πεπραμένο
ἐπὶ λύσει: Χ.

52. IG II² 2711
Chasias

ὅρος χωρίο
υ πεπραμέν
ου ἐπὶ λύσει
Ⲣ ΗΗΗ
Η.

53. *Hesperia* 7 (1938) 93, no. 14
Rough marble

ὅρος χωρίο[υ]
πεπραμένου
ἐπὶ λύσει: ⲢΗ̣
Κίρωνι Πιθεῖ.

The name may be Kimon rather than Kiron.

54. Δελτ. 11 (1927/8) παρ. 51, no. 163
Athens, fieldstone

ὅρος χωρίο
πεπραμένο

ἐπὶ λύσει Εὐ
τράωνι ἐκ Κε
ραμέων
Γ᾽.

55. IG II² 2704 (II 1146 — I J I viii, no. 55)
Peiraieus, marble

[ὅρ]ος χωρίου
[π]επραμένου
ἐπὶ λύσει ΗΓ᾽
Χρώμωνι Φυ
λασίωι.

56. IG II² 2709 (II 5,1150 b)
Spata

[ὅρος χω]ρίου
[πεπρα]μέν[ου]
[ἐπὶ λύσ]ει | —
— — νιε[ῖ]
— Η

57. IG II² 2658 (M 1372 — I J I viii, no. 25 bis)
Eleusis, local stone

ὅρος χω
ρίο πεπρ
αμένο ἐπ
ὶ λύσει πα
ιδὶ Καλλισ
τράτο : Η —

58. IG II² 2706
Peiraieus, white marble

ὅρος χ[ωρίου]
πεπραμ[ένου]
ἐπὶ λύσει
᾽Επικρά
τει Οἰῆ[θεν].

59. IG II² 2707
Rough stone

> ὅρος χ[ωρίο]
> πεπραμ[ένο]
> [ἐ]πὶ ⟨λ⟩ύσει
> ...δώρωι
> [Στει]ριεῖ.

60. IG II² 2708 (II 5,1143b — IJ I viii, no. 51 and 25 ter)
Acropolis, marble

> [ὅρος χω]
> ρίου π[ε]
> πραμέν
> ου ἐπὶ λ
> ύσει Δοξ
> ////////

61. IG II² 2714 (II 5,1143c)
Sunion, limestone

> ὅρος χωρίου
> πεπραμένου
> ἐπὶ λύσει.

62. IG II² 2715
White marble

> [ὅρος χ]ωρίου
> [πεπρα]μένο
> [ἐπὶ λύ]σει.

63. IG II² 2716
White marble

> ὅρ[ος χω]ρ[ίου]
> πεπραμέ[νου]
> 〚.πι.....〛

The letters πι are still visible in an erasure that originally
read ἐπὶ λύσει.

64. IG II² 2717 (II 1115 — I J I viii, no. 33)
Marble

> ὅρος [χωρ]
> ίο πε[πρα]
> μέν[ο ἐπὶ]
> [λύσει —]

65. IG II² 2727
Acharnai, marble, 312/1 B. C.

> ἐπὶ Πολέμω
> νος ἄρχον(τος). ὅρ
> [ο]ς χωρίου πεπρα
> μένου ἐπὶ λύσει
> [Λ]ύκωνι Στειριεῖ
> [κ]ατὰ συν[θή]
> [κ]ας κειμ[έν]
> [ας πα]ρὰ —
> — — ιεῖ.

66. *Kerameikos* 20
Bluish stone

> ὅρ[ος χωρί]
> ο πε[πραμέ]
> νο [ἐπὶ λύσε]
> ι Πρ......
> ?

67. IG II² 2740 (II 5,1151 b — I J I viii, no. 56)
Peiraieus, marble

> [ὅρο]ς οἰκιῶν
> πεπρα[μένω]
> ν ἐπὶ λ[ύσει]

68. IG II² 2731 (II 1129 — I J I viii, no. 46)
Peiraieus, bluish marble

> [ὅρος οἰκία]ς [πε]
> [πρα]μέ[ν]ης ἐ[πὶ]

[λύσ]ει: 'Ακροβ[ί]
λωι Λακι[ά]
[δει] ΧΧΧ.

69. IG II² 2729
West base of the Acropolis

ὅρος οἰκί
ας πεπραμ
ένης ἐπὶ
λύσει ΧΧ
'Αριστοδήμωι
'Αφιδνα[ίωι].

70. IG II² 2743 (II 1119 — I J I viii, no. 38)
Western slope of Munychia, blue marble

ὅρος οἰκίας
πεπραμένης
ἐπὶ λύσει ἐραν
ισταῖς τοῖ
ς μετὰ Παν
ταρέτου 'Αλ
ωπεκῆθεν
ΧΓ HHH.

71. *Hesperia* 10 (1941) 54, no. 18A — 309/8 B. C.

[ἐπὶ Δη]μητρίου ἄρχον
[τος· ὅρ]ος οἰκίας περαμ
[ένης] ἐπὶ λύσει : ΓHH
[ἐρα]νισταῖς.

This text was deleted and no. 152, dated 308/7 B.C., was
inscribed immediately below.

72. *Hesperia* 10 (1941) 54, no. 17
Marble

ὅρος
[οἰ]κίας πεπραμένη[ς]
ἐπὶ λύσει
ΧΓ.

73. IG II² 2732 (II 1120 — I J I viii, no. 39)
Peiraieus, stoichedon

[ὅρος οἰ]κία
ς πεπραμέν
ης ἐπὶ λύσε⟨ι⟩
’Αρχενομ[ίδ]
[η]ι Χ.

74. IG II² 2733
Marble

ὅρος οἰκίας πε
πραμένης ἐ
πὶ λύσει Σωκ
λεῖ Λαμπτρ
εῖ 𐅋ΗΗΗ.

75. IG II² 2737
Eleusis, bluish marble

ὅρ[ος]
οἰκίας πεπ
ραμένης ἐπ
ὶ λύσε[ι] 𐅋ΗΗ.

76. IG II² 2744 (M 1740)
West foot of the Acropolis, marble, 315/4 B. C.

ἐπὶ Πραξι[β]
ούλου ἄρχον-
τος· ὅρος οἰκία
ς πεπραμένη
ς ἐπὶ λύσει Λυ
σικλεῖ ’Αθμονε
ῖ 𐅋ΗΗ.

77. IG II² 2730 (II 1127 — I J I viii, no. 45)
Acropolis, marble

[ὅρος] οἰκίας πεπρ
[αμέ]νης ἐπὶ λύ

[σ]ει Γ⌐ Ἀρχε
δήμωι Αἰ
γιλιεῖ.

78. IG II² 2736 (II 1125 — IJ I viii, no. 43)
Athens, marble

ὅρος οἰκ[ί]
ας πεπρα
μένης ἐπὶ λ
ύσει ΗΗΗΗ.

The creditor's name originally appeared after line 4 but
was then deleted.

79. IG II² 2728

ℎόρος
οἰκίας
πεπραμ
ένης ἐ
πὶ λύσει
Διοκλ
εῖ ΗΗΓ⌐
ΔΔΔΔ.

80. 81. IG II² 2735 (II 1116 — IJ I viii, nos. 34 and 35)
Rough stone

80 — ὅρος οἰκίας πεπραμένης
ἐπὶ λύσε⟨ι⟩ Μενεφίλωι Ἰκαριεῖ
ΗΗΓ⌐ΔΔ.
81 — ὅρος οἰκήματος
[π]επραμένου
ἐπὶ λύσει Φα[ύ]λλωι
Ἰϝαριεῖ ΗΗ.

The second horos was inscribed in a second hand, immediately following the first.

82. IG II² 2682 (M 1369)
    Marble

> [ὅ]ρος οἰκία[ς]
> πεπραμέν-
> [η]ς ἐπὶ λύσει
> [Μα]λθάκει τῆι
> [Λεω]στράτου
> [θυγα]τρὶ ᾽Αλωπε
> [κῆθε]ν προικὸς
> — — —'Η

82A. *Polemon* 3 (1947/8) 133, no. 10 (reprinted REG 63 [1950]
     156)
     Marathon

> [ℎόρ]ος χωρίο[υ]
> πεπραμέ[νου]
> ἐπὶ λύσει π
> [ροι]κὸς — —
> — — —

83. IG II² 2734 (II 1131 — I J I viii, no. 48)
    Athens

> [ὅρος] οἰκίας
> [πεπρ]αμένης
> [ἐπὶ λύ]σει Νικο
> ....ωι Λυσαν
> [δρίδ]ου — —

84. IG II² 2739 (II 5,1143 d)
    Acropolis, marble

> ὅρος
> οἰκίας π
> επραμ[έ]
> νης
> [ἐπὶ λύ]σ̣[ει]
> ..ο —

85. IG II² 2745 (II 1133 — IJ I viii, no. 49)
Athens, marble, 315/4 B. C.

[ἐπὶ] Πραξιβού
[λου] ἄρχοντος·
[ὅρος οἰ]κίας πε
[πραμένης ἐπὶ λύ]
[σει — — —]

86. IG II² 2742
Athens, marble

[ὅρ]ος οἰκίας καὶ κ[οπρ]
ῶνος πεπραμ[ένων]
ἐπὶ λύσει ΕΓ —
ΤΕ' ⟨'Ελ⟩ευσι[νί]
ωι ⲐΗΗΗ.

87. IG II² 2752 (II 5,1123b)
Near Dipylon, limestone

ὅρος οἰκίας καὶ ἐργασ
τηρίων πεπραμένων
ἐπὶ λύσει τῶν ἐντ⟨ὸ⟩ς
τείχους καὶ τοῦ ἔξω
τείχους λιθοργεί⟨ο⟩υ
Φιλίππωι Αἰξωνεῖ
Τ.

88. IG II² 2747 (II 1122 — Syll. 1191 — M 1373 — IJ I viii,
no. 41)
Marble, well cut letters

θεοί.
ὅρος ἐργασ
τηρίου καὶ ἀν
δραπόδων πε
πραμένων ἐπὶ
λύσει Φείδων
ι Αἰξωνεῖ : Τ.

This stone was found in the remains of an ancient mine near
Thorikos.

89. IG II² 2748 (II 1123 — IJ I viii, no. 42)
In the mining region of Sinterni, marble

ὅρος ἔργα
στηρίου
καὶ ἄνδρα
πόδων πε
πραμένων
ἐπὶ λύσει Σ
μικύθωι [Π]α
[ιαν]ιεῖ?

90. IG II² 2749 (II 1104 — IJ I viii, no. 26)
Near Markopulo, rough stone

[ὅρος ἐργαστηρίο]
πεπραμένο ἐπὶ λύσε⟨ι⟩
καὶ ἀνδραπόδων Ϝ⟨Η⟩Η
Πυθοκρίτωι ʻΑμαξαντε⟨ῖ⟩.

The reconstruction in line 1 is justified by the mention of slaves.

91. IG II² 2746 (II 1145 — IJ I viii, no. 54)

[ὅρος] ἐργ
[αστη]ρίων
[πεπρ]αμέ
[νων] ἐπὶ λ
[ύσει —]

92. IG II² 2750
Laureion, limestone

ὅρος κ̣[α]
μίνου καὶ
ἐδάφων
πε[πραμέ]
[νων ἐπὶ λύ]
[σει —]

93. IG II² 2683
    Marble

> [— — — —]
> [— — —]έν
> [..ἐπὶ λύ]σει Λυσ
> [ιστράτ]ηι 'Ανδ —
> [— — — —]
> [θυγατρὶ προικός]

In the Corpus, the opening lines are restored, without any justification, to read [ὅρος χωρίου καὶ / οἰκίας πεπραμ]έν / [ων ἐπὶ] κτλ. The restoration of the final line is also highly dubious.

94. IG II² 2692 (II 5,1114 d)
    Blue stone

> ὅρος [χωρίου καὶ οἰκί]
> ας πεπ[ραμένων ἐπὶ]
> λύσει [— — Πε]-
> ργασῆθε[ν —, Εὐαγ?]
> γέλωι Ο [— — —,]
> Μνησαγ[όραι — —]
> ρωι Ⴊ, Δ [— —]
> Περγασ[ῆθεν — —]
> Μνησι[— — —]
> τι — —

95. IG II² 2738
    Marble

> ὅρο[ς — — π]
> επραμ[έν..ἐπὶ λύ]
> σει ΧΗΗ.

The Corpus, following Ziebarth, inserts οἰκήματος in the first line. The rarity of this word in the *horoi* compels rejection of that suggestion.

96. IG II² 2742 a
West base of the Acropolis, limestone

[ὅρος]
— —
[—] ηπ
[. .] πεπρ
αμένων
ἐπὶ λύ[σ]
ει —

The Corpus reads, lines 2–4, without adequate justification:
[οἰκίας / καὶ κ]η π / [ων].

97. IG II² 2753 (II 1117 — I J I viii, no. 36)
White marble

[ὅρος]
[— — πεπραμέ]
[ν. . ἐ]πὶ λύσε[ι]
[Κα]λλίππωι ᾿Ε[ρ]
[οιά ?]δει, Πεισι
[— — —]

98. IG II² 2754 (II 5,1150 c)
Eleusis, local stone

ὅρο[ς — —]
πεπρα[μέν. .]
ἐπὶ λύσε[ι]
Δημ[— —]
ΙΕΓ

99. IG II² 2755
Marble

ὅρος [— —]
πεπρ[αμέν. .]
[ἐπὶ λύσει —]

100. IG II² 2756 (II 1143 — I J I viii, no. 52)
Chasani, marble

ὅρος [— —]
πεπρ[αμέν..ἐ]
π[ὶ λύσει —]
[— —]

101. IG II² 2757
Marble
Only a few letters remain, probably restored as follows:
[ὅρος — —] N [— — πε]πρα[μέν..] ἐπ[ὶ λύσει — —]

B. AMORGOS

102. IG XII 7,55 (Syll. 1200 — M 1385)
Some miles east of Arkesine, blue marble, c. 300 B. C.

θεοί·
ἐπ' ἄρχοντος Φανοκράτους· μηνὸς
'Ανθεστηριῶνος· ἀπέδοτο Νική
ρατος καὶ 'Ηγεκράτη καὶ ὁ κύριο[ς]
5   Τελένικος Κτησιφῶντι Πυθίπ
που τὰ χωρία καὶ τὴν οἰκί[α]ν κ[α]ὶ
τὸγ κέραμον ἄπαντα ἃ ἔχε[ι] διε
λόμενος Νικήρατος πρὸς τὸν
ἀδελφὸν 'Ανθίνην καὶ τὰ χωρία
10   ἃ ἐπρίατο Νικήρατος παρὰ Ἰσχυρί
ωνος ἄπα[ν]τα καὶ τὰ χωρία ἃ ἔχει
θέμενος Ν[ικήρ]ατος παρὰ 'Εξακέσ
του ἄπαντα [ἀ]ργυρίου δραχμῶν
πεντακισχιλιῶν ἐπὶ λύσει·
15   ὑποτελεῖ δὲ μίσθωμα Νικήρατος
Κτησιφῶντι καθ' ἕκαστον ἐνιαυ
τὸν ἀργυρίου δραχμὰς πεντα
[κ]οσίας ἀτελεῖς.

The absence of the word ὅρος and the unusual detail set
this text apart. In a narrow, technical sense, it is perhaps no
horos at all, yet its inclusion seems easily justified.

C. LEMNOS

103. *Annuario* 15/16 (1932/3, publ. 1942) 305, no. 11
Mudro (Hephaistia), hardly after 480 B. C. (?)

·[ℎόρος]
χωρίο
καὶ οἰ[κ]
ία[ς] π[επ]
ρα[μέν]
ο[ν] ἐπὶ [λ]
ύσ[ει ᾽Α]
γων⟨ο⟩
[τ]ίμω[ι ? — —]

Four numerals, HHHH, appear on the right side of the stone. On the reading and date, see Chap. I, note 26.

104. IG XII 8,18
Kome (Hephaistia), end of the fourth century B. C.

ὅρος χωρίου κα
ὶ οἰκίας πεπρα
μένων ἐπὶ λύσε
[ι — — —]
ω[ι] ῾Ραμνο[υσίωι]
XXHHH ἐπὶ ἄρχ[ον]
τος Νικοδώρου
κατὰ τὰς συνθή
κας τὰς παρὰ Πα
τροφῶντι Φαλ
ηρεῖ.

The numerals in line 6 appear in IG XII Supp.

105. *Annuario* 15/16 (1932/3, publ. 1942) 306, no. 12 (reprinted
REG 62 [1949] 42)
Hephaistia, dark stone, found in five fragments

ὅρος χωρίο
πεπραμένο
ἐπὶ λύσει

ὑπὸ Νικίο
Εὐαινέτωι
'Ερχιεῖ [τῶι]
[δεινὶ — —]
[Διομ]ειεῖ
[Διοδώ]ρωι 'Ερ
[χιεῖ]
— — Χ.

106. *Annuario* 15/16 (1932/3, publ. 1942) 309, no. 13 (reprinted
REG 62 [1949] 42)
Hephaistia, middle of the fourth century B. C.

[ὅρ]ος χωρ
[ί]ου πεπρα
μένου ἐπὶ [λ]
ύσει Μεν[εκ]
λίδει 'Αμ[αξ]
αντεῖ Ⱶ.

107. 108. IG XII 8,19
Kome (Hephaistia), end of the fourth century B. C.

107 — ἐπὶ Νικοδώρου ἄρ[χον]
τος· ὅρος χωρίου καὶ ο[ἰκί]
ας πεπραμένων ἐπὶ
λύσει Χ: δραχμῶν ὀρ
γειῶσι τοῦ 'Ηρακλεί[ου]ς
τοῦ ἐ[ν] Κόμει κατὰ τὸ γρα
μματεῖον τὸ ὀργειωνι
κόν.

108 —   ἐπὶ 'Αρχίου
ἄρχοντος· ὅρος χωρί
ου καὶ οἰκίας πεπρα
μένων ἐπὶ λύσει
[...]Η δραχμῶν ὀργε
ῶσι τοῦ 'Ηρα[κλ]εί[ου]ς
τοῦ ἐν Κόμει κατὰ τὸ γρ

αμματεῖον τὸ [ὀργει]ω
νικόν.

The two texts run on without a break, no. 107 ending after three letters in line 8 and no. 108 continuing thereafter.

109. IG XII 8,21 (M 1375 — IJ I viii, no. 59)
Mudro (Hephaistia), tufa, end of the fourth century B. C.

ὅρος
[χ]ωρίο
πεπραμ
ἐνο ἐπὶ λ
ὑσει ὀργ
εῶσι ΗΗΗΗ.

110. IG XII 8,20
Voroskopo (Hephaistia), tufa, end of the fourth century B. C.

[— — —]
[— —]π̣ε
[πραμέ]ν̣ων ἐ
[πὶ λ]ύ̣σει ἐρα
[νιστ]αῖς τοῖς
[μετ]ὰ̣ Χαιρ
[— —]

The editor's reconstruction of the opening, [ὅρος χωρίο / καὶ [οἰκίας], is a pure guess.

D. SKYROS

111. IG XII Supp. 526 (*Athen. Mitt.* 59 [1934] 72, no. 25)
Lava, first half of the fourth century B.C.

ὅρος
χωρίο
πεπραμ
ἐνο ἐπὶ
λύσε[ι].

E. *PRASIS EPI LYSEI* OR SALE ?

Athens

112. IG II² 2763 (II 1110 — M 1376 — IJ I viii, no. 60)
Pikermi

> ὅρος χωρίο πε
> πραμένο ἑρα
> νισταῖς τοῖς
> μετὰ Καλλ[ι]
> τέλος ΗΗ
> ΗΗΔΔ.

113. IG II² 2764
Peiraieus, marble

> [ὅρος χωρίου καὶ]
> [οἰ]κίας π[επραμέ]
> νων ἑρα[νισταῖς]
> ΧΧΧ τοῖς [μετὰ —]
> νος Λευκ[ονοέως]
> — — ΛΙΤ — —

114. *Hesperia* Supp. 7 (1943) 3, no. 2
Pnyx

> [ὅρος]
> [ο]ἰκίας π[επρ]
> αμένης ἑρα[ν]
> [ι]σταῖς τοῖς μ[ετ]
> ὰ Τιμοσστράτο ῾Α[μα]
> [ξαν]τέως ΧΧ Διε[ύ]
> [χει Μυρ]ρινοσ[ίωι].

The editor, A. E. Raubitschek, writes: "Most of the readings and restorations are uncertain."

Lemnos

115. IG XII 8,22 *(Syll.* 1193)

Hephaistia, rough tufa, poorly cut, fourth century B. C., but later than nos. 107—110

ὅρος χωρί
ο καὶ οἰκίας πε
πραμένου π
αντὸς 'Επιγό
νωι 'Αγκυλῆ(θεν)
⌐ΗΗΗ.

III. *APOTIMEMA*

A. PUPILLARY TYPE

1. Athens

116. IG II² 2657 (II 1138 — *Syll.* 1186 — M 1365 — I J I viii, no. 5)
Acharnai, marble, 302/1 B. C.

[ἐ]πὶ Νικοκλέου
ς ἄρχοντος· ὅρο
[ς] χωρίων καὶ οἰ
[κ]ίας καὶ τοῦ ὕδα
5 [τ]ος τοῦ προσόν
[τ]ος τοῖς χωρίοι
[ς κ]λήρων δυεῖν
[ἀπ]οτετιμημέν
[ων π]αισὶν ὀρφα
10 [νοῖ]ς τοῖς Χαρί
[ου ἰ]σοτελοῦς Χ
[αιρ]ίππωι καὶ Χ
[αρί]αι.

117. IG II² 2649 (II 1135 — I J I viii, no. 4)
Marathon

ὅρος χωρίου
καὶ οἰκίας ἀποτ[ί]

μῆμα παιδὶ ὀρφ[α]
νῶι Διογείτονος
Προβα(λισίου).

118. IG II² 2650 (II 5,1141c — IJ I viii, no. 9)
Keratea, fieldstone

[ὅρ]ος χωρίου καὶ
[οἰ]κίας ἀποτίμη
μα παιδὶ Καλλί
ου Δειραδιώτ
ου.

119. IG II² 2651
Markopulo, limestone

ὅρος χωρίο καὶ
οἰκίας ἀποτίμη
μα παισὶ ᾿Εργοκλέ
ος Κοπρε[ί]ο.

120. *Hesperia* 10 (1941) 52, no. 14
Marble

[ὅρ]ος χωρ[ί]
[ο]υ̣ καὶ οἰκί
[α]ς ἀποτιμ
[ή]ματος π
[α]ιδὶ Φιλοκλ
[έους].

121. IG II² 2642 (II 1106 — M 1364 — IJ I viii, no. 1)
Mesogaia

ὅρος
χωρίο ἀποτι
μήματος Θε
αιτήτο παιδὶ
Κηφισοφῶντι
᾿Επικηφισίο.

122. IG II² 2643 (II 1107 — I J I viii, no. 2)
Southeastern Athens, marble

> ὅ[ρος χωρίο ἀπο]
> τιμήμα[το]
> ς Διονυσοδ
> ώρο Παλλη
> νέως πα[ίδ]
> ων.

123. IG II² 2644 (II 1151 — I J I viii, no. 7)
North of the Parthenon, marble

> [ὅρος]
> χωρί[ου ἀποτί]
> μημα [παιδὶ ὀρφα]
> νῶι 'Ιππ[— —]
> ουσ[ίου].

124. IG II² 2645 (II 5,1114b)
White marble

> [ὅρος χωρ]
> [ί]ο ἀποτιμή
> ματος παίδω[ν]
> Μακαρέως 'Αμ
> φιτρο(πῆθεν) Λυσιστ
> ράτο, Πατρο
> κλέος.

125. IG II² 2647
Eleusis, bluish marble

> ὅρος
> χωρίου
> [ἀ]ποτιμή[μα]
> [το]ς παισὶν [Εὐ]
> [θυ]κράτου
> ['Αμ]φιτροπῆ[θεν].

126. Δελτ. 14 (1931/2) παρ. 31, no. 2
Eleusis, white marble

> ὅρος χωρί[ου]
> ἀποτίμημα τ
> [οῖ]ς παισὶν Πυθ
> οδήλου Φαλη
> ρέως.

127. IG II² 2654
Spata, marble

> [— — — ἀπο]
> τι[μήματος Δωρ]
> οθέο ῾Ιπ[ποτομά]
> δο παισὶν {῾Ιπ[π]
> οτομάδε⟨ι⟩} Δω
> ροθέω⟨ι⟩ ῾Ιπποτομ[ά]
> δε⟨ι⟩, Θιλοδήμ⟨ω⟩ι ῾Ιππο[τ]
> ομάδει ⌐ΗΗΗ.
> ἐπὶ Χαιρικλείδ[ο]
> [ἄρ]χοντος δε —
> — —

Kirchner, in IG, has a lengthy restoration at the beginning:
[ἐπὶ - - / ἄρχοντος· ὅρος χω/ρίο καὶ οἰκίας ἀπο]/τι [μήματος].
The assumption that land and a house were involved is
unjustified. Even the assumption of an initial date is open
to question; see Appendix II.

128. IG II² 2652 (II 5,1141 d — IJ I viii, 9 bis)
Kato Liossa, marble

> [ὅρος χωρίου] καὶ ο
> [ἰκίας ἀποτετι]μημέ
> [νων παισὶν] ὀρφανο
> [ῖς — —] ῾Αλαιέως
> — — — Σωσικρ
> [άτει — —]

129. IG II² 2653 (II 1114 — IJ I viii, no. 3)
Laureion, marble

ὅρος
ἀποτιμ
ήματος
Εὐβοίο
παί[δ]ων
'Οῆ[θεν].

2. Amorgos

130. IG XII Supp. 331 (RP 63 [1937] 316, no. 2)
Arkesine, end of the fourth century B. C.

εἰς ἐνιαυτὸν ἐπ[ὶ]
Κλεισαγόρου ἄρχοντ⟨ο⟩
ς τõ μισθώματος.
ὅρος ἀποτιμήματος ἐν [τ]
5   οἷς Δεξιβίο τῶν Σίμω[ν]
ος θυγατρῶν Σιμών[η]
ς Δεμοδίκης· μισθωτ
ὴς Δεξίβιος ἀπετί[μ]ησε
'Αριστότιμος Ξα(νθιάδο) κατὰ τ
10   ρίτον μέρος, ἐπιπεμ
ψάντων τῶν ἀρχόν
των Ξανθιππίδο Ξαν
θιπ(πίδο), Πραξικλέος Θεο
γνῶτο — —

The first three lines are much more deeply cut than the
emainder.

3. Naxos

131. IG XII Supp. 194
Fourth century B. C.

[ὅ]ρος χωρίων καὶ
οἰκίας καὶ κεράμου

ἀποτετιμημέν
ων τοῖς παιδίοις
5   τοῖς Ἐπίφρονος τοῦ
ἀρχαίου ΧΧΧΓ καὶ
τῶν μισθωμάτων
τετρακοσίων δρα
χμῶν τοῦ ἐνιαυ
10   [το]ῦ ἑκάστου ἐπὶ
....ήτου τούτου
[δὲ τοῦ χω]ρίου ἅπα
[ντα τετι]μήται
[κ]αὶ τὰ ἐν Ἐλαι
15   οῦντι καὶ τὰ
ἐμ Μέλανι.

On the restoration of line 13, see Chap. IV, note 26.

B. DOTAL TYPE

1. Athens

132. IG II² 2679 (II 1137 — *Syll.* 1187 — M 1367 — IJ I viii,
    no. 17)
    Spata, marble

ἐπὶ Εὐξενίππου ἄρ[χ]
οντος (305/4)· ὅρος χωρίων
καὶ οἰκιῶν ἀποτιμη
μάτων προικὸς Ξέναρ
5   [ί]στει Πυθοδώρου Γαρ
γηττίου θυγατρί, τ
[ὸ] κατὰ τὸ ἥμυσυ καὶ τ[ὸ]
ἐκ τούτου γιγνόμεν
ον αὐτεῖ εἰς Λεώσ
10   τρατον ἄρχοντα (303/2)
ΧΧΓΗΗ/////Ͱ.

133. IG II² 2659 (II 5,1142c — IJ I viii, no. 18)
    Keratea, marble

ὅρος χωρίου
καὶ οἰκίας ἀπ
οτίμημα προ
ικὸς 'Αρχίππηι
ΤΧΧ.

134. IG II² 2662 (II 1128 — I J I viii, no. 14)
Plain of Thria, marble

ὅρος χωρίου καὶ ο[ἰ]
κίας προικὸς ἀπο
τίμημα Τιμοδίκε[ι]
Φιλίππου 'Αναγυρ(ασίου)
θυγατρὶ ΧΧΧΧ⸗.

135. IG II² 2660 (II 1149 — I J I viii, no. 20)
Spata

ὅρος χωρίου καὶ
οἰκίας ἀποτίμη
μα προικὸς Πυ
θοστράτει Με
νάλκου 'Αναφλ
υστίου ἰατρ[οῦ]
ΧΧΧ.

135 A. Hesperia 19 (1950) 23
Ikaria, rough schist

ὅρος χωρίου καὶ
οἰκίας ἀποτίμημα
προικὸς Φανομάχει Κτήσωνος
ἐκ Κερ(αμέων) ΧΧΧ.

136. IG II² 2661
Spata, marble

ὅρος χω[ρίου]
καὶ οἰκίας [ἀπο]
τίμημα πρ[οικὸς]
ΧΧ 'Αρχεστ[ρά]
τει Τολμαίο[υ 'Ι]

καριείως θ[υγα]
τρί.

137. IG II² 2663 (II 5,1142e — IJ I viii, no. 10 bis)
Porto Raphti

[ὅρ]ος χωρίου
[καὶ ο]ἰκίας
[Με]νεστρά
[τηι] προικὸς
5 [Φιλ]οκράτ
[ους] Προσπα
[λτί]ου θυγα
[τρὶ] ἀποτίμ
[ημα] ΧΓ.

138. IG II² 2664 (II 5,1142d — IJ I viii, no. 11)
Near Trachones, white marble

ὅρος
χωρίου καὶ οἰκ[ίας]
ἀποτίμημα προι[κὸς]
Νικομάχει Πολυκλέο[υς]
Φηγαέως θυγατρί.

139. IG II² 2665
Areopagos (?), marble

ὅρος χωρίο
καὶ οἰκίας
ἀποτίμημα
προικὸς Στ
ρατονίκει.

140. IG II² 2667 (II 5,1142b — IJ I viii, no. 13)
Dionyso, rough stone

[ὅρ]ος χωρ[ίου]
[κ]αὶ οἰκίας ἀποτ[ίμη]
[μα] προικὸς [.]ρω

..κει Κλεισ

..ΞΛ|'Ω.. Ο

Ο

Lines 3—5 probably read [Π]ρω[το/δί]κει Κλεισ[θέ/ νου]ς Αἰ[ξ]ω[νέ]ω[ς] (Preuner).

141. AJP 69 (1948) 202, no. 2
Anavyso, rough marble, rudely cut

ὅρος
χωρίο : ἀπο
τιμήματο
ς : Ἱπποστρ
άτει : προ
ικὸς ₱ΗΗ.

142. IG II² 2668 (II 5,1142f)
Keratea

ὅρος [χ]ωρίο[υ]
ἀποτ[ί]μη[μ]α προι
κὸς Ξενοκρατ[εί]
αι Χ₱ΗΗΗ.

143. IG II² 2676 (II 1150 — IJ I viii, no. 21)
Southern slope of the Acropolis

[ὅρος]
[οἰκ]οπέ
δων ἀποτε
τιμημένων
προικὸς ₱
'Ε fiss. πικρατεί
fiss. αι.

144. IG II² 2669 (II 1142 — IJ I viii, no. 19)
Munychia, marble

ὅρος χ[ωρίου]
προικὸ[ς ἀποτι]
μημα[— —]

ρείας
ΝΑΣΘ

145. IG II² 2674
Chalandri, marble

ὅρος χωρίου
ἀποτετιμη
μένου πρ
οικὸς Θεα
νοῦς.

146. IG II² 2670 (II 1113 — *Syll.* 1188 — M 1366 — IJ I viii,
no. 10)
Sochoria (between Marusi and Chalandri), marble

ὅρος χωρίο προικὸς
Ἱπποκλείαι Δημοχά
[ρ]ος Λευκονοιῶς Τ·
[ὅσ]ωι πλείονος ἄξι
5   [ον] Κεκροπίδαις
[ὑπό]κειται καὶ Λυκ
[ομί]δαις καὶ Φλυεῦ
[σι].

147. *Hesperia* Supp. 7 (1943) 1, no. 1
Marble

ὅ[ρ]ος οἰκίας ἀποτε[τιμ]
ημένης προικὸς Ε[ἰρη ?]
νεὶ Ἀντιδώρου Λευ[κονοι]
ἕως θυγατρὶ Χ δρα[χμῶν·]
5   ὅσωι πλέονος ἀξία ἐ[τιμήθ]
η Ἀγλαοτίμει ὑπόκε[ιται]
ΗΗ καὶ Γεφυραίοις ΗΗ[...]
ΗΗΗΙ καὶ ἐπὶ τοῖς α[...]
[..]υ[.....]τευμ[......]

148. IG II² 2671
Amynia, rough stone

ὅρος οἰκίας ἀ[ποτ]ίμημα πρ[οικὸς]
Πατροκλείαι θυγατρὶ Παντ— —
Φρεαρ(ρίου) ΧΓ.

149. IG II² 2672
     Marble

[ὅρος]
[οἰ]κία[ς ἀποτί]
[μημα προικὸς —]
σ[τ]εῖ Θεοκρίτ
[ο]υ θυγατρὶ
    Γ rasura?
    κληρ- postea add.

150. IG II² 2673 (II 1124 — M 1368 — IJ I viii, no. 12)
     Athens, marble

[ὅρ]ος οἰκίας
ἐν προικὶ ἀπο
τετιμημέ
νης : ΗΗΗ :
ʽΑγνοκλείαι.

151. *Hesperia* 3 (1934) 65, no. 57
     Athens, marble

ἐ[πὶ — —]ων[— ἄρχ]
οντος· ὅρος ο[ἰκίας Φιλο]
υμ⟨έ⟩νει Τη[......]
Δηκελέως π[ροικὸς]
[ἀ]ποτίμημ[α —]

The name was restored by A. Raubitschek, in *Hesperia* 11
(1942) 313. The archon's name is a matter of dispute. Meritt
tentatively proposed Chairondas (338/7 B.C.); Dow and
Travis, "Demetrios of Phaleron" 163-64, suggest Phano-
machos (260/59 B.C.).

152. *Hesperia* 10 (1941) 54, no. 18 B
     Athens, marble, 308/7 B. C.

[ἐπὶ Και]ρίμου ἄρχοντος·
[ὅρος ο]ἰκίας προικὸς ἀπ
[οτίμη]μα Σιμάλει
— —

This text was preceded on the stone by no. 71, which was
deleted to make way for the present *horos*.

153. IG II² 2675 (II 1132 — IJ I viii, no. 15)
Athens (?), marble

[ὅρ]ος οἰκίας [καὶ]
[κ]ήπου ἀποτετ[ιμ]
ημένων προικ[ὸς]
τἔι Διοδώρου θυ[γ]
ατρὶ Καλλιστράτ
ει ΧΓΗΗ.

2. *Amorgos*

154. IG XII 7,56 (IJ I viii, no. 23)
Arkesine, bluish marble, 3rd century B. C.

ὅρος οἰκιῶν [— — —]
〚///〛 ἀποτε[τιμημ]έ[νων ἐπ' ἄ]
ρχοντος Κριτοβούλου ὑπὸ 'Ε[ξα]
κέστου Κλεινοκράτει Τιμαγόρου
5   〚///////////〛 πρὸς
μέρος τῆς προικὸς δραχμὰς
〚Χ〛 Χ 〚Χ///////////〛
〚//〛 κατὰ συνθήκας τὰς παρὰ 'Αρι[σ]
[τ]ονίκωι.

The editors gratuitously restored καὶ κήπων τῶν in line 1.

155. IG XII 7,57 (*Syll.* 1189 — M 1370 — IJ I viii, no. 24)
Arkesine (found on the Acropolis), white marble, c. 300 B.C.
[ὅρος οἰκιῶν καὶ κήπων τῶν πρ]
ὸς ταῖς οἰκίαις, τῶν ἀποτετι

μημένων Νικησαρέτηι εἰς τὴ
ν προῖκα, καθιερωμένων καὶ ἁ
νακειμένων τῆι Οὐρανίαι Ἀ
5 φροδίτει τῆι ἐν Ἀσπίδι ὑπὸ Νι
κησαρέτης τῆς γυναικὸς {τ}
τῆς Ναυκράτους καὶ κυρίου
Ναυκράτους καὶ κατὰ τὰς δι
αθήκας τὰς κειμένας ἐν τῶι
10 ἱερῶι τῆς Ἀφροδίτης καὶ παρ' Ε
ὑνομίδει τῶι ἄρχοντι καὶ π
αρὰ τῶι θεσμοθ[έ]τει Κτησι
φῶντι.

Ἀφ(ροδίτης)

In a sense, this is a boundary-stone of property dedicated
mortis causa rather than a *horos* marking hypothecation. Yet
it is sufficiently "mixed" in character to warrant inclusion in
the present collection. The name of the goddess in the final
line appears in the form of a monogram. Ziebarth, "Neue
Hypothekeninschriften" 673, noted that all previous editions
(including I J) had omitted the words καὶ κυρίου Ναυκράτους
in lines 7–8, through an error in transcription. All earlier
interpretations are therefore necessarily wrong. For the date,
see A. Wilhelm, in *Jahreshefte* 7 (1904) 110.

3. Naxos.

156. IG XII Supp. 195 — c. 300 B. C.

[ὅ]ρος οἰκίας ἀπ[ὸ κε]
ράμου καὶ σκευ[ῶν τῶν ἐν]
τῆι οἰκίαι πάντω[ν τῶν]
ἀποτετιμημ[ένων τῆι δεινὶ]
5 ἐν προικὶ ἐπ' ἄρχ[οντος Τιμα]
γόρου: XႲ: χιλίων μ[ὲν οἰκή]
σεως, πεντακοσί[ων πάντων]
τῶν σκευῶν.

4. Uncertain and Miscellaneous

a. Athens

157. IG II² 2646 (II 5, 1130b)
Acropolis, limestone (?)

[— — —]παι [...]
[....]μάντου Μυ
[— — —] θώνδου
ΧΧΧΧ.

In the IG, the text is restored: [ἀποτιμήματος] παι[δὸς/
ʼΑδει]μάντου Μυ/[ρρινουσίου —]θώνδου / ΧΧΧΧ.
This reading is not only gratuitous; it leaves the final letters
θώνδου in an impossible position.

158. IG II² 2648 (II 1153 — IJ I viii, no. 8)
Athens

[ὅρος χ]ωρί[ου ἀ]ποτ[ίμ]ημα Τ[ει]σίο|υ παι]δὶ ʼΑ[ρίσ]-
τωνι ?   (Koehler)

159. IG II² 2655 (II 1141 — IJ I viii, no. 6)
Athens, marble

ἐπὶ Εὐβ[ούλου]
ἄρχοντο[ς· ὅρος]
ᴅοἰκίας καᴉ[ὶ τοῦ ὕδατος]
τοῦ προσόν[τος ἀπ]
οτιμήμα[τος]
ʼΑρχίαι Φ — —

Athens had two archons named Eubulos, one in 345/4 B.C.,
the other in 272/1.

160. IG II² 2656
Marble, 265/4 B. C.

[ἐπὶ Φιλι]ππίδου [ἄρχον]
[τος· ὅρος χ]ωρίου ἀποτ[ιμ]
— — —

Dow and Travis, "Demetrios of Phaleron" 161-62, report that examination of the stone by A. Raubitschek and J. V. A. Fine reestablished the earlier reading of the archon's name, first suggested by Sauciuc, in preference to the name, Simonides (311/0 B.C.), given by Kirchner in IG.

161. IG II² 2677 (II 1152 — IJ I viii, no. 22)
Athens, marble

> ὅρος οἰκί[ας καὶ ἐρ]
> γαστηρί[ου ἀποτε]
> τιμημέν[ων — —]
> Μελίττ[— — —]
> δου Ερ — —
>
> — — —

The editors all insert the word προικός in the lacuna in line 3, place a dative ending ηι on the name in line 4, and add θυγατρί in line 6. These restorations rest on the assumption that the *apotimema* was restricted to dotal and pupillary uses; see Chap. IV.

162. IG II² 2678 (II 1136 — IJ I viii, no. 16)
Athens, marble, 305/4 B. C.

> ὅρος οἰκί[ας]
> ἀποτιμήμ[α]
> [τ]ος ἐπ᾽ [Ε]ὐξεν
> [ίπ]που: XX.

163. IG II² 2767 (M 1741)
Markopulo

> ὅρος χωρίου ἀποτίμημα ἐπὶ συνθήκαις
> Διονύσωι ⌐ΗΗ ⌐.

164. *Hesperia* 3 (1934) 65, no. 58
Athens, marble

> ὅρ[ος]
> ἀποτ[ιμή]
> ματος [..]
> ι..στ[..]
> — θε —

b. Naxos

165. IG XII Supp. 193 (SEG II 500)
Third century B. C.

[ἐπὶ ἄρχοντ]ο[ς? — — ὅρος οἰκίας καὶ]
[κήπου] κ[α]ὶ κεράμου ἀμ[φορέων — —]
[ἀποτ]ετιμημένων ᾿Αρτ — — —
...ἰω[ν ἐ]πὶ το[ῖ]ς ᾿Αντ [— κτήμασιν —]
5   [...ί]ππ[ωι.......]ασια — — —
.... ὡς ἐπὶ ἔτη ἑξ — — —
.... ἀργυρίου δραχμῶν — —
.......τα[κισ]χιλίων κα[τὰ συγγραφὴν]
[ἤν ἔχει ......]ω... ΓΩΝ [— τό]
10   [κου τ]οῦ ἐνιαυτοῦ [ἐ]κάσ[του ᾿Αττικῶι? νο]
[μίσματ]ι δραχμῶν χ[ιλίων τετρακοσίων, τριμήν]
[ου δὲ τρ]ιακοσίων πεντή[κοντα ἀτελῶν]
[παντὸς φόρο]υ, ὧν ἄρχει [μὴν — —]
[— — —]ς ἕως ἀ[ν — —]

This text is reproduced precisely as it appeared originally in SEG and again in the IG, with the fanciful restorations by W. Crönert. Wilhelm suggested the following for lines 3–4: ἀρ⟨γ⟩[υρίου δραχμῶν — — — / κοσ (or χιλ)]ίω[ν]; and Crönert, by way of example: ᾿Αρ[τεμισίαι, ἀνθ᾿ ὧν ἔδωκε / δανε]ίω[ν] κτλ. I have not used this inscription in the discussion, for it seems impossible to reconstruct with any degree of assurance. I am not fully convinced that it is a *horos* at all.

IV. MISCELLANEOUS AND DUBIOUS
A. HOPELESS FRAGMENTS
I. *Athens*

166. IG II² 2695
Near Spata, marble

[— — Σ]οφοκλε[ῖ]
[᾿Ιππ]οτομάδει
— — ⟨Ρ⟩Η

— — σκλεῖ Αἰθ[α]
[λίδηι —]

[ὅρος χωρίου / καὶ οἰκίας / πεπραμένων / ἐπὶ λύσει], the Corpus reading for the beginning, is not warranted.

167. IG II² 2710
Western base of the Acropolis, white marble

νεί : Η.

The original editor, E. Ziebarth, called this a *horos* from the form of the stone. His proposed opening is gratuitous: [ὅρος χω/ρίου πεπρ/αμένου ἐπὶ λύσει].

168. IG II² 2768
Mandra, bluish marble

ΚΛΟΝΑ [— κατὰ συνθή]
κ[ας τ]ὰς κειμένα
ς [παρ]ὰ ΚΜΔΙΗΠ
᾿Α[σ]ω[π]οκλέους ᾿Αθ
μονεῖ καὶ τὰς [παρὰ]
Πρωτοκλεῖ —

169. IG II² 2769
Limestone

[— — κατὰ]
τὰς συ[νθήκας]
τὰς κειμέ[νας παρὰ —]
πώραι ῾Ιερω[ν —]

170. IG II² 2770
Peiraieus, marble

ωι Ⱶ
ἐπικλή
ρω[ι]
νι

171. *Kerameikos* 21
Kerameikos, poor marble

> ασίωι Ϝ κατὰ τὰς συν
> θήκας αἳ κεῖνται παρὰ
> Πρωτέαι 'Εξηκέστου
> 'Ανακαιεῖ.

Werner Peek, the editor, proposes the following opening lines: [ὅρος χωρίου πε/πραμένου ἐπὶ λύ/σει τῶι δεινὶ 'Αναγυρ]/ ασίωι. He justifies the restoration on the ground that shorter first lines are characteristic of the *horoi*. This argument is not valid.

2. Amorgos

172. IG XII 7,59
Arkesine, blue marble, *c.* 300 B. C.

> [θ]εοί·
> [ὅρος οἰκία]ς καὶ χωρί[ων —]
> — —

173. IG XII 7,60
Arkesine, blue marble, *c.* 300 B. C.

> [— — μηνὸς Βοη]δρομιῶνο[ς]
> [— — — καὶ χ]ωρίων τῶν
> [— — —] μναῖς π[..]
> [— — —] τῶν χω[ρίων]
> 5   [— — — κε]ιμένω[ν —]
> πολ
> ρων
> ο

Only the right half of the stone is preserved. The editor suggests restorations for the left half which I have not bothered to reproduce, including the word ἀποτετιμημένων in line 3 and the reading [ὑποκε]ιμένω[ν] in line 5.

B. PROBABLY NOT HYPOTHECATION-STONES

1. Athens

174. IG II² 2766
Marble

ὅρος
χωρίο Λυ
σίππης.

175. IG II² 2666
Marble

ὅρος χωρ[ί]
ο καὶ οἰκία
ς προικὸ
ς Ναυσ
ικρίτη[ι].

176. IG II² 2765 (II 1109 — M 1381 — IJ I viii, no. 67)
Northern part of the city

ʰόρος οἰκία
ς καὶ χωρίο Τιμ
οστράτης 'Ανακ
αίαθεν τῆς Βό
ωνος ἀδελφῆς
'Ανακαιῶς, μητρὸ
[ς ⸺ ⸺] Κηφι
[σιῶς].

177. IG II² 2680
Marble, 313/2 B. C.

ἐπὶ Θεοφ[ρά]
στου ἄρχον[τ]
[ο]ς· ὅρος χω
ρίου ἀπὸ το[ῦ]
μέρος τοῦ
χωρί: ⊢H / / /

178. IG II² 2751 (II 1121 — IJ I viii, no. 40)
Peiraieus, marble

ὅρος κή[που καὶ]
ἀνδραπόδ[ων].

2. *Syros*

179. IG XII 5,707 (DGE 784 — M 1382 — IJ I viii, no. 68)
Rough limestone, third century B. C.

ʹΗγησοῦ
τῆς Κλεομ
όρτου θυγατρὸ
[ς] προὶξ τὸ χωρί
ον.

180. IG XII 5,1105

ʹΑρχιδίκης τῆς Δε
ξικράτου θυγατρὸς
προὶξ ἡ οἰκία.

The tables that follow present in summary fashion the information about the nature of the property, the amount of the obligation, the number of creditors (a word to be understood in the very broad sense of anyone to whom money is owed or may be owed at some future time), and the presence or absence on the stones of a date and a reference to a written agreement. Only 154 *horoi* were considered (nos. 1-111, 116-156), those which are sufficiently complete to lend themselves to such analysis and which unquestionably mark security relationships. Several introductory notes are necessary.

(1) Attic and island *horoi* are treated together since they differ very little in essential content. Throughout the book, variations are indicated when necessary.

(2) All entries are based on the readings that are printed in the body of the text-collection. No distinction has been drawn between fully preserved texts and editorial restorations where the latter are certain. Separate notations have been made in all cases of doubt or suspicion.

(3) Plural and singular forms have been retained systematically for all types of property mentioned.

(4) With almost perfect uniformity, the *horoi* use the word *chorion* for landed property and avoid the more descriptive terms available in the Greek language. "Land" has been chosen for the English rendition as the correspondingly neutral, non-descriptive word. A detailed examination of the kinds of land concealed behind the toneless language of the texts appears in Chapter V.

(5) A few *horoi* reveal the deletion of a portion of the numeral indicating the amount of the obligation, presumably because some of the debt had been liquidated. I have chosen the smaller number and have indicated that fact in the notes whenever the total picture is affected.

(6) When a group appears as the creditor, it is treated as a single individual and included in the appropriate column in the tables, rather than under "multiple creditors."

(7) When a woman and her guardian (*kyrios*) appear on the stones, I have tabulated them as a single individual.

(8) Multiple creditors are indicated in the *horoi* in several ways. For purposes of tabulation, the differences have been ignored except in the cases of nos. 32, 146, and 147. The first of the three announces a *prasis epi lysei* and then an *apotimema*, the other two a dotal *apotimema* followed by a *hypotheke*. They have been tabulated on the basis of the first-named transaction in each instance, as if the other did not exist. A discussion of these stones and of the problem of multiple creditors generally appears in Chapter VIII.

Table A   Breakdown of *Horoi*

Marking *Hypotheke* Obligations

Type of Property	No. of *Horoi*	Debt (in drachmas) Range Maximum	Minimum	Median	Value not stated or lost	No. of Creditors None named	1	Dated *Horos* Yes	No	Reference to a Written Agreement Yes	No
Lands, house, garden, & equiment ..	1				1	?[1]			1		1
Land, garden & well	1			300		?		?		1	
Land & house	1			800			1	1		1	
Land[2]	1			2,000			1	1			1
Houses & garden	1			90			1	1		1	
House	4[3]	1,000	200	200	1		4	2	2	2	2
Workshop ...	1			750	1				1		1
Total	10	2,000	90	525	2	2	6	4	5	5	5

1. No. 8 (from Amorgos). I have placed a question mark here because the answer depends on the interpretation of the text; see the discussion in Chap. VII, sect. 4.
2. I have included *horos* no. 3 despite the absence of a verb meaning hypothecation.
3. In no. 10, a Lemnian stone, the word used is οἴκημα. It appears on one other *horos*, no. 81, a *prasis epi lysei* text. I have not tried to distinguish between οἰκία and οἴκημα in these instances.

Table B Breakdown of *Horoi* Marking *Prasis epi lysei* Obligations

Type of Property	No. of *Horoi*	Debt (in drachmas) — Range: Maximum	Minimum	Median	Not stated	Lost or doubtful	No. of Creditors: 1	2	3	5	If several creditors: No. where only one amount	No. where separate debts	Not stated	Lost or doubtful	Dates *Horos*: Yes	No	Reference to a Written Agreement: Yes	No
Lands, gardens, house	1				1		1									1		1
Lands & houses	1					1		1							1		1	
Lands, house & roof[1]	1			5,000			1				?				1			1
Land & two houses	1			3,000					1		1				1			1
Land, house & garden	1			5,000			1								1			
Land & house[2]	28	7,000[3]	200[4]	2,000		6	16	3[5]		1[6]	4[7]	1	3	4	4	24	4	24
Land	32	6,000	150	1,000	9	4	20	1	1	1	1	2	7	2	1	31	1	30
Houses	1					1								1		1		1
House[8]	19	3,000	200	700		4	14						3[9]	2	3	16	1	18
House & privy (?)	1			800			1									1		1
House & workshops	1			6,000			1									1	1	
Workshops	1					1								1		1		1
Workshop & slaves	3	6,000	700	?			3									3		3
Smelter & surface land[10]	1					1								1	1			?
Total	92	7,000	150	1,050	10	18	58	5	2	2	6	3	13	11	13	79	8	81

Footnotes on next page

+ 10 too fragmentary to analyze

Notes to Table B

1. No. 102 from Amorgos. On roofs in the *horoi*, see Chap. V, sect. 5.
2. No. 39 is badly broken and the nature of the property involved is uncertain. The restoration proposed in IG is highly dubious because it includes the name of the debtor, unprecedented in an Attic *horos*, as the original editor, Ziebarth, "Neue attische Grenzsteine," *Sitz. Berlin* (1898) 782, no. 26, had already seen. I have therefore included this text in the category "house," though that leaves the problem of restoration unsolved.
3. In no. 15 the amount appears as ⌐XX, subsequently deleted. The largest unchanged reading is 6,000 drachmas in no. 30.
4. No. 28 now reads HH, two additional 100-drachma signs having been deleted. The lowest unchanged figure is 300 drachmas in no. 29.
5. No. 35 is included here although the restoration of the names, and hence the number of creditors, are somewhat uncertain.
6. In no. 94 only portions of the names are legible but the total number of creditors seems quite certainly to be five.
7. In no. 18, the property is made over to "Hagnodemos and the co-suretors." The presence of sureties does not change the fact that there was but one creditor in the principal obligation.
8. The word οἴκημα appears in no. 81; see note 3 to Table A. See further note 2 above regarding *horos* no. 39.
9. No. 78, included here, originally did have a creditor's name inscribed but it was subsequently deleted.
10. No. 92, found in Laureion, reads κάμινος καὶ ἐδάφη, on which see briefly Chap. V, note 45, and Crosby, "Laureion Mines" 195.

Table C   Breakdown of *Horoi*
Marking Pupillary *Apotimema* Obligations

Type of Property	No. of Horoi	Amount of Debt stated		No. of Children[1]		Dated Horos	
		Yes	No	One	More than one	Yes	No
Lands, house, & water ..	1		1		1	1	
Lands, house & roof[2]	1	1			1		1
Land	6		6	2	4		6
Land & house	5		5	3	2		5
Unidentified or uncertain	3	1	2		3	1	1[3]
Total	16	2	14	5	11	2	13[3]

Notes to Table C

1. About as often as not, the stone gives the father's name but not the name of the child. It is therefore impossible to analyze the number of children more precisely, since, when their names are not given, we have only the number of the word παῖς to go by.
2. No. 131 from Naxos. On roofs in the *horoi*, see Chap. V, sect. 5.
3. No. 130, an Amorgian stone, does give a date in the first three lines. It is not clear, however, whether these lines are actually part of the *horos* or not. The word ὅρος opens the fourth line.

Table D   Breakdown of *Horoi*
Marking Dotal *Apotimema* Obligations

Type of Property	No. of *Horoi*	Debt (in drachmas) Range Maximum	Minimum	Median	Not stated	Lost or doubtful	Dated *Horos* Yes	No	Reference to a Written Agreement Yes	No
Lands & houses	1			4,000[1]			1			1
Land & house ..	9	8,000	1,500	3,000	2	1		9		9
Land	5	6,000	1,800	5,200[2]	1	1		5		5
Building lots[3] ..	1			500				1		1
House & gardens	1				1[4]			1		1[4]
House & garden	1			1,700				1		1
House, roof & equipment[5] ..	1			1,500[5]			1			1
House	6	1,000	300	750		2	2	4		6
Uncertain[6]	1					1[6]		1	1	
Total	26	8,000	300	1,700	4	5	5	21	1	25

1. In no. 132, one of the most troublesome of the *horoi*, the property evaluation of 4,000 drachmas, which has been deduced from the text, may not be the correct figure.
2. This figure appears in no. 141, which is very badly preserved. The editor, D. M. Robinson, indicates complete confidence in his reading, however.

3. No. 143 is the only *horos* with the word οἰκόπεδον.
4. No. 155, from Amorgos, is a complex stone, marking property which was used to secure a dowry and which was then consecrated by will to Aphrodite by the husband and wife together. As a dedication-stone, it made no reference either to value or to a written agreement, in the sense of a contract between dowry-giver and dowry-taker. There is reference to διαθήκαι, clearly the articles (testament) establishing the dedication. I have therefore listed the stone among those not mentioning a written agreement.
5. No. 156, from Naxos, is unique in that the 1,500-drachma evaluation is broken down into 1,000 drachmas for the house and 500 for the equipment. On roofs in the *horoi*, see Chap. V, sect. 5.
6. No. 154, from Amorgos, is full of deletions. The nature of the property cannot be restored. The amount was originally 3,000 drachmas, apparently, and was later reduced to 1,000.

APPENDIX II

FERGUSON'S THEORY OF THE LEGISLATION OF DEMETRIOS ON *HOROI*

In discussing the law code which he believes Demetrios of Phaleron promulgated in 316/5 B.C., Ferguson, *Hellenistic Athens* 43, says that the function of the section on real property was to "reduce the embarrassing uncertainty which often existed in Athens as to the titles or liabilities of property. What his remedies were we cannot say definitely, but perhaps it was required that the originals of all contracts involving the testamentary disposition, sale, donation, or mortgaging of houses or land should be dated precisely and deposited with reliable third parties. Certainly the copies published during the next decade or two in Attica and in the cleruchies [by this phrasing, Ferguson apparently means the *horoi*] exhibited significant changes in these particulars. His aim here, which was obviously to protect business men in making investments, was accordingly consistent with his general policy."

This quotation is a compressed (and somewhat more cautious) statement of a thesis that Ferguson had developed at length in his article, "Laws of Demetrius," published in the same year as the book (unless otherwise indicated, all further references are to the article), and reaffirmed some thirty years later by Erich Bayer, *Demetrios Phalereus der Athener* [*Tübinger Beiträge zur Altertumswissenschaft* 36 (Stuttgart and Berlin 1942)] 48—51, who contributes nothing but his enthusiasm to the discussion, and by Dow and Travis, "Demetrios of Phaleron." Ferguson was led to the theory by his observation that no dated *horos* was unquestionably to be placed before 315/4 B.C. (a point to which we shall return) and that, of the relatively small number of dated *horoi*, the largest number (it is now five) fall in precisely that year. The theory seems untenable on grounds of both inner logic and economic considerations. In view of its broad implications, an analysis in some detail is necessary.

1. Even if we assume that Dow and Travis have successfully demonstrated that all the dated *horoi* fall in the years 315/4 and after, they have proved the wrong point. To support Ferguson's

thesis it is necessary to show not that *horoi* were not dated before Demetrios introduced that requirement, but that none was *undated after* the promulgation of the law. At least, the latter must be shown for the years preceding the democratic restoration of 307 B.C., an embarrassing date in any event; Dow and Travis write, p. 165, note 58: "It is worth noting that the democratic government restored in 307 B.C. did not repeal Demetrios' laws on property transfers, if one may judge from the fact that several boundary-stones [a misconception of the legal *horoi* that runs through the article] of the third century B.C. mentioning dates and contracts are now extant." It is admittedly impossible to make the required demonstration for the undated *horoi*, and editors seem agreed that a substantial number fall well into the third century.

Elsewhere we have seen that Ferguson's idea that Demetrios introduced the dating and filing of wills and donations is easily disproved (see Chap. II, note 83, and sect. 3 generally). Dow and Travis, pp. 164—65, note, furthermore, that the majority of the dated stones make no mention of a written agreement, from which they conclude that, though the agreement and its deposit for safekeeping with a reliable third party were mandatory, a statement to that effect on the *horos* was not necessary. That interpretation fails to explain why any *horos* should make reference to a written agreement (see Chap. II, sect. 3).

2. The absence of dated *horoi* prior to 315/4, if true, actually argues against Ferguson's explanation of the reason for Demetrios' requirement. If the date had a protective function, why had no creditor thought of adding one before Demetrios insisted on his doing so? The creditor himself, it must be remembered, prepared the stone and set it up on his debtor's property. Dow and Travis saw this objection (p. 165) but refused to draw the necessary conclusion from it. Ferguson writes (p. 266): "The inscription on the ὅροι was of course not an official, not *the* legal, record of indebtedness: it was simply an advertisement made in the interest of third parties, or by a creditor interested in having the fact of a loan known to his debtor's neighbors in order to secure himself for the future against a possible denial of obligation.... The sole purpose that the specification of the time of contracting a loan could have served was to facilitate a search and above all establish publicly the sequence of several loans secured by a single piece of realty, and thus safeguard investors." We need not re-examine the material in Chap. II, sect. 2, in detail to reply to this account. Ferguson agrees that the *horoi* did

not serve as decisive evidence. But what was "*the* legal record of indebtedness" and what sort of "search" would a date on the *horoi* facilitate? Either Ferguson believes that there was some sort of title registry, which would have rendered the *horoi* entirely unnecessary, or he has in mind the written agreement of the transaction, in which case the *horoi* could not have performed the function he has suggested unless they invariably gave the name of the man with whom the agreement had been deposited for safekeeping.

On p. 270, Ferguson says that Demetrios "aimed to provide the courts with a working basis for settling disputes over real estate" by requiring that the agreement be deposited with third parties "who were, doubtless, made legally responsible for their safe-keeping." He can offer no evidence of any kind for this statement, nor any valid arguments against the negative evidence presented in Chap. II, sect. 3. (Note should be taken of the equally unsupported statement of Schulthess "Συνθήκη," 1166, writing of the period before Demetrios, "*Hingegen ist wesentlich und doch wohl gesetzlich vorgeschrieben die Deposition des Vertrages bei einer Drittperson.*")

How little value the addition of a date would have had in case of fraud is demonstrated by Demosthenes' suit against Onetor, on which see Chap. II, at note 37, and Chap. VIII, note 7. The fraud which Demosthenes charged was an elaborate one, involving a fictitious divorce, the placing of *horoi* without just cause and subsequent juggling of the *horoi* in order to change the amount of money claimed and the precise definition of the property supposedly put up as security. The date of the alleged divorce was one of the points at issue. Surely a man who had carried his fraudulent acts this far — whether or not Demosthenes was reporting accurately is immaterial — would not have shrunk from the further step of inscribing a false date on the stone.

3. Ferguson admits that the dating requirement was an imperfect device to accomplish Demetrios' basic aim. "What Theophrastus had urged upon the ideal legislator," he writes, *Hellenistic Athens* 43, "the public registration of all transfers — Demetrius did not indeed enact." If Theophrastus were Demetrios' teacher and the inspiration behind his legislation, why did the latter fail to carry out so important a proposal (on which see Chap. II, note 25)? Ferguson's explanation, "Laws of Demetrius" 270, is that to have done so "would have doubled the work of administration and led to violent interferences with the traditional ways of doing business." Not only is this explanation out of keeping with Ferguson's own conception

12*

of the character of Demetrios and his rule and with the "violent interferences" that must have followed his sumptuary legislation, but it contradicts the very reasons Ferguson gives for the ruling. If Demetrios' aim, "consistent with his general policy," was "obviously to protect business men in making investments," why did he shrink from steps that might have achieved such a purpose and remain satisfied with minor measures of no genuine significance? And who would have objected? Surely not the people on whose support Demetrios could count, the men of means who could have no real objection to the establishment of a central public-record and public-notice system if they genuinely felt the need for one to protect "their investments."

4. One advantage of dating *horoi*, Ferguson thinks (p. 266), would be to "establish publicly the sequence of several loans secured by a single piece of realty." He cites particularly *horos* no. 41, which names five creditors and gives a separate amount for each. The order of entry, Ferguson says on p. 266, decided the priority of claims, hence a date was needed on the stone. A date is unnecessary if the order of entry was the decisive point; in any event, this conception of multiple creditors is untenable, as has been shown in Chap. VIII (see particularly at notes 8—11 for *horos* no. 41). Nor is it necessary to repeat the objections to the "investment" approach, without which, it may be noted, the entire analysis falls at once, since that was the supposed motive for Demetrios' legislation (see generally Chap. VI, latter part of sect. 2; Chap. VII at notes 52—53).

5. The fact remains that five of the nineteen (twenty-two if we include nos. 160, 162, and 177) dated *horoi* fall in the year 315/4 B.C., and there is some possibility that the remainder all date in subsequent years. Dow and Travis sought to establish the point that no *horos* can be dated earlier. Some comments on their analysis are necessary: (a) They include the Lemnian *horoi*, nos. 104, 107, and 108 (to which no. 10 should now be added), under the erroneous assumption that the archons named were Athenian, not Lemnian; see Chap. I, note 25. (b) IG II² 2630 is a boundary-stone, not a hypothecation-stone, and does not belong in this discussion at all. (c) Their list includes two still unpublished *horoi* from the Agora, Inv. I 5579 and 5873, dated 301/0 and *c.* 267/6 B.C., respectively; they give neither the text nor an indication of the content of these *horoi*. (d) *Horos* no. 3 is dated in the archonship of Theophrastos. Athens had two archons by that name, one in 340/39 B.C. and the other in 313/2. Dow and Travis, p. 166, say frankly that the Fer-

guson thesis is the sole basis for deciding in favor of the later date. The same situation exists with *horos* no. 159, though in this case they had a squeeze at their disposal. (e) Their reading of the archon's name in no. 13 as Nikodoros is debatable and to be explained largely by a desire to fit it into the Ferguson thesis. A similar situation exists with *horoi* nos. 151 and 160. (f) *Horos* no. 127 has the archon Chairikleides of 363/2 B.C. in lines 9—10, and Kirchner in IG assumed that an earlier archon's name appeared in the opening lines, which are lost. Dow and Travis argue, p. 161, that "it is easy to imagine" that the "first text contained no date," and that a subsequent transaction took place which was dated precisely in order to distinguish it from the original one. The end of the stone is also gone, so that the entire discussion is speculative, but there can be no objection in principle to their explanation.

Even if one or two of the *horoi* are more probably dated before 315/4 B.C., the original observation by Ferguson cannot be ignored. I have no concrete explanation to offer but the answer probably will be found in the years of political disturbance and conflict of the end of Alexander's reign and of the period between his death and the assumption of power by Demetrios of Phaleron. The sudden appearance and equally rapid disappearance of a particular type of inscription in a particular community is no rare phenomenon. Two examples may be noted from the material used in our discussion: the lists of the freedmen's bowls (see Chap. VII at notes 71—78) and the Olynthian "deeds of sale" (see Chap. III, note 21). Political conditions in general or a specific incident may give rise either to a new procedure or to a desire to record on stone a practice that was not new. Only rarely do we have information that would even suggest the reasons. But it is unnecessary to assume that some profound social, economic, or legal change has taken place in each instance, and certainly not that there has been special legislative enactment. The danger of rushing to the legislative explanation has been demonstrated by Wilhelm's disproof of the conclusions drawn by Ferguson, among others, from the eight inscriptions granting noncitizens the right to own realty but limiting the monetary value of the property they could acquire; see Chap. V at note 47.

APPENDIX III

NEW *HOROI* FROM THE AGORA

The new Agora *horoi* mentioned in Chap. I, note 14, were publish-ed, while the present volume was in press, by John V. A. Fine, *Horoi. Studies in Mortgage, Real Security, and Land Tenure in Ancient Athens* [*Hesperia* Supp. 9 (1951)] Chap. I. Fine also gives the texts of two previously unpublished Epigraphical Museum *horoi*. In his second chapter, he reprints all *horoi* previously pub-lished elsewhere than in IG. Included are four, from Attica, pub-lished by Werner Peek in *Athen. Mitt.* 67 (1942) 35-36, nos. 38-40, 43, to which I have not had access. The total of published *horoi* is now 222, of which 40 are uncertain or hopelessly fragmentary.

Nothing in these texts or in Fine's discussion has caused me to alter my views in any significant way. I therefore reprint the new documents with few comments. The texts have been arranged and numbered on the principles stated in Appendix I. Fine's and Peek's numbers are given in parentheses (Fine II means Fine, Chap. II). At the end of this Appendix, I shall note four revisions of previously published *horoi* indicated by Fine.

I. *Hypotheke*

3A. (Peek 43, Fine II 27) Marble, *c.* 259/8 B. C.

ἐπὶ Λυκέου ἄρχ[οντος]
ὅρος χωρίου καὶ [οἰκίας ὑποκειμέν]
ων Σαλαιπίωι Σι — — —
Χ δραχμῶν τι[μῆς — — —]
είου κατὰ συν[θήκας τὰς κειμέν]
ας παρὰ Λάχη[τι — — —]

II. *Prasis epi lysei*

18A. (Fine 17) Marble

ὅρος χωρί[ου]
καὶ οἰκίας [πε]

πραμένης ᾽Α[σ]
φαλ[ει ἐ]π[ὶ λ]ύσ[ει]
ο — — — vacat εν
ΧΧΧ οφειλ — —

21A. (Fine 12) Two fragments of white marble

[ὅρο]ς χωρίου καὶ οἰκίας
[πεπ]ραμένων ἐπὶ λύ[σει]
προ[ικ]ὸς ΧΧ
Μ[......κ]αὶ κυρίω[ι]
Δ[..... Με]λιτεῖ.

This is the fifth *horos* linking *prasis epi lysei* with a dowry (see Chap. IV at note 59). If the readings and restorations in lines 4–5 are correct — and Fine stresses the difficulty — this is the second appearance of a woman's *kyrios* on a dotal *horos*. The other, no. 155 from Amorgos, explicitly indicates added complications. The father's name, however, is frequently stated on the stones marking dotal *apotimemata* (see Chap. IV at note 55); perhaps the *kyrios* was named here because the father had died prior to his daughter's marriage. Note should also be taken of Fine's statement that "there may have been other numerals after the ΧΧ in line 3. That part of the inscription is badly mutilated; possibly the line was deliberately erased...."

31A—B. (Fine 26) Two marble fragments found in the wall of a modern house

[ὅρ]ος [— —]
[καὶ οἰ]κ[ο]πέδο[υ]
[πε]πραμένων
[ἐπ]ὶ λύσει ΧΗΗΗ
[ἐ]ρανισ{σ}ταῖς τ[ο]
[ῖ]ς μ[ε]τὰ Βλεπαίο[υ].

Fine restores χωρίου in line 1, but οἰκίας seems more probable with οἰκόπεδον (a word found only in *horos* no. 143). The numeral in line 4 and all of lines 5–6 were inscribed in a second hand. Underneath, Fine and J. H. Kent detected signs of a deleted text, reading in line 4, Ḥ; line 5, ΔΔΙ; line 6, κ'τ. A seventh line, which Kent believes to have been engraved by the first hand, remains on the stone: νος Βατῆθεν. Presumably this is another instance of a "double" *horos* (see Chap. II, end of sect. 2).

39A. (Fine 15) Marble

ὅρο[ς οἰκίας]
καὶ χ[ωρίου πεπρ]
αμ[ένων ἐπὶ λύ]
σ[ει — —]
— — —

39B. (Fine Add. I a, p. 24)

ὅρος χω[ρ]
[ί]ου καὶ οἰκ[ί]
[α]ς πεπρα[μ]
[ένω]ν ἐπ[ὶ]
[λύσει —]
— — —

51A. (Peek 40, Fine II 19) Limestone

ὅρος χ[ωρίο]
πεπραμέν
ο ἐπὶ λύσει
Εὐθυμέν[ει]
ΓΗΗΗΗ
Εὐωνυμ[εῖ].

Fine writes: "Peek believes that line 6 was inscribed at some later time."

66A. (Fine 14) Marble

[ὅ]ρος οἰκ[ιῶν πεπρα]
μένω[ν ἐπὶ λύσει]
[—]εν — — —
[Π]αια[νι]ε̣[ῖ]
Χ.

Fine states that originally there may have been other numerals in line 5.

66B. (Fine 11) Bluish stone

> ὅρος
> χωρίο[υ]
> πεπραμ[ένου]
> [ἐπὶ λ]ύσ. [ι —]
> — — —

Fine's comment is: "Line 3 was either erased or has been badly worn. At the lower right, part of the word λύσει seems to be visible, but it is strange that no other traces of a line 4 are discernible."

66C. (Fine 24) Marble

> [ὅρος χωρί]
> ου πε[πραμ]
> ένου — — —
> τετ — — —

66D. (Fine 27) Blue limestone

> [ὅρος χωρ]ίο
> [πεπρα]μένο
> [ἐπὶ λ]ύσ[ει]
> [— —] ι ’Ανα
> [φλυ]σ[τ]ί[ωι].

67A. (Fine 23) Poor marble

> ὅρος οἰκίας
> πεπραμέν
> ης ἐπὶ λύσει
> τῶι δήμωι τ
> ῶι Κεραμέω
> ν ΧΧΧ.

82B. (Fine 25) Gray stone

> [ὅρο]ς χω[ρί]
> [ου] πεπρ[α]

[μ]ένου [..]

[.]ικοσ — —

— — —

Fine reads προικός in line 3/4. Because of the infrequency of προικός in *prasis epi lysei* texts I should prefer a proper name, but I have been unable to find one in a brief search.

85 A. (Fine 10) Blue-white marble

[ὅρο]ς οἰκίας [πε]

[πρα]μένη[ς ἐπὶ]

[λύσει — — —]

85 B. (Fine 18) Marble

[ὅ]ρο[ς]

[ο]ἰκίας [ἐπὶ]

λύσει πεπ[ρα]

[μ]ένη[ς —]

— — —

85 C. (Fine 20) Marble, inscribed on two faces

Face a: [ὅ]ρος οἰ[κ]

[ί]ας πε[πρ]

[αμένης —]

— σσ —

— —

Face b: 'Αρίστω[ν]

ος Γαργη[τ]

[τίου — —]

— — —

86 A. (Fine 16) Marble

ὅρος κοπ[ρῶνος]

[κ]αὶ οἰκημ[ατίου]

[πεπ]ρ[αμένων ἐπὶ]

[λύσει — —]

— — —

"Above the first line," writes Fine, "transcribed here there are certain marks on the stone which could be traces of letters. Thus this inscription may have begun with an archon's name."

92 A. (Fine 19) Unworked marble

[ὅρο]ς οἰκίας καὶ κα
[π]ηλείου καὶ κήπ
ου πεπραμένων
ἐπὶ λύσει Καλλίπ
πωι Φαληρεῖ : Ρ.

The small sum is further evidence for the conclusion suggested in Chap. V, end of sect. 4, that shops seem to have had no more value than buildings called simply "houses."

101 A. (Fine 9) Marble

[ὅρο]ς
[χωρίου καὶ] οἱ
[κήματος] πε
[πραμένων ἐ]
[πὶ λύσει —]

— — —

101 B. (Fine 13) Marble

[ἐπὶ — —ἄρ]χον[τος]
[ὅρος — —] πεπρ[αμέ]
[ν . . ἐπὶ λύσει — — —]

— — —

Fine's restoration of χωρίου in line 2 is gratuitous.

101 C. (Fine 21) Marble

— — ρ — —
[— πε]πρ[αμέν —]
[—] καὶ ʽΗρ[—]
[—] Θυμαι[τάδηι —]
φράτρα[ι — —

— — —

II E. *Prasis epi lysei or Sale?*

114A. (Fine 28) Marble

[ὅρο]ς οἰκίας π[ε]
[πρα]μένης Δι[ο]
[τίμ?]οι Μελιτεῖ
[τιμ]ῆς ἧς ἐνεγύη[σε]
5   [ἀραβ]ῶνα τοῦ ἐράν[ου]
[τοῦ π]εντακοσιοδρ[άχ]
[μου] πληρώτρια Δη
[μὼ? ἕ]ως ἂν διεξ
[ἔλθηι].

I reprint the text exactly as restored by Fine "with great
hesitation and many doubts." He translates as follows: "Horos of a house sold to 'Diotimos' of Melite, for the price of
which he has pledged his deposit (payment, contribution) in
the five hundred drachma eranos loan. 'Demo' is plerotria
until the loan shall have expired."

That both the restoration and the interpretation are impossible is certain. It is sufficient to point to two of several
misconceptions of basic legal institutions.

(1) The ἐγγύη was an institution whereby someone guaranteed the performance of an obligation by a second party,
not self-performance; see Partsch, *Bürgschaftsrecht* 63–65 and
passim. Furthermore, it was personal suretyship, not the
pledge of an object.

(2) In support of his restoration of [ἀραβ]ῶνα in line 5 and
his translation, Fine writes: "It is true that the basic meaning
of ἀρραβών is 'the earnest,' i.e., part-payment of the price in
advance..., but it may be legitimate to assume that the
word could also signify more generally the ideas of deposit,
payment, contribution, etc." But "earnest" is not merely the
basic meaning of the word, it is the *only* one known in the
sources. Moreover, the assumption of a broader meaning
rests on a failure to distinguish between an earnest of a
future action by the person making the payment, an *arrhabon*,
and a contribution to an *eranos*-loan, in which the person
receiving the money assumes an obligation for the future,
namely, repayment.

114B. (Fine Add. I b, p. 25) Kerameikos

ℎό[ρος]
χωρίο
πεπρα
μένο.

On the initial *h*, see Chap. I, note 20. Fine seems uncertain whether the text ended with line 4 or not.

III. *Apotimema*

A. *Pupillary Type*

120. A (Fine 5) Marble

ὅρος
[χ]ωρίο
[κα]ὶ οἰκία
[ς ἀ]ποτιμ
[ήμ]ατος
[πα]ιδὸς
— τ λ —
— —

126 A. (Fine 4) Marble

[ὅρο]ς χω[ρίου]
[ἀπο]τίμ[ημα]
[. . .]οκλε[— —]
[πα]ιδὶ Τι[— —]
[Λ]αμπ[τρέως].

126 B. (Peek 38, Fine II 4) Gray limestone

ὅρος χωρίου ἀπο
τιμήματος παι
σὶ τοῖς Εὐθυκρά
τους Ἐρχιέως.

126 C. (Peek 39, Fine II 5) Liopesi, gray limestone

ὅρος χωρίο ἀποτ[ίμημ]
α Τιμοκράτος Π[αια]
νιῶς παισί.

129 A. (Fine 2) Marble

> [ὅρος —]
> [— ἀποτι]
> [μ]ήματο[ς]
> [Δ]ωρο[—]
> [.]ωνο[ς] πα
> [ἰ]δων Φιλο
> κλέος κα[ἰ]
> Φ]ιλόργο.

Fine's restoration of χωρίο in line 1/2 is gratuitous.

B. Dotal Type

152 A. (Fine 6) Marble, 301/0 B. C.

> [ἐ]πὶ Κλεάρ[χου]
> [ἄ]ρχοντος ὅρ[ος]
> [οἰ]κίας προικ
> [ὸς ἀ]ποτίμη
> [μα —]χα —
> — — —

This is one of the two then unpublished, dated *horoi* listed by Dow and Travis (see Appendix II).

III B 4. *Uncertain and Miscellaneous*

164 A. (Fine 3) Marble, 267/6 B. C.

> ἐπὶ Πει[θιδήμου ἄρ]
> χοντος [ὅρος —]
> ἀποτίμη[μα —] -
> 'Αντιφίλ[— —]
> Προξέν[—].

This is one of the two then unpublished, dated *horoi* listed by Dow and Travis (see Appendix II). There is no way of determining whether παιδὶ or προικὸς should be restored in line 3, as Fine recognizes though he nevertheless chooses the former and includes the text under the pupillary *apotimemata*. His restoration of χωρίου in line 2 is equally gratuitous.

IV. *Miscellaneous and Dubious*
A. *Hopeless Fragments*

166 A. (Fine 32) Marble

[ὅρο]ς ἐργασ
[τηρί]ων τῶν
[ἀνοι]κοδομη
[μέν]ων καὶ [ἀν]
[δρα]πόδ[ων —]

— — —

171 A. (Fine 1) Marble

ὅρο[ς —]
οἰκία[ς —]
Φρα[—]
σιω[—]
— —.

Fine reconstructs, with no discoverable justification:

ὅρο[ς χωρίου καὶ]
οἰκία[ς ἀποτίμημα]
Φρα[— — παι]
σὶ ᾿Ω[αθεν —]
— —.

171 B. (Fine 22) Marble

ὅρος [— —]
[.]α[— —]
[..]μένω[ν —]

— — —

— — —

Fine reconstructs: ὅρος [χωρίου / κ]α[ὶ οἰκίας πεπ/ρα]μέ-νω[ν ἐπὶ/λύσει — —/— — —]. Obviously the verb could also be ἀποτετιμημένων and there is no basis for his restoration of χωρίου καὶ οἰκίας.

171C. (Fine 29) Marble

ὅρος
about 4 lines erased
X.

171D. (Fine 30) Marble

— —δ[— —]
ϛ 'Ἐρχι[έω]
ϛ

"Two considerations," writes Fine, "namely that the inscription ends with what is presumably a demotic..., and that the bottom of the stone was left rough, probably for insertion in the ground..., suggest that this is a fragment of a horos mortgage stone."

171E. (Fine 31) Marble

ⲂΗΗ 'Α[π]
ολλ[ο]δ[ῶρωι ?]
Κυδαθ[ηναιεῖ].

171F. (Fine 33) Whitish limestone

[ὅρο]ϛ συνοικία[ϛ]
ΣΤΗΣΠ
'Τ\

IV. B. *Probably Not Hypothecation Stones*

175A. (Fine 7) Marble

ὅρος
οἰκίας
προικὸς
'Ἀρχίλλ[ηι]
Ⲃ — —

The bottom of the stone has not been preserved and it is possible that the missing portion contained the word *apotimema* in some form. Otherwise, this stone probably marked a dowry in real property, evaluated in monetary terms as required by law (see Chap. IV at note 63), not a security transaction. Fine (p. 118, note 20) raises the latter possibility, too, though he includes the text among the new dotal *apotimemata*.

175 B. (Fine 8) Marble, found in the wall of a modern house

[ὅρο]ς
[χ]ωρίο
[π]ροικός.

Corrected Readings

23. (Fine II 21) The text is inscribed in six lines, not five as Peek had given it.

54. (Fine II 20) The creditor's name should be read as Εὐτέλωνι, not Εὐτράωνι.

126. (Fine II 6) Lines 2–3 read ἀποτιμήματ/ος παισίν instead of ἀποτίμημα τ/[οἷ]ς παισίν.

151. (Fine Add. II b, pp. 25-27) J. H. Kent suggests that the disputed archon is Charias, which would date the *horos* in 415/4 or 164/3 B.C. Fine comments that the earlier date is impossible from Ferguson's argument (see Appendix II), that the other "is suspiciously late, but is not impossible."

(written January, 1952)

Notes to Chapter I

1. It is unnecessary to examine the still disputed question whether the *antidosis* ever led to an actual exchange of property or was merely a formal challenge serving to initiate judicial determination of which party should perform the liturgy. For a detailed examination of the source material and conflicting theories, see W. A. Goligher, "Studies in Attic Law II. The Antidosis," *Hermathena* 14 (1907) 481–515. A less complex analysis will be found in L. Beauchet, *Histoire du droit privé de la République athénienne* 3 (4 vols., Paris 1897) 722–37.

2. [Demosthenes], *Against Phainippos* 42.5. In the final clause, I have retained the reading now generally accepted, with Blass' deletion: ὅπως μὴ ὕστερον ἐνταῦθα χρέως γενόμενον [ἐπὶ τῷ χωρίῳ] ἀναφανήσεται. (All translations are my own unless otherwise indicated.)

3. *Ibid.* 42.28.

4. An old, but still useful, survey of Greek boundary practices will be found in Paul Guiraud, *La propriété foncière en Grèce jusqu'à la conquête romaine* (Paris 1893) 181–87. Though this book is still the only complete study of real property in ancient Greece, it has become quite antiquated and its chief weakness, Guiraud's imperfect understanding of juristic matters, stands out more and more sharply with new discoveries and our increasing knowledge of Greek law. Nevertheless, it hardly needs saying that no student of the subject can fail to read the book with profit.

5. DGE 688 A 6–16. On the inscription, see P. Haliste, "Zwei Fragen zum Katasterwesen in Platons 'Gesetzen,'" *Eranos* 48 (1950) 93–106, at pp. 98–106.

6. The *horoi* are cited according to the numbers assigned them in Appendix I. In translations, parentheses indicate words not found in the Greek text that seem necessary for clarity in the English.

7. See also IG II² 1183, line 29.

8. The fact that not one pair of *horoi* marking the same legal transaction has been found is not impressive as evidence one way or the other. The details will be found in H. T. Wade-Gery, "Horos," *Mélanges Gustave Glotz* 2 (2 vols., Paris 1932) 877–87, at pp. 878–80. Wade-Gery proposes a complex etymology leading to a primitive meaning of "watchman" as the explanation of the two uses of *horoi*. The same idea was put forth independently by W. J. Woodhouse, *Solon the Liberator. A Study of the Agrarian Problem in Attika in the Seventh Century* (London 1937) 105, note 5. The possible correctness of this etymology is irrelevant, for it is the approach that is faulty. Whatever the archaic meaning of the word, fourth and third-century Athenians knew it to mean "definition" or "limit," and that is how they used the word in common speech, in

literature, and in the technical language of science, philosophy, and music. The idea of employing the ubiquitous boundary-stones for some additional purpose is such a simple and obvious one that it requires no complicated philological justification.

9. See Erich Ziebarth, "Neue attische Hypothekeninschriften," *Sitz. Berlin* (1897), at p. 670; D. M. Robinson, in *Hesperia* 19 (1950) 23; cf. IG I² 94, lines 23–25, quoted in Chap. VII, note 35; P. Graindor, in MB 25 (1921) 111–12, on IG XII 5,1100.

10. IG II² 2631 and 2632; for the Greek text and a discussion, see Chap. VII, sect. 3. That the use of boundary-stones for public notice was not limited to Athens is easily demonstrated by reference to nos. 155, 179, and 180 in Appendix I; to the inscription from the region of Erythrai in Asia Minor, first published in a posthumous article by Bernard Haussoullier, "Loi inédite d'Erythrées," RP 53 (1928) 191–99, and then re-edited with a considerably different interpretation by W. H. Buckler, "Une borne ionienne," RP, 3 ser., 8 (1934) 293–98; or to the text from Poiessa on the island of Keos, *Syll.* 964A.

11. In a combination such as "bound by markers," it was simple to substitute the generic word "stele" for *horos*: στήλας ὁρισάμενοι, Xeno-phon, *Anabasis* 7.5.13. Cf. the frequent use of στήλη, not ὅρος, for boundary-marker in the mine-lease inscription, IG II² 1582.

12. In the *editio minor* of IG, the *horoi* appear under the general heading, *termini*, subdivided into *termini fundorum publicorum et sacrorum viarum sepulcrorum* and *termini fundorum pignoratorum*, which cannot be translated in any other way than "boundary-stones of public and temple lands, roads, graves" and "boundary-stones of pledged lands." *Terminus* is the precise Latin equivalent of *horos* in the two meanings, boundary and boundary-stone, but it cannot be given the transferred sense of "mark of legal encumbrance." Further, *fundus* is too narrow and *pignus* is wrong on a key point of law. Precise classification there-fore requires that the legal *horoi* be elevated to independent rank (not kept a subdivision of *termini*) under some such rubric as *lapides praediorum hypothecae nomine obligatorum*. (Cf. Gaius' phrasing, *Digest* 22.4.4: *In re hypothecae nomine obligatae*; also 20.1.4; 20.4.11.2; 20.4.12 pr., references I owe to Dr. Adolph Berger.) Kirchner has been followed recently by, among others, Werner Peek, editor of the inscriptions in vol. 3 of *Kerameikos: Ergebnisse der Ausgrabungen* (Berlin 1941). Peek headed this particular section *Horos-Steine* and did not even bother to introduce any subheadings. Other examples of the confusion are given in Chap. II, note 49. The distinction was properly made by Th. Thal-heim, "Ὅροι," PWRE 8 (1913) 2414–16, in an article otherwise not always reliable. The late Greek and Byzantine lexicographers, who were perfectly familiar with boundary-stones, usually limited their definitions to the long obsolete legal-encumbrance type. The *Etymologi-cum Magnum* had it quite right, however: ὅρος σημαίνει δύο· τὰ ὅρια καὶ τῆς χώρας τὰ τέλη, καὶ σανίδιον τὸ ἐπιτεθέμενον ταῖς οἰκίαις καὶ τοῖς χωρίοις ἐγκαταπηγνύμενον τοῖς ἐνεχυριαζομένοις πρὸς ἃ ὀφείλουσιν οἱ δεσπόται.

13. The Liddell-and-Scott Lexicon also treats boundary-stones and legal *horoi* as subdivisions in the same general category. For the latter we read: *"pillar* (whether inscribed or not, cf. Harp.) *set up on mortgaged property*, to serve as a bond or register of the debt.*"* The available evidence indicates that these *horoi*, unlike the boundary-stones, were always inscribed; in fact, their very reason for existence would have been nullified by the absence of an inscription. The editors of Liddell-and-Scott have apparently used a corrupt reading in the Harpocration manuscripts, properly rejected by Dindorf in favor of the reading found in the Epitome and in Suidas. The latter runs as follows: ὅρος· οὕτως ἐκάλουν οἱ Ἀττικοὶ τὰ ἐπόντα ταῖς ὑποκειμέναις οἰκίαις καὶ χωρίοις γράμματα, ἃ ἐδήλουν (or δηλοῦντα) ὅτι ὑπόκεινται δανειστῇ. (Cf. *Lexeis rhetorikai, Anecdota Bekker* I 285.12, on which see Chap. II, note 27, and the references to ἄστικτον χωρίον, Chap. II, note 42.) The corruption came with the words χωρίοις γράμματα, which were replaced by χωρὶς γράμμα in A, χωρὶς γραμμάτων in BC, and χωρὶς γράμματος in the Aldine. Confirmation of the correct reading comes from another passage in Harpocration: ἄστικτον χωρίον· τὸ μὴ ὑποκείμενον δανειστῇ· ὅταν γὰρ ὑποκέηται, εἴωθεν ὁ δανείσας αὐτὸ τοῦτο δηλοῦν διὰ γραμμάτων ἐπόντων τῷ χωρίῳ. τὸ δ'αὐτὸ καὶ ἐπ' οἰκίας γίνεται.

14. The complete list follows:

Athens — IG II² 2642–2770; *Athen. Mitt.* 59 (1934) 42, no. 4; Δελτ. 11 (1927/8) παρ. 51, no. 163; 14 (1931/2) παρ. 31, no. 2; παρ. 33, no. 4; Ἑλληνικά 8 (1935) 223, no. 3; *Hesperia* 3 (1934) 65, nos. 57–8; 7 (1938) 93, no. 14; 10 (1941) nos. 14, 16–18; 13 (1944) 19; 19 (1950) 23; Supp. 7 (1943) nos. 1–2; *Kerameikos* 19–21; AJP 69 (1948) 201–4, nos. 1–3; *Polemon* 3 (1947/8) 133, no. 10.

Amorgos — IG XII 7,55–60, 412; XII Supp. 331.

Lemnos — IG XII 8,18–22 (no. 18 corrected in IG XII Supp.); *Annuario* 15/16 (1932/3, publ. 1942) 305–9, nos. 11–13.

Naxos — SEG II 500; IG XII Supp. 194–95.

Skyros — IG XII Supp. 526.

Syros — IG XII 5,707, 1105.

Actually, the stones from Syros are not *horoi* at all. Some 30 *horoi* found in the Agora have not yet been published and the texts were not available to me. [See Appendix III.]

Six of the stones contain two distinct texts each. They will be treated as if each text were entirely independent and a separate number has been assigned to each; see Chap. II, end of sect. 2.

The only complete collection ever assembled (text, translation, and commentary) is in I J I viii. That collection included 70 texts, of which no. 66 has, upon later re-examination of the stone, proved to be no *horos* at all (IG XII 5,50), and their nos. 16, 40, 60, 67, and 68 are being eliminated from the present discussion (see the following footnote). That leaves 64 texts, compared with the 154 that constitute our present base. Good selections will be found in *Syll.* and M, nos. 1168–98, 1200 and 1364–82, 1738–41, respectively.

15. The twenty-eight stones eliminated from general consideration are nos. 112–115, 157–180. The texts are reproduced in Appendix I and

they have been brought into the discussion whenever necessary. All statistics are calculated on the basis of 154 *horoi*, however, to the exclusion of this group of twenty-eight.

16. See note 13 above.

17. The close link between Athenian law and Amorgian has been frequently noted ever since the discovery of a group of inscriptions, IG XII 7,66–70, dealing with money borrowed by the *polis* of Arkesine on Amorgos about 300 B.C. (see further Chap. VII, sect. 2), for the contractual provisions are nearly identical with those of Athenian bottomry contracts, especially the agreement in [Demosthenes], *Against Lakritos* (no. 35). Students have seen in this parallel strong proof of the existence, by the end of the fourth century B.C., of a more or less universal commercial law in the Greek world. Thus, Walter Ruppel, "Zur Verfassung und Verwaltung der amorginischen Städte," *Klio* 21 (1927) 313–39, writes at p. 323, note 2: "*Ich gehe auch nicht näher auf die Klauseln der oft behandelten Schuldverträge ein, weil es sich bei ihnen um Anwendung gemeingriechischer Rechtsgepflogenheiten in internationalen Verkehr handelt, nicht um Gesetzesrecht der amorginischen Poleis.*" But the *horoi* weaken the evidentiary value of the loan inscriptions. If Amorgos took over the peculiarly Athenian use of *horoi*, even though that practice did not become general among the Greeks, then it is possible that the provisions of the loan agreements may represent a similar borrowing from Athens, equally limited in the extent of its spread. For the prevailing view see, for example, L. Goldschmidt, "Inhaber-, Order- und exekutorische Urkunden im classischen Alterthum," *ZSS* 10 (1889) 352–96, at pp. 360–79; Ludwig Mitteis, *Reichsrecht und Volksrecht* (Leipzig 1891) 177–79, 404–9.

18. For a brief indication of Athenian influence on Priene, see F. Hiller von Gaertringen, *Inschriften von Priene* (Berlin 1906) x, xiii–xiv. Egon Weiss, *Pfandrechtliche Untersuchungen* I (2 vols., Weimar 1909–10) 32–33, cites no. 42 of the Priene inscriptions as proof of the low value of *horoi* as evidence of hypothecation, but the inscription refers to boundary-stones, not hypothecation-stones.

19. The dating question has been very much complicated by an argument put forth by W. S. Ferguson, "The Laws of Demetrius of Phalerum and Their Guardians," *Klio* 11 (1911) 265–76, and reaffirmed by Sterling Dow and A. H. Travis, "Demetrios of Phaleron and His Lawgiving," *Hesperia* 12 (1943) 144–65. Their thesis is examined in Appendix II.

20. In his introductory note to the *Termini* in IG I², Hiller von Gaertringen indicates the impossibility of dating the earlier *horoi* precisely, hence the decision to publish them all in the post-fifth-century volumes. Too much has been made of the fact that the initial aspirate letter *h* appears on fourth-century *horoi*, even after the letter had been dropped by the official spelling reform of 405/4 B.C. Actually it is found only on nos. 51 and 79, probably on no. 49, and on no. 176, which is not a *horos* of the legal type (see further Chap. VI, note 23).

The *h* has also been restored in no. 103, a Lemnian stone, because of the early fifth-century date assigned to it by the editor, and in no. 82A. Altogether they make up a very small number when compared with the boundary-stones, some 25 per cent of which retained the *h* after the date of the spelling reform, and with the much more numerous eccentricities in grammar and orthography. In no. 14, for example, all three creditors are from the deme Halai and the demotic is spelled three different ways. The explanation for the persistence of the aspirate is probably to be found in the fact that the *horoi* were private "documents," often engraved by untutored people, and not in "conservative formalism" as Wade-Gery, "Horos" 877, note 2, would have it. Cf. the inconsistency in the use of the *h* in vase inscriptions, discussed by Paul Kretschmer, *Die griechischen Vaseninschriften ihrer Sprache nach untersucht* (Gütersloh 1894) 155–61, or the orthographic irregularities in both public and private documents of the fifth century B.C. discussed by W. S. Ferguson, *The Treasurers of Athena* (Cambridge, Mass., 1932) 175–78.

21. Isaeus, *On the Estate of Philoktemon* 6.36. This is the sole reference to *horoi* in the extant works of Isaeus. I am unable to agree with the argument of Wade-Gery, "Horos" 883, note 1, that the passage does not suggest that the procedure was either rare or new at the time. All that Isaeus says about *horoi* is καὶ ὅροι τεθεῖεν. The full passage is about an attempted fraud that is now quite incomprehensible; see William Wyse, *The Speeches of Isaeus* (Cambridge, Eng., 1904) 525. Such a text can hardly be adduced as evidence for the antiquity or novelty of an institution.

22. The reference appears in Harpocration, s.v. ἀστικτον χωρίον, who uses the word *grammata*, not *horos*. The context (given in note 13 above) makes it more than probable that the two words were here conceived as synonyms.

23. Solon, frag. 36, quoted in Aristotle, *Constitution of the Athenians* 12.4. I shall deal with the Solonic *horoi* in a separate article. For a full discussion of the older literature, see W. Vollgraff, "De origine hypothecae in iure attico," *Mnemosyne* n.s. 50 (1922) 213–23. Recently, Woodhouse, *Solon*, chaps. X and XI, has revived an old theory that the Solonic *horoi* marked encumbrance of the land by *prasis epi lysei*, a view enthusiastically supported by N. Lewis, "Solon's Agrarian Legislation," AJP 62 (1941) 144–56, and by Kurt von Fritz, "The Meaning of ʿΕΚΤΗΜΟΡΟΣ," AJP 61 (1940) 54–61, "Once More the ʿΕΚΤΗΜΟΡΟΙ," AJP 64 (1943) 24–43.

24. Note should be taken that *Digest* 43.24.22.2 is not a reference to *horoi*, as some scholars have thought; see Weiss, *Untersuchungen* I 64–65.

25. A month name also appears in one of the texts eliminated from discussion, no. 173. Two *horoi* from Lemnos, nos. 104 and 107, specify the archonship of Nikodoros and virtually all commentators since C. Fredrich, the original editor, have taken it for granted that the reference is

to the Athenian Nikodoros, archon in 314/3 B.C. Mario Segre has properly rejected the assumption and included Nikodoros among the small number of Lemnian archons whose names are known, along with Archias of no. 108 and Menaichmos of no. 10. None of the Lemnian archons can be assigned to a specific year.

26. The two fifth-century stones are no. 103, dated by its editor as probably before 480 B.C., and no. 105, of the end of the century. Mario Segre's knowledge of Lemnian stones is not to be taken lightly, but it should be noted that the reading and suggested dating of the earlier of the two are both based on a drawing, not on the stone or even a squeeze. The stone was found in many little fragments by G. Ricci, who made the reconstruction and drawing. Segre did not see the stone. It seems advisable to suspend judgment and not lean too heavily on this one text, which, as reconstructed, documents the existence of real security by *prasis epi lysei* a century earlier than any other known source. The presence of names with Athenian demotics also supports the view of Segre and others that there was an Athenian cleruchy on the island before 446 B.C.

The Lemnian *horoi* and their dating will have to be restudied together with the very fragmentary inscription, IG II² 30, an Athenian decree of 386/5 B.C. regarding the cleruchic land in Lemnos. S. Luria has proposed restorations which would indicate a prohibition against the alienation, hypothecation, or lease of this land (lines b 4,7). His restorations are given, with bibliography, in SEG III 73; see also Luria, "Bemerkungen zu Aristot. AΘHN. ΠOΛIT. 1–16," *Raccolta di scritti in onore di Giacomo Lumbroso* (Milan 1925) 305–15, at pp. 311–14. (On IG I² 1, which Luria links with IG II² 30, see the new text and recent bibliography in SEG X 1.)

27. Thus, U. E. Paoli, "La 'datio in solutum' nel diritto attico," SIFC, n.s., 10 (1933) 181–212, at pp. 206–9, somewhat contemptuously replied to LaPira's criticism that he had failed, in a volume under review, to study the *horoi* adequately, by insisting on their paucity of content. Even the editors of IJ, who collected the *horoi* with care, tend in their commentary to fall back on the traditional approach of concentrating on a select few for analysis. They are followed by E. Caillemer, "Horos," *Dar.-Saglio* III, 1 (1899) 264–67. The chapter entitled "Die Horoi" in H. F. Hitzig, *Das griechische Pfandrecht* (Munich 1895) 67–72, was too brief and sketchy even when written; subsequent finds have rendered much of it out-of-date. A parallel chapter (pp. 206–10) concludes the section on Greek law in D. P. Pappulias, Ἡ ἐμπράγματος ἀσφάλεια κατὰ τὸ ἑλληνικὸν καὶ τὸ ῥωμαϊκὸν δίκαιον (only vol. 1 published, Leipzig 1909), but it is much sketchier than Hitzig's and ends on a note of complete confusion with boundary-stones.

28. A careful reading of Hitzig, *Pfandrecht*, suggests that he was constantly troubled by the failure of the source material to fit into neat patterns. Though Hitzig drew the patterns nevertheless, he was continually compelled to qualify and to note the disappearance of rigid lines of demarcation; see especially pp. 7–13, 88–92. Published in 1895,

his book laid the foundation for the modern study of Greek hypothecation. Subsequent studies have tended to move away from Hitzig's
doubts and cautions, with the notable exceptions of Ernst Rabel, *Die
Verfügungsbeschränkungen des Verpfänders* (Leipzig 1909), and A.
Manigk, "Hyperocha," PWRE 9 (1916) 292–321, towards greater and
greater rigidity and dogmatism; see the remarks by Manigk, *ibid.*
307–8.

A kind of climax has been reached with the publication of U. E.
Paoli, "Ipoteca e ἀποτίμημα nel diritto attico," *Studi di diritto attico*
(Florence 1930) 141–94, with its intricate legal constructs, including
the introduction of hypothetical and fictitious stages in the history of
the institutions in order to overcome the absence of essential documentation. This work must be read together with two strongly critical
reviews, by V. Arangio-Ruiz in AG 107 (1932) 246–51 and by Giorgio
LaPira in BIDR 41 (1933) 305–320, and with Paoli's replies to the
criticism (in which he held his ground except for minor concessions on
details), "Sul diritto pignoratizio attico," AG 108 (1932) 161–78, and
"Datio in solutum." The objections raised by Arangio-Ruiz and LaPira
have apparently not struck home, for, beginning with a wholly favor-
able review by Egon Weiss in ZSS 52 (1932) 443–45, students have
been turning to Paoli's monograph more and more frequently as the
standard reference on the subject.

It is regrettable that the editors of PWRE chose to publish a number
of articles on individual Greek words rather than one general discussion of the Greek law and practice of security. As a result, all that
one can find on the subject in PWRE is an assortment of snippets; and
it must be said, snippets of poor quality, *e.g.*, Th. Thalheim's article,
"Ὑποθήκη," 9 (1916) 412–14. E. Ziebarth's article, "Pfandrecht,"
Supp. 7 (1940) 981–83, is merely an assemblage of unrelated sentences
and citations, chiefly about Hellenistic law.

29. See, for example, Arthur Nussbaum, *Lehrbuch des deutschen Hypothekenwesens nebst einer Einführung in das allgemeine Grundbuchrecht*
(2 ed., Tübingen 1921) 45–53; Theodor Rohlfing, "Hypothek," *Rechtsvergleichendes HWB* 4 (1933) 267–320, at pp. 267–73. The link in the
title of Nussbaum's book between the hypothec and the *Grundbuch* is
noteworthy, for it lays bare a difference between the ancient Greek and
the modern continental institution of a fundamental, qualitative character. (In the present volume, "real security" means "security in the
form of real property" and nothing more; no suggestion of real rights,
rights *in rem*, is intended or in any way to be implied.)

30. For *apotimao* and *piprasko epi lysei* I have always written "put up as
security," followed by the Greek equivalent in parenthesis. See Chaps.
III and IV for a detailed discussion of the language of hypothecation
and for the reasons underlying the choice of English words and phrases.

31. That no comparative study has been made of the Anglo-American
mortgage and Greek security need hardly be said. For an appreciation
of the uniqueness of the mortgage, rooted as it was in feudal property
relations and transformed slowly and tortuously by centuries of activ-

ity in the Courts of Chancery, see R. W. Turner, *The Equity of Redemption: Its Nature, History and Connection with Equitable Estates Generally* (Cambridge, Eng., 1931), or the succinct and rather tart account in F. W. Maitland, *Equity* (rev. ed. by John Brunyate, Cambridge, Eng., 1947) 179–205. For the difference between the mortgage and Roman or modern continental practices, see H. D. Hazeltine's prefatory essay to the Turner volume, entitled "The Roman *Fiducia cum creditore* and the English Mortgage"; W. W. Buckland and A. D. McNair, *Roman Law & Common Law: A Comparison in Outline* (Cambridge, Eng., 1936) 239–49; Rohlfing, "Hypothek" 267–68. On the continental mortgage during the Middle Ages, see, *e.g.*, H. Van Werveke, "Le mort-gage et son role économique en Flandre et en Lotharingie," RB 8 (1929) 53–91.

Notes to Chapter II

1. This argument, based on the pattern of the texts, has been generally accepted since Hitzig, *Pfandrecht*; see especially his pp. 9–11. It has recently been challenged by Paoli, "Ipoteca," whose conception of Greek hypothecation rests basically on the belief that transfer of possession is the key. To maintain that position, Paoli must introduce the notions of "symbolic" and "legal" possession, as distinct from physical, *de facto* possession (pp. 164–65, 187–94, and again "Datio in solutum" 187–91). It is true that the idea of possession has been complicated — more properly, confused — by such conceptions in modern law; see, for example, Frederick Pollock and R. S. Wright, *An Essay on Possession in the Common Law* (Oxford 1888); Albert Kocourek, *Jural Relations* (2 ed., Indianapolis 1928) Chap. XX; briefly Rupert Cross, "Larceny de Lege Lata," LQR 66 (1950) 496–510. But such subtleties were unknown to the Athenians, to whom possession meant occupation, detention, precisely as the word is understood by any layman today. In reply to Paoli, it is sufficient to refer to the effective criticisms by Arangio-Ruiz and LaPira cited in Chap. I, note 28. Some details of Paoli's analysis will be taken up in the course of the present chapter. A substantial portion of Paoli's evidence comes from bottomry cases. As indicated briefly in Chap. V, at notes 17–19, bottomry is economically and juristically distinct from land-secured credit transactions and should not be introduced into an analysis of the nature of real security.

2. Hence the proposed restoration in *horos* no. 39, which would introduce the debtor's name, is unacceptable. The creditor's name is omitted often enough to make a mockery of Paoli's "symbolic possession" (see the previous note), for of what value could such a symbol be when it does not even indicate whose it is?

3. This will be apparent from the discussion of the *apotimema* in Chap. IV. In his review of Paoli's work, LaPira (p. 308) correctly noted that the Paoli thesis falls on this point.

4. Fritz Pringsheim, *The Greek Law of Sale* (Weimar 1950) 105, cites one of the Amorgian *horoi*, no. 102, as the first of six available examples of Type II in his formal classification of Greek sale contracts. But a *horos* cannot be evidence of the *form* of the agreement itself. Nor can no. 102 be considered in isolation from all the others, as Pringsheim does. He comments further: "This is not a simple contract of sale, but a mortgage, an ὠνή ἐπί λύσει [on this discarded term, revived by Pringsheim, see Chap. III, note 17], with the usual clauses. Since the mortgagee as the creditor neither pays a price nor takes over any duties a declaration by the debtor, the vendor, is sufficient." Obviously the creditor does pay a price — the loan — and he does take on the duty of releasing the property if the debtor returns the money. From his reasoning, Pringsheim would be unable to explain the fact that the common practice was to name the creditor on the *horoi*, not the debtor (a fact which he apparently ignores). He uses the same reasoning to incorporate the Delphic manumission inscriptions in Type II, and then contradicts himself on p. 108 to allow for those manumission texts that use Type III.

5. [Demosthenes], *Against Phainippos* 42.5,28; see above, pp. 3–4. Paoli, "Ipoteca," does not mention the Phainippos oration until almost the end of his monograph (p. 190) and does not return to it in either of his two follow-up articles. By that point, he has proved to his own satisfaction that *horoi* were affixed after the creditor took possession and he dismisses the counter-evidence of this oration as merely a sign that "symbolic" possession was sufficient in some instances.

6. Demosthenes, *Against Spudias* 41.5–6; see the analysis in Chap. IV, sect. 2. This oration is explained away by Paoli, "Datio in solutum" 187–91, as "legal" possession, not actual.

7. Demosthenes, *Against Aphobos II* 28.17–18 (the 2,000-drachma figure is not given here but in *Against Meidias* 21.78–80). It is noteworthy that though Demosthenes retains possession, he says τὰ ὑποκείμενα ... τῶν ὑποθεμένων ἐστίν. The language used is an excellent illustration of the danger of trying to determine the precise legal (and often even the factual) situation from an author's choice of such words as "to be" or "to have"; see further immediately below. This passage also has interest as the main evidence in Pappulias' unsuccessful attempt, 'Ασφάλεια 81, to disprove the traditional view that in case of default the creditor had a right to seize the whole of the hypothecated property, not merely enough to satisfy his monetary claim. For the correct interpretation of the text and a bibliography, see Paoli, "Ipoteca" 160–61.

8. [Demosthenes], *Against Polykles* 50.13,61; cf. *Against Nikostratos* 53.13. When we read in Xenophon, *Symposium* 4.31, τὰ ἔγγαια οὐ καρποῦμαι, we have no way of determining, without further informa-

tion, the reason for the failure to obtain "the fruits." Yet Paoli, "Diritto pignoratizio" 171, has no hesitation in citing the passage as further proof of his theory that possession went to the creditor in hypothecation.

9. [Demosthenes], *Against Timotheos* 49.12.

10. In none of the examples given is a *prasis epi lysei* involved, insofar as we can tell. The Pantainetos case, however, is clear proof that the owner retained possession in that type of security transaction; see Chap. III, sect. 2. *Horos* no. 102, one of the exceptions noted in the opening of this chapter, offers an exact parallel. See also IG II² 1183, lines 28–30, quoted in Chap. VII, at note 33, though that inscription makes no reference to *prasis epi lysei*. In Demosthenes' dispute with Onetor we do seem to find the argument that his remaining in possession is proof that the owner had not hypothecated the property. For an alternative interpretation, see the discussion of the case in Chap. IV, sect. 2.

11. The Greek is ὥστε (or ἐφ᾽ ὧιτε) ἔχειν καὶ κρατεῖν. (On the interchangeability of ὥστε and ἐφ᾽ ὧιτε, see Michel Lejeune, *Observations sur la langue des actes d'affranchissement delphiques* [diss. Paris 1939] Chap. II.) It is noteworthy that in no. 1 the creditor is not named but referred to as ὁ θέμενος, in no. 2 as ὁ ὑποθέμενος, whereas in no. 10 he is named but not labeled. I intend to publish a detailed analysis of the phrase, ἔχειν καὶ κρατεῖν, which will show why I have selected the somewhat equivocal translation, "to have and to have power," rather than the customary "to have (possess) and to own." That κρατεῖν does not necessarily mean "to own" is clear from such passages as Herodotus 2.136; Isaeus, *On the Estate of Kiron* 8.2; [Demosthenes,] *Against Lakritos* 35.25, *Against Timotheos* 49.11; Xenophon, *Memorabilia* 2.7.2; Polybius 12.16.4. Note Alkiphron, *Letters* 1.16: οὐκ ᾔτησά σε ἃ ἔχεις, ἀλλ᾽ ἃ μὴ ἔχεις. ἐπεὶ δὲ οὐ βούλει ἃ μὴ ἔχεις ἕτερον ἔχειν, ἔχε ἃ μὴ ἔχεις. The full significance of this letter, quoted here in full, is clear from the two which precede it.

12. See Emil Szanto, "Hypothek und Scheinkauf im griechischen Rechte," WS 9 (1887) 272–96, as republished in his *Ausgewählte Abhandlungen* (Tübingen 1906) 74–92, at p. 78. Szanto's point that these were contractual provisions, not statutory, seems to have been ignored in the more recent literature as various attempts have been made to fit the three *horoi* into a pattern that would permit no exceptions. A favorite interpretation has been that the creditor is to "have and have power" only in case of default, but that such a statement would be absurdly superfluous is shown by Paoli, "Ipoteca" 153–54. Paoli's critics have here fallen into his error of trying to force every single text to fit an absolutely unbending rule, instead of recognizing that the very fact and character of the exception support their critique of his over-all analysis. With these three stones, Paoli links no. 102, which reveals how the debtor had originally acquired each of the three units being put up as security (*prasis epi lysei*). One unit, says the stone, he had

as creditor in hypothecation (ἃ ἔχει θέμενος) and Paoli takes that to mean he had possession while the debt was still in force. Paoli's interpretation is possible (cf. Demosthenes, *Against Aphobos I* 27.24–29, involving slaves), but it is more likely that there had been default and transfer of ownership. The phraseology is very cryptic, to be sure, but cf. IG II² 43, lines 35–42, on which see briefly Chap. VI, note 5.

The editors of I J introduce the term *antichresis* for these few cases in which possession goes to the creditor, and they have been followed by Kirchner in IG II². *Antichresis* is a Greek word known only from one papyrus and from Roman juristic literature to describe a transaction in which the creditor obtains the use and fruits of the hypothecated property in lieu of interest; see Raphael Taubenschlag, *The Law of Greco-Roman Egypt in the Light of the Papyri, 332 B.C.–640 A.D.* I (2 vols., New York and Warsaw, 1944–49) 216–20. The objection to its application to the Greek world of pre-Roman times is twofold. First, the word is not known in any source of this period. Guiraud, *Propriété foncière* 278, cites Aristotle, *Nicomachean Ethics* 5.2.13, 1131a4, but that is a false reference. In enumerating voluntary transactions, Aristotle distinguished between *daneismos* and *chresis*, that is, between loans for profit and loans for use, more precisely, between loans with and loans without interest. In neither instance does the lender receive the use of the pledged property in return for his money. The second objection is that there is no solid evidence in the texts to show that the practice of giving the creditor the use of realty in place of interest was at all current. That may have been the situation with the slaves Demosthenes' father had taken over, perhaps also in the extremely difficult passage in Isaeus, *On the Estate of Philoktemon* 6.33, but these are isolated and unclear cases. R. Dareste, in the notes accompanying his translation of the private orations of Demosthenes (2 vols., Paris 1875), sees *antichresis* in *Against Onetor I* 30.26–30, and *Against Spudias* 41.3–6 (followed here by Walter Erdmann, *Die Ehe im alten Griechenland* [*Münchener Beiträge* 20 (Munich 1934)] 315–16), but his view rests on a clear misinterpretation of both orations. Weiß, *Untersuchungen* I 22, speaks of an "*antichretische Pfand*," but it is significant that he can cite no non-papyrological source apart from [Lysias], *Against the Co-Associates* 8.10, on which see Chap. III, note 50, and Chap. VII, note 56.

13. Isocrates, *Against Euthynus* 21.2. In the Guillaume Budé ed., vol. 1 (Paris 1928), G. Mathieu and E. Brémond translate ὑπέθηκε as "*vendit à réméré*" (the standard French rendition for *prasis epi lysei*). They offer no comment but are apparently operating under an old misconception that transfer of possession was characteristic of *prasis epi lysei* and not of *hypotheke*. E. F. Bruck, *Die Schenkung auf den Todesfall im griechischen und römischen Recht* [only vol. 1 published, *Studien zur Erläuterung des bürgerlichen Rechts* 31 (Breslau 1909)] 76–89, examines in detail eight cases from the fifth and fourth centuries B.C. of gifts made in the event of death (summarized pp. 89–91), several of which were motivated by the presence of a threat and accompanied by the condition that, should the giver survive the threat, the gift is

withdrawn. The striking point for our purpose is that in some there was immediate transfer of possession, in others not. Nikias chose a fictitious hypothecation as an alternative way of accomplishing the same end, namely, to prevent his property from falling into the hands of his enemies if he were killed.

14. See Hazeltine, *"Fiducia* and Mortgage" lxi–lxii. For the legal complications that followed the shift from possession by the creditor to possession by the debtor in Stuart England, see Turner, *Equity of Redemption,* Chap. V. On some modern aspects of the general problem, see Theodor Rohlfing, "Antichrese," *Rechtsvergleichendes HWB* 2 (1929) 232–35.

15. See Chap. VI, sect. 2. Hazeltine, *ibid.,* writes: "The growth of the equity of redemption as an estate meant that the security-idea was fully victorious over the earlier idea of strict legal forfeiture of the *res* for non-payment at a set day; while the retention of possession by the debtor, on principles of hypothecation, further accentuated the conception of security for debt." In ancient Athens, however, retention of possession by the debtor existed along with the forfeiture (see Chap. VIII), a neat illustration of the need for a consideration of Greek law in order to check generalizations that seem valid when, as is customary, comparative studies are limited to Roman, Germanic, and English jurisprudence.

16. On the role of the neighbors, see Josef Partsch, "Die griechische Publizität der Grundstücksverträge im Ptolemaërrechte," *Festschrift für Otto Lenel* (Leipzig 1923) 77–203, at pp. 88–98 (the first part of this monograph deals largely with the Greek cities, despite the title); Egon Weiss, *Griechisches Privatrecht* (only vol. 1 published, Leipzig 1923) 246–52; cf. the non-legal material in L. Radermacher, "Beiträge zur Volkskunde aus dem Gebiet der Antike," *Sitz. Vienna* 187,3 (1918), at pp. 3–17. For an introduction to modern forms of public notice (with excellent bibliographies), see Percy Bordwell, "Land Transfer," EnSS 9 (1933) 127–31; Caesar Predari, "Grundbuch" and "Kataster," *Rechtsvergleichendes HWB* 3 (1931) 786–807 and 4 (1933) 707–9, respectively. The German *Grundbuch* marks the furthest development of such requirements for all transactions affecting realty.

17. The description in Aristotle, *Constitution of the Athenians* 47.2–48.2 (47.2 corrected by A. Rehm, in *Philologus* 86 [1931] 118–19) of the way records were kept by the *poletai* and *apodektai* is most revealing. In the first place, the whole procedure was designed to fulfill a police function; as soon as payments were made, records were erased. Secondly, Aristotle devotes a relatively inordinate amount of space to describing a method of recording accounts receivable that is taken for granted by every young file clerk today. See further *ibid.* 53.4–7; [Demosthenes], *Against Theokrines* 58.50.

18. One need only read [Demosthenes], *Against Eubulides* (orat. 57), especially §§ 26 and 60, or Demosthenes, *Against Boiotos I* (orat. 39), to appreciate the low level of deme record-keeping. The best account

of the work of the demarch, the responsible official in the deme, remains B. Haussoullier, *La vie municipale en Attique* [*Bibl. Éc. fr.* 38 (Paris 1884)] Chap. III, though it requires considerable correction. See also his excellent summary and discussion of the Eubulides case on pp. 38–51. On the lists of citizens, see Weiss, *Privatrecht* 369–83, and the additional material in J. J. E. Hondius, "A New Inscription of the Deme Halimous," BSA 24 (1919/21) 151–60 (the inscription is republished with one important correction as SEG II 7), and "Quid sit τὸ κοινὸν γραμματεῖον," *Mnemosyne* 50 (1922) 87–90.

19. The existence of an Athenian land register or cadaster is frequently assumed, for example by A. M. Andreades, *A History of Greek Public Finance*, trans. by C. N. Brown (only vol. 1 published, Cambridge, Mass., 1933) 341, on the sole basis of Harpocration, δήμαρχος:...τὰς ἀπογραφὰς ἐποιοῦντο τῶν ἐν ἑκάστῳ δήμῳ χωρίων. But *apographe* in Attic juridical parlance most often means "denunciation" and it is with the *apographe*-procedure that this function of the demarch is linked, not with land or assessment lists; see the evidence in J. H. Lipsius, *Das attische Recht und Rechtsverfahren* 2 (3 vols, Leipzig 1905–15) 302, note 12. Haussoullier, *Vie municipale* 110–14, also misinterprets the passage to mean a property record and then writes several pages of admitted guesswork and supposition, confirmatory evidence being wholly absent. Even the more cautious formulation of Guiraud, *Propriété foncière* 299 (followed by Beauchet, *Droit* III 75–76, and then largely contradicted III 337–42), "*Les textes grecs font de fréquentes allusions sinon à des cadastres proprement dits, du moins à des espèces de livres fonciers,*" cannot be supported by the sources. In his ensuing discussion, Guiraud is able to cite very few texts (not "*fréquentes allusions*"), not one of them Athenian. The complete absence of cadasters, in the technical sense of land registers kept for taxation or other public purposes, is indicated for the Greek city-states even in Hellenistic times, by Egon Weiss, "Kataster," PWRE 10 (1919) 2487–93, at cols. 2487–9, and by André Déléage, "Les cadastres antiques jusqu'à Dioclétien," *Études de papyrologie* 2 (1934) 73–228, at pp. 79–81.

20. Henri Francotte, *Les finances des cités grecques* (Paris 1909) 37–40, though conceding Lipsius' point that the Harpocration passage quóted in the previous note stems from a confusion in terminology, nevertheless finds evidence of a cadaster in the fact that some of the agreements whereby demes leased land to private individuals specified who was to pay the *eisphora* on the land, and sometimes even on what evaluation (*timema*). (These agreements are summarized in another context in Chap. VII, middle of sect. 2.) But his logic is faulty, for these clauses indicate not that there was an assessment-list but, quite the contrary, that there was none and that the deme-landlord wished to take no risk that the tenant change the value the deme had placed on the holding. Georg Busolt, *Griechische Staatskunde* 2 (3 ed., 2 vols., second vol. revised by Heinrich Swoboda, Munich 1920–26) 968, note 2, makes the same argument, without referring to Francotte. Busolt adds several references to a land register in Plato, *Laws*, but Plato's proposal

for recording the landholdings in his ideal state obviously proves
nothing about Athenian practice; the argument to the contrary by
Josef Bisinger, *Der Agrarstaat in Platons Gesetzen* [*Klio*, Beiheft 17
(1925)] 17–18, rests on a clear misunderstanding of the *timema*.

21. In this context, cf. the remarks of Kurt Latte, *Heiliges Recht* (Tübingen 1920) 27–28, on the use of the oath in the *antidosis*; see also his
pp. 96–99.

22. [Demosthenes], *Against Polykles* 50.8. On "visible" property, see
further Chap. V, sect. 1. Four additional texts revealing the absence of
land registers by their silence in the matter may be noted. There is no
reference to a cadaster in [Demosthenes], *Against Kallikles* (orat. 55),
in which the issue was a dispute over a watercourse between owners of
adjoining properties. In [Demosthenes], *Against Euergos and Mnesibulos* 47.34, the speaker reports how, in order to determine whether a
family estate had been divided or not, information he needed to take
proper legal action, he made personal inquiry through one of the
members of the family; cf. *Against Boiotos II* 40.58–59. The defendant
in Lysias, *On the Sacred Olive-Tree* (orat. 7, *c*. 395 B.C.), charged with
the crime of having uprooted one of the publicly owned olive trees (of
which there were many located on privately owned land) on his farm,
replies that there were no "sacred" trees on his estate and buttresses
his contention by the deposition of witnesses and the evidence, both
positive and negative, of his neighbors; see especially §§ 9–11, 18.

23. Theophrastus, *Laws* (frag. 97 Wimmer), quoted in Stobaeus, *Flori-
legium* 44.22 (sections 1–4 deal with public notice). The most recent
edition, excellently annotated, is in V. Arangio-Ruiz and A. Olivieri,
Inscriptiones Graecae Siciliae et infimae Italiae ad ius pertinentes
(Milan 1925) 240–49. Translations are available in French in R. Dareste,
La science du droit en Grèce (Paris 1893) 305–12, and in German in
K. F. Hermann, *Lehrbuch der griechischen Rechtsalterthümer*, 4 ed. by
Th. Thalheim (Freiburg and Tübingen 1895) 146–52. The most recent
discussion is Pringsheim, *Sale* 134–42, primarily concerned with §§ 4
and 7. On the correct title of the work, see H. Bloch, "Studies in
Historical Literature of the Fourth Century B.C. III. Theophrastus'
Nomoi and Aristotle," *Harvard Studies in Classical Philology*, Supp. 1,
Studies Presented to William Scott Ferguson (Cambridge, Mass., 1940)
355–76, at p. 357, note 4.

24. *Ibid.* § 1. The passage also mentions the 1 per cent payment to the
city: καὶ τὸν πριάμενον ἑκατοστὴν τιθέναι τῆς τιμῆς . . . καὶ ὁ δικαίως ἐωνημένος
φανερὸς ᾖ τῷ τέλει. The translation and interpretation of the latter are
widely disputed, specifically as to whether the *hekatoste* was necessary
for the legal validation of the sale; for the various views, see F. von
Woess, *Untersuchungen über das Urkundenwesen und den Publizitäts-
schutz im römischen Ägypten* [*Münchener Beiträge* 6 (1924)] 14, note 3,
and the review by Ernst Rabel in ZSS 45 (1925) 521. The primitive
character of the whole requirement has troubled legal historians no
end, for, on the surface, little protection is afforded third parties

against fraud; see, for example, Walter Schwahn, "Der Hauskauf in Athen," *Hermes* 69 (1934) 119–20; or Georg Simonetos, "Das Verhältnis von Kauf und Übereignung im altgriechischen Recht," *Festschrift Paul Koschaker* 3 (3 vols., Weimar 1939) 172–98, at pp. 188–89. Supporting evidence is lacking one way or another. Until further proof is available, I am loath to reject the testimony of Theophrastus simply in order to bring Athenian practice to a level more consonant with the sentiments of modern jurists.

When P. Vogt, "Hypereides' erste Rede gegen Athenogenes," WS 16 (1894) 169–217, at pp. 212–13, argues that the absence of a 60-day delay in the slave sale in that case throws doubt on the accuracy of Theophrastus, he has either overlooked the real-property limitation of the requirement or he has made the error of considering Athenogenes' "perfumery" real property, whereas it was in fact nothing but three slaves together with some tools and supplies; see J. H. Lipsius, "Zu Hypereides Rede gegen Athenogenes," *Philologus* 55 (1896) 39–45, at p. 45, and the detailed discussion of the transaction in Chap. V, sect. 4. Nor is it relevant to cite Hesychius, ἐν λευκώμασιν: ἔθος ἦν τὰ πιπρασκόμενα χωρία ἢ σώματα δημοσίᾳ ἀπογράφεσθαι ἐν σανίσι λευκαῖς, οἱ δὲ πυξίοις κεχρισμένοις λευκᾷ γῇ τὰ ὀνόματα καὶ τῶν κτημάτων καὶ τῶν ἀνδραπόδων καὶ τῶν πριαμένων αὐτά, ἵν' εἴ τις βουληθῇ αἰτιάσασθαι ἐπ' ἀδείας ἔχοι ἐντυχὼν τῷ λευκώματι. Hesychius names no cities in which this practice was followed, nor have we any supporting evidence (public notice of manumission is something quite different from public notice of sale) in other sources. That there was no such inscription, even temporary, of slave sales in Athens can be considered certain from the complete silence of the sources, most notably perhaps in Theophrastus and in [Demosthenes], *Against Nikostratos* (orat. 53).

25. Theophrastus, *Laws* § 2: ἐστὶ πάντ' ἢ τὰ πλεῖστα δὶ ἔλλειψιν ἑτέρου νόμου τίθεται· παρ' οἷς γὰρ ἀναγραφὴ τῶν κτημάτων ἐστὶ καὶ τῶν συμβολαίων, ἐξ ἐκείνων ἔστι μαθεῖν εἰ ἐλεύθερα καὶ ἀνέπαφα καὶ τὰ αὐτοῦ πωλεῖ δικαίως· εὐθὺς γὰρ καὶ μετεγγράφει ἡ ἀρχὴ τὸν ἐωνημένον. Just what sort of record is meant by *anagraphe* is debatable; see briefly the footnote following. The assumption by Hitzig, *Pfandrecht* 51–52, and others that συμβόλαια here means security transactions is totally unwarranted linguistically; see briefly Lipsius, *Attisches Recht* II 694, note 62. There is no evidence anywhere in the sources of the existence of a register of security obligations. In his *Euboean Oration* 7.124, Dio Chrysostom speaks of an ἀναγραφὴ τῶν συμβολαίων and in the more detailed statement in the *Rhodian Oration* 31.51, he enumerates sales (land, boats, slaves), loans, manumissions, and gifts, but not security transactions. The two passages together make it quite clear that compulsory registration of sales was generally unknown in the Greek cities even at the end of the first Christian century.

26. The most thorough discussions of public notice and its legal aspects will be found in Partsch, "Publizität," and Weiss, *Privatrecht*, Chaps. VIII (Das Publizitätsprinzip) and IX (Archive). For a briefer account, see Weiss, "Grundbücher," PWRE Supp. 3 (1918) 848–64. Weiss clearly draws the distinction between archives, in which records are placed for

safekeeping and reference, and the *"Publizitätsprinzip,"* in which some form of governmental participation is a necessary part of the legal validation of the transaction. (He errs, strangely enough, when in *"Grundbücher"* 863–64 and *Privatrecht* 279–81 he speaks of *horoi* as a *"Publizitätsform,"* for the setting up of *horoi* was a purely private action.)

The prevailing over-all view of Greek publicity and notice is the negative one of Partsch. His sharpest and most persistent critic has been Ernst Schönbauer, beginning with *Beiträge zur Geschichte des Liegenschaftsrechtes im Altertum* (Leipzig and Graz 1924). For our purposes it is sufficient to note the methodological fallacies in Schönbauer's work. He operates from two interrelated premises: (1) that it is proper to approach the law of the Greek cities from Hellenistic Egypt, and (2) that the Greeks, having "racial" unity, had a *"Stammesrecht."* The first five chapters of his *Liegenschaftsrecht* are therefore devoted to Egypt, where the existence of land registers and official participation in real-property transactions are easily proven. There he worked out his distinction between *anagraphe* and *katagraphe*. Chapter VI then opens with the statement that, having developed his central concept *"intuitiv,"* he now turns to Greece *"zu fragen, ob diese Zeugnisse mit der obigen Deutung in Einklang zu bringen sind"* (p. 109). Even then he makes no independent study of the sources but merely comments on the well-known inscriptions discussed in the standard manuals. More specifically, he rests entirely on the chief sources cited in Weiss, *Privatrecht*. (On p. 124, Schönbauer gives his only citation to the Tenos "register of sales," one of the most important texts for his argument. In the citation, he gives the wrong IG volume number, XII 2 instead of XII 5, and adds in a footnote at that point, "Vgl. Weiss, 259." Weiss cites the inscription correctly dozens of times in his *Privatrecht*, but on p. 259 there is a typographical error, ·XII 2 for XII 5.) Schönbauer concludes with a discussion of the way in which the records mentioned by Theophrastus were organized and decides that, unlike Egyptian practice, they were arranged by property rather than by person (*Realfolien*, not *Personalfolien*). Presumably intuition remained his guide. Schönbauer's numerous later publications in the field have been devoted to an increasingly violent polemic, chiefly against A. B. Schwarz and somewhat less so against Ernst Rabel, on the *anagraphe-katagraphe* problem in the papyri; for the references, see Raphael Taubenschlag, *Law* I 240–50. A convenient summary of the discussion will be found in Walter Hellebrand, *"Ὠνή,"* PWRE 18 (1939) 417–37, at pp. 419–27; see also the important review article by Wolfgang Kunkel in *Gnomon* 3 (1927) 145–65. It should be understood that every author cited in this note works from Hellenic to Graeco-Egyptian law and back again, and that not even Schönbauer attempts to demonstrate the existence of genuine public records of land transfers in Athens. Finally, as a curiosity we might note that Orth, "Landwirtschaft," PWRE 12 (1925) 624–76 (an article far below the standards of PWRE) writes in cols. 638–39 that Athens had *Grundkataster* (ἀπογραφαί) as far back as the time of Solon and that *Hypothekenbücher* (ἀναγραφαί) were introduced for tax purposes by the reforms of Nausinikos in 377 B.C. It need hardly be added that he offers no evidence.

27. *Lexeis rhetorikai, Anecdota Bekker* I 285.12: ἕνεκα τοῦ μηδένα συμβάλλειν τοῖς προκατεσχημένοις. I have used the rather equivocal "held" for προκατεσχημένος, though the meaning is clearly "encumbered" (Hitzig, *Pfandrecht* 70, writes *"verhaftet"*). Though *symballein* may mean "to lend," the broader interpretation is preferable here in order not to anticipate a major legal problem in the field of creditors' rights. The other lexical statement of purpose, Etymologicum Genuinum, s. v. ἄστικτον (R. Reitzenstein, *Inedita poetarum graecorum fragmenta* [*Index Lectionum in Academia Rostochiensi* 1890/1] p. 8), says: ἵνα μὴ πλανηθεὶς ἕτερος ὡς ἔτι καθαρῷ αὐτῷ δανείση. A much briefer and quite inaccurate definition of *horos* appears in *Dikon onomata*, another of the lexica published in *Anecdota Bekker*, I 192.5. The contrast is but one of many illustrations of the wide difference in quality and value among this group of lexica, a subject that has not been examined systematically. It is therefore misleading to cite these works only as *Anecdota Bekker* or Lexica Segueriana (occasionally, worse still, Lexicon Seguerianum), after the names of the editor and a former owner of the MS, respectively, as if they all made up a single, coherent lexicon. See, *e.g.*, K. Latte, "Zur Zeitbestimmung des Antiatticista," *Hermes* 50 (1915) 373-94.

28. Cf. IG II² 2631 and 2632, discussed in Chap. VII, beginning of sect. 3.

29. The details are summarized in the tables in Appendix I. On the important question of the rarity of dates, see Appendix II.

30. On both these points see Chap. VIII at notes 20–23, and Appendix II.

31. IG II² 1183, lines 28–30; for the text and further discussion, see Chap. VII at note 33.

32. The material is presented in Chap. VII, end of sect. 2.

33. In two instances we do have orations on both sides of a private-law dispute, though in neither case were the speeches delivered in the same lawsuit. The pairs are Demosthenes, *For Phormio* (orat. 36) and *Against Stephanos I* (orat. 45), and Isaeus, *On the Estate of Hagnias* (orat. 11), coupled with [Demosthenes], *Against Makartatos* (orat. 43). The existence of two orations has proved to be a hindrance rather than a help in discovering the facts; see Chap. V, note 28.

34. See especially Werner Kamps, "Une affaire de fraude successorale à Athènes," *Annuaire de l'Institut de philologie et d'histoire orientales et slaves* 6 (1938) 15–27, at pp. 15–17. The classic demonstration of the technique of argumentation in the orators is still Wyse, *Isaeus*, though one may question his firm belief that Isaeus never had a client who was in the right.

35. [Demosthenes], *Against Timotheos* 49.12.

36. Plutarch, *Demosthenes* 15.

37. Demosthenes, *Against Onetor II* 31.1–7,12–13. Demosthenes also makes much of the fact that Aphobos remained in possession of the property; on this, see the discussion of the case in Chap. IV, sect. 2.

38. [Demosthenes], *Against Phainippos* 42.5,28.

39. The dowry issue is discussed *ibid.* 26–27. The speaker's efforts to knock this item from the inventory have no connection with *horoi.* We may ignore the extraordinarily complicated legal problem of property rights in the dowry at the various stages in a Greek woman's marital career.

40. *Ibid.* 28–29. See Chap. VIII, note 4, for a brief account of the difficulty in determining the exact significance of the key words in this passage.

41. Friedrich Blass, *Die attische Beredsamkeit* III,1 (3 vols. in 4, 2 ed., Leipzig 1887–98) 507–8, calls attention to the "poor preparation" of the case as one proof that the oration is not authentic. I do not dispute the decision, universally accepted, that Demosthenes did not write this speech. But I do question the validity of this particular proof, which goes to the heart of the methodological problem in using the orations as source material. The private orations were neither treatises on law nor models of rhetoric, but forensic speeches. They were planned according to the logic of the courtroom (which is quite different from the logic of the law) and that kind of logic has always been *sui generis.*

42. Illustrations are rare, but that fact does not seem to weaken the significance inherent in the usage. For ὁρίζω, see [Demosthenes], *Against Timotheos* 49.61, and Pollux, *Onomasticon* 9.9. (Demosthenes, *Against Onetor II* 31.5, is sometimes included in this context but there the connotation is the actual affixing of the horoi.) Ἄστικτος in this sense is known only from the lexica, but its Attic use cannot be questioned since they cite sources. The fullest entry appears in the Etymologicum Genuinum, beginning with a definition, ἄστικτον· οὕτως Ἀττικοὶ ἐκάλουν τό ἐλεύθερον χωρίον καὶ μὴ ὑποκείμενον χρηστῆ, and ending, after some explanation, with a four-line quotation from Menander (frag. 1 Demianczuk). See also Harpocration (who cites Lysias, *Against Aeschines the Socratic*), Suidas, Pollux, *Onomasticon* 3.85, and Hesychius, *s.vv.* ἄστικτον and ἐστιγμένην οἰκίαν.

43. Demosthenes, *Against Onetor II* 31.1–7,12–13, and *Against Stephanos I* 45.28,35, respectively.

44. See in general G. M. Calhoun, "Documentary Frauds in Litigation at Athens," CP 9 (1914) 134–44.

45. [Demosthenes], *Against Phainippos* 42.5,28. No valid argument can be drawn from the frequency with which hypothecation is mentioned in the literature without any reference to *horoi.* Two illustrations will suffice. Nothing is said about *horoi* in [Demosthenes], *Against Nikostratos* 53.10,13, because there, as so often, the fact that the property was encumbered is not in dispute. To mention *horoi* would have been obviously superfluous. Aristotle, *Constitution of the Athenians* 56.7, indicates the role of the archon in the leasing of the property of minor

orphans (for the text and discussion, see Chap. IV, sect. 1) without saying anything about *horoi*. In a brief enumeration of the functions of the
archon, the omission of such a minor detail (one among several ignored
in this particular section) is meaningless.

46. The famous passage in Aristotle, *Rhetoric* 1.15,1376a33, on how to
argue for or against a document as the situation may require, deserves
mention here. It is interesting to note that in American law there is one
situation, pledge of bulky goods, in which a device strikingly like the
horoi may serve as "sufficient evidence of assumption of control to
create a pledge"; see American Law Institute, *Restatement of the Law
of Security* (St. Paul 1941) 20 (hereafter cited as *Restatement: Security*).

47. See Chap. VII, end of sect. 2, for the suggestion that *horoi* were not
used when small sums were involved. No extant *horos* indicates an
amount below 90 drachmas.

48. This point is of considerable importance in connection with Ferguson's thesis, discussed in Appendix II.

49. Legal historians, with their natural concern for the full ramifications
of each institution, almost inevitably tend to stress disputes and court
action unduly. In denigrating the evidentiary value of the *horoi*, they
lose sight of the fact that their objections, sound as they are, can be
applied with equal weight to any document. A demonstration that
they lacked final authority in a courtroom is not be be confused with
the question of the regularity of their use. Such a confusion is apparent,
for example, in IJ I pp. 138–41. In the same vein, Hitzig, *Pfandrecht*
71, dismisses the orations against Phainippos and Timotheos in two
words; the arguments based on the existence of *horoi* are *"übertrei-
bende Äußerungen."* A position most nearly like the one I have taken
will be found in the brief discussion in Lipsius, *Attisches Recht* II
696–97, though he makes the strange error of citing the following four
texts as his evidence that *horoi* were customarily used — Theophrastus,
Characters 10.9; IG II² 1165, lines 21–22; IG II² 2492, lines 23–24; and
IG II² 2631, each of which refers to boundary-stones and has nothing
whatever to do with hypothecation-stones. In Theophrastus, *Characters* 10.9 (also erroneously cited by Liddell-and-Scott under hypothecation-stone), the penny-pincher "checks the *horoi* every day to see
that they remain in place." Cf. the same use of the word in IG II² 1165,
line 21, or Plato's parallel characterization of the miser who encroaches
beyond his neighbor's boundaries (*Laws* 843C): ὃς δ'ἂν ἐπεργάζηται τὰ
τοῦ γείτονος ὑπερβαίνων τοὺς ὅρους.

50. IG II² 43. Lines 12–14 were chiseled out, presumably to eliminate
remarks aimed at Sparta; see Silvio Accame, *La lega ateniese del secolo
IV A.C.* [*Studi pubblicati dal R. istituto italiano per la storia antica* 2
(Rome 1941)] 49–53. Several changes were also made in the list of
member cities.

51. No. 154 has other deletions as well, not all of them explicable; see
Chap. IV at note 56. Adolf Wilhelm, *Beiträge zur griechischen In-*

schriftenkunde [*Sonderschriften des österreichischen Institutes in Wien* 7 (Vienna 1909)] 50, notes that an alteration had also been made in the numeral in *horos* no. 163.

52. In publishing *horos* no. 63 (IG II² 2716), Kirchner followed the original editor, Erich Ziebarth, and overlooked the fact that upon re-examination of the stone, Th. Sauciuc, *Jahreshefte* 15 (1912) Beib. 24, had discovered the letters πι in the erasui ϶.

53. A precise parallel is to be found in the Pantainetos case, on which see Chap. III, sect. 2.

54. How Kirchner was able to determine that the 1,100-drachma obligation was the earlier of the two is a mystery.

55. Nos. 81 and 10 are the only *horoi* containing the word *oikema*, which has the root-meaning of "little house" but a wide variety of uses. I have no satisfactory explanation for its appearance in no. 81. A possible clue may exist in the Tenos register, IG XII 5,872, § 47, where the property is described as follows:... ἐν τῶι ἄστει ἐν τόνωι ἑβδόμωι τὸ μετέωρον οἴκημα τὸ ἐπ[ὶ τἔ]ι εἰσόδωι κα[ὶ κ]έραμον τὸν ἐπόντα καὶ θύρας τὰς ἐπούσας καὶ δίοδον εἰς τὴν οἰκίαν. Cf. § 31: ... τῆς οἰκίας τῆς ἐν ἄ[στ]ει ἡ ἦν πρό-τε[ρον τοῦ δεῖνος τὸ μετέ]ωρον καὶ ὑπότυπον.... D. Pappulias, "Zur Ge-schichte der Superficies und des Stockwerkeigentums," ZSS 27 (1906) 363–64, suggests that in § 47 the buyer acquired only an upper story, a passageway, the roof, and doors, not "*Grund und Boden.*" He cites Herodotus 2.148: οἰκήματα δ'ἔνεστι διπλᾶ, τὰ μὲν ὑπόγαια, τὰ δὲ μετέωρα ἐπ' ἐκείνοισι. The virtually unprecedented use of *oikema* in *horos* no. 81 may perhaps indicate either separate "*Stockwerkeigentum*" or pos-sibly a small "bungalow" not part of the "main house" of *horos* no. 80. See further Chap. V, sect. 5.

56. No attempt to answer these questions is possible without a full dis-cussion of the complex legal problem of multiple charges, which are taken up in brief and very tentative fashion in Chap. VIII. To com-plete the present section on changes in the stones, we should note the additions and deletions at the end of no. 13, which I do not understand, and the equally puzzling deletion in line 3 of no. 159.

57. See, for example, I J I p. 129.

58. Weiss, *Privatrecht* 433–34, notes that in this respect the law drew no distinction between major transactions, the conveyance of land for example, and trifling actions.

59. Demosthenes, *Against Spudias* 41.5–6. Contrast the reference to *grammata* in § 9, where another intra-family transaction is involved. This word does not mean "contract" either, but unilaterally prepared documents. The distinction is clear from Demosthenes, *For Phormio* 36.18–19,36, where Demosthenes derides the contention of his oppon-ent, Apollodoros, that he was having difficulty proving his case be-cause the latter's mother, at Phormio's instigation, had caused the

necessary *grammata* to disappear. Clearly these were informal records prepared by Pasion, unlike the will which the latter had deposited with other people according to the usual procedure (§ 7).

60. For other illustrations, see Erdmann, *Ehe* 311–14. On the other hand, written agreements are known in some purely intra-family dealings, as in Lycurgus, *Against Leokrates* 23.

61. [Demosthenes], *Against Timotheos* 49.5; see briefly B. Laum, "Banken," PWRE Supp. 4 (1924) 68–82, at cols. 78–79. Cf. the long argument in §§ 50–52, where Apollodoros replies to the defense, which apparently claimed that one of the loans, for 1,000 drachmas, had been made not to Timotheos but to a Boeotian nauarch. In a series of rhetorical questions, Apollodoros demands the names and testimony of the slaves who would have handled the copper allegedly pledged for the money. Slaves, he says, would have been essential in such a transaction. Of agreements there is not a word. Cf. [Demosthenes], *Against Kallippos* 52.4–7, and note 59 above. To speak of these memoranda as "bankers' contracts," as does R. J. Bonner, *Evidence in Athenian Courts* (Chicago 1905) 23,40, is to suggest a misleading picture of the legal rules as well as of business practice generally in Athens. Nearly a century ago A. Philippi, "Über die demosthenische Rede gegen Timotheos," *Jahrbücher KP* 93 (1866) 611–20, correctly questioned the evidentiary worth of Greek bank records.

62. See Louis Gernet, "Sur les actions commerciales en droit athénien," REG 51 (1938) 1–44, at pp. 30–32, for further documentation. I have followed Gernet's views rather closely here, though I am not prepared to accept his thesis that the growth of a distinct "commercial law" can be traced in Athens, analogous to the development of the Roman *ius gentium* procedurally if not substantively. Pringsheim, *Sale* 43, correctly notes that "even Theophrastus' description shows that documents were not usual in Greece," but he then goes on to stress that the "line of development" led "from oral to documented agreements," without considering differences in practice according to the material content of the transaction. He attributes the continuing Athenian preference for witnesses as the only proper evidence to "a predilection for publicity which is congenial to the ideas of the πόλις. Even private agreements have to be made publicly"; cf. p. 45: "...especially if it was not a private instrument, but sealed and given into custody of a trustworthy custodian or an official record office...." This is a strange conception of publicity, yet it lies at the heart of Pringsheim's theory of the Greek contract. On the role of verbal understandings in suretyship, see Josef Partsch, *Griechisches Bürgschaftsrecht* (only vol. 1 published, Leipzig and Berlin 1909) 147, 154, who writes: "*Solche Urkunden über Bürgschaften* [i.e., contracts between the suretor and the creditor] *neben einem privatrechtlichen Schuldvertrage sind bei den Rednern und in den Papyri m.W. noch nicht belegt....*"

63. On this point, see Chap. VI, sect. 1.

64. For a discussion of *horos* no. 154, see Chap. IV at note 56. Note should also be taken here of no. 163, which is too cryptic to be analyzed.

65. Reasons for rendering οἱ μετά as "those with" are given in Chap. VII, note 7.

66. Dow and Travis, "Demetrios of Phaleron" 160, incorrectly include this pair in their list of *horoi* mentioning a contract. (On their analysis of this entire group of stones, see Appendix II.) Cf. the orgeonic lease, IG II² 2501, lines 20–22.

67. IG II² 1183, lines 27–32; see above at note 31.

68. Chapter VII is devoted largely to this question. On the lease of land by public and quasi-public bodies, by far the best study is Otto Schulthess, "Μίσθωσις," PWRE 15 (1932) 2095–2129, though, as Schulthess himself indicates, it is by no means complete either in documentation or in analysis. Unfortunately, he was unable to benefit by the valuable new readings and analyses of some of the most important inscriptions by Adolf Wilhelm, "Attische Pachturkunden," APF 11 (1935) 189–217; the appropriate citations will be made in the present volume as the occasion arises. In view of the excellence of the Schulthess study, it is difficult to understand the recent publication of Sibylle von Bolla, "Pacht," PWRE 18,4 (1949) 2439–83. Presumably the justification was that Schulthess explicitly left the papyri out of account and limited his analysis to the Greek cities. But why then repeat his work, with a marked deterioration in quality, under the subtitle, "Griechisches Recht einschließlich der gräco-ägyptischen Papyri" (cols. 2439–74)? A. Herdlitczka, "Miete," PWRE Supp. 6 (1935) 375–95, expressly refrains from entering the Greek field because of the excellence of the Schulthess article.

On the matter of written agreements in the leasing of land by public and quasi-public bodies, it is sufficient to note that the lease of the theater belonging to the deme Peiraieus, IG II² 1176, lines 18–21 (*c.* 360 B.C.), provides that a copy of the contract (*synthekai*) and the name of the person with whom it was deposited be inscribed on the stele. A similar provision has been restored, with some probability, in IG II² 1168, lines 23–25, a fragment of a tribal decree on leases, of unknown date. All the other lease documents that make any reference to publication restrict themselves to stelae, variously located, though the word *synthekai* also appears in IG II² 2492, lines 29–30; IG II² 2501, line 20; Πραγματεῖαι Ἀκαδ. Ἀθηνῶν 13, fasc. 2 (1948) 5, line 27; each time clearly referring to the terms as inscribed on the stones we have.

We know next to nothing about the leasing of land owned by individuals in Athens. The agreements were not engraved on stone. The scattered references in the orations permit no study of the procedures. Hence there seems to be no adequate basis for Schulthess' conclusion, "Μίσθωσις" 2099, that rental agreements between individuals were customarily in writing, though he concedes that verbal arrangements were permissible.

69. In addition to the fourteen *horoi* discussed in this section, references
to contracts appear in three fragments, nos. 168, 169, and 171. In each
of the three that reference is all that remains of the stone, so that no
analysis is possible. A note of caution should be raised, however,
against being too certain that these are fragments of *horoi* and not of
some other kind of document. No. 168 is particularly suspect because
the indication is that there were two copies of the agreement, each
deposited with another person; cf. the dedication-stone, no. 155, discussed immediately below.

70. I use the word "pledge" solely for security transactions in which
possession of the security is with the creditor for the duration of the
obligation; see *Restatement: Security* 1–2, 5–9.

71. Demosthenes, *Against Pantainetos* 37.5,7,25–26,29. The contract was
not submitted in evidence; see the account in Chap. III, sect. 2.

72. *Ibid.* 37.16. See briefly Ernst Rabel, "Nachgeformte Rechtsgeschäfte,"
ZSS 27 (1906) 290–335; 28 (1907) 311–79, at XXVIII 354.

73. [Demosthenes], *Against Polykles* 50.61. There is no need to consider
the text and its various interpretations in the present context. What is
notable is the phrase, κατὰ τὰς συγγραφάς, where we should have
excepted συνθήκας. Gernet, "Actions commerciales" 39, has found it
particularly embarrassing because of his stress on *syngraphe* as the
typical "literal contract" of the "commercial law." His explanation of
the use of the word here, if I understand him correctly, is to be found in
the executory clause, a concept, he says, which was closely linked with
the maritime *syngraphe* in the minds of the Athenian people. In
[Demosthenes], *Against Apaturios* (orat. 33), on the other hand, the
word *syngraphe* appears but twice (§§ 12,36), whereas *synthekai* is
used repeatedly. Again Gernet must explain away the choice, this time
(p. 24, note 2) because the speaker deliberately avoided *syngraphe*
"*justement parce que c'est celui qui figurait dans la loi*" dealing with
the *dikai emporikai*. Obviously a proper study of these terms, based on
an analysis of every known use, would be invaluable. A good introduction, and admittedly no more than that, is provided by Otto Schulthess, "Συνθήκη," PWRE Supp. 6 (1935) 1158–68.

74. Demosthenes, *Against Aristogeiton I* 25.69–70. For a convenient
summary of the literature on the authenticity of the oration, see
G. Mathieu in the Guillaume Budé edition, 4 (1947) 134–39.

75. The literary references are assembled in Bonner, *Evidence* 61–66,
though with inadequate analysis. Bonner is too concerned with a comparison of Athenian and Anglo-American rules of evidence and he
seems to miss the basic implication in the strong Greek preference for
oral testimony.

76. Aristotle, *Rhetoric* 1.15,1376a33. Gernet, "Actions commerciales" 36,
note 1, overreaches himself, in an otherwise sound analysis of the characteristic Athenian reluctance to produce documents in evidence,

when he argues that Aristotle, in enumerating the types of evidence, means by *synthekai* the understanding reached by the parties rather than the written agreement. Aristotle's stress on the depositee can refer only to the latter.

77. Isaeus, *On the Estate of Kleonymos* (orat. 1). I have indicated a slight doubt as to which official had the document because in §§ 3, 14, 18, 21, 22, and 25, Isaeus uses ἀρχή, in §§ 14, 22, and 25, ἄρχοντες; only in § 15 does he mention an *astynomos* as the person who brought the document to the dying man's house. Richard Häderli, *Die hellenischen Astynomen und Agoranomen vornehmlich im alten Athen* (Leipzig 1886) [reprinted from *Jahrbücher KP*, Supp. 15] 82, gives a complete list of references to agreements, loosely defined, kept by the *astynomoi*. With the exception of the Isaeus passage, all deal with agreements in which the state itself has a direct interest. Furthermore, it is the only Athenian text in the list. That hardly warrants Häderli's summary remark: "*Endlich sind noch die Verträge zu erwähnen, welche unter den Auspicien der Astynomen sowohl wie der Agoranomen abgeschlossen wurden; es sind theils Staats-, theils Privatverträge.*" Plato's proposal, *Laws* 847B, to give the *astynomoi* authority to adjudicate work agreements, which Häderli cites in this context, is completely irrelevant, both because it says nothing about prevailing practice and because it has nothing to do with written documents or their preservation. (On the impossibility of dating the Isaeus speech, see Wyse, *Isaeus* 178–79; Karl Münscher, transl. of Isaeus, ZVR 37 (1919) 32–328, at p. 55.)

78. Diogenes Laertius, *Lives of the Philosophers* 10.16. It should be stressed that it was an earlier *dosis*, not the will itself, which Epicurus filed; see Bruck, *Schenkung* 130–32.

79. For the date, see A. Wilhelm in *Jahreshefte* 7 (1904) 110.

80. In the *horoi* marking a dotal *apotimema*, the wife's name always appears in the dative. I have translated, "put up as security to Nikesarete," although, the legal situation of property rights in a dowry being so complicated in Greek law, it would perhaps be better to write, "put up as security for the dowry of Nikesarete." See further in Chap. IV, sect. 2.

81. Ruppel, "Amorginische Städte" 321, generalizes from this text, for which I know no Amorgian parallel. He calls the thesmothete the "*Archivbeamter.*" But then what are the *chreophylakes* of IG XII 7,3, line 36, also from Arkesine in Amorgos, dated in the first half of the fourth century B.C.? Without entering into a discussion of the *chreophylakes* I should like to note several points. (1) This one inscription in which they are mentioned in Amorgos (for instances elsewhere, see R. Dareste, "Le ΧΡΕΩΦΥΛΑΚΙΟΝ dans les villes grecques," BCH 6 [1882] 241–45) deals with judgment-debts, precisely the context in which Aristotle, *Politics* 6.5.4,1321b34 (and again briefly 6.5.12, 1322b33) speaks of ἑτέρα δ'ἀρχὴ πρὸς ἣν ἀναγράφεσθαι δεῖ τά τε ἴδια συμβόλαια καὶ τὰς κρίσεις ⟨τὰς⟩ ἐκ τῶν δικαστηρίων, as a reading of the full passage shows (the only such general reference, furthermore, in the lite-

rature). (2) Whatever the function of the *chreophylakes* in Amorgos may have been, it could not have included registration of the kinds of transactions noted on *horoi*. If the failure to mention these officials in *horos* no. 155 is inconclusive because of its special nature, the specific indication of a contract deposited with a private individual in *horos* no. 9 is decisive. Official registration of contracts would have rendered safekeeping of copies by individuals, and the *horoi* themselves, superfluous. (3) The Amorgian *chreophylakes* had no counterparts in Athens.

Still another Amorgian *horos*, no. 8, enumerates the encumbered property as lands, a house, gardens, and ἐπικύρβια ἐνέχυρα. No other use of ἐπικύρβια is known. Hitzig, *Pfandrecht* 18, note 2, suggested that here it was equivalent to σκευή, but his interpretation has been universally rejected for the proposal of Bruno Keil, *Die solonische Verfassung in Aristoteles Verfassungsgeschichte Athens* (Berlin 1892) 59, note: "*auf einer Urkunde verzeichnet.*" Keil's translation is of course based on the Solonic κύρβεις. It should be pointed out that the precise meaning of κύρβεις has been a mystery for over two thousand years; see H. Swoboda, "Κύρβεις," PWRE 12 (1925) 134–36, and the complete source collection in L. B. Holland, "Axones," AJA 45 (1941) 346–62. The link between the Solonic κύρβεις and the *hapax legomenon*, ἐπικύρβια, is tenuous. Even if one were to insist on the notion of documentation, furthermore, Liddell-and-Scott's "registered on κύρβεις," is an unwarranted, though only implicit, extension to the idea of public recording. That interpretation would leave the untenable situation, with reference to *horos* no. 8, in which the state took official cognizance of pledged movables but not of encumbered realty.

82. See Weiss, *Privatrecht* 397. In suggesting the presence of a *donatio mortis causa* in all three instances, I am following the lucid analysis of Bruck, *Schenkung* 125–36. His further conclusion is not convincing that official approval and registration of all *donationes mortis causa* were required by law throughout the Greek world. His evidence is very thin and of dubious value, as Bruck virtually concedes at the end. The one Athenian source he attests is Plato, *Laws* 847B, the irrelevance of which is indicated in note 77 above.

83. Note must also be taken of Harpocration, δόσις: ἰδίως μὲν λέγεται παρὰ τοῖς ῥήτορσι συμβόλαιον γραφόμενον ὅταν τις τὰ αὐτοῦ διδῷ τινι διὰ τῶν ἀρχόντων, ὡς παρὰ Δεινάρχῳ. There is no agreement among commentators on the meaning of this isolated sentence, either as to the type of transaction covered by the word *dosis* or as to the extent of the official action indicated. That *dosis* is restricted to matters of family law seems most probable from other uses of the word. In any event, there is no indication in Harpocration of a broad obligatory procedure. The Deinarchus speech which he used is lost. Nothing in the extant orations can be related to his definition, unless it be the Isaeus speech we have been discussing, and there the non-obligatory situation is certain. Ferguson, "Laws of Demetrius" 267, argues from the silence of the orators that new legislation by Demetrios of Phaleron was at the base of the Harpocration text, but that is an untenable and unsupported idea; see Weiss, *Privatrecht* 397.

84. It is worth noting that not even settlements of legal disputes out of court were officially recorded, despite the public element obviously involved; see Artur Steinwenter. *Die Streitbeendigung durch Urteil, Schiedsspruch und Vergleich nach griechischem Rechte* [*Münchener Beiträge* 8 (1925)] 123–24, 128. Cf. on wills B. Kübler, "Testament," PWRE, 2 ser., 5 (1934) 966–1010, at col. 983.

85. The foregoing discussion has gone into considerable detail because of the persistent attempt to find a trend towards governmental intervention in so isolated an instance as the deposit of a document in the Metroon by Epicurus. Even a careful scholar like Bruck writes, *Schenkung* 131, that Epicurus' resorting to the Metroon rather than to the *astynomoi* (as had Isaeus' client), *"hängt mit der in späterer Zeit immer stärkeren Inanspruchnahme gerade dieses Archivs zu privaten Zwecken zusammen."* The proof, he adds, will be found in Bruno Keil, *Anonymus Argentinensis* (Straßburg 1902) 192. But the only texts Keil can cite are Diogenes on Epicurus' *dosis* and IG II² 1327, line 27 (*c.* 178/7 B.C.). Of the latter, he says, *"hundert Jahre später deponirt ein Orgeonencollegium dort* [*i.e.*, in the Metroon] *gar ein Steinstele."* The group involved is the *orgeones* of the Mother Goddess and the Metroon is not the state archive at all but a sanctuary of the *orgeones*, privately owned, located in the Peiraieus; see Curt Wachsmuth, *Die Stadt Athen im Alterthum* 2 (2 vols., Leipzig 1874–90) 158; W. S. Ferguson, "The Attic Orgeones," *Harvard Theological Rev.* 37 (1944) 61–140, at pp. 107–15. Thus we are left with Epicurus alone, once again. On the public Metroon, then, we can say no more than did W. Kroll, "Metroon," PWRE 15 (1932) 1488–90, at col. 1490; *"Daß auch private Urkunden im Metroon hinterlegt werden konnten, zeigt das Testament Epikurs."* Kurt Latte, "Thesmotheten," PWRE, 2 ser., 6 (1936) 33–37, not having *horos* no. 17 at his disposal, has not a word to say about an archival function of the thesmotetes. The discovery of one *horos* does not warrant a revaluation of their activities. Ferguson, "Laws of Demetrius," attributes a basic change in the law to Demetrios of Phaleron, which he explains in terms of broad economic and political policy; on that theory, see Appendix II.

86. U. Wilamowitz-Moellendorf, *Aristoteles und Athen* 1 (2 vols., Berlin 1893) 236, note 100. Cf. Plato, *Laws* 766 E.

Notes to Chapter III

1. On execution in Greek law, see particularly Weiss, *Privatrecht*, Bk. IV, elaborately documented and with full bibliographies, and briefly, "Katenechyrasia (κατενεχυρασία)," PWRE 10 (1919) 2495–2512. (Weiss, "Exekution," PWRE Supp. 6 [1935] 56–64, discusses personal execution in Greek law at cols. 56–59, but merely cites the earlier article for real execution.) The one difficulty to be noted is in Weiss' not separating city-state material from papyrological sources. Few institutions demand sharp differentiation among different places and eras in Greek history more obviously than does execution. See H. Swoboda, "Beiträge zur griechischen Rechtsgeschichte. II. Über die altgriechische Schuldknechtschaft," ZSS 26 (1905) 190–280, especially pp. 190–234; Partsch, *Bürgschaftsrecht* 193–200. The survival of personal execution in many Greek communities and the continuation right through the Hellenistic age in Aetolia, Crete, and elsewhere of the notion of the rightlessness of the stranger, unless he is protected by an *asylia* treaty, would seem to require at least a major qualification of the idea of a fundamental unity in Greek law.

2. See the illuminating comments in Mitteis, *Reichsrecht* 413–19, with particular reference to the so-called executory clause in contracts, rather than to execution generally. John H. Wigmore, "The Pledge-Idea: A Study in Comparative Legal Ideas," *Harvard Law Rev.* 10 (1896/7) 321–50, 389–417; 11 (1897/8) 18–39, finds the origin of security in the forfeit characteristic of primitive exchange in a society that knows no credit, and apparently not in the evolution of forms of execution against defaulting debtors. It is unnecessary for us to examine this or other possible theories of origins, which would take us back centuries before the time limits fixed for this study, since the link between security and execution is undeniable when we reach the classical period. Wigmore's article may still be read with great profit, especially for his demonstration of the values and limitations of the comparative method, despite the many inaccuracies in detail that fifty years of further research have brought to light. For a brief restatement of Wigmore's views, with particular emphasis on newer researches in Roman law, see his "The Pledge-Mortgage Idea in Roman Law: A Revolutionary Interpretation," *Illinois Law Rev.* 36 (1941/2) 371–93; and the comments by Ernst Rabel, "Real Securities in Roman Law: Reflections on a Recent Study by the Late Dean Wigmore," *Seminar* 1 (1943) 32–47.

3. See the brief closing remarks in Chap. I.

4. In Demosthenes, *Against Spudias* (orat. 41), ἀποτιμάω and ἀποτίμημα are the sole words used for the security transaction which was at issue, but θέντες ἐνέχυρα appears in § 11, when a pawnbroking operation is indicated. Cf. the use in a metaphorical context of θείς and θέμενος for the parties giving and receiving an ἐνέχυρον in Plato, *Laws* 820E; τὰ μὲν ἐνέχυρα κεῖται αὐτῶν in [Demosthenes], *Against Euergos and Mnesi-*

bulos 47.54; ἐνέχυρον τίθησιν in Aristophanes, *Plutus* 451 (cf. *Ecclesiazusae* 755); and the additional references in notes 7 and 17 below, and in Chap. VI, note 61. IG XII Supp. 533, an early third-century B.C. text from Dystos in Euboea, begins as follows: [ἂν] τις ὠνῆται γῆν ἢ οἰκίαν ἢ τιθῆται [ἢ ὑ]ποτιθῆται.... The original editor, E. Ziebarth, "Hypothekinschrift aus Dystos," *Philologus* 83 (1928) 204–7, at pp. 205–6, noted that, although there is usually no distinction between τίθημι and ὑποτίθημι, one must be intended here. On the basis of Isaeus, *On the Estate of Dikaiogenes* 5.21, he concluded that τιθῆται in this instance referred to *prasis epi lysei*. (The Isaeus passage is given in note 51 below.) Egon Weiss, "Tempelinschrift aus Dystos über Haftungsübernahme," *Byzantinische Zeitschrift* 30 (1929/30) 638–40, at p. 639, and Paoli, "Ipoteca" 144, prefer to base the distinction between the two words on whether the creditor or debtor had possession of the pledged property. Whichever interpretation is correct — and I see no basis for deciding on what was obviously a matter of local linguistic practice — the more important point is that as a rule τίθημι and ὑποτίθημι are used interchangeably in the field of legal security. It is enough to cite *horoi* nos. 1 and 2 (see Chap. II, note 11) or the use of ὑποθεμένωι in IG II² 43, line 40, followed by τιθῆται in line 41/42 (see Chap. VI, note 5). Herodotus 2.136 writes ὑποτιθέντι τοῦτο τὸ ἐνέχυρον, whereas, as we have seen, τίθημι is the usual verb in this construction. Note should also be taken of κατέθηκεν in *horos* no. 9, an Amorgian stone. One lexical passage, too, may be cited, Harpocration, θέσθαι· ἀντὶ μὲν τοῦ ὑποθήκην λαβεῖν Ὑπερείδης ἐν τῷ πρὸς Ὑγιαίνοντα... (cf. *Lexeis rhetorikai, Anecdota Bekker* I 263.32).

5. Other forms are also found from time to time, such as ὑπόθεμα, ὑπόθημα, and ὑπόθεσις. The only Attic examples I know are in Menander. *Anonymous Antiatticista, Anecdota Bekker* I 115.1, says: ὑπόθεσιν, ἀντὶ τοῦ ὑποθήκην· Μένανδρος (cf. *Lexeis rhetorikai, ibid.* 312.22, without citation). The word ὑπόθημα appears in Menander, *Arbitration* 288 (329 Körte³), used for a ring put up to cover a gambling loss. This text, isolated though it is, supports the suggestion made in Chap. VII at note 38, that there may be other instances in the sources in which the appearance of *hypotheke* or even *apotimema* may nevertheless indicate the use of personal property for security, not realty; cf. note 7 below.

6. To the best of my knowledge, the verb ἐνεχυράζω and the noun ἐνεχυρασία are used only to indicate execution, never a security transaction. A striking illustration is to be found in Aristophanes, *Clouds* 239–41. Strepsiades says to Socrates: βουλόμενος μαθεῖν λέγειν. ὑπὸ γὰρ τόκων χρήστων τε δυσκολωτάτων ἄγομαι, φέρομαι, τὰ χρήματ' ἐνεχυράζομαι. Earlier in the play (lines 34–35), Strepsiades had already informed the audience of the difficulties which were to lead him to Socrates for help: ... ὅτε καὶ δίκας ὤφληκα χἄτεροι τόκου ἐνεχυράσεσθαί (MSS: ἐνεχυράσασθαί) φασιν. Following an erroneous tradition that goes back to the scholia, Paoli, "Ipoteca" 158, treats the situation as one in which a pledge is in the possession of the creditor. But W. J. M. Starkie,

in his edition of the *Clouds* (London 1911), had already noted that
ἐνεχυράζω means "to distrain," whereas "to hand over as security" for
payment ·is ἐνέχυρα θεῖναι. For the former, he cites [Plato], *Axiochos*
367B, Demosthenes, *Against Timokrates* 24.197, Aeschines, *Against
Ktesiphon* 3.21. Another illustration is Aristophanes, *Ecclesiazusae*
565–67, where Praxagora, enumerating the blessings that her plan
will bring to Athens, says: μὴ λωποδυτῆσαι, μὴ φθονεῖν τοῖς πλησίον, μὴ
γυμνὸν εἶναι, μή πένητα μηδένα, μὴ λοιδορεῖσθαι, μὴ 'νεχυραζόμενον φέρειν.
V. Ehrenberg, *The People of Aristophanes* (2 ed., Cambridge, Mass.,
1951) 233, translates the final words "taking in pawn" and draws an
incorrect comparison with ἐνέχυρα θήσων of line 755. The latter is a clear
reference to pawning, the former to seizure of goods by a creditor following default. For epigraphical illustrations of the use of ἐνεχυράζω, see
the quotation from IG II² 2492 in Chap. VII, note 36 (cf. also note 30).
The point to much of the plot of the *Clouds* would disappear if Strepsiades had given the creditors property as a pledge for his debts. What
could Socrates then teach him that would be of use? And what would
be the meaning of the repeated references to court proceedings (*e.g.*, lines
239–41, 1254–58, 1267–78) and to Strepsiades' being able to outwit the
witnesses of Pasias, one of the creditors (lines 1151–53, 1213–27)? Pasias
would have retained the pawned goods and that would have been the
end of the story.

7. Examples are given throughout the volume when appropriate. One
illustration of an attempt to build sharp categories from the terms may
be noted here. Fritz Pringsheim, *Der Kauf mit fremdem Geld* (Leipzig
1916) 22, concludes a survey of the known bottomry cases with the
point that maritime loans were ordinarily secured by the ship and
cargo together or the cargo alone, and in two instances perhaps by the
ship alone, though the facts are not certain. In note 8, he writes: *"Das
Pfand am Schiffe heißt* ἐνέχυρον *... während für das Warenpfand nur*
ὑποθήκη *vorkommt."* For the former he cites only [Demosthenes],
Against Dionysodoros 56.3, for the latter [Demosthenes], *Against
Phormio* 34.6,7,8,22, and *Against Lakritos* 35.52; then he adds that
34.50 and 35.18 are *"unsicher"* and that we should consult *"übrigens
die einzigen Stellen, in denen das Wort* [ὑποθήκη] *überhaupt bei Demosthenes begegnet."* The chain of reasoning runs something like this:
(1) We do not know definitely that the ship alone was ever used as
security. (2) A sharp terminological distinction can be made to differentiate security in the ship alone from security in the cargo. (3) Only
three orations can be cited for both types in any event, and even they
include passages the meaning of which is uncertain. We may add that
[Demosthenes], *Against Apaturios* 33.12, puts an end to the entire
effort; see note 17 below. In this volume I have not considered security
in bottomry transactions for reasons indicated in Chap. V at notes 17–19.

8. The figure 10 is not quite precise. *Horos* no. 3, found in Acharnai, has
no verb and no. 9, from Amorgos, has κατέθηκεν. On the other hand,
a *hypotheke* is specifically indicated in no. 146 and again in no. 147;
neither is included in this figure as indicated in Appendix I in the
introductory notes preceding the Tables.

9. The statistical validity of this distribution seems reasonably well established. Nevertheless, the possible effects of chance in the results of excavation cannot be ignored. Half a century ago, the collection published in I J included 4 *horoi* marking *hypotheke* obligations, 35 for *prasis epi lysei*, and 24 for *apotimema*. Hitzig, *Pfandrecht* 5, who grouped *apotimema* and *hypotheke* as one form of security, could therefore see a balance among the types that has been completely destroyed by subsequent finds. (Hitzig wrote 25 rather than 35 as the number of the *prasis epi lysei* stones, a typographical error no doubt.) Paoli, "Ipoteca," whose contempt for the value of the *horoi* as evidence has already been indicated, Chap. I, note 27, not only ignores the statistics and the problems they raise but also ignores the institution of *prasis epi lysei* itself, except for two or three casual remarks.

10. See below, note 17.

11. The practice of the late Greek and Byzantine lexicographers is very revealing in this connection. They ignored the word *hypotheke*, of course, because it was in common use when they were writing. *Horos* and *apotimema* they explained in some detail, since they found both words, obsolete and unintelligible in their day, used by the Attic orators on whose works their dictionaries and word-lists were largely based. But on *prasis epi lysei* they maintained a complete silence, not because the institution was still a familiar one but because that combination of words did not appear in the classical literature. *Prasis* or *lysis* standing by itself required no definition. Pollux, *Onomasticon* 8.142 (Hypereides, frag. 193 Blass), ῾Υπερείδης δὲ ἐν τῷ πρὸς Χάρητα ἔφη ἀποδόμενος ἀντὶ τοῦ ὑποθείς, is no exception. He had noted the use of ἀποδίδωμι without the appended ἐπὶ λύσει, and indicated that in that passage it meant "hypothecate," not "sell" (see further Chap. VIII, note 16).

12. See Chap. II, end of sect. 1 and beginning of sect. 3.

13. See further Chap. VI, beginning of sect. 2.

14. It should be evident that in suggesting the possibility of greater flexibility in the *hypotheke*, I do not share the interpretation of either Hitzig, *Pfandrecht* 9–14, or Pappulias, ᾿Ασφάλεια *passim*, who approach the question from a very different (and exclusively juristic) point of view.

15. See P. Chantraine, "Conjugaison et histoire des verbes signifiant vendre (πέρνημι, πωλέω, ἀποδίδομαι, ἐμπολῶ)," RP, n.s. 14 (1940) 11–24. The fullest analysis of the terminology of sale will be found in Pringsheim, *Sale*, especially pp. 93–98, 111–26; it is intricate and often highly tendentious.

16. On this sense of ἐπί see R. Kühner, *Ausführliche Grammatik der griechischen Sprache* II,1 (3 ed. by F. Blass and B. Gerth, 2 vols. in 4, Hannover and Leipzig 1890–1904) 501.

17. The use of the word *lysis* in Demosthenes, *Against Pantainetos* 37.5, is no exception to this statement. In Lysias, *On the Injury* 4.13, we read ἐπὶ τῇ ἐκ τῶν πολεμίων λύσει πραθείη. The reference here is to ransom of a prisoner from the enemy and has nothing to do with *prasis epi lysei* as legal security. The new inscription mentioned is *Hesperia* 10 (1941) 14, no. 1, on which see Chap. VIII at notes 13–19. Hitzig, *Pfandrecht* 4, note 1, writes: "...*in der Rede d. Demosth. c. Apatur. liegt eine* πρᾶσις ἐπὶ λύσει vor, *das Geschäft wird aber auch* θέσις 12 (896), *das Objekt* ἐνέχυρον 10 (895) *genannt.*" The "*auch*" is misleading since nowhere in the oration does the term πρᾶσις ἐπὶ λύσει appear. If the transaction actually was a *prasis epi lysei*, that is a deduction drawn from the facts, not from the language. Pappulias, Ἀσφάλεια 14, cites § 10 of the same oration as his one source for *prasis epi lysei* in his opening chapter on the terminology of security. His method is altogether puzzling in this chapter, for, beginning with the very first reference on p. 13 for ἐνέχυρον (Athenaeus, *Deipnosophists* 11.508F and *P. Fay.* 12), Pappulias seems deliberately to avoid classical citations wherever possible.

Pringsheim, *Sale* 117–18, argues from the absence of the term πρᾶσις ἐπὶ λύσει that "ὠνὴ ἐπὶ λύσει would be more appropriate." The shift in terminology is important for his theory of the evolution of the Greek sale contract, which we need not examine. It should be noted, however, that the phrase πρᾶσις ἐπὶ λύσει is at least suggested by the recurring formula of the *horoi* despite Pringsheim's attempt to argue this evidence away, whereas ὠνέομαι ἐπὶ λύσει is altogether unknown. *Hesperia* 10 (1941) 14, no. 1, which Pringsheim overlooked, suggests that the entire attempt to draw significant juristic conclusions from the linguistic usage is ill-founded in this instance. In that inscription we find ἀποδομένο (line 23) and πριαμένων — ἐπὶ λύσει (lines 33–34) used synonymously in identical contexts; see Chap. VIII, note 13, for the Greek text.

18. SEG IV 62. For a full commentary, see the edition in Arangio-Ruiz and Olivieri, *Inscriptiones* no. 17, together with the reviews by Kurt Latte, in *Gnomon* 3 (1927) 371–72, and Otto Gradenwitz, in ZSS 47 (1927) 494–95.

19. Franz Cumont, "Le plus ancien parchemin grec," *RP* 48 (1924) 97–111, reprinted with almost the identical commentary in Cumont, *Fouilles de Doura-Europos (1922–1923)* (Paris 1926) 286–96; see also P. M. Meyer, in ZSS 46 (1926) 339. In line 6, we read ἀπέδοτο λύσιμα κατὰ τὸν ν[όμον]. In the papyri, the term ὠνὴ ἐν πίστει appears occasionally and it is commonly assumed that its meaning is the same as *prasis epi lysei*, transformed for some reason to the "buyer's" viewpoint. The nature of the institution in the papyri is far from clear. The best account is still that of Mitteis in Ludwig Mitteis and Ulrich Wilcken, *Grundzüge und Chrestomathie der Papyruskunde* II, 1 (2 vols. in 4, Leipzig and Berlin 1912) 135–41; cf. Taubenschlag, *Law* I 206–7. There is no certain parallel in the Greek cities, but a probable case of ὠνὴ ἐν πίστει is IG VII 3376, a manumission inscription from Chaironea

of the first half of the second century B.C. For the various views, see
Pringsheim, *Sale* 187–89, and Erich Guenter, *Die Sicherungsübereignung
im griechischen Rechte* (diss. Königsberg 1914) 52–53.

20. See sect. 1 above. A very significant question of method is raised by
the terminological problem. Hitzig, for example, says in the preface of
his *Pfandrecht* (p. IV): "*Meine Schrift beschäftigt sich mit griechischem
Pfandrecht; ich habe mich nicht auf das attische Pfandrecht beschränkt,
sondern andere griechische Rechte berücksichtigt; ich bin dabei ausge-
gangen von den Bemerkungen, die Mitteis, Reichsrecht und Volksrecht,
pg. 61ff. gemacht hat; das Pfandrecht liefert einen neuen Beweis für die
Richtigkeit des dort gesagten.*" Though he adds a caution about possible
local variations (not always noted by later scholars), he proceeds to
shuttle from city to city as a text becomes available for his analysis.
That such a procedure destroys any possibility of seeing significant
variations that may lie concealed beneath a superficial similarity in
language or external form is soon apparent. After indicating the
frequency of *prasis epi lysei* in the Attic *horoi* and suggesting a
distinction between this type of security and the *hypotheke*, Hitzig
continues (p. 12): "*Auch die Betrachtung der außerattischen Quellen ergibt dasselbe Bild.*" The only other references he is able to give for
prasis epi lysei, however, are *horoi* from Amorgos and Lemnos (neither
SEG IV 62 nor the Doura parchment were available when he wrote).
Then he lists illustrations of *hypotheke* from Mykonos, Delos, Delphi,
Naxos, Ephesos, Amorgos, Kyme, Thera, and Kos, and concludes
(p. 13): "*So stehen Hypothek und* πρᾶσις ἐπὶ λύσει *im griechischen Rechte
nebeneinander,*" without realizing (as the remainder of his work demonstrates) that if he has proved anything from the terminology, it is that
hypotheke and *prasis epi lysei* did *not* exist side by side throughout the
Greek world. Guenter, *Sicherungsübereignung* 16, writes, without sub-
mitting any evidence: "*Aus den zahlreichen Quellen ergibt sich, daß die
πρᾶσις ἐπὶ λύσει vom 5. bis 2. Jahrh. v. Chr. ein im griechischen Rechts-
kreise wohl bekanntes und weit verbreitendes Rechtsinstitut war.*"

21. *Tenos* — IG XII 5,872 (with a few added notes in IG XII Supp.),
dated between 266 and 233 B.C. by Paul Graindor, in MB 14 (1910) 52;
cf. M. Holleaux, in BCH 54 (1930) 247, note 6. On the complex network
of transactions hidden behind the facade of sales in this so-called
register of land sales, see especially Rabel, "Nachgeformte Rechtsgeschäfte," XXVIII 312–17, 354–55. A complete analysis of this lengthy
document is very much needed. That *prasis epi lysei* was involved in
some of the entries can be demonstrated not only from the content but
also from the language in § 30, ἣν ἐπρίατο... κα[τ]ὰ δάνειον, and § 46,
ἃ ἀπέδωκε Φῶκος ᾿Αθηνάδει δανειζόμενος παρ᾽ ᾿Αθηνάδου 1400⊦. Cf. *P.A.-M.
Desrousseaux* of 75 B.C., lines 11–13; περὶ ὧν καὶ [ὑπ]έθεντο οἱ αὐτοὶ τῶι
Πετεσούχωι καθ᾽ ἑτέραν ἑξαμάρτυρον ὁμολογίαν πρά[σεως] βοῦς [θ]ηλείας πρὸς
ἀσφ[ά]λειαν τοῦ δανείου, translated by the editor, P. Jouguet: "*Dette
pour laquelle ils ont vendu en garantie à Petesouchos une vache, selon un
autre contrat à six témoins.*"

Sardis—Sardis, vol. VII, part 1, *Greek and Latin Inscriptions*, by
W. H. Buckler and D. M. Robinson (Leiden 1932) no. 1, originally

edited by Buckler and Robinson, with translation and lengthy commentary, in AJA 16 (1912) 11–82. The date has been disputed. Originally the editors set it at *c.* 300 B.C., but following objections by various scholars, some of whom placed it as late as the middle of the second century B.C., Buckler and Robinson in their re-publication suggest *c.* 200 B.C. for the actual inscription and perhaps as much as half a century earlier for the original transaction. Nothing in the two-column text, of which the upper ten lines were chiseled out, says explicitly that the document deals with a *prasis epi lysei* (the mere presence of the word ἀπολύσασθαι in line II 2 proves nothing). A strong argument has been made for so identifying it, but I prefer to reserve judgment. Too many difficulties remain to be explained before a final determination can be made. In any event, the complex transaction described took place under the monarchical land tenure regime of Hellenistic Asia Minor, so different in essence from the land system of the Greek cities that only the most cautious comparisons may be made. Certainly this inscription cannot serve as the key to the *prasis epi lysei* of the Athenian *horoi* in the present state of our knowledge.

Olynthus — TAPA 62 (1931) 42, no. 2, one of a group of inscriptions from Olynthus published as "deeds of sale," reads, lines 7–8: βεβαιωταὶ Ἀντίδοτος Θεοδώρου, Νίκων Ἡδωνέος ἐνιαυτὸν ἐπὶ ἀπόλυσιν. Altogether, 15 texts have been published in this group by D. M. Robinson, all from the years just prior to the city's destruction in 348 B.C., as follows: TAPA 59 (1928) 225–32; 62 (1931) 42–53, nos. 2–4; 65 (1934) 124–31, nos. 3–6; 69 (1938) 47–56, nos. 3–9. A nearly hopeless fragment was published by Robinson in *Excavations at Olynthus* 2 (Baltimore 1930) 101. Possibly related are three other inscriptions: M 1386, with further comments by Paul Perdrizet, "Études amphipolitaines," BCH 46 (1922) 36–57, at pp. 36–40; the stone edited by Adolf Wilhelm, "Neue Beiträge zur griechischen Inschriftenkunde I," *Sitz. Vienna* 166,1 (1910) 42, no. 8, with comment by P. Roussel in BCH 53 (1929) 18; and Δελτ. 9 (1924/5) παρ. 40. Though the series of Olynthian texts appears to be a group of deeds of sale inscribed on stone, it appears that in some, at least, other transactions lie concealed beneath the sale appearance. In the one stone singled out here, warranty ἐπὶ ἀπόλυσιν may very well indicate *prasis epi lysei*, though Robinson thinks not.

22. For an indication of the failure of the late Greek and Byzantine lexica to consider *prasis epi lysei*, see note 11 above.

23. On the phrase, "which Nikeratos has as pledgee" (ἃ ἔχει θέμενος), see Chap. II, note 12. On the participation of Hegekrate and her *kyrios*, see Chap. VI, note 22. For ἀποδίδωμι instead of πιπράσκω, see Chap. VIII, note 16.

24. Demosthenes, *Against Pantainetes* (orat. 37). For the date, see Blass, *Beredsamkeit* III 1,478. This is one of the rare instances in which Blass misunderstood the facts and issues completely. He missed the essential point, that the transaction was a *prasis epi lysei*, an error that is widespread among non-juristic commentators; cf., for example, Engelbert

Drerup, "Über die bei den attischen Rednern eingelegten Urkunden," *Jahrbücher KP*, Supp. 24 (1898) 223–365, at pp. 323–25, or G. M. Calhoun, *The Business Life of Ancient Athens* (Chicago 1926) 167–70.

25. The combinations in these loans are worth noting, three creditors and two debts the first time, two creditors and two amounts the second. On the significance of such combinations in the *horoi*, see Chap. VIII. The relationship among the creditors in the Pantainetos case has often been misinterpreted; see Chap. V, note 110.

26. *Ibid.* 5: καὶ γὰρ ἐώνητ' ἐκεῖνος αὐτὰ τούτῳ παρὰ Τηλεμάχου τοῦ πρότερον κεκτημένου.

27. "In a given period" is ἔν τινι ῥητῷ χρόνῳ, *ibid.* Reference to the additional clauses appears in §§ 5–7, 25–26, 29.

28. *Ibid.* 13–16. "...we were rightfully..." is ἡμεῖς δ'εἰκότως ἐφαινόμεθ' ὧν ἐωνήμεθα κρατεῖν. The word for "seller" is always πρατήρ, on which see below, note 33.

29. *Ibid.* 31: ἃ γὰρ ἡμεῖς πέντε καὶ ἑκατὸν μνῶν ἐωνήμεθα, ταῦθ' ὕστερον τριῶν ταλάντων καὶ δισχιλίων καὶ ἑξακοσίων ἀπέδου σύ· καίτοι τίς ἂν καθάπαξ πρα-τῆρά σ' ἔχων σοὶ δραχμὴν ἔδωκε μίαν; The two best MSS, S and A, read ἀπεδόμεθα in place of ἐωνήμεθα. The choice is immaterial, since Nikobulos and Euergos both "bought" and "sold" the property for 10,500 drachmas at different times. From § 30, I prefer ἀπεδόμεθα; its rejection by the editors may be attributed to their misunderstanding of the legal situation. On καθάπαξ πρατήρ, see immediately below.

30. *Ibid.* Arg. 2: καὶ ἦν τοῦτο τῷ μὲν ἔργῳ τόκος, τῷ δ'ὀνόματι μίσθωσις.

31. Paoli, "Ipoteca" 152, misreads the possession situation in this case, as was indicated by LaPira in his review, in BIDR 41 (1933) at p. 301.

32. Demosthenes, *Against Pantainetos* 37.30. Hitzig, *Pfandrecht* 106, note 2, comments that Nikobulos seems to be saying "*daß normal ge-wesen wäre, wenn die Sprecher an Pantainetos zurück, und dieser selbst dann weiterverkauft hätte.*"

33. The word πρατήρ merits careful study. It is used 14 times in this oration. According to Konrad Schodorf, *Beiträge zur genaueren Kennt-nis der attischen Gerichtssprache aus den zehn Rednern* (Würzburg 1904) 93, the only other use in the extant works of the Attic orators is in Isaeus, *On the Estate of Aristarchos* 10.24. There the MS actually reads πρακτήρ, changed to πρατήρ by Stephanus (followed by all modern editors). Whatever the correct reading may be, the context is again one of proving the legitimacy of one's holding, title in other words; see note 51 below. Demosthenes' preference for "to be a vendor" rather than "to sell" in the Pantainetos oration can best be explained by this emphasis on warranty. The only other Athenian citation of πρατήρ as "seller" in Liddell-and-Scott is Plato, *Laws* 915C–D: ἐὰν δὲ ὡς αὑτοῦ ἐφάπτηται ζῴου καὶ ὁτουοῦν ἢ τινος ἑτέρου τῶν αὑτοῦ χρημάτων, ἀναγέτω μὲν ὁ ἔχων εἰς πρατῆρα ἢ τὸν δόντα ἀξιοχρέων τε καὶ ἔνδικον ἤ τινι τρόπῳ

παραδόντα ἄλλῳ κυρίως.... A remarkable parallel appears in one of the mid-third-century Milesian *asylia* treaties with various Cretan cities, *Milet* I 3,140 B 40–42: ἐάν τις Μιλησίων ἐγ Γόρτυνι ἢ Γορτυνίων ἐμ Μιλήτωι ἐφάπτηται σώματος ἢ δούλου ἢ ἐλευθέρου, ἂμ μὲν ἀνάγηι ὁ ἔχων πράτορι ἀξιόχρεωι ἢ εἰς πόλιν ἔνδικον.... The warranty idea is again unmistakable. Further clarification comes from *Synagoge, Anecdota Bekker* I 467.1 (= Suidas, s.v.): αὐτομαχῆσαι: ὅταν ἀντιποιῆταί τις οἰκίας ἢ χωρίου, καὶ εἴη ὁ πεπρακὼς μὲν ἀξιόχρεως, ὥστε δοκεῖν ἀποτῖσαι ⟨ἂν? Rehm⟩ τὴν ζημίαν καὶ (sc. ὥστε, Rehm συνίστασθαι τὴν δίκην πρὸς τὸν ἀντιποιούμενον, βούλοιτο δὲ ὁ διακατέχων τὴν οἰκίαν ἢ τὸ χωρίον ἴδιον αὐτῷ γένεσθαι ἀγῶνα πρὸς τὸν ἀμφισβητοῦντα, τοῦτο αὐτομαχῆσαι λέγεται. As usual, *Dikon onomata, ibid.* I 184.13, has a shorter and less accurate definition. On the legal procedure indicated in these texts, see Max Kaser, "Der altgriechische Eigentumsschutz," ZSS 64 (1944) 134–205, at pp.161–79, with a complete collection of sources and full bibliography.

Liddell-and-Scott's one non-Athenian citation is the Tenos "register" of sales, IG XII 5,872, where the word πρατήρ appears over and over again with the unequivocal meaning of "warrantor" and *not* "seller," as the lexicon has it. Liddell-and-Scott has no definition, πρατήρ = warrantor (for a similar error with regard to προπώλης, see Chap. VI, note 46).

That Libanios understood the warranty emphasis in the Pantainetos case is apparent. He writes, Arg. 2: καὶ γίνεται πρατὴρ καὶ βεβαιωτὴς τοῖς δευτέροις δανεισταῖς ὁ πρότερος δεδανεικὼς ὁ Μνησικλῆς, ὁ τὰς ὠνὰς ἔχων; and again, Arg. 4: πάλιν δ'οὐκ ἐθελόντων τῶν δανειστῶν ὠνεῖσθαι τὰ κτήματα, εἰ μὴ πρατῆρες αὐτοὶ καὶ βεβαιωταὶ γίγνοιντο Νικόβουλος καὶ Εὔεργος. The usual Greek word for "to warrant," βεβαιόω,, appears once in the oration proper, § 12: καὶ τοῦ Μνησικλέους βεβαιοῦντος ἡμῖν. Here, as often in the literature, it ha the general sense of "confirm," not the narrow, technical meaning of "warrant title."

34. See Partsch, *Bürgschaftsrecht* 356–58 (pp. 340–58 remain the best account of Greek warranty in general along with the more detailed discussion by Pringsheim, *Sale,* Pt. III, Chap. V).

35. Cf. the lexical passage on αὐτομαχῆσαι quoted in note 33 above, and Dio Chrysostom, *Rhodian Oration* 31.50.

36. Demosthenes, *Against Pantainetos* 37.50: καὶ ἐφ' οἷς δανείσασθαι μὲν οὐδεπώποτ' ἠδυνήθης ἑκατὸν μνῶν πλέον, πέπρακας δὲ καθάπαξ τριῶν ταλάντων καὶ δισχιλίων.... The figures are rounded off here, a characteristic device of the orators. The correct amounts are 10,500 and 20,600 drachmas, respectively.

37. The significance of this arithmetic is properly stressed by Wyse, *Isaeus* 431. One other *horos* marking a *prasis epi lysei*, no. 27, may also indicate an interest-figure; see Chap. VI, note 66.

38. Demosthenes, *Against Pantainetos* 37.31,50. The word is καθάπαξ.

39. Fortified by the use of the word θέσις to describe what is quite certainly a *prasis epi lysei* in [Demosthenes], *Against Apaturios* 33.12, and by Pollux, *Onomasticon* 8.142, ' Ὑπερείδης δὲ ἐν τῷ πρὸς Χάρητα ἔφη ἀποδόμενος ἀντὶ τοῦ ὑποθεῖς, legal historians have generally agreed, if somewhat reluctantly, that the Greeks understood *prasis epi lysei* to fall within the framework of security and not sale; see Hitzig, *Pfandrecht* 3–4; Rabel, "Nachgeformte Rechtsgeschäfte" XXVIII 354–55; Weiss, *Untersuchungen* I 10–12 and *passim*. That was certainly Libanios' understanding of the Pantainetos transaction when he wrote, Arg. 1: ὕστερον δ'ἀπαιτούμενος τὸ ἀργύριον ὁ Πανταίνετος δευτέρους λαμβάνει δανεισ-τὰς τόν τε παραγραφόμενον νῦν Νικόβουλον καὶ Εὔεργόν τινα, καὶ τούτοις ὑποθήκην δίδωσι τὸ ἐργαστήριον καὶ τὰ ἀνδράποδα. To explain the sale aspect, Libanios added, Arg. 2: γραμματεῖον δ'οὐχ ὑποθήκης, ἀλλὰ πράσεως γράφεται. A striking analogy is offered by early modern English law, as summarized by Hazeltine, "*Fiducia* and Mortgage" xliv: "The introduction of the proviso for reconveyance appears to have some historical connection with the attempt to treat the mortgage transaction as a sale of land with an option of buying it back.... If by means of these instruments the transaction could be treated as a sale with option of repurchase the debtor's rights would be lost immediately upon his default. On the principles of 'once a mortgage, always a mortgage,' it was held by the chancery, however, that if such a transaction was in fact intended merely as a security, it was nothing but a mortgage."

A determined attempt to remove *prasis epi lysei* from the category of security and place it under sale was made by Guenter, *Sicherungsübereignung*. We need not seek to refute his fine-spun legalisms in detail, however, first because the entire argument rests on the assumption that Greek legal institutions can be pigeonholed into neat, clear-cut juristic categories (an assumption that is untenable for ancient Greece and not even as valid for modern law as Guenter seems to think), and second because the recent publication of *Hesperia* 10 (1941) 14, no. 1, cuts the ground from under him entirely, as it has rendered much writing on the subject of *prasis epi lysei* obsolete. This inscription is discussed briefly in the text immediately below and at length in Chap. VIII at notes 13–19. (The recent study by I. A. Melotopoulos, "Πρᾶσις ἐπὶ λύσει," *Polemon* 4 (1949) 41–72, was not available to me.)

40. Maitland, *Equity* 182.

41. [Demosthenes], *Against Apaturios* (orat. 33). On the date, see Blass, *Beredsamkeit* III 1,572–74. The main argument for considering the key transaction to be a *prasis epi lysei* rests on § 8: λαβὼν δὲ [ἐγὼ] τὰς ἑπτὰ μνᾶς παρὰ τοῦ Παρμένοντος, καὶ τὰς τρεῖς ἃς προσειλήφει οὗτος παρ' ἐκείνου, ἀνθομολογησάμενος πρὸς τοῦτον, ὠνὴν ποιοῦμαι τῆς νεὼς καὶ τῶν παίδων, ἕως ἀποδοίη τάς τε δέκα μνᾶς.... It is worth noting that, though the unnamed speaker identifies himself as a professional moneylender and though a banker is also involved, the implication is clear that these were interest-free, "friendly" loans. Further, though a ship served as security, the loan was not a bottomry loan in the usual sense.

42. *Ibid.* 12. It would take us beyond the bounds set for this discussion to examine the legal problem created by this seemingly forced sale of the hypothecated property. That is but one of half a dozen perplexing legal questions raised in this oration, none of which has been satisfactorily answered. That the sale of Apaturios' ship cannot be generalized into a rule of Greek security transactions is recognized by all scholars.

43. *Hesperia* 10 (1941) 14, no. 1, lines 1–39. See further Chap. VIII at notes 13–19.

44. The second *prasis epi lysei* is identified in lines 33–34, from the "buyer's" point of view, by πριαμένων ἡμῶν . . . ἐπὶ λύσει, the first simply by the verb ἀποδομένο (line 23), thus confirming Pollux, *Onomasticon* 8.142, quoted in note 11 above. Four *horoi*, nos. 112–115, say "sold"; see Chap. VII at notes 68–70.

45. Cf. the "paired" *horoi*, nos. 80–81, discussed in Chap. II, end of sect. 2. One of the complications in the Pantainetos case that I disregarded in my summary because it was not germane to the main thread was the account, by no means a lucid one, of an added encumbrance Pantainetos had placed on the property by borrowing an unidentified amount from unidentified lenders while first Mnesikles and then Nikobulos and Euergos "held" the property by *prasis epi lysei* (Demosthenes, *Against Pantainetos* 37.12). This raises the whole question of primary and secondary security obligations, on which see Chap. VIII. Both the Pantainetos case and the new *Hesperia* text show decisively, in my judgment, that whatever the law and the practice may have been on this question, they approached *prasis epi lysei* under the law of guaranty, not of sale.

46. See further Chap. II, end of sect. 2.

47. On *horos* no. 71, see Chap. VI, near the end. When Hitzig, *Pfandrecht* 10, writes, "*bei der* πρᾶσις ἐπὶ λύσει *war Fixierung des Termins nicht nötig, weil ja sofort Eigentum überging*," and Rabel, "Nachgeformte Rechtsgeschäfte" XXVIII 354, adds that failure to specify a terminal date means that there is no time limit to the seller-debtor's right to redeem his property, they reveal the magnetic power of the word "sale" in *prasis epi lysei*, for the statements are not meaningful. They are merely saying that if the agreement provides no terminal date for payment, there is no terminal date. Why should that be more noteworthy in *prasis epi lysei* than in any other security transaction, or in an unsecured loan for that matter? Loans without a terminal date are not unknown; see, for example, the various loans by Pasion to Timotheos, [Demosthenes], *Against Timotheos* (orat. 49), or the two-talent loan made by the speaker's grandfather in the fifth century B.C., which eventually led to the legal dispute of Lysias, orat. 17, known from the manuscript under the impossible title, Δημοσίων ἀδικημάτων. Ultimately, the duration of the typical *prasis epi lysei* is a matter of the prevailing Athenian practice with regard to loans, and it will be argued at the end of Chap. VI that the practice was one of short-term

obligations. I see nothing in the available evidence to require a modification of that conclusion for *prasis epi lysei*.

48. Isaeus, *On the Estate of Philoktemon* 6.33–34. The key passage is οἰκίαν δὲ ἐν ἄστει τεττάρων καὶ τετταράκοντα μνῶν ὑποκειμένην ἀπέλυσε τῷ ἱεροφάντῃ. It is often mistranslated as "redeemed from the hierophant," whereas Wyse, *Isaeus* 521, has shown that ἀπολύω in the active is always used for the creditor who gives a release.

49. This has been the generally accepted view since Hitzig, *Pfandrecht* 9, note 1. Wyse, *Isaeus* 521, expresses doubts because of the word ὑποκειμένην. But such terminological precision is not to be expected. On the other hand, Hitzig's suggestion that the appearance of *lysis* is always a sign of *prasis epi lysei* is untenable in the light of the common use of the word in all kinds of relationships that are subject to dissolution.

50. [Lysias], *Against the Co-Associates* 8.10. For a bibliography on the meaning of the passage, see Guenter, *Sicherungsübereignung* 44–47. It is significant that Guenter must lay so much stress on this miserable text. In the first place, the whole character of the oration is uncertain; see Chap. VII, note 56. In the second place, the transaction may well have been an ordinary pledge, as Hitzig, *Pfandrecht* 96–97, and others have argued. The main argument for holding it to be a *prasis epi lysei* rests on the words, κάμνοντα τὸν ἵππον ἀνάγειν με βουλόμενον Διόδωρος οὑτοσὶ ἀποτρέπειν ἐπειρᾶτο. Now ἀνάγειν εἰς πρατῆρα is a technical term for an action to compel cancellation of a sale, for instance in the case of a slave with a concealed defect. (Cf. the passages and bibliography cited in note 33 above and, above all, Hypereides, *Against Athenogenes* 5.15, which Guenter overlooks though it is his best parallel.) Hence Gernet and Bizos, in the Guillaume Budé edition, translate, "*je voulais intenter l'action rédhibitoire.*" And, therefore, says Guenter, the original transaction must have been a *prasis epi lysei*, for only in case of sale could there have been an action of cancellation. (He also introduces the erroneous idea of a time limit, for which there is not a shred of evidence in the passage.) But we cannot be sure that the speaker, more properly the writer, was using technical juristic language; this was not a forensic speech and it is generally a poor specimen of the speechwriter's art. Nor do we know anything about the rights of a creditor in an ordinary pledge transaction; specifically we know nothing about the procedure available to him if the pledged object should prove to be defective. Finally, we have no evidence of the existence of special actions for cases arising from hypothecation. If the ordinary property actions were used, as is generally agreed, why not the ἀνάγειν εἰς πρατῆρα too when appropriate? In sum, this text hardly demonstrates that *prasis epi lysei* was a sale transaction, qualitatively distinct in the legal system from security transactions.

51. In Isaeus, *On the Estate of Dikaiogenes* 5.21, we read: οὐδὲ γὰρ πρὶν ἡττηθῆναι τὴν δίκην εἶχεν ὧν ἡμεῖς δικαζόμεθα, ἀλλ' οἱ παρὰ τούτου πριάμενοι καὶ θέμενοι, οἷς ἔδει αὐτὸν ἀποδόντα τὴν τιμὴν ἡμῖν τὰ μέρη ἀποδοῦνα

(cf. § 22). In *On the Estate of Aristarchos* 10.24, we find: καίτοι δίκαιον, ὦ ἄνδρες, ὥσπερ τῶν ἀμφισβητησίμων χωρίων δεῖ τὸν ἔχοντα ἢ θέτην ἢ πρα-τῆρα (MS: πρακτῆρα) παρέχεσθαι ἢ καταδεδικασμένον φαίνεσθαι.... It seems unnecessary to enter into the many debates over the meanings of πριά-μενοι καὶ θέμενοι in the former and θέτην in the latter, since, no matter how interpreted, the passages do not contribute to the present discussion. On the former, see Wyse, *Isaeus* 429–37, and Paoli, "Ipoteca" 155. On the latter, I agree with Münscher, who translates on p. 283, "*der sie ihm durch Adoption vermacht hat,*" for θέτην, basing his translation on Harpocration and Photius, *s.v.*, and *Lexeis rhetorikai, Anecdota Bekker* I 264.3, and thus linking the passage with the texts cited above in note 33. For an alternative view, see Wyse, *Isaeus* 668–69; Kaser, "Eigentumsschutz" 185. Suggestions have also been made that *prasis epi lysei* may be meant in IG II² 1172 and 2498, but the proposals are unwarranted; see Chap. VII, notes 39 and 38, respectively.

52. This point is discussed in detail in the latter part of Chap. VI.

53. On the question of interest-bearing and interest-free loans, see the latter part of Chap. VI. Guenter, *Sicherungsübereignung* 30, writes: "*Gleichzeitig mit dem Eigentume erhält der Käufer bei der* πρᾶσις ἐπὶ λύσει *auch den Besitz und die Nutznießung an der auf Lösung ihm ver-kauften Sache.*" For this erroneous generalization he cites secondary references only and a study of the latter will show that the conclusion is unwarranted even from their citation of sources. Then he goes on to the Pantainetos case and *horos* no. 102, from which he concludes (p. 31): "*Diese Rückübertragung von Besitz und Nutzung an den Ver-käufer ist sehr häufig bei der* πρᾶσις ἐπὶ λύσει *erfolgt.*" For that, the evidence (in note 3) is: "*So die übereinstimmende Ansicht in der Literatur,*" followed by some Roman-law parallels.

Notes to Chapter IV

1. Two points should be noted regarding the terminology: (1) occasionally the prefix *apo* was ignored (see note 51 below); and (2) *apotimao* is sometimes, though rarely, used to mean "to evaluate" in fields other than legal security (see note 44 below).

2. In the translation the first three lines of the stone have been omitted. On those lines and on two linguistic peculiarities of the text, see notes 25 and 54 below.

3. Aristotle, *Constitution of the Athenians* 56.7: μισθοῖ δὲ καὶ τοὺς οἴκους τῶν ὀρφανῶν καὶ τῶν ἐπικλ[ήρων], ἕως ἄν τις τετταρ]αικαιδεκέτις γένηται, καὶ τὰ ἀποτιμήματα λαμβάν[ει]. In Athenian law, a child became an orphan through the loss of the father. An *epikleros* was an orphaned girl who had no brothers.

4. Harpocration, ἀποτιμηταὶ καὶ ἀποτίμημα καὶ ἀποτιμᾶν καὶ τὰ ἀπ᾽ αὐτῶν:
οἱ μισθούμενοι τοὺς τῶν ὀρφανῶν οἴκους παρὰ τοῦ ἄρχοντος ἐνέχυρα τῆς μισθώσεως παρείχοντο· ἔδει δὲ τοῦ ἄρχοντα ἐπιπέμπειν τινὰς ἀποτιμησομένους τὰ
ἐνέχυρα. τὰ μὲν οὖν ἐνέχυρα τὰ ἀποτιμώμενα ἐλέγοντο ἀποτιμήματα, οἱ δὲ πεμ-
πόμενοι ἐπὶ τῷ ἀποτιμήσασθαι ἀποτιμηταί, τὸ δὲ πρᾶγμα ἀποτιμᾶν. The definition goes on to the dotal *apotimema*; see at notes 29 and 34. The
word *misthosis* may mean either the lease-agreement or the rental.
Harpocration probably meant the latter, but I have translated the
word as "lease" because, as will be indicated later in this section, the
security guaranteed the return of the property as well as the rental
payment. Similar definitions, with but insignificant variants in wording, are to be found in Suidas, *s.v.*; *Synagoge, Anecdota Bekker* I
437.15; Scholia to Demosthenes, *Against Onetor II* 31.11.

5. In his original publication of SEG IV 73, a fourth or third-century
bronze tablet from Terina, Domenico Comparetti, "Tabello testa-
mentarie delle colonii Achee di Magna Grecia," *Annuario* 2 (1916) 219–
66, at pp. 241–42, proposed an incorrect interpretation involving the
pupillary *apotimema*; see Arangio-Ruiz and Olivieri, *Inscriptiones* no.
21; Latte, in his review of the latter volume, in *Gnomon* 3 (1927) 372–
75; and Werner Kamps, "La fiducie dans le droit de Grande-Grèce et
l'origine de la *mancipatio familiae*," RHD, 4 ser., 15 (1936) 142–55.

6. The only systematic discussion of the *misthosis oikou* is Otto Schulthess, *Vormundschaft nach attischem Recht* (Freiburg 1886) 139–73, 209–
20. It is not entirely satisfactory, partly because of the many digres-
sions into problems of leases in general and of interest rates and partly
because of its exclusive concern with juristic questions. Half a century
later, Schulthess wrote a brief, slightly revised, summary of his
analysis, "Μίσθωσις" 2111–14, which is the best introduction available; see also Weiss, *Untersuchungen* I 129–38. No one, to my knowledge, has examined the social and economic implications of the
institution, a study well worth making even if the nature of the available sources probably will not permit very conclusive findings.

7. Demosthenes, *Against Aphobos I* 27.15,40,42; II 28.1,7; cf. *Against
Onetor I* 30.6.

8. See Otto Schulthess, *Die Vormundschaftsrechnung des Demosthenes*
(Program Frauenfeld 1899) 38–39.

9. Lysias, *Against Diogeiton* 32.23. On the date, see Gernet and Bizos in
the Guillaume Budé ed., II 187.

10. The permissive character of *misthosis oikou* when not required by
testament is also clearly implied in Lysias, frag. 43 (Thalheim), preserved in Dionysius, *On the Orations of Isaeus* 8; Isaeus, *On the Estate of
Dikaiogenes* 5.10-11, *On the Estate of Apollodoros* 7.6, *On the Estate of
Kiron* 8.41–42, and *On the Estate of Hagnias* 11.34. The sole text which
seems to say, on the contrary, that *misthosis oikou* was required by law,
is in the suspect third oration of Demosthenes against Aphobos,
29.29: ... καὶ τὸν οἶκον οὐκ ἐμίσθωσε τῶν νόμων κελευόντων καὶ τοῦ πατρὸς

ἐν τῇ διαθήκῃ γράψαντος .... Here the question of authenticity goes far beyond authorship. If it can be demonstrated that the speech was not written by Demosthenes and not delivered in his suit against his guardians, then it must be completely rejected as a rhetorical exercise of late though uncertain date, and hence of no value as a source of information about fourth-century Athenian institutions. A full analysis, with detailed bibliography, will be found in G. M. Calhoun, "A Problem of Authenticity (Demosthenes 29)," TAPA 65 (1934) 80–102. Calhoun concludes that the speech is genuine despite such glaring errors as the inclusion of Demosthenes' uncle Demon among the guardians. Unfortunately, Calhoun completely overlooked § 29. The statement that the law requires *misthosis oikou* is certainly wrong. Further, this is an error Demosthenes himself could not have made in the light of his treatment of the problem in the two authentic speeches against Aphobos. It is not difficult to see how a later rhetorician, neither well versed nor much concerned with the law, could have misinterpreted Demosthenes' statement (27.58): τούτῳ γὰρ ἐξῆν μηδὲν ἔχειν τούτων τῶν πραγμάτων, μισθώσαντι τὸν οἶκον κατὰ τουτουσὶ τοὺς νόμους. All that this means is that the guardians could have leased the estate in the manner prescribed by law, presumably the same law or body of laws cited by Lysias, *Against Diogeiton* 32.23, in the passage just quoted. It does not mean "as the law orders." Taken with the other errors, this mistake fully justifies the conclusion that the third oration against Aphobos is a school exercise or practice speech; see Schulthess, "Μίσθωσις" 2112, who quite properly objects to any milder formulation, such as *"mindestens eine rednerische Übertreibung,"* as Lipsius, *Attisches Recht* II 346, note 25, phrases it. Lipsius considers the speech unauthentic and yet persistently cites it as a source, a procedure that is self-contradictory, as Calhoun, *ibid.* 99, noted.

Lysias, *Against Diogeiton* 32.23, indicates that the law on orphans also permits the guardian to buy land with money that is included in the estate. In Lysias, frag. 91 (Thalheim), preserved in Suidas, *s.v.* ἔγγειον, we read: τοῦ νόμου κελεύοντος τοὺς ἐπιτρόπους τοῖς ὀρφανοῖς ἔγγειον τὴν οὐσίαν καθιστάναι, οὗτος δὲ ναυτικοὺς ἡμᾶς ἀποφαίνει. That the law was permissive, not mandatory, on this point too is clear, for example, from Demosthenes' complaint against his guardians. The fragment preserved by Suidas is therefore either misquoted, taken out of context, or wrong in some other respect; see Gernet and Bizos in their ed., II 183, note 3.

Finally, it should be noted that these references to laws do not contradict the point made repeatedly in this volume that the Athenian law of security was guided by practice, not by statute. We are dealing here with a body of regulations concerning orphans and their property. In that context, the law set up procedures for the leasing of property under certain conditions, and for the taking of security (apotimema) to protect the orphan's future rights. There is little doubt that, once the security was offered and accepted by the archon, further procedures involving the security itself followed the regular practice of Athenian hypothecation.

11. Demosthenes, *Against Nausimachos and Xenopeithes* 38.23, discussed more fully immediately below; cf. Isaeus, *On the Estate of Hagnias* 11.34; Harpocration and Suidas, *s.v.* φᾶσις; *Lexeis rhetorikai, Anecdota Bekker* I 313.20, 315.16. In Demosthenes, *Against Aphobos I* 27.15, however, he says merely that his uncle Demochares remonstrated (ἐποιήσατο λόγους) with the guardians for their failure to lease, despite his claim that it was ordered in the will.

12. Lysias, *Against Diogeiton* 32.23.

13. Demosthenes, *Against Nausimachos and Xenopeithes* 38.7,23. Paoli, "Ipoteca" 166–67, who argues vigorously that it was liquid and "business" property, not land, that was leased, cites this text as proof of his view, overlooking the outcome of the transaction. He also ignores Isaeus, *On the Estate of Hagnias* 11.34, on which see the following note. Of his further references, the Aphobos case and Lysias, *Against Diogeiton* 32.23, are subject to the alternative interpretation indicated in the text; Isaeus, *On the Estate of Menekles* 2.29, and Demosthenes, *Against Aphobos I* 27.58 (which deals with a parallel cited by Demosthenes), are probably legitimate illustrations; Demosthenes, *Against Aphobos II* 28.2, is quite irrelevant (see note 23 below).

14. I do not understand why Lipsius, *Attisches Recht* 348, note 28, writes: "*Daß auch einzelne Teile des Vermögens verpachtet werden konnten, folgt aus Isaios a.a.O.* [i.e., 2.9] *nicht, darf aber auch nicht mit Schulthess S. 148f in Abrede gestellt werden.*" He presents no evidence. Ironically, the sole exception to the otherwise invariable *misthosis oikou* is in Isaeus, *On the Estate of Hagnias* 11.34, where we find μίσθωσις χρημάτων in reference to property much of which is in land. This is but another illustration of the arbitrary use of χρήματα by Isaeus. The property at issue is half an estate, that is, one brother's share. Insofar as the latter is concerned, the half-share is his *oikos*; hence this instance is no exception to the rule. It is unfortunate that some translators still persist in rendering *oikos* as "house," as in the recent translation of Aristotle's *Constitution of the Athenians* by Kurt von Fritz and Ernst Kapp (New York 1950), where we find (56.7) "leased out the houses of orphans." *Lexeis rhetorikai, Anecdota Bekker* I 315.16, reads μεμισθωκότων τὰς οἰκίας τῶν ὀρφανῶν, but that is a copyist's error. In the Harpocration passage quoted in note 4 above, the MSS read οἰκίας, corrected to οἴκους by Dindorf on the basis of the Epitome and the identical entries in Suidas and others. On the distinction between οἶκος and οἰκία, see in particular Xenophon, *Oeconomicus* 1.5; 6.4.

15. Isaeus, *On the Estate of Menekles* 2.9. Schulthess had sought to dispute the validity of this evidence in *Vormundschaft* 148–49, but later withdrew his objections, "Μίσθωσις" 2112.

16. Though the proof that the guardian could himself be the lessee is limited to Isaeus, *On the Estate of Philoktemon* 6.37, and much of that account is hopelessly unintelligible (as we shall see shortly), Schulthess, *Vormundschaft* 146, note 2, is surely correct when he writes: "*Daß wirklich die Vormünder selber die Pacht übernehmen wollten, steht in der*

Stelle, wir können sie lesen, wie wir wollen." (His citation of *Syll.* 364, lines 53–55 [Ephesos *c.* 300 B.C.], as a parallel instance outside of Athens rests on a misunderstanding of the basic character of the inscription.) Wyse, *Isaeus* 526–27, disputes Schulthess, but his only argument is that a guardian would be in an "anomalous position" as lessee. This is not the only instance of Wyse's rejection of an argument in Isaeus because it would be improbable or implausible under late nineteenth-century social and economic conditions.

17. Isaeus, *On the Estate of Philoktemon* (orat. 6). For a guide through the almost unbelievably complicated history of this family dispute, see Wyse, *Isaeus* 483–88, with important corrections, based on a fundamentally new approach, by Kamps, "Affaire de fraude."

18. *Ibid.* 36–37.

19. Wyse, *Isaeus* 525, says, "If the judges...comprehended the design which he attributes to his opponent, they were more acute than modern commentators," and Münscher, in his translation at p. 178, note 1, agrees emphatically. Kamps, "Affaire de fraude" 33, fits the story into his general explanation but makes no effort to unravel the difficulties.

20. For other references to public lease or sale ἐν τῷ δικαστηρίῳ, see IG II² 1669, lines 8 and 21; Aristotle, *Constitution of the Athenians* 47.3; and, by implication, *Hesperia* 10 (1941) 14, no. 1, discussed in Chap. VIII at notes 13–19.

21. Cf. Demosthenes, *Against Nausimachos and Xenopeithes* 38.23: οὐκ ἐμίσθωσαν ἡμῶν τὸν οἶκον, ἴσως ἐροῦσιν. οὐ γὰρ ἐβούλεθ' ὁ θεῖος ὑμῶν Ξενοπείθης, ἀλλὰ φήναντος Νικίδου τοὺς δικαστὰς ἔπεισεν ἐᾶσαι αὐτὸν διοικεῖν.

22. The seemingly exceptional passage is Isaeus, *On the Estate of Menekles* 2.9. For the various views, see Paoli, "Ipoteca" 168. I am frankly unable to understand the passage.

23. Hitzig, *Pfandrecht* 38, calls attention to the phrasing in the Harpocration passage quoted in note 4 above: "It was necessary for the archon to send persons to evaluate the securities." "Send," Hitzig says, can mean only that the property consisted of realty, for movables could have been brought in by the lessee for evaluation. The same verb, ἐπιπέμπω, appears in *horos* no. 130. Cf. IG I² 94, line 7: καὶ τὸς ὁριστὰς (boundary surveyors) ἐπιπέμψαι ὁρίσαι τὰ ℎιερὰ ταῦτα. Paoli, "Ipoteca" 168–69, adds two references, one admittedly uncertain, which prove merely that in those particular cases the security offered was realty. His third reference involves a misunderstanding. In Demosthenes, *Against Aphobos II* 28.2, the orator is seeking to counter one argument made by Aphobos. The latter had said that in the will of the elder Demosthenes there was a specific request that the estate should not be leased, because, Aphobos explained, the grandfather had been inscribed as a defaulting state debtor and *misthosis oikou* proceedings would reveal the estate and hence open the risk of confiscation. Demosthenes

begins his answer as follows: νῦν δὲ τεκμηρίοις μεγάλοις ἐπιδείξομεν ὡς οὔτ' ὤφειλεν οὔτ, ἦν κίνδυνος οὐδεὶς ἡμῖν φανερὰ κεκτημένοις τὰ ὄντα. Paoli translates the ending, "*non vi era per noi alcun pericolo se (in conseguenza della* μίσθωσις) *fossimo venuti in possesso di beni immobili.*" But the danger, according to Aphobos, was in revealing Demosthenes' *oikos* (this is the issue of "visible" and "invisible" property discussed in Chap. V, sect. 1), not the property to be put up as security by a lessee. The root of the error lies in Paoli's view, to which repeated reference has been made, that in an *apotimema* transaction possession of the security is immediately transferred to the creditor. In the same vein, he argues that since the security always consisted of realty, Aristotle's language — the archon "receives" the *apotimema* — indicates a *pignoris capio*. The obvious reply to this conception of the *apotimema* is to ask first why anyone should lease one holding for a period of years only to give up possession of another worth at least as much, and second who would manage the *apotimema* if the guardian would not or could not administer his ward's own estate.

24. On the implications of the non-citizen's being barred from the land, see Chap. VI, sect. 1.

25. In note 2 above, it was indicated that there was difficulty in interpreting the first three lines of *horos* no. 130, which precede the word *horos* itself. These lines read: εἰς ἐνιαυτὸν ἐπ[ὶ] / Κλεισαγόρου ἄρχοντ⟨ο⟩ /ς τὸ μισθώματος. The original editor, Jeanne Vanseveren, in RP 63 (1937) 315, no. 2, notes that the three lines are larger and deeper than the rest. Though she says nothing about the hand, the photograph seems to indicate that everything on the stone was inscribed by the same stonecutter. Mlle. Vanseveren suggests either that the stone had previously been used for some other purpose and was not fully erased, or that the opening lines were the end of a summary of the lease-agreement which the person who set up the *horos* chose to publicize on the stone along with the notice of the *apotimema*. The first alternative seems most unlikely because it is difficult to understand the failure to destroy the three final lines of a discarded text before re-using the stone. The other alternative would explain the failure of the *horos* proper to specify the kind of property put up as security. However, *horos* no. 129, found in Laureion, also omits a description of the property and it is possible to explain both omissions as examples of the carelessness that runs through the *horoi* and nothing more than that. Furthermore, in the light of our analysis of the *misthosis oikou* it is difficult to find a reason for inscribing the lease-agreement, unless it be the one noted before, that is, the tendency in Amorgos to be explicit about "borrowed" legal institutions.

26. Professor John Day suggests that in no. 131 lines 13–14 be restored ἄπα / [ντα τετι]μήται, rather than ἄπα / [ν ἀποτετί]μηται as published in IG XII Supp. The use of τετιμήται in place of ἀποτετίμηται is defensible; see note 51 below. Note should also be taken of the use of the singular χωρίου in line 12, as against the plural in line 1, to be explained, I think, by the notion of "property" inherent in the context of

line 12. *Horos* no. 127, the beginning and end of which are lost, is important for a consideration of the problem of dated *horoi*; see Appendix II.

27. Since the discovery of *horos* no. 131, there is no need to discuss further whether the *apotimema* guaranteed both interest and principal or only the interest.

28. Schulthess, *Vormundschaft* 166, writes that, *"bei* μίσθωσις *ließ sich eine solche* [*i.e.*, amount of the obligation] *eventuell aus dem Pachtzins berechnen."* Not only does he overlook the fact that return of a specific piece of property was guaranteed (as does Hitzig, *Pfandrecht* 70), the value of which cannot be calculated from the rental and need not be calculated in any event, but he is indulging in the common exercise of estimating the normal "rate of capitalization" in ancient Greece (pp. 150–56). All such efforts are doomed to failure, in my opinion, not only because of the lack of available information but, more important, because they rest on the assumption that "capitalization" was a Greek economic concept; see further Chap. V, note 89.

29. Harpocration, ἀποτιμηταί: ... εἰώθεσαν δὲ καὶ οἱ τότε, εἰ γυναικὶ γαμουμένῃ προῖκα διδοῖεν οἱ προσήκοντες, αἰτεῖν παρὰ τοῦ ἀνδρὸς ὥσπερ ἐνέχυρόν τι τῆς προικὸς ἄξιον, οἷον οἰκίαν ἢ χωρίον. For other lexical references, see note 4 above.

30. See Erdmann, *Ehe* 332–39; cf. comments in Chap. VI, note 26.

31. See, *e.g.*, Demosthenes, *Against Onetor I* 30.7. On this point, see Weiss, *Untersuchungen* I 73–77. Weiss' account of the dotal *apotimema*, though the most complete, rests on a misconception of the essential nature of the *apotimema* because he did not perceive the significance of the act of evaluation.

32. The clearest instances are Isaeus, *On the Estate of Pyrrhos* 3.8–9,35–38, 78 (to be studied in the light of the analysis in Rabel, "Nachgeformte Rechtsgeschäfte" XXVIII 331–32); Demosthenes, *Against Aphobos I* 27.15–16; and [Demosthenes], *Against Neaira* 59.51–54. The literature offers other references to dowries apparently unsecured by *apotimema*, but unless the context is one in which the inclusion or exclusion of the reference is essential to the argument, as in the three orations cited, failure to mention an *apotimema* is without significance. H. J. Wolff, "Marriage Law and Family Organization in Ancient Athens," *Traditio* 2 (1944) 43–95, at p. 60, uses Harpocration to bolster his astounding notion that property given as dowry could serve at the same time "to secure the claim for restitution of the dowry." He reaches this conclusion by confusing the verb *apotimao* in *horos* no. 155 with *entimao* (see note 63 below) and therefore mistranslating, "valued for Nicesarete into her property," although on p. 55, note 66, he criticizes several translators of Demosthenes for making precisely that error in rendering *Against Spudias* 41.27–28, and refers to *horos* no. 155 as evidence that *apotimao* "is a well-known technical expression to denote the pledging of property for a debt." He misinterprets *horos* no. 126 in the same way, having failed to note no. 147 (see Chap. VIII, note 1).

33. Demosthenes, *Against Aphobos I* 27.17; [Demosthenes], *Against Neaira* 59.51–52; see G. Billeter, *Geschichte des Zinsfußes im griechisch-römischen Altertum bis auf Justinian* (Leipzig 1898) 46–56.

34. Harpocration, ἀποτιμηταί: ... ὁ δ'αὐτὸς λόγος καὶ ἐπὶ τῶν ἄλλων ὀφλημάτων.

35. IG II² 2498, lines 3–6.

36. IG II² 1172, lines 20–22. For the text and a discussion of this inscription and the one cited in the previous note, see Chap. VII, end of sect. 2.

37. A translation of the complete *horos* is given in Chap. II at note 64. On the *eranoi*, see Chap. VII, sect. 4. Note should also be taken of *horos* no. 162, which reads: "*Horos* of a house put up as security (*apotimema*) in (the archonship) of Euxenippos, 2,000 (drachmas)." Here too we are probably dealing with neither a dotal nor a pupillary *apotimema*. In IG II², Kirchner classifies no. 162 among the dotal *apotimemata*, no. 163 among the *incerta*, and no. 160, a hopeless fragment, among the pupillary *apotimemata*.

38. See Chap. VIII.

39. Hitzig, *Pfandrecht* 46, 112, and Weiss, *Untersuchungen* I 71, miss the essence of the dotal *apotimema* when they say, in Weiss' words, that "*diese Hypothek das ganze Vermögen des Ehemannes ergriff.*" They rest their argument primarily on Hitzig's gratuitous insertion of the word ἀπετίμησε in a lacuna in the Tenian inscription, IG XII 5,873, line 9 (lines 12–13 indicate that the text is probably not a dowry register at all) and on a misinterpretation of *horos* no. 102 (see Chap. VI, note 22).

40. See Chap. VI, end of sect. 2.

41. Speaking of the dotal *apotimema*, Hitzig, *Pfandrecht* 42–43, writes: "*Die zur Dos gegebene Gegenstände werden geschätzt, damit im Falle der Unmöglichkeit der Rückgabe in natura über den Wert nicht gestritten werden könne ... und damit ein Maßstab für das Pfandobjekt gegeben sei; der griechische Ausdruck für diese Schätzung ist* ἐντιμᾶσθαι" (citing Pollux, *Onomasticon* 8.142). He is here confusing two distinct operations, the evaluation of the security and the evaluation of a non-monetary dowry. He apparently overlooked the definitions of ἐνετιμᾶτο in Harpocration and Suidas, both of whom say correctly, ἐνετιμᾶτο διαφέρει τοῦ ἀπετιμᾶτο; see further note 63 below. It should be noted that my interpretation of the grounds for the *apotimema* does not exclude the possibility of exceptional cases, such as the provision of the deme Plotheia mentioned in the text. In the latter, I believe that the reason for *apotimema* lies in the small sums involved.

42. One illustration will suffice, all the more striking because it comes from a work of the highest caliber. In IJ I 123, the section headed, "Du classement des inscriptions hypothécaires," begins as follows, after a brief introductory paragraph: "*Nous distinguerons tout d'abord les*

hypothèques, ou plus exactement les garanties, auxquelles les Athéniens réservaient le nom d' ἀποτιμήματα. *Le grammarien Harpocration leur a consacré un article très précis et très net....*" A French translation of the Harpocration definition follows, but it omits the sentence, "The same word (is used) also in the case of other debts." The omission is indicated by three dots, but in the Greek text given in note 1 on p. 124, even the dots are dropped. Then comes a restatement: "*Les* ἀποτιμήματα *doivent donc être divisés en deux classes: hypothèques de mineurs, hypothèques de femmes mariées.*" The lost sentence from Harpocration is never recovered.

43. See, *e.g.*, Paoli, "Ipoteca" 173.

44. In one or two texts, such as Isaeus, frag. 29 (Thalheim), quoted in Dionysius, *On the Orations of Isaeus* 13, the use of *apotimao* or *apotimema* is too generalized and the context too vague to warrant any discussion. In [Demosthenes], *Against Nikostratos* 53.20, a debtor, unable to repay a loan, ἐναπετίμησεν a slave to the creditor in its stead. Paoli, "Datio in solutum" 200–1, takes this to refer to an *apotimema* and uses the passage to support his general theory that the *apotimema* was a *datio in solutum* and not the establishment of a security obligation (see further the following note). F. A. Paley and J. E. Sandys, ed., *Select Private Orations of Demosthenes* (2 vols., 3 ed., Cambridge, Eng., 1896–8), in a note to the text, write, "the compound ἐναποτιμάω is in the present passage applied to the debtor's transference of a part of his property in valuation in lieu of direct payment of his debt," and they cite as comparable Dio Cassius 41.37.3. (There is a fourth ed. of Paley and Sandys, but it was not available to me.) Liddell-and-Scott defines ἐναποτιμάω as "take in payment at a valuation," citing the same two texts. (See also note 63 below.) There can be little doubt that this is the correct definition and that no hypothecation was involved. Herodotus 5.77 uses ἀποτιμάω in the sense of "to have a price (or value) fixed" for the release of prisoners of war: χρόνῳ δὲ ἔλυσάν σφεας διμνέως ἀποτιμησάμενοι.

45. Demosthenes, *Against Onetor* I and II (orats. 30 31). Paoli has laid great stress on this dispute as evidence that the *apotimema* obligation came into being not when the dowry was given to the husband but at the moment its return by the latter fell due, in other words, that the transaction was a *datio in solutum* and not the creation of a security obligation assuring a payment at some future date; see "Ipoteca" 173–78, 180–81, 192–93, "Datio in solutum" 192–99. The heart of his argument is that Demosthenes' main proof of his contention that Onetor's claim was fraudulent was the alleged fact that Aphobos continued in possession of the property. This argument, says Paoli, demonstrates that *apotimema* meant immediate transfer of the property to the creditor (in this case, to Onetor if he were telling the truth). It is unnecessary to reply to Paoli's analysis in detail, for it has already been indicated (see especially Chap. II, sect. 1) that the institution of the *apotimema* would have been economically impossible unless the debtor retained possession and that this is proved by the very nature

of the *horoi*. It is worth noting, however, as LaPira showed in his review of Paoli, in BIDR 41 (1933) 192–93, that the possession argument is raised by Demosthenes to prove that the alleged divorce itself never took place (see especially *Against Onetor I* 30.26–30). If there had been no divorce, then obviously Onetor's claim to the property by *apotimema* was fraudulent since repayment of the dowry was not due. The direct link between possession and *apotimema* that Paoli seeks to establish requires his taking material out of this broader context. See also note 23 above on Paoli's misreading of Demosthenes, *Against Aphobos II* 28.2, again in connection with his theory of transfer of possession.

46. The MSS give the deme as Thria; the correction to Teithras is made from a dedication, *Hesperia* 6 (1937) 341, which also reveals the younger daughter's name, Kleiokrateia.

47. Demosthenes, *Against Spudias* 41.5: τὴν οἰκίαν ταύτην ἀποτιμῶμαι πρὸς τὰς δέκα μνᾶς; § 6, τελευτῶν διέθεθ' ὅρους ἐπιστῆσαι χιλίων δραχμῶν ἐμοὶ τῆς προικὸς ἐπὶ τὴν οἰκίαν.

48. See Rudolf Burgkhardt, *De causa orationis adversus Spudiam Demosthenicae (XLI)* (disś. Leipzig 1908) 26–27.

49. Demosthenes, *Against Spudias* 41.6.

50. It is of some interest, from the standpoints of language and institution, to draw a comparison with the so-called "dowry register" from the island of Mykonos, *Syll.* 1215. The editors are unusually indefinite about the date of the inscription but I gather that shortly after 200 B.C. is about right. The inscription gives various details about individual dowry transactions, including amount, indebtedness, etc. In its present state, the stone has eight complete entries and four fragmentary ones. In three of the eight, only part of the dowry has been paid to the husband, but of these three one alone indicates that security has been provided for the balance. Entry no. 4 (lines 15–20) reads in part: τῶν δὲ τριακοσίων [δρα]χμῶν ὑπέθηκε Καλλίξενος Ῥοδοκλεῖ τὸ οἴκημα τὸ ἐμ πόλει. The verb *timao* appears elsewhere in the inscription (line 8) in reference to the monetary evaluation of the trousseau (not of property offered in security): ἐσθ[ὴ]ν δὲ τετιμημένη διακοσίων δραχμῶν.

51. *Ibid.* Arg. I: ... τὴν οἰκίαν τῆς ἄλλης οὐσίας ἐξελεῖν, καὶ ταύτην εἰς τὸ χρέος δοῦναι. What the preposition ἀπό adds to τιμάω is the idea of "off," "asunder," in other words, the separation of the evaluated property (figuratively, not literally) from the rest. This linguistic nicety should not be overstressed, for τιμάω and τίμημα are used once in a while without the prefix in reference to *apotimema* transactions. (A parallel is the synonymous use of μισθόω and ἀπομισθόω in IG I² 94, lines 6,11–12, or in Lysias, *On the Sacred Olive Tree* 7.9,10,11,17, together with ἐκμισθόω in § 4.) Harpocration writes (cf. Suidas): τίμημα· ἀντὶ μὲν τοῦ ἐνέχυρον καὶ οἷον ἀποτίμημα Λυσίας ἐν τῷ ὑπὲρ Καλλίου [frag. 52 Thalheim]: "οὗτοι δὲ φάσκοντες πλείονος μισθώσασθαι καὶ τίμημα κατα-

στήσασθαι." Demosthenes, *Against Onetor II* 31.6 (quoted in Chap. VIII, note 7) uses τιμάω for the evaluating in a dotal *apotimema*; the reconstruction of the verb in *horos* no. 147 is certain, I think, and likely in no. 131 (on which see note 26 above). The noun *timema*, used in the sense of *apotimema*, has been restored in IG II² 1172 with virtual certainty (see Chap. VII, note 42). This interchangeable use of τιμάω and ἀποτιμάω, rare as it is, has been the cause of some confusion and misunderstanding (see notes 45, 50, 63 in this chapter). Stress must therefore be laid on the infrequency with which τιμάω is used in this sense and on the necessity for accepting a security meaning only when the context demands one.

52. See above, note 47.

53. In Demosthenes, *Against Spudias* 41.3, for example, the dowry is given to the husband, but in *Against Stephanos I* 45.28, to the wife. Wolff, "Marriage Law" 57, has recently argued that ἐπιδίδωμι 'Αρχίππη in the latter passage should be translated "I give him (the husband) as dowry on behalf of Archippe." He draws a sharp distinction between ἐπιδίδωμι, "to give (the husband a dowry)" and δίδωμι, "to give (the wife a trousseau)," but the supposed distinction is removed by Demosthenes himself in the sentence immediately following the one Wolff quotes. Wolff's attempt to unravel the legal complexities of the Athenian dowry is generally unsatisfactory, as is evident from the two following statements: "The conclusion is that the husband was the κύριος of any sort of dowry property, and the one who might dispose of it" (p. 60). "The dowry in principle always belonged to the estate of the family to which the woman herself belonged, and its destiny was determined by the purposes which it served within the framework of the classical Athenian family system" (p. 62).

54. Naming of the children (more correctly, identifying them, since they are not actually named) in the *horoi* marking pupillary *apotimemata* is not a comparable procedure, since, if they are males, they will in fact take over the property (their own or the security in substitution) upon reaching majority. Most often the word παῖς appears in the dative, but in *horoi* nos. 122, 124, 129, and 130 (θυγατρῶν in this one case) it is in the genitive. I see no significance in this variation.

55. See Chap. II, sect. 1.

56. It was indicated in Chap. II, note 80, that linguistically it would be proper to read "put up as security for Kleinokrate" instead of "to Kleinokrate." In view of the wife's inability to "own" the property in any complete sense, the preposition "for" can also be defended on substantive grounds. Nevertheless, I have preferred to retain "to" in order to have the *horoi* marking a dotal *apotimema* consistent with the others. In all other *horoi* in which a name appears, it is in the dative (with the meaningless exceptions noted above, note 54), and the case unmistakably indicates the person "to whom" the security has been given, the creditor, in other words.

16*

57. Hitzig, *Pfandrecht* 45, followed by Weiss, *Untersuchungen* I 23–24, suggested, on the basis of Demosthenes, *Against Onetor II* 31.5, that in the arrangement, "*der Dosbetrag geteilt wird und die Teilbeträge auf verschiedene Objekte versichert werden.*" Some form of payment in installments is also reflected in *horos* no. 132. I cannot unravel the mystery of this text, which has been endlessly debated; for the various views, see IJ pp. 133–35; Billeter, *Zinsfuß* 53–56; Pappulias, Ἀσφάλεια 63–66. One fact stands out without dispute, however, that the woman's father and his deme are both named, and this is a powerful reason for believing that the *apotimema* was put up by the husband.

58. *Horos* no. 156 says ἐν προικί rather than the customary προικός; so does no. 150. No. 155 has εἰς τὴν προῖκα (see Bruck, *Schenkung* 134–37, for an analysis of the transaction). Demosthenes writes ἀντὶ τῆς προικός in *Against Onetor I* 30.26 and II 31.11 but ἐν ᾧ in II 31.3 (whereas Libanios in Arg. I has εἰς τὴν προῖκα). It seems to me that no distinctions can be drawn from the choice of preposition in any one text, as Paoli, "Datio in solutum" 194–95, seeks to do from the use of ἀντί.

59. Kirchner in IG II² published three, nos. 49, 82, and 93, all under the rubric, *hypothecae pro dote uxori*, not under *prasis epi lysei*, again illustrating the weakness of his classification. Further, he included no. 57, which reads, "*Horos* of land put up as security (*prasis epi lysei*) to the son of Kallistratos, ――― (amount lost)," among the pupillary *apotimemata*. This is incorrect if I am right in believing that *apotimema* was the mandatory form of security in *misthosis oikou*; see above at note 22.

60. Wigmore, "Pledge-Idea" XI 19, note 7: "When the husband, lessee, etc., gave a hypothec for a possible default, it was essential that a specific portion of land, etc., should be set apart and 'appraised' as the equivalent thus predetermined, *i.e.* to be accepted, for better or for worse, as the ultimate satisfaction." In modern juristic literature, the three main theories are the following: (1) Hitzig holds that *apotimema* is merely a kind of *hypotheke*; see especially *Pfandrecht* 5–9. (2) Pappulias holds that the essence of *apotimema* is not in the evaluation but in the idea of substitution, whereas the *hypotheke* was collateral security (that is, in case of default the creditor was entitled to the amount of the debt, no more and no less); see his Ἀσφάλεια, Pt. I, *passim*, and the clear, though uncritical, summary in the review of the book by Ludwig Mitteis, in ZSS 30 (1909) 442–51. Against Pappulias, see particularly Leo Raape, *Der Verfall des griechischen Pfandes besonders des griechisch-ägyptischen* (Halle 1912) 1–48, who comes closest to the position I have taken (see pp. 12–13), though he approaches the problem in purely juristic terms (see the brief criticisms in Chap. VIII, note 8). Note should be taken of the reviews by E. F. Bruck, in ZSS 33 (1912) 551–69, who concludes (p. 558) that the sources do not permit a decisive answer in favor of either Pappulias or Raape; and by P. Koschaker, in KVJ 50 (1912) 507–20, and A. Manigk, in PhW 34 (1914) 205–13, who are much more negative in their judgments of Pappulias, correctly so, in my opinion. (3) Paoli has a particularly complex theory that four distinct institutions are all called *apotimema*. For a

convenient summary, see his "Diritto pignoratizio" 166–67. In general, see Chap. VIII for a brief consideration of some of the major legal problems.

61. Demosthenes, *Against Spudias* 41.7: ... ὅσα (or εἰς ἃ) ἀπετίμησεν, εἶναι δίκας οὔτ' αὐτοῖς οὔτε τοῖς κληρονόμοις. That would seem to apply to the debtor, the man who gave the *apotimema*, but § 10, λαβὲ δή μοι πρῶτον μὲν τὸν νόμον, ὃς οὐκ ἐᾷ τῶν ἀποτιμηθέντων ἔτι δίκην πρὸς τοὺς ἔχοντας, seems to refer to the creditor. Τοὺς ἔχοντας cannot mean those in physical possession of the property but those who "have" the *apotimema* in the sense of "have the contingent right to the property," just as Aristotle, *Constitution of the Athenians* 56.7, spoke of the archon "receiving" the *apotimema* in *misthosis oikou*; see Burgkhardt, *Adversus Spudiam* 29–30.

62. See the summary in Burgkhardt, *Adversus Spudiam* 25–30. Since then, the only new thesis put forth has been Paoli's which is based on his untenable idea that the plaintiff had possession in law as a result of a *datio in solutum*; see, e.g., "Datio in solutum" 190–91.

63. Isaeus, *On the Estate of Pyrrhos* 3.35: ὅπου γάρ, ἐάν τις τι ἀτίμητον δῷ, ἕνεκα τοῦ νόμου, ἐὰν ἀπολίπῃ ἡ γυνὴ τὸν ἄνδρα ἢ ἐὰν ὁ ἀνὴρ ἐκπέμψῃ τὴν γυναῖκα, οὐκ ἔξεστι πράξασθαι τῷ δόντι ὃ μὴ ἐν προικὶ τιμήσας ἔδωκεν. Because of the linguistic difficulty, some editors have amended νόμου to γάμου. Either reading gives the same basic sense; see Wyse, *Isaeus* 312–14, who successfully rejects attempts to challenge the passage as a gloss. For instances of the evaluation in money of dowries or trousseaus given in kind, see *Syll.* 1215, line 8 (note 50 above); Demosthenes, *Against Spudias* 41.27; and [Demosthenes], *Against Euergos and Mnesibulos* 47.57. The last-named text is sometimes cited incorrectly as an illustration of a dotal *apotimema*, whereas it refers to the giving of the dowry itself and its evaluation; see the references in Wolff, "Marriage Law" 54, note 60. In this connection, it is worth noting Pollux, *Onomasticon* 8.142: ἐντιμήσασθαί ἐστιν, ὅταν τις προῖκα διδοὺς τιμήσηται ὁπόσου δεῖ; and Harpocration (= Suidas), ἐνετιμᾶτο: Δημοσθένης ἐν τῷ πρὸς Σπουδίαν [41.27]· τὸ ἀπετιμᾶτο διαφέρει τοῦ ἐνετιμᾶτο· ὅταν μὲν γὰρ πρός τι ποσὸν ἀργύριον ἀποτίμημα λαμβάνῃ τις, ἀποτιμᾶσθαι λέγεται· ὅταν δὲ ἐν εἴδεσί τισι λογίσηταί τις μέρος τι τοῦ ἀργυρίου, τοῦτο λέγεται ὡς ἐνετιμήσατο.

Notes to Chapter V

1. Aristotle, *Politics* 2.4.12,1267b9. The more commonly cited text for Aristotle's "classification" of wealth is *Rhetoric* 1.5,1361a12, but various editors have raised serious questions about the manuscript readings in that passage and, though it is somewhat more detailed than the *Politics* text, it adds nothing substantial to the present discussion. Cf. the enumeration in Xenophon, *Memorabilia* 2.4.2: house, farm (ἀγρός),

slaves, cattle, and furnishings (σκευή). Xenophon does not include money because the reference is to acquisition of wealth rather than to possessions.

2. Xenophon, *Poroi* 4.7, says of furnishings (ἔπιπλα): "When someone possesses enough for his house, he most certainly would not buy more."

3. In other words, the Greek cities knew *Tiermiete*, not *Viehpacht*, to follow the distinction drawn in German legal systems. Sibylle von Bolla, *Untersuchungen zur Tiermiete und Viehpacht im Altertum [Münchener Beiträge* 30 (Munich 1940)] 29–30, says that in antiquity *Viehpacht* was an *"Institut mit universalrechtlichem Charakter"* to be found in virtually all societies. The sole proof she can adduce for the city-states consists of two anecdotes, one in Diodoros (8.7) and the other in Pausanias (4.4.5), suggesting the opposite conclusion, namely, that *Viehpacht* was to all intents and purposes unknown in the city-state world.

4. For the details, insofar as we have them, see Busolt, *Staatskunde* I 352–58.

5. See Johannes Hasebroek, *Staat und Handel im alten Griechenland* (Tübingen 1928) 31–35. (An English translation by L. M. Fraser and D. C. MacGregor is available under the title, *Trade and Politics in Ancient Greece* [London 1933].)

6. An interesting study could be made of the geographical distribution of the honorary decrees in which the right of pasturage is added to the right to own land and houses. Such precision in the language of the decrees is a significant reflection of the economy of the states involved. The fact that not one such decree has been found in Athens, for example, is a measure of the insignificance of pasturage there, not just an accident as suggested by Paul Gerhardt, *Die attische Metoikie im vierten Jahrhundert* (diss. Königsberg 1933) 71, note 165. For a brief survey of the available references to rights of pasture, see L. Robert, "Épitaphe d'un berger à Thasos," *Hellenica* 7 (1949) 152–60, at pp. 156–57.

7. Aristotle, *Constitution of the Athenians* 52.1. In 47.2, where he is also speaking of the *poletai*, Aristotle uses the generic word *ousia*.

8. See, for example, SEG X 238 = *Hesperia* 8 (1939) 69, no. 23 (a group of six fragments, several of which had previously been published as IG I² 325 and 326) or *Athen. Mitt.* 66 (1941) 232, no. 5. For further details, see Busolt, *Staatskunde* II 1141–43.

9. The documentation will be presented in a separate publication.

10. "Visible" is usually φανερός, less frequently ἐμφανής; "invisible" is ἀφανής (and the verb ἀφανίζω). I am preparing a special study of this terminology and its social and economic implications. Probably the best available analysis will be found in J.C.A.M. Bongenaar, *Isocrates' Trapeziticus vertaald and toeglicht* (Utrecht and Nijmegen

1933) 234–39. Citations in the Attic orators are collected by Schodorf, *Gerichtssprache* 90–92 (a work that is useful but not always reliable).

11. Aeschines, *Against Timarchos* 1.101; cf. Demosthenes, *On the Symmoriai* 14.25; Deinarchos, *Against Demosthenes* 1.70.

12. Isaeus, *On the Estate of Hagnias* 11.43. An excellent illustration of the flexibility of the antinomy is Isocrates, *Trapezitikos* 17.7, where the speaker, a young man from the Bosporus, reports that he and the banker Pasion decided that he would reveal to the representatives of his king his "visible money" (τὰ μὲν φανερὰ τῶν χρημάτων) but conceal the sums on deposit with Pasion.

13. Xenophon, *Hellenica* 5.2.10. Xenophon writes τὰ ἐμφανῆ κτήματα, perfect documentation of the impossibility of pinning classificatory labels on the Greek words.

14. In the treaty between Athens and Selymbria following Alcibiades' capture of that city in 409 B.C., restitution of real property is specifically indicated; IG I² 116, lines 14–18: ἃ δὲ ἀπόλετο ἐν τõι πολέμοι [χρέματα ’Αθεναί]ον ἒ τõν συμμάχον ἢ εἴ τι ὀφελ[όμενον ἒ παρακ]αταθέκεν ἔχοντός το ἔπραχσα[ν οἱ ἄρχοντες], μὴ ἔναι πρᾶχσιν πλὴγ γ͞ες καὶ οἰ[κίας.] On the date of this inscription and the most recent bibliography, see M. N. Tod, *A Selection of Greek Historical Inscriptions* 1 (2 vols., vol. 1 in 2 ed., Oxford 1946–48) pp. 217, 265; SEG X 132.

15. IG IX² 192.12–14. The Aetolian League adopted a series of decrees granting inviolability (*asylia*) and guarantees against raids and reprisals to various communities, all in the closing decades of the third century B.C. Provisions parallel to the one quoted in the text appeared in some, if not all, these decrees; for a complete list of these and comparable *asylia* decrees and a bibliography, see M. Rostovtzeff, *The Social & Economic History of the Hellenistic World* (3 vols., Oxford 1941) 198–201 and the pertinent notes. Rostovtzeff misses the significance of the terminology when he mistranslates the key lines of IG IX² 4 to read: "...the chief magistrate in office shall exact such property as has been visibly carried off, and for property that has been made away with the councillors shall pass sentence of such fine as they may think fit...." See Hans Benecke, *Die Seepolitik der Aitoler* (diss. Hamburg 1934) 18–19, and generally 17–31.

Kaser, "Eigentumsschutz" 154–58, interprets the distinction between the two types of action to be one based on whether rightful ownership was disputed or not. This view, which he incorrectly attributes to Ernst Rabel, is untenable linguistically as well as juristically. The "visible-invisible" explanation is much simpler and more consonant with the socio-economic picture; see Weiss, *Privatrecht* 491–94. In general, Kaser gives a very valuable analysis (pp. 154–56) of the ἀφανής-ἐμφανής antinomy within the special context of the δίκη εἰς ἐμφανῶν κατάστασιν.

All the then available source material dealing with the restitution of property following return from exile will be found, systematically assembled and analyzed, in Paul Usteri, *Ächtung und Verbannung im griechischen Recht* (Berlin 1903) 118–58. There is no comparable treatment of the material discovered in the last half-century.

16. The existence of slaves may explain why the terms "movable" and "immovable" as applied to property are unknown in Greek literature before the later Roman Empire. Slaves are "movable" and yet they differ in every respect, economically and physically, from all other forms of "movable" goods. See generally A. A. Schiller, "*Res mobiles, immobiles* and *se moventes*," *Atti del Congresso internazionale di diritto romano a Roma* 2 (Pavia 1935) 429–48. The suggestion of Michel Feyel, in BCH 66/67 (1942/3) 185, note 2, that Greek legislation distinguished animate property (slaves and livestock) from inanimate, is not well-founded as a generalization.

17. In every case known to us, maritime loans were secured by the ship or cargo. See Pringsheim, *Kauf* 18–27, and especially 18–22, where he effectively proves that [Demosthenes], *Against Polykles* 50.17, is not a reference to a bottomry loan at all, and hence no evidence that such loans were made without the security of the ship or cargo. A convenient summary of the five bottomry cases preserved in the Demosthenic corpus will be found in G. M. Calhoun, "Risk in Sea Loans in Ancient Athens," JEBH 2 (1930) 561–84, though it is not always reliable on juristic matters.

18. [Demosthenes], *Against Dionysodoros* 56.3 (cf. the rhetoric in the opening of the oration). The final words in the Greek are οὔτε τὸ ἐνέχυρον καθίστησιν εἰς τὸ ἐμφανές, a reference to the δίκη εἰς ἐμφανῶν κατάστασιν. In his discussion of that form of action, Kaser, "Eigentumsschutz" 150–58, reveals how in that respect bottomry is a problem quite apart from any other type of transaction, although he is not directly concerned with that point.

19. See the warning raised by Rabel, *Verfügungsbeschränkungen* 24. In view of the use Paoli makes of bottomry cases in his "Ipoteca," it is worth noting that in another article published in the same volume, "Il prestito marittimo nel diritto attico," *Studi* 9–137, he has a three-page chapter entitled, "La garanzia nel prestito marittimo" (pp. 118–20), which he himself summarizes in the following brief statement: "*Sommario. — Carattere eccezionale della garanzia marittima (Rinvio).*"

20. Dionysius, *On the Orations of Lysias* 32 (often published as the Argument to Lysias, orat. 34). See G. Mathieu, "La réorganisation du corps civique athénien à la fin du Vᵉ siècle," REG 40 (1927) 65–116, at pp. 104–11.

21. Unless otherwise indicated, Athenian population figures are those of A. W. Gomme, *The Population of Athens in the Fifth and Fourth Centuries B.C.* (Oxford 1933).

22. Thus, Wilamowitz, *Aristoteles und Athen* II 226–30, holds 5,000 to be too high, whereas Gomme, *Population* 27, thinks it much too low.

Gomme errs seriously when he assumes that "landless population" is a synonym for thetes, whose number at this time he places in the neighborhood of 11,000 (men aged 18–59). Wilamowitz demonstrated that many landowners were not wealthy enough to provide themselves with arms and were therefore classed as thetes.

23. Max Wagner, *Zur Geschichte der attischen Kleruchien* (diss. Tübingen 1914) 50–51.

24. This is the argument of Gomme, *Population 27*.

25. [Demosthenes], *Against Timotheos* 49.11.

26. [Demosthenes], *Against Polykles* 50.8.

27. The family tree is given in a diagram in J. Kirchner, *Prosopographia Attica* 1 (2 vols., Berlin 1901–03) no. 2921, reproduced in Wyse, *Isaeus* 671.

28. The two orations are Isaeus, *On the Estate of Hagnias* (no. 11) and [Demosthenes], *Against Makartatos* (no. 43). On the basis of a deposition in the latter (§ 31), the text of which has been preserved in the manuscripts, the two speeches have been dated 359/8 and about 342 B.C., respectively, by most scholars. With the discovery of the anonymous historical fragment known as the *Hellenica Oxyrhyncha*, which fixes the capture and death of Hagnias in 396 or 395 (§ 2.1), the traditional dates must be discarded for considerably earlier ones. The new dating also compels reconsideration of the authenticity of the depositions found in a few of the private orations in the Demosthenic corpus, supposedly proved beyond question by Drerup, "Urkunden." For other evidence of the dubious character of the depositions in the oration against Makartatos, see R. J. Bonner and Gertude Smith, *The Administration of Justice from Homer to Aristotle* 2 (2 vols., Chicago 1930–38) 98–100.

29. Alfred E. Zimmern, *The Greek Commonwealth* (4 ed., Oxford 1924) Pt. III, Chap. III, is well worth reading for its appreciation of the paramount role of landed property in Greek life and Greek psychology.

30. See Auguste Jardé, *Les céréales dans l'antiquité grecque* [only vol. 1 published, *Bibl.Éc.fr.* 130 (Paris 1925)] 120–22.

31. See p. 3. Busolt, *Staatskunde* I 180, note 1, places the figure at 300 hectares (about 740 acres) and he is followed by A. Raubitschek, "Phainippos [3]," PWRE 19 (1938) 1591, and Rostovtzeff, *Hellenistic World* 1181. Gustave Glotz, *Le travail dans la Grèce ancienne* (Paris 1920) 300, says 315 hectares (about 780 acres). (An English translation of Glotz's work is available, London 1926.) None of these scholars indicates how he arrived at his result. Jardé, *Céréales*, is uncertain. On p. 48 he says the estate was 390 hectares (about 965 acres); on p. 78 he gives the same figure as the maximum; and on p. 121 he gives 300 hectares (about 740 acres) as the minimum.

32. On Aristophanes: Lysias, *On the Property of Aristophanes* 19.29; on Alcibiades: Plato, *Alcibiades I* 123C.

33. Demosthenes, *Against Leptines* 20.115. Plutarch, *Aristeides* 27.1, mentions only the 100 *plethra* of orchard land.

34. Isaeus, *On the Estate of Dikaiogenes* 5.22. IG I² 376, re-edited with a new fragment, *Hesperia* 12 (1943) 28, no. 6 (=SEG X 304), and dated *c.* 424/3 B.C. by A. E. Raubitschek, lists the leases of sacred Athenian property in Euboea. Acreage is given. The only fully legible entry (line 4) records three γύαι of cleared land at a rental (annual?) of 90 drachmas.

35. The current connotation of the word "class" validates the objection raised against the commonly used phrase, "Solonic classes," by Edgar Salin, "Der 'Sozialismus' in Hellas," *Bilder und Studien aus drei Jahrtausenden – Eberhard Gothein zum siebzigsten Geburtstag* (Munich and Leipzig 1923) 15–59, at p. 44, note 1.

36. Glotz, *Travail* 296–97. A differently conceived calculation, basically comparable in the end result, is given by Orth, "Landwirtschaft" 636–37.

37. IG II² 30, a nearly hopeless fragment dealing with cleruchic property in Lemnos in the year 386/5 B.C., makes an unmistakable reference to Solonic ratings in line a 12; see Chap. I, note 26, for a bibliography on this inscription, and Busolt, *Staatskunde* II 840, note 1, for a summary of the available material on the Solonic classification in the fourth century. More generally on these ratings in the fifth and fourth centuries, see Ulrich Kahrstedt, *Studien zum öffentlichen Recht Athens I. Staatsgebiet und Staatsangehörige in Athen* (Stuttgart and Berlin 1934) 250–55.

38. On the techniques of agriculture and pasturage, see Jardé, *Céréales* 19–30; Rostovtzeff, *Hellenistic World* 1186–1200; and the neglected work of R. Lefebvre des Noëttes, *L'attelage, le cheval de selle à travers les âges* 1 (2 vols., Paris 1931) Chaps. I–II. Jardé begins his concluding section in this way (p. 190): "*Ce qui semble ressortir le mieux de notre étude, c'est que l'agriculture grecque en général, la culture des céréales en particulier ne se sont modifiés qu'à peine durant les temps historiques. C'est par une illusion, facile à comprendre, qu'on s'est figuré l'agronomie grecque en perpétuel progrès.*" F. M. Heichelheim, *Wirtschaftsgeschichte des Altertums* 1 (2 vols., Leiden 1938) 386, writes that the fifth and fourth centuries B.C. saw a notable increase in agricultural "*Rationalisierungsmaßnahmen*" and he cites the lease inscription, IG II² 2493 (dated 340/39 B.C.), as proof of the use of the three-field system. But even if Heichelheim's conclusion about this one text is correct, and it probably is not, he has succeeded only in establishing a single exception to what remained the prevalent method throughout Greek history, the two-field, fallow system; see Jardé, *ibid.* 85–87; Rostovtzeff, *ibid.* 1617, note 142. It is sufficient to note that Xenophon takes the two-field system for granted in his *Oeconomicus*. On the absence of rationalization,

see Gunnar Mickwitz, "Economic Rationalism in Graeco-Roman Agriculture," *English Historical Rev.* 52 (1937) 577–89.

39. See, *e.g.*, Glotz, *Travail* 308. The most thorough attempt to analyze the material is Jardé, *Céréales* 61–105. Despite his care and precision (even to the extent of a 24.7 per cent estimate for the total area under production, p. 78), Jardé succeeds chiefly in proving the futility of this type of calculation, in my judgment. The great inscription, IG II² 1672, which reports the payments of the first-fruits to Eleusis, gives very exact figures (see Jardé, *ibid.* 36–60). Unfortunately, they are reported by tribes, not demes, and hence are not very helpful in the present context. The figures do, however, help to confirm in a general way the view that farming was very widely dispersed throughout Attica. Note should also be taken of the effect of the frequent raids in the third century B.C., which led to an exodus of some proportions from farmlands on the border, thereby causing a reduction in the total land under production for reasons having nothing to do with agronomy; see W. S. Ferguson, "The Priests of Asklepios," *Univ. of Calif. Publ. in Class. Phil.* I (rev. ed., 1907) 131–73, at pp. 161–62.

40. See Wilhelm Larfeld, *Griechische Epigraphik* (3 ed., Munich 1914) 148–53. For excellent illustrations of the movement of stones in modern times, with rich bibliographic material, see Louis Robert, *Études épigraphiques et philologiques* (Paris 1938) 219–23, and "Hellenica. XIV. Pierres errantes," RP, 3 ser., 13 (1939) 181–98; see also Michel Feyel, "Inscriptions erratiques," *Contribution à l'épigraphie béotienne* [*Publ. de la Fac. des Lettres de l'Univ. de Strasbourg* 95 (Paris 1943)] 51–66.

41. No. 12, found in the deme Ikaria, deals with lands in Anthreion, an unidentified place name, as well as gardens and a house. No. 14, found in the modern village of Vari, in the territory either of the ancient deme of Halai Aixonides or of Anagyrus, reads in part "house and land and house in the city." No. 87, a limestone slab discovered near the Dipylon Gate, is worth quoting in full: "*Horos* of a house and workshops put up as security (*prasis epi lysei*), those within the (city) walls and the stoneworking establishment outside the walls, to Philippos of Aixone, one talent." An Amorgian stone, no. 8, and a Naxian, no. 131, give local place names (translations are given in Chap. VII, at note 60, and Chap. IV, at note 26, respectively).

42. See the illustrations given by Adolf Wilhelm, "Neue Beiträge zur griechischen Inschriftenkunde III," *Sitz. Vienna* 175,1 (1913) no. 15, at pp. 4–7. An Athenian example is IG I² 376, re-edited with a new fragment, *Hesperia* 12 (1943) 28, no. 6 (=SEG X 304).

43. Thus, the land-lease inscription, IG II² 2498, put up by the deme itself, specifically refers to pasturage rights, a most unusual reference in this type of Athenian document.

44. In the decree of 333/2 B.C., IG II² 337, granting the merchants of Kition the privilege of obtaining land in the Peiraieus on which to

erect a sanctuary to Aphrodite, the word *chorion* (line 41) could best be rendered "building lot."

45. Cf. *ibid.* Demosthenes, *Against Stephanos I* 45.33, referring to Phormio's lease of Pasion's bank, asks the rhetorical question: ἔστιν οὖν ὅστις ἂν τοῦ ξύλου καὶ τοῦ χωρίου καὶ τῶν γραμματείων τοσαύτην ὑπέμεινε φέρειν μίσθωσιν? Here *chorion* can at most mean *"emplacement,"* to use Dareste's French equivalent. We might also note its use in Antiphon the Sophist, frag. 54 (Diels), in the sense of a spot where money was buried. In the mine-lease records of the *poletai* for the year 367/6 B.C., *Hesperia* 10 (1941) 14, no. 1, the word *chorion* appears several times in the statements of the location and boundaries of individual mines. Margaret Crosby, the editor of the stone, always translates the word as "field" and in his "Addendum: A Topographical Note," which follows on pp. 28–30, John Young takes it for granted that the reference is to farms, a most unlikely interpretation. Recently, in "The Leases of the Laureion Mines," *Hesperia* 19 (1950) 189–312, at pp. 193–94, Miss Crosby has revised her view and recognized that in the mine-lease inscriptions *chorion* is merely a synonym for the more common *edaphe*; in this context, both words refer to the privately owned surface-land underneath which the ore was mined (as in *horos* no. 92), despite the elaborate arguments of E. Schönbauer, "Vom Bodenrecht zum Bergrecht," ZSS 55 (1935) 183–225, at pp. 197–207. Among earlier writers, see Édouard Ardaillon, *Les mines du Laurion dans l'antiquité* [*Bibl. Éc. fr.* 77 (Paris 1897)] 173–74; Kahrstedt, *Staatsgebiet* 27–29.

46. Xenophon, *Poroi* 2.6. The decree for Theogenes is IG II² 206; cf. II² 53, 130, 554. For non-Athenian examples, see IG VII 7, 8, and 14 (Megara).

47. The texts are IG II² 706, 732, 786, 801, 810, 835, 862, and 947. The readings and restoration of these inscriptions, all badly mutilated, were completely revised by Adolf Wilhelm, "Attische Urkunden II," *Sitz. Vienna* 180,2 (1916), no. 5, pp. 9–23 (the new readings are given in the Addenda and Corrigenda of IG II²). All discussions of these documents in works prior to 1916 must be re-examined in the light of Wilhelm's study and some rather broad historical generalizations discarded, as, for example, those in Guiraud, *Propriété foncière* 153–54, or in W. S. Ferguson, *Hellenistic Athens* (London 1911) 245–46.

48. See particularly the list for the year 414/3 B.C., at least six fragments of which have so far been discovered; they are assembled by B. D. Meritt in *Hesperia* 8 (1939) 69, no. 23 (including those previously published as IG I² 325 and 326), reprinted as SEG X 238. Cf. the fragment of a list of the first half of the fourth century, IG II² 1580.

49. The literalness of the stone copy is demonstrated decisively by *Hesperia* 10 (1941) 14, no. 1, with its unnecessary repetition of the rather lengthy "boundaries" of the house and its use of direct discourse to indicate the claims made against the property by several creditors; see Chap. VIII at note 13.

50. In the light of Xenophon's statement, *Poroi* 2.6, that there are many vacant sites within the city walls (with the further implication that they have no significant monetary value), I cannot take very seriously his argument, *ibid.* 4.50, that, if the city adopts his plan for intensified exploitation of the Laureion mines, a large population will be attracted to the district, with the effect, among others that οἵ γε χῶροι οὐδὲν ἂν εἶεν μείονος ἄξιοι τοῖς κεκτημένοις ἐνταῦθα ἢ τοῖς περὶ τὸ ἄστυ. J. H. Thiel, in his ed. (Vienna 1922), speaks of a veritable boom in urban realty, but I know of no supporting evidence. Note should also be taken of the fact that the word *oikopedon* sometimes means not the building-site but the building itself: Thucydides 4.90.2; Plato, *Laws* 741C.

51. See Chap. IV, at note 28, and sect. 5 of the present chapter.

52. There are not enough island *horoi* for a comparable breakdown. We may merely note that among the Lemnian stones, 3 mark land alone, 4 land and a house, and 1 a house alone.

53. The two *horoi* are nos. 6 and 75, the former dated in 291/0 B.C. Cf. Demosthenes, *Against Meidias* 21.158.

54. [Demosthenes], *Against Phainippos* 42.6.

55. See Gomme, *Population* 37–48.

56. This point is missed by Gomme, *ibid.*, in his otherwise excellent analysis of the available evidence (apart from the *horoi*) for the "urbanization" trend in Athens. Thus, on p. 45, he writes: "These figures illustrate ... the migration from the country to the town." Then he adds the following footnote: "This must not however be exaggerated; there is plenty of evidence in Demosthenes and Isaeus that men continued to live in the country and cultivate the land; and the figures for the corn production of Attica in 329 ... show that the land was well-cultivated." Land may be well-cultivated even under absentee landowners. In this connection, note the significance of the use of the word *astoi* to mean the Eupatrids, the aristocrats, in early Greece, when there were no urban communities at all; see the material assembled by Busolt, *Staatskunde* II 778, note 4.

57. Plato, *Laws* 680E–681A, assumes this to have been the primitive condition of group existence.

58. Aristotle, frag. 558 (Rose), in Athenaeus, *Deipnosophists* 348B.

59. Xenophon, *Hellenica* 5.2.5,7. Somewhat later, 7.5.14–15 (under date of 361 B.C.), he describes how Epaminondas caught the population of Mantinea outside the walls, at work in their fields during the harvest. Cf. 5.4.3 for Thebes in a parallel situation.

60. For the non-resident tenants, see BCH 21 (1897) 553, no. 2, reprinted in part as DGE 485, and substantially corrected by Michel Feyel, in BCH 58 (1934) 501–5 and 60 (1936) 175–77. For the farm broken up into 22 lots, see the inscription originally published by A. Keramo-

poullos, Δελτ. 14 (1931/2) 12, no. 1–2, lines A36–58, re-edited and completely reinterpreted by Feyel, BCH 60 (1936) 177–183, 389–415. It is unfortunate that this most important group of texts, which have undergone a series of re-editions and revisions, is not published together in corrected form in any single book or article. The complete list, with revised dates, is given in Feyel, *Polybe et l'histoire de Béotie au IIIe siècle avant notre ère* [*Bibl. Éc. fr.* 152 (Paris 1942)] 235.

61. *Syll.* 141, which does not include the list of the settlers that was inscribed on the stone, for which see the original edition by J. Brunšmid, *Die Inschriften und Münzen der griechischen Städte Dalmatiens* (Vienna 1898) 2. This document is extraordinarily interesting in many respects, since it specifies the amount and type of land given to the colonists and restricts alienability; see Adolf Wilhelm, "Neue Beiträge III," no. 15, pp. 3–18. A comparable allocation of rural land and a house in the city was made by Zeleia in Asia Minor to various individuals after a change in the political structure of the city in 334/3 B.C. or soon thereafter, SGDI 5533, on which see Wilhelm, *ibid.* 5–6; and by the Cretan city of Kydonia when it provided property for several *proxenoi*, probably in the second half of the third century B.C., IC II x, 1. (This list of illustrations is not intended to be complete.)

62. See, for example, [Demosthenes], *Against Neaira* 59.39–42. Cf. Aeschines, *Against Timarchos* 1.105, discussed shortly below.

63. It is most significant for the whole question of how to evaluate the supposedly factual material in the orators that any attempt to piece together a reasonably consistent picture from the two orations, mentioned earlier, that deal with the same family estate, a generation apart, is doomed from the start. The two stories simply do not agree on point after point. There is some evidence that the land held by groups, both public and private, most of which centered around one or more cults, tended to remain static for long periods; see, for example, the two inscriptions published by W. S. Ferguson, "The Salaminioi of Heptaphylai and Sounion," *Hesperia* 7 (1938) 1–74, the first of which is dated in 363/2 B.C. (the property in question certainly had been in the hands of the *genos* long before this time) and the other in 260/59 (by W. K. Pritchett and B. D. Meritt, *The Chronology of Hellenistic Athens* [Cambridge, Mass., 1940] xx). But even if this is so, it follows from the character and function of these associations and cannot be used as evidence of the general economic trend.

64. The most famous fifth-century fortunes were the 200 talents of Kallias, the son of Hipponikos, and the 100 of Nikias; see Lysias, *On the Property of Aristophanes* 19.47–48. To be sure, Lysias argues that the generally reputed figures were exaggerated. But he has need to argue the point in the case at hand and he did not himself hesitate, in another oration, to have the speaker claim that his family's wealth before the Peloponnesian War was 80 talents (*For Euandros* 26.22). Besides, the few available fourth-century figures over 10 or 15 talents are also matters of public repute, no more reliable a source of information than it was 100 years earlier.

65. [Demosthenes], *Against Phainippos* 42.4.

66. Aeschines, *Against Timarchos* 1.105; cf. Dio Chrysostom, *On Kingship IV* 4.91. This "typology" is more realistic than Aristotle's. The enumeration of possible holdings reads as follows in the Greek: οὐκ οἰκία, οὐ συνοικία, οὐ χωρίον, οὐκ οἰκέται, οὐ δάνεισμα. Cf. Isaeus, *On the Estate of Menekles* 2.27: εἰ δὲ περὶ χρημάτων ἐστὶν ὁ λόγος αὐτῷ, ἐπιδειξάτω ὑμῖν ὁποῖον χωρίον ἢ συνοικίαν ἢ οἰκίαν κατέλιπεν ἐκεῖνος. It will be apparent from the ensuing discussion why I prefer to translate *synoikia* as "multiple-dwelling" rather than the usual "lodging-house" or "tenement-house." Cf. Billeter, *Zinsfuß* 25, note 1.

67. The material on Pasion's multiple-dwellings is scattered among the various orations for and against Apollodoros in the Demosthenic corpus. See particularly *For Phormio* 36.34, *Against Stephanos I* 45.28, and *Against Nikostratos* 53.13. There are so many difficulties, including outright contradictions, in the Apollodoros speeches that I feel no certainty that the passages deal with two buildings and not one.

68. Isaeus, *On the Estate of Philoktemon* 6.19–21.

69. Isaeus, *On the Estate of Kiron* 8.35. It is unnecessary to follow those editors who have emended the manuscript reading of δισχιλίας for the value of the house leased out.

70. Gomme, *Population* 26. The residences of metics were concentrated in a few demes; see U. Wilamowitz-Moellendorf, "Demotika der attischen Metoeken," *Hermes* 22 (1887) 107–28, 211–59, at pp. 116–21, and the summary in Gerhardt, *Metoikie* 15–17.

71. In discussing Euktemon's *synoikiai*, Isaeus explicitly labels them brothels. The link between *synoikiai*, foreigners, and vice is taken for granted in the sources; see Aeschines, *Against Timarchos* 1.43. That the Peiraieus was also a center of wealthy citizens, incidentally, is clear from the material in Wachsmuth, *Stadt Athen* II 150–56.

72. Xenophon, *Poroi* 3.12; cf. 4.49.

73. The best example of house rental by wealthy citizens is IG II² 1590, a listing of the properties of Athena Polias leased out in 343/2 B.C. Six entries are preserved, all of house leases, five to citizens, one to a metic. The annual rental was high, ranging from 126 to 175 drachmas. Kirchner's notes in IG also indicate that the tenants were men of some prominence in the life of the city.

74. IG II² 1183, lines 28–29.

75. *Hesperia* 5 (1936) 393, no. 10, lines 117–53, sale of a confiscated *synoikia* in the Peiraieus below Munychia. The three adjoining houses, it may be worth noting, are each called *oikia* in the inscription.

76. Aeschines, *Against Timarchos* 1.124. Some editors have excluded this sentence as a later gloss, but its authenticity seems clearly defensible from the context, to which we shall return in a moment.

77. Nos. 73, 68, and 70, respectively. The confiscated *synoikia* in the Peiraieus already referred to, *Hesperia* 5 (1936) 393, no. 10, lines 117–53, was sold by the *poletai* at auction, in about 342/1 B.C., for 3,705 drachmas and 2 obols. The price is very suspicious, first because the odd sum is most unusual in such sales, second because it equals precisely the amount of the debt to the state plus the 100 per cent penalty, in default of which the building had been confiscated.

78. See Chap. VI, end of sect. 2.

79. Aeschines, *Against Timarchos* 1.124.

80. It is not insignificant that the sole use of the word in Herodotus (4.14) is for a laundry; in Aristophanes (*Knights* 744) for a butcher's shop. For other examples of fifth-century usage and a discussion of the close link between *ergasterion* and shopkeeping, see Ehrenberg, *People of Aristophanes* 125–28.

81. In fact, the word does not appear in any extant work of Aristotle's. The sole occurrence listed in H. Bonitz, *Index Aristotelicus* (separately paged in vol. 5 of Aristotle, *Opera*, ed. Academia Regia Borussica [Berlin 1870]), is in the post-Aristotelian *Oeconomica* 2.2.2,1346b7. Nor was the word ever used by Plato, according to G. A. F. Ast, *Lexicon Platonicum sive vocum Platonicarum* (3 vols., Leipzig 1835–38).

82. Aeschines, *Against Timarchos* 1.101.

83. See Ardaillon, *Mines* 59–89. It is necessary to reiterate the point made by Ardaillon, p. 172, that *ergasterion* is never used for a mine, which is always *metallon* in the sources. The sole use of the word *ergasterion* in the extant works of Isaeus, *On the Estate of Pyrrhos* 3.22, is in a mining context.

84. *Horos* no. 92 does not use the word *ergasterion* but κάμινος καὶ ἐδάφη, which means "a smelter and (surrounding) grounds"; see note 45 above.

85. In *horos* no. 90, the word *ergasterion* has been restored because slaves were also included in the encumbered property.

86. No. 161 is one of the *horoi* not included in the tabulations in Appendix I because of its fragmentary condition.

87. The word *ergasterion* has also been restored by the editor in no. 2, erroneously as I have indicated.

88. [Demosthenes], *Against Olympiodoros* 48.12–13.

89. The so-called third oration against Aphobos is, in my judgment, spurious and cannot be used as evidence for Athenian institutions of the fourth century B.C.; see Chap. IV, note 10. The best summary of the facts, as alleged by Demosthenes, remains that of Arnold Schaefer, *Demosthenes und seine Zeit* 1 (2 ed., 3 vols., Leipzig 1885–87) 270–302. The most ambitious analysis is Walter Schwahn, *Demosthenes gegen*

Aphobos. Ein Beitrag zur Geschichte der griechischen Wirtschaft (Leipzig and Berlin 1929), but it is worthless. In order to fit Demosthenes' account, and particularly his figures, to his own preconception of the character of the Athenian economy, Schwahn emends the text, applies modern bookkeeping techniques (not always without contradictions) and, where all other devices fail, simply dismisses certain statements by the orator as lies. Schwahn's main conclusions have been demolished by Friedrich Oertel, "Zur Frage der attischen Großindustrie," RhM 79 (1930) 230–52. But Oertel also attempts to make calculations of rate of profit and similar estimates which are impossible because they rest on the fallacy that fourth-century Athenians must have thought and operated in the same way as a modern businessman, even if on a quantitatively lower level. Similar attempts have been made by Arnaldo Momigliano, "La εἰσφορά e la sostanza di Demostene," *Athenaeum*, n.s. 9 (1931) 477–96, and by J. Korver, "Demosthenes gegen Aphobos," *Mnemosyne*, 3 ser., 10 (1941/2) 8–22. Cf. the calculations of the income, outgo, and rate of profit of a large agricultural operation in Jardé, *Céréales* 157–64, on Phainippos' estate.

90. Demosthenes, *Against Aphobos I* 27.9.

91. Max Weber, "Agrarverhältnisse im Altertum," *HWB der Staatswissenschaften* 1 (3 ed., Jena 1909) 52–188, reprinted in his *Gesammelte Aufsätze zur Sozial- und Wirtschaftsgeschichte* (Tübingen 1924) 1–288; see p. 9 (all references to this article are to the republication). Cf. Gunnar Mickwitz, "Zum Problem der Betriebsführung in der antiken Wirtschaft," *Vierteljahrschrift* 32 (1939) 1–25, at pp. 20–21.

92. Schwahn, *Demosthenes gegen Aphobos* 15–18, cannot permit such a conclusion; he therefore tampers with the text and locates certain concealed figures giving him a value of 9,300 drachmas for materials and tools, neither of them mentioned by Demosthenes. This is pure fantasy; see Korver, "Demosthenes gegen Aphobos" 17–18, who, however, proposes emendations of his own because he is dissatisfied with the value of the slaves as given by the orator.

93. Demosthenes 27.24,25,32, and 10 respectively. Johannes Hasebroek, "Nochmals ΠΥΡΓΟΣ 'Wirtschaftsgebäude,'" *Hermes* 57 (1922) 621–23, has demonstrated that the *pyrgos* mentioned in [Demosthenes], *Against Euergos and Mnesibulos* 47.56, was a special workroom within the house, a use of the word also known from the papyri. Perhaps the πύργος καὶ οἰκία in the mine-lease records for 367/6 B.C., *Hesperia* 10 (1941) 14, no. 1, lines 74–75, is a similar reference.

94. Xenophon, *Memorabilia* 2.7.2–12. For other illustrations of a man's residence serving as his workshop, see Herodotus 1.68; IG III 3, 69. The reference in Lycurgus, *Against Leokrates* 55–58, may be comparable, but there is also the possibility that the coppersmiths owned by Leokrates did not work in the house — nothing is said in the speech about an *ergasterion* — but were hired out to other producers. Some scholars have tried to get around the fact that Demosthenes' inheritance did not include a special workshop by suggesting that the 50–odd

slaves were hired out. This explanation flies in the face of the evidence, especially in 27.30–31. See Oertel, "Großindustrie" 231–33, a decisive analysis despite which Korver, "Demosthenes gegen Aphobos" 20, has revived the old explanation.

95. Demosthenes elsewhere uses the word *ergasterion* in a metaphoric sense that is particularly cogent in this context. In *Against Boiotos I* 39.2, he speaks of an *ergasterion* of sycophants, an invidious use of the word strongly reminiscent of the English colloquial use of "crew." Cf. *Against Boiotos II* 40.9.

96. Demosthenes, *Against Aphobos I* 27.26 and II, 28.12, respectively. Cf. 27.19, where slaves and *ergasterion* are used synonymously in the same passage.

97. *Ibid.* 27.18. For identical reasoning about mines and farms, see Xenophon, *Poroi* 4.4–5. It should be noted that the furniture makers were in Demosthenes' estate as security for a loan the orator's father had made, and he treats them as a second *ergasterion*.

98. Weber, "Agrarverhältnisse" 9; cf. Oertel, "Großindustrie" 239, 249–50; more generally, Salin, "'Sozialismus' in Hellas" 52–55. Somewhat connected with the present discussion is the fact that the Greek language had no word equivalent to "contractor" or "entrepreneur" as they are used in the modern business world. Ἐργοδότης and ἐργολάβος have a purely juristic connotation; they distinguish between the party who has work done and the party who does it (either by himself or through slaves or employees). Hence the ἐργοδότης may be a public official, the ἐργολάβος a contractor in our sense. A basic misconception of Greek economy is involved, therefore, when Robert Pöhlmann, *Geschichte der sozialen Frage und des Sozialismus in der antiken Welt* I (2 vols., 3 ed. by F. Oertel, Munich 1925) 172, writes: "*Der Arbeitgeber* (ἐργοδότης) *und der Arbeitnehmer* (ἐργολάβος) ... (*seien*) *scharf getrennte Klassen.*" Cf. the use of γεωργός to mean farmer and farm owner, indiscriminately; see Aristotle, *Politics* 6.2.5,1319a6; Demosthenes, *On the Crown* 18.41, *On the Embassy* 19.314.

99. Hypereides, *Against Athenogenes* 5.6,9,10,19.

100. *Ibid.* 7–9.

101. *Ibid.* 15; cf. § 22. See also Chap. II, note 24.

102. See Chap. II, note 24, for an illustration of the difficulties that arise from failure to understand this point. See the account in Demosthenes, *On the Crown* 18.169, of the destruction of the booths in the market-place when the news of the fall of Elatea reached Athens in 338 B.C.; and the interpretation by Charles D. Adams, "Τὰ Γέρρα Ἐνεπίμπρασαν, Demosthenes xviii, 169," *CP* 16 (1921) 1–11. Xenophon's summary, *Agesilaos* 1.26, of the remarkable arms production organized in Ephesos in 395 B.C. suggests that the work was done either in the open or in booths.

103. There seems no need to enter into the legal aspects of the manu-
facturing establishments operated by Lysias and his brother since
from the sources now available, it appears impossible to determine
whether they did or did not receive ἔγκτησις (the right to own
realty), and if so, when. See Friedrich Ferckel, *Lysias und Athen* (diss.
Würzburg 1937) 54–63, and Michel Feyel, "Sur quelques inscriptions
attiques et ioniennes de la première moitié du IVᵉ siècle," RP, 3 ser., 19
(1945) 116–161, at pp. 158–61, and the older literature cited by them.
Michel Clerc, *Les métèques athéniens* [*Bibl. Éc. fr.* 64 (Paris 1893)] 432,
says simply and characteristically, "*Il est certain qu'il* [i.e., Lysias]
jouissait de l' ἔγκτησις."

104. See the material in W. L. Westermann, "Sklaverei," PWRE Supp. 6
(1935) 894–1068, at cols. 915–16.

105. Not one extant *horos* that had been affixed to an *ergasterion* mentions
a written agreement, on which see Chap. II, sect. 3.

106. *Hesperia* 5 (1936) 393, no. 10, lines 105–110.

107. IG II² 2496.

108. IG II² 2501.

109. Demosthenes, *Against Pantainetos* (orat. 37). For a detailed discussion, see Chap. III, sect. 2.

110. Pantainetos also carried on mining operations in a mine leased from
the state. Modern editors and translators persist in confusing the mine
and the mill; for the correct distinction see Ardaillon, *Mines* 102–4.
The two creditors supplied unequal parts of the loan, Nikobulos the
plaintiff 4,500 drachmas and Euergos 6,000. Ever since Augustus
Boeckh, *Die Staatshaushaltung der Athener* 1 (3rd ed. by Max Fränkel,
2 vols., Berlin 1886) 86, most historians have assumed that Euergos'
loan was on the *ergasterion*, Nikobulos' on the slaves. They argue from
§ 21, where Nikobulos says οὐκοῦν ὡς μὲν ἀφῆκέ με πάντων, ὅτ' ἐγιγ-
νόμην τῶν ἀνδραπόδων πρατήρ, ἐπέδειξα, and from Xenophon, *Poroi*
4.23, which seems to indicate that slaves working in the mines cost,
on the average, about 150 drachmas each. There are many objections, however. § 21 can be interpreted as merely one more
illustration of Demosthenes' saying "slaves" when he means workshop
(see above, at notes 90–93; on the difficult sense of πρατήρ, see Chap.
III, note 33). Xenophon does not actually give the average price as 150
drachmas, and scholars who have dealt with the passage have reached
various figures, none of which, though they all revolve around 150,
would produce 4,500 drachmas when multiplied by the 30 slaves that
Pantainetos owned. Further, the whole transaction involves a loan
with real security in the form of *prasis epi lysei*, not a true sale, and
there are indications that the actual worth of the mill and slaves was
roughly twice the amount of the debt. Finally, there are various
passages in the oration in which the two loans are treated as a single
transaction (*e.g.* §§ 10, 12). Cases in which two or more men contribute

unequal shares of a loan are not unknown, as is clear from the *horoi* (and indicated in the Tables in Appendix I); cf. [Demosthenes], *Against Apaturios* 33.6. And the difference in the constituent parts results from a variety of factors, but not from a separation of the debtor's property into distinct units, each guaranteeing one of the loans. For a correct statement of the legal relationship between the two creditors in the Pantainetos case, see Hitzig, *Pfandrecht* 117-19.

111. [Demosthenes], *Against Timotheos* 49.11-12.

112. The two inscriptions are published in *Hesperia* 7 (1938) 1-74, with a detailed commentary by W. S. Ferguson (see note 63 above for the full reference and the dates). On the topographical questions, see H. A. Thompson, *ibid.* 75-76, and J. S. Young, in *Hesperia* 10 (1941) 163-69. I have summarized no. 1, lines 16-19; no. 2, lines 11-38.

113. See, *e.g.*, Lysias, *Against Diogeiton* 32.4: "Diodotos and Diogeiton, judges, were brothers, having the same father and the same mother, and they divided the invisible property but held the visible in common (ἐκοινώνουν)."

114. See Egon Weiss, "Communio pro diviso und pro indiviso in den Papyri," *APF* 4 (1908) 330-65 (with scattered material on the Greek cities, especially at pp. 331-38); J. H. Thiel, "Iets over retributies en burenrecht in de Grieksche Oudheid," *Tijdschrift voor Rechtsgeschiedenis* 6 (1925) 225-35 (too uncritical of such accounts as the one in [Aristotle], *Oeconomica* 2.2.4,1347a4, of Hippias' confiscating the upper stories of private houses); and the material in Chap. II, note 55. The most interesting examples are to be found in the Tenos inscription, IG XII 5,872, §§ 12,21,22,24,38, and 41. Weiss, *ibid.* 331, note 2, has shown that, in §§ 22 and 24 at least, the description leaves no doubt that the property in question remained a physical unit though legally divided. The basic explanation which he gives for the practice — and it applies to many of the Aegean islands — is the need to enclose farms in stockades for protection against pirates. The protective wall and blockhouse (πύργος) were naturally retained intact and the ownership shared when the farm itself was "divided" among two or more men.

115. For a translation of *horos* no. 130, see Chap. IV at note 2. Cf. Isaeus, *On the Estate of Hagnias* 11.34, for the lease of the one-half that was an orphan's share of the paternal estate (see briefly Chap. IV, note 14). On the slight possibility that *horos* no. 81 indicates a *prasis epi lysei* of part of a house, see Chap. II, note 55.

116. In no. 86, the property is defined as an οἰκία καὶ κ[οπρ]ών. The latter may be a privy or a dung-pit. If the latter is meant, then we must consider the possibility of an easement rather than of outright ownership of a thing. Cf. the lease agreement, IG II² 2496, of about the middle of the fourth century B.C., in which the property is described (lines 9-11) as τὸ ἐργαστήριον τὸ ἐν Πειραεῖ καὶ τὴν οἴκησιν τὴν προσοῦσαν αὐτῶι καὶ τὸ οἰκημάτιον τὸ ἐπὶ τοῦ κοπρῶνος.

117. See IG I² 94, lines 34–37; IG II² 2494, lines 8–11, with suggestions by Wilhelm, "Pachturkunden" 205, and G. Klaffenbach, in *Sitz. Berlin* (1936) 382, note 2. Cf. the fragment of a decree by the *orgeones* of Bendis, IG II² 1361, lines 8–12, dated after the middle of the fourth century B.C., and a contemporaneous orgeonic lease, Πραγματεῖαι ᾽Ακαδ. ᾽Αθηνῶν 13, fasc. 2 (1948) 5, lines 11ff. (known to me only from the republication by J. and L. Robert, in REG 63 [1950] 148–49).

118. IG II² 2499, lines 11–14, 30–37. None of the other extant Athenian lease agreements has a comparable provision. Πραγματεῖαι ᾽Ακαδ. ᾽Αθηνῶν 13, fasc. 2 (1948) 5, lines 11–23, is not comparable because the proviso deals with a building to be erected by the tenant. J. H. Kent, "The Temple Estates of Delos, Rheneia, and Mykonos," *Hesperia* 17 (1948) 243–338, at p. 293, notes that in Delos the "inventories of the Hieropoioi list several kinds of farm buildings, and for each one it is carefully noted whether it is a building 'with a door' (τεθυρωμένος) or 'without a door' (ἄθυρος)."

119. *Horos* no. 165, a hopelessly broken stone from Naxos, has κεράμου ἀμ[φορέων] in line 2. The restoration is far from certain, here as throughout the text, but if it is correct, then the reference is to clay jars and not to a roof. In the Tenian inscription, IG XII 5,872, we find the explicit statement in § 22, τοῦ κεράμο[υ τῆς στέγ]ης and simply *keramos*, in § 23; cf. § 47, quoted in Chap. II, note 55.

120. Kent, "Temple Estates" 293, draws the wrong conclusion, I think when he writes: "It was evidently the custom in ancient Greece to regard all wooden architectural parts of a farmhouse as part of the household furniture, and an Attic lease of 306/5 B.C. shows that in the case of rented farms the woodwork was usually the property of the tenant." The Attic lease is unique in this respect (see note 118 above), so that, if we are to argue anything from the clause about the wood-work it is precisely the opposite of Kent's conclusion. The lease, by its explicitness, probably shows that the woodwork was usually *not* the property of the tenant. It is of some interest to indicate, as Kent does (page 293, note 181), that "even today the lessees of the Rheneian farms, which are owned and leased by the municipality of Mykonos, are obliged to furnish their own doors."

121. The *horos* begins with the words, "*horos* of a house, including the roof and the furnishings in the house," whereas the monetary allocation ignores the roof, presumably because it was considered part of the furnishings. For the complete translation, see Chap. IV at note 58.

122. On this phrase, see Chap. II, note 81.

123. As illustrations of the great difficulty encountered in trying to prevent the disappearance of movables in other kinds of legal trans-actions, such as execution following a judgment or an *antidosis*, see Lysias, *On the Property of Aristophanes* 19.31; Demosthenes, *Against Onetor I* 30.28; and [Demosthenes], *Against Phainippos* 42.6–7,30.

124. *Horos* no. 178 reads in full: "*Horos* of a garden and slave(s)." The editors give no indication that other words were deleted. I have no suggestion to offer about this stone or its significance. References to the pawning of slaves are very rare, probably because an owner would not surrender possession of productive slaves except in an emergency. By giving them up, he seriously weakens his economic position and hence his opportunity of repaying the debt and releasing the slaves from pledge. The one important case known is that of Demosthenes' father and the slaves he received in pledge and kept for years, discussed in sect. 4 above. Such a text as [Demosthenes], *Against Euergos and Mnesibulos* 47.74,77, is irrelevant because the slaves were seized by the creditors without prior agreement in the form of hypothecation. The creditor's right to seize property in satisfaction of a debt extends to all types, slaves included, regardless of the debtor's preference.

125. See Westermann, "Sklaverei" 911–15.

Notes to Chapter VI

1. Demosthenes, *For Phormio* 36.6: μισθούμενος οὖν ὅδε τὴν ἐργασίαν αὐτὴν τῆς τραπέζης καὶ τὰς παρακαταθήκας [λαμβάνων], ὁρῶν ὅτι μήπω τῆς πολιτείας αὐτῷ παρ' ὑμῖν οὔσης, οὐχ οἷός τ'ἔσοιτ' εἰσπράττειν ὅσα Πασίων ἐπὶ γῇ καὶ συνοικίαις δεδανεικὼς ἦν, εἵλετο μᾶλλον αὐτὸν τὸν Πασίωνα χρήστην ἔχειν τούτων τῶν χρημάτων ἢ τοὺς ἄλλους χρήστας, οἷς προειμένος ἦν. καὶ οὕτω διὰ ταῦτ' ἐγράφη εἰς τὴν μίσθωσιν προσοφείλων ὁ Πασίων ἕνδεκα τάλαντα, ὥσπερ καὶ μεμαρτύρηται ὑμῖν. Both the translation of ἐργασία as "income" and Blass' deletion of λαμβάνων are supported by § 13: τὰς παρακαταθήκας καὶ τὴν ἀπὸ τούτων ἐργασίαν αὐτὴν ἐμισθώσαντο.

2. Demosthenes, *Against Stephanos I* 45.29–36.

3. I have ignored the extraordinary complications raised by this dispute over the lease of a bank, with its far-reaching implications for our understanding of many aspects of fourth-century Athenian economics and law. One crucial point is the absence of any legal distinction between the bank and the banker, in other words, the total lack of a corporate idea. Otherwise Phormio as lessee would have had no difficulty with the guaranties in real property. He says at one point in *For Phormio* 36.50: "And Sosimos and Timodemos and the other bankers, who, when they had to settle with those to whom they were in debt, all gave up (some of) their (own) property." (I have accepted the emendation proposed by W. Rennie, in CR 28 [1914] 267–68, of ἐξέστησαν ἅπαντες τῶν ὄντων for the MS ἀπάντων.) To my knowledge, no one has made the thorough analysis of the dispute between Apollodoros and Phormio that the issues merit. There is a casual presentation in J. Hasebroek, "Zum griechischen Bankwesen der klassischen Zeit," *Hermes* 55 (1920) 113–74, at pp. 140–1, 161–2, 166–7, 170–3. The

juristic problem inherent in Pasion's transfer of obligations is discussed without concern for the full legal situation by Gernet, "Actions commerciales" 42–43. Calhoun, *Business Life* 109, states correctly that there is no distinction between bank property and the banker's personal wealth and then proceeds to ignore this fact completely, speaking constantly of "firms" and "established institutions." Any study of the dispute will have to give serious consideration to H. Schucht, "Über die Echtheit attischer Rednerurkunden (Demosth. 45,31; 45,28; 46,21; 46,14)," PhW 39 (1919) 1120–28, 1143–51.

4. Aristotle, *Rhetoric* 1.5,1361a21. The phrase is δόσις καὶ πρᾶσις. In this context, *dosis* actually means much more than is usually associated with the English word "gift"; it includes any form of alienation of property without a quid pro quo, above all, by testament and adoption. See Bruck, *Schenkung* 109–12; Lipsius, *Attisches Recht* II 561–62. Erich Ziebarth, "Δόσις", PWRE 5 (1905) 1598–1603, suffers from an imbalance that creates a false impression of the proper implications of the word. He devotes only a few lines to wills and *donationes mortis causa*, the typical transactions, and the balance to the so-called Hellenistic family foundations, in which he was interested at the time he wrote the article.

5. IG II² 43, lines 37–41: ... ἐγκτήσασθαι ἐν τ[α]ῖς τῶν συμμάχων χώραις μήτε οἰκίαν μήτε χωρίον μήτε πριαμένωι μήτε ὑποθεμένωι μήτε ἄλλωι τρόπωι μηθενί. The combination ἐγκτήσασθαι ὑποθεμένωι is difficult. Most probably it is an elliptical way of saying that Athenians shall not be permitted to accept real property in allied territory as security because the potential consequence is foreclosure and thereby the acquisition of property. Lines 41–42 read: ἐὰν δέ τις ὠνῆται ἢ κτᾶται ἢ τιθῆται τρόπωι ὁτωιōν.... Accame, *Lega ateniese* 60, without comment translates: "*se un Ateniese acquista per via di compera o sotto qualche altro titolo un immobile o ne riceve uno in annullamento d'un credito....*" For the earlier lines, he gives "*se il possesso deriva da una vendita quanto se deriva da costituzione d'ipoteca....*" This is a paraphrase, not a translation, and the "*annullamento d'un credito*" is an indication of the potential result of τιθῆται, not its meaning.

6. Another exceptional text, IG II² 1289, is discussed in Chap. VII at note 46. Pringsheim, *Sale* 183, writes: "Restrictions and prohibitions of alienation regularly refer to sales and mortgages." His own evidence reveals that "and mortgages" is erroneous.

7. Aeschines, *Against Ktesiphon* 3.21. It would be futile to list the scores of available texts. For the sake of diversity, mention may be made of the testaments of Plato and Theophrastus in Diogenes Laertius, *Lives of the Philosophers* 3.41 and 5.53, respectively, and the clause in the lease of land by the deme Aixone, IG II² 2492, lines 9–12, which provides that during the 40-year term of the lease, the deme will neither sell nor lease the property to anyone else.

8. Demosthenes, *Against Stephanos I* 45.28,35.

9. Hypereides, *Against Athenogenes* 5.8–9. This interpretation of the
function of the suretor here is correctly argued by Partsch, *Bürgschaftsrecht* 322, and Pringsheim, *Sale* 171, against the views that this
text offers evidence of suretyship in sale contracts (for which there is
no parallel in the sources) or of warranty.

10. Wilamowitz, "Metoeken" 215, note 1.

11. See Weiss, *Privatrecht* 171–89, on the legal disabilities of non-citizens
generally, with full source references and bibliographies.

12. These figures do not take into account names of women appearing on
the stones without the father's name, for a woman had no demotic. Nor
do they include the names of men with whom the actual contract was
deposited. Legally they could be citizens or non-citizens; actually, no
identifiable non-citizens appear among them.

13. The Lemnian *horoi* have five identifiable names of individual creditors and one of a debtor, all with Athenian demotics. This in no way
affects the problem under discussion, for all these men were cleruchs
and cleruch-land was treated as part of the Athenian domain; see the
material in Kahrstedt, *Staatsgebiet* 32–41.

14. The best testimony is Xenophon, *Poroi*. For a brief comment with
additional references, see Karl von der Lieck, *Die xenophontische
Schrift von den Einkünften* (diss. Cologne 1933) 28–29. See also the
material in Henri Francotte, *L'Industrie dans la Grèce ancienne*, 1
(2 vols., Brussels 1900–1) 215–20.

15. See Gernet, "Actions commerciales" 14–20.

16. Xenophon, *Poroi* 2.6; 3.12. Rudolf Herzog, "Zu Xenophons Poroi,"
Festgabe für Hugo Blümner (Zurich 1914) 469–80, at p. 471, explains
this limitation as the expression of a desire to prevent metics from
misusing the right of property *"zum Hypothekenwucher"* (so also Lieck,
Von den Einkünften 35–36). Such a view misreads the economic
picture. Nowhere in this period do we find the hostility to the man
who lends on real security that the view requires. Xenophon was
reflecting a much more profound conviction, that the ownership of
land was an inalienable privilege of citizenship. He was not concerned
with the problem of usurious moneylending at all.

17. Unfortunately, the historians who have been concerned with the
metic population of Athens seem to have overlooked the critical
significance of their basic economic disability, their separation from the
land. Neither Clerc, *Métèques*, for example, nor Th. Thalheim, "Εγ-
κτησις," PWRE 5 (1905) 2584–85, nor Hans Schaefer, *Staatsform und
Politik* (Leipzig 1932) 35–57, nor H. Hommel, "Metoikos," PWRE 15
(1932) 1413–58, raises the question of the relative frequency or infrequency of grants of the privilege of land ownership. When Hommel
writes (col. 1440) that from the conquest of Athens by Demetrios in
294 B.C., the notion of metic became meaningless because citizenship

itself had only *"munizipiale Bedeutung"* thereafter, he reveals a remarkable indifference to anything but the narrowest political implications. His discussion of *enktesis* appears only in the section called "Terminologie," concerned with legal definitions.

Still another effect of the failure to see the significance of the land question may be indicated. Drawing the wrong generalization from the Pasion-Phormio agreement, Calhoun, *Business Life* 103, concludes: "The great bulk of the money lent by banks, however, seems to have been secured by first mortgages on real property." He is then led to the following generalization, clearly a reflection of present-day notions of investment: "It would appear from this that Athenian bankers were very conservative in making loans, as they had need to be, since most of them apparently operated upon a rather slight margin." Calhoun thus ignores the position of the non-citizen with respect to land ownership. Then he argues (pp. 113–15) that the *dikai trapezitikai*, about which nothing is known from the sources, "were primarily for the recovery of loans made by banks" and were introduced "to protect and encourage the employment of capital." But if most bank loans were land-secured, such special protection would have been quite unnecessary.

18. For a summary of the rules regarding legal transactions entered into by men of unsound mind, etc., see Weiss, *Privatrecht* 235–38, Erich Berneker, "Παρανοίας γραφή," PWRE 18 (1949) 1275–78.

19. Isaeus, *On the Estate of Aristarchos* 10.10. Cf. Aristophanes, *Ecclesiazusae* 1024–25: ἀλλ' οὐ κύριος ὑπὲρ μέδιμνόν ἐστ' ἀνὴρ οὐδεὶς ἔτι; the scholiast cites the law in explanation of this metaphor, which means "he is no better than a woman." See generally Erdmann, *Ehe* Pt. I.

20. That "guardian" is not an absolutely precise rendition of *kyrios* is true, but it is less misleading than "master," recently proposed by Wolff, "Marriage Law" 46, note 22.

21. IG XII 5,872, with a few added notes in IG XII Supp.

22. No. 8 is one of the more perplexing *horoi*; it will be discussed in Chapter VII, sect. 4. The word for "agrees" here is συνεπιχωρούσης. Such words appear rather frequently in legal texts where the authorization of a third party is necessary in order to eliminate possible legal disputes, arising chiefly from family-law situations; see W. L. Westermann, "Extinction of Claims in Slave Sales at Delphi," JJP 4 (1950) 49–61. Another Amorgian stone (no. 155) marks property which a woman and her husband acting as her *kyrios* consecrate to Aphrodite; the property, says the stone, had been hypothecated to the woman as a dotal *apotimema*. Arguing by analogy, the editors of I J, I pp. 135–36, and Weiss, *Untersuchungen* I 71, explain the woman's intervention in nos. 8 and 102 on the ground of rights she had in the property by *apotimema*. There is nothing in the text of no. 8 to argue for or against this view, but no. 102 explicitly enumerates the ways in which the property had originally been acquired by the man (partly by division

of a family estate, partly by purchase, and partly by hypothecation), leaving no room for a dotal *apotimema*, and there is no indication that the two were man and wife anyway. The explanation given in IJ must be rejected, therefore, though no alternative presents itself. A full translation of no. 102 is given in Chap. III, beginning of sect. 2.

23. Two Attic stones, nos. 174 and 176, are sometimes erroneously included among the *horoi*, whereas they are boundary-stones marking the property of women. No. 176 was apparently necessary because of a complicated family property situation; see IJ I pp. 126 and 137, and Erdmann, *Ehe* 328, note 7. No. 174 has but three words in the Greek, saying "*Horos* of the land of Lysippe." In IG, Kirchner publishes the two among the *termini fundis emptis appositi*, without any possible justification. The original editor of no. 174, H. J. W. Tillyard, in BSA 11 (1904/5) 69, no. 14, writes with considerable probability that "this stone seems to refer to the dowry of Lysippe." Substantiation comes from the two boundary-stones from Syros, nos. 179 and 180, which say explicitly that the property marked was the dowry in each case. No. 181 is included by Guiraud, *Propriété foncière* 242, among the then known cases of land given as dowry in lieu of money. Incidentally, neither stone from Syros has the word *horos*. Finally, note should be taken of no. 175, which has the word *proikos* but no verb. The probability is that the word *apotimema* was omitted through an oversight as in no. 146.

24. See Table D in Appendix I. We may disregard the four *horoi* indicating the guaranty of dowries by *prasis epi lysei* rather than by *apotimema*. Three give no figure, the fourth, no. 49, gives 1,050 drachmas.

25. For a full discussion of the evidence and of the views of previous scholars, see Arnaldo Biscardi, "I rapporti tra ΠΡΟΙΞ ed ΕΓΓΥΗΣΙΣ nel diritto matrimoniale attico," SIFC, n.s. 11 (1934) 57–80, and, more briefly, Erdmann, *Ehe* 303–6.

26. The economic and social aspects of the dowry in ancient Greece deserve more thorough study than they have yet received. Erdmann, *Ehe* 300–341, is devoted almost entirely to legal questions and is not completely adequate. Erdmann tends to generalize from isolated texts and he is not always reliable either in his summary or in his interpretation of the texts. On pp. 319–321, he gives illustrations of dowries of varying sizes, presented quite unsystematically and loosely. A convenient list, also incomplete, will be found in Wyse, *Isaeus* 243. I have not been able to consult a recent volume of J. M. Sontis, Προὶξ κατὰ κλασσικὸν καὶ Βυζαντινο-ρωμαϊκὸν χρόνον.

27. Demosthenes, *Against Stephanos I* 45.66.

28. [Andocides], *Against Alcibiades* 4.13–14; Plutarch, *Alcibiades* 8.2.

29. The sums provided by men on their deathbeds as "dowries" for their wives have been excluded deliberately. Several of these grants were well over 6,000 drachmas. The elder Demosthenes, for example, gave

his wife to Aphobos along with 8,000 drachmas and the use of the house, and his daughter, aged five, to Demophon with a dowry of 12,000 drachmas payable at once; Demosthenes, *Against Aphobos I* 27.5. Pasion on his deathbed apparently gave his wife in marriage to Phormio with money and property worth some 20,000; Demosthenes, *Against Stephanos I* 45.28. None of these cases is comparable with the figures we are examining because of the added factor of guardianship that is involved. The larger sums were understood to be a form of insurance of the guardian's goodwill and honesty in the performance of his duties. The rather complicated instructions for the care of Herpyllis that Aristotle placed in his will are illuminating in this connection; Diogenes Laertius, *Lives of the Philosophers* 5.13-14.

The huge dowries in Menander are to be rejected, too, as a comic exaggeration; see Ferguson, *Hellenistic Athens* 68. They do not warrant the generalization which Rostovtzeff, *Hellenistic World* 163, draws from them: The Athenian "bourgeois" of the end of the fourth century B.C. "gives a decent but not excessive dowry, usually of one, two, three, or four talents of silver, sixteen being the maximum." Even if one shares Rostovtzeff's view that Menander, along with Theophrastus and Diogenes Laertius, offers a "vivid picture of the life of an Athenian citizen of the time" (cf. also his pp. 118-19), the notion that one to four talents would be a "decent but not excessive dowry" is simply untenable.

30. Isaeus, *On the Estate of Hagnias* 11.40. The end of the first sentence reads ὥστε εἶναι μὲν [οὐχ] ἱκανά, λῃτουργεῖν δὲ οὐκ (or μὴ) ἄξια. Reiske's emendation, the deletion of οὐχ, is necessary to the sense and has been accepted by all modern editors. Cf. Isaeus, *On the Estate of Pyrrhos* 3.49.

31. Plutarch, *Aristeides* 27.1; cf. the 3,000-drachma dowry in Plato, *Epistles* XIII 361E. O. Schulthess, "Φερνή," PWRE 19 (1938) 2042-50, at col. 2046, misses the point of Plutarch's story when he cites the dowering of Aristeides' daughters as evidence that "*zur Zeit der Redner war auch bei Minderbegüterten eine Mitgift von 30 Minen üblich.*" His approach to the question is so altogether unrealistic that he can write: "*Sogar bei ärmlichen Leuten betrug sie 10, 20, 25 Minen.*"

32. [Demosthenes], *Against Makartatos* 43.54 (cf. Isaeus, *On the Estate of Kleonymos* 1.39). I have already indicated in Chap. V, note 28, the general problem of the authenticity of the laws quoted in this speech. A quite different version of the "Solonic" law on the dowering of thetic *epikleroi* seems to have been mentioned by the late third-century B.C. grammarian, Aristophanes of Byzantium, in a fragment preserved in Eustathios, *Commentary on the Iliad and Odyssey* 1246.10: αὕτη δέ, φησίν, ἐπὶ τὸν πλησίον τοῦ γένους πορεύεται κατὰ νόμον ἀναγκάζοντα τοῦτο· καὶ ὁ μὴ αἱρούμενος γῆμαι πέντε μνᾶς ἀποτίνει, ὡς ἔταξε Σόλων. ἐν δὲ τοῖς ἐπικαινισθεῖσι νόμοις μετέδοξε τοῦτο ὡς μικρόν, καὶ ἐγένοντο δέκα μναῖ. See the ed. of the fragments of Aristophanes by A. Nauck (Halle 1848) 194, frag. 39.

33. Diogenes Laertius, *Lives of the Philosophers* 5.63 and 5.72, respectively.

34. Demosthenes, *Against Spudias* 41.3 and *Against Onetor II* 31.1–3, respectively.

35. See Chap. VIII, at note 13, for the full text and translation.

36. See Gomme, *Population* 17–19.

37. It would be doubly wrong to compare the figures on the *horoi* with the few figures we have from other sources as to the total wealth of specific individuals, some of which run to sums far beyond those with which we are dealing. The great majority of the *horoi* mark one specific piece of property. In the few that indicate more than one "house" or "land," there is no way of our knowing the number or the nature of the units. No ground is established, therefore, for comparing the monetary sums on the *horoi* with the known monetary value of a total holding. Furthermore, it is perfectly possible that two or more of the extant *horoi*, not to mention the untold numbers that are no longer in existence, indicated the encumbrance of the property of the same owner, with one unit hypothecated to one creditor and another to a second, or third.

38. See, for example, the excellent summary in Nussbaum, *Lehrbuch* 190–99; Fritz Schulte, "Land Mortgage Credit: Agricultural, General," EnSS 9 (1933) 43–47.

39. The most thorough discussions of this problem will be found in the legal literature. Basic are the works of Josef Partsch; see particularly his review of D. P. Pappulias, ʿΙστορικὴ ἐξέλιξις τοῦ ἀρραβῶνος ἐν τῷ ἐνοχικῷ δικαίῳ, in GGA (1911) 713–32, reprinted in his *Aus nachgelassenen und kleineren verstreuten Schriften* (Berlin 1931) 262–80, at pp. 262–66; and "Mitteilungen aus der Freiburger Papyrussammlung 2. Juristische Texte der römischen Zeit," *Sitz. Heidelberg* 7 (1916) no. 10, at pp. 15–17. For a good summary with full bibliography, see Hellebrand, "Ὠνή" 427–29, 433–34. The most recent and most complete account is Pringsheim, *Sale*, Pt. II, Chaps. V–VIII, Pt. III, Chaps. I–II. Because of their exclusive concern with the legal problems, the jurists tend to ignore the question of the relative frequency and socioeconomic significance of credit operations in real property transfers. This becomes evident in the reluctance with which Hellebrand concedes the unimportance of the exceptions; it approaches absurdity in the elaborate argumentation with which Simonetos, "Kauf und Übereignung" 177–87, attacks Partsch's fundamental conception in order to make room for the rarest of exceptions, obviously most insignificant in terms of the general practice. Pringsheim, *Sale* 247, says that the "concept of sale on credit was familiar to Greek law," but the only documentation he can present outside the papyri (and apart from the *arrhabon*, on which see the text and notes immediately following) are the slave sale in Lycurgus, *Against Leokrates* 23; [Aristotle], *Oeconomica* 2.2.8,1347b3, a corrupt and unintelligible passage on which Pringsheim

concedes that "certainty is impossible"; *Syll.* 742, an Ephesian inscription of 85 B.C., which need not be interpreted in this way at all; and Plato's prohibition of credit sales in the *Laws*, 849E and 915D–E.

40. Isaeus, *On the Estate of Kiron* 8.23.

41. Aristotle, *Politics* 1.4.4–5,1259a3. It should be noted that a briefer version of the same story in Diogenes Laertius, *Lives of the Philosophers* 1.26, taken from the third-century B.C. philosopher and historian, Hieronymos of Rhodes, omits all reference to the *arrhabon*.

42. The *arrhabon* is mentioned repeatedly in Theophrastus, *Laws* §§ 4 and 6.

43. Harpocration, s.v. βεβαιώσεως, with a general reference to two speeches by Lysias — this passage is reproduced in the *Lexeis rhetorikai, Anecdota Bekker* I 219.33 (for a summary of the various theories and explanations this passage has evoked, see the article, not convincing in its own contribution, by P. J. Reimer, "Zur δίκη βεβαιώσεως bei Harpokration," Mnemosyne, 3rd ser., 9 [1940/41] 153–56).

44. The one exception of note was in the sale of realty confiscated by the state. Buyers were given five years in which to pay for houses, ten for land; Aristotle, *Constitution of the Athenians* 47.3. This exception is irrelevant to the present discussion because the state did not participate in hypothecation; see Chap. VII, sect. 2. The *arrhabon* has produced an enormous amount of polemical writing among modern jurists, which takes on an Alice-in-Wonderland quality in the light of the fundamental insignificance of the institution they are debating. The prevailing view is that of Partsch, who held that no sale, at least of real property, was legally binding until the full purchase price had been paid, that therefore the *arrhabon* did not create an enforceable sale-purchase contract, that, in case the buyer failed to consummate the transaction, only the amount of the deposit itself, not the full purchase price, was forfeited, and that, in case of default by the vendor, the buyer had a legal remedy for the return of the deposit, perhaps with a penalty; see the references in note 39 above, and now, in greatest detail, Pringsheim, *Sale*, Pt. III, Chap. IV.

The opposing view, that the Greeks developed the consensual sale contract, has been maintained against Partsch by G. Cornil, "Die Arrha im justinianischen Recht," ZSS 48 (1928) 51–87, at pp. 70–73; and H. R. Hoetink, "Quelques remarques sur la vente dans le droit grec," *Tijdschrift voor Rechtsgeschiedenis* 9 (1929) 253–70. It is the nature of Hoetink's reasoning that is particularly interesting. Conceding the pitiful character of the evidence, he is finally reduced to the argument that so commercial a people as the Greeks must have had a consensual sale contract, a perfect *petitio principi*.

45. Pringsheim, *Sale* 163–64, tries to argue this stone away because on its face it contradicts one of his theses. "The only interpretation warranted by the words," he writes, "is that the price is still owing. If the land had been mortgaged or otherwise encumbered this would be indicated in the inscription itself. That is a rule to which there is no exception." But

horos no. 146 is an exception, and if there is one, there can be two. Generally speaking, Pringsheim is correct when he criticizes editors of the *horoi* who too often give explanatory notes to the effect that the debt originated in a credit sale, *e.g.*, Kirchner in IG II² re *horos* no. 7. This practice cannot be supported either by the texts themselves or by the information available from other sources. If the four stones, nos. 112–115, in which the verb appears without the qualifying *epi lysei* marked actual sales rather than *praseis epi lysei*, though I have suggested the contrary in Chap. VII at notes 68–70, then there was no security transaction at all and the stones were not *horoi* as we are using the word. Similarly, the deletion of the words *epi lysei* from the stone, no. 63, some time after its original inscription merely indicates that the debtor had defaulted and the creditor taken over the property. Again this transaction tells us nothing about the reason for which the land was offered in security originally.

46. See Pringsheim, *Sale* 172–73. It is wrong, therefore, to see in the *horoi* and other epigraphical references to hypothecation evidence of a highly developed *"Güterhandel,"* as, for example, does Ziebarth, "Dystos" 207. Similarly Hitzig, *Pfandrecht* 36–38, ranks sale second in his list of underlying transactions, a list which in general gives a false picture of Greek credit operations. Busolt, *Staatskunde* I 179, speaks of land as a *"Gegenstand der Spekulation,"* especially after the destruction and ruin of the Peloponnesian War. As proof, he cites (1) the story of Ischomachos' father in Xenophon, *Oeconomicus* 20.22, a moralistic tale absolutely unique in Greek literature that proves the great rarity of land speculation, if anything; and (2) the extensive landholdings of Pasion noted in Demosthenes, *For Phormio* 36.5,36. There is nothing in the oration to indicate land speculation on Pasion's part, however, and the implication in Busolt's phrasing that the banker took advantage of the bankruptcy of many peasants to buy farmland cheaply at the end of the Peloponnesian War is unwarranted. We do not know when Pasion, an ex-slave, obtained the right to own realty, but it is probable that when Isocrates' *Trapezitikos* (orat. 17) was written, between 394 and 391 B.C., Pasion was not yet a citizen; see Hans Schaefer, "Pasion [2]," PWRE 18,4 (1949) 2064–68, at col. 2065. Alkiphron, *Letters* 1.26, is of course not evidence for the era under discussion. It is perhaps significant, nevertheless, that the professional moneylender there described demanded that the purchaser hypothecate all his property, not merely the farm at Kolonos he wished to buy. Finally, it is worth noting that there was no word in ancient Greek meaning "broker" or "seller of land"; see the list of 67 different "seller" words compiled from the lexica (especially Pollux, *Onomasticon* Bk. 7) by Heichelheim, *Wirtschaftsgeschichte* I 346–47. Liddell-and-Scott mistranslates προπώλης as *"one who buys for another* or *negotiates a sale, broker,"* whereas the word means "warrantor," as was demonstrated forty years ago by Partsch, *Bürgschaftsrecht* 344, 354 note 3; see Pringsheim, *Sale* 441.

47. The fourth-century B.C. lease of a garden owned by the *orgeones* of the Hero Physician, Πραγματεῖαι ᾽Ακαδ. ᾽Αθηνῶν 13, fasc. 2 (1948) 5,

lines 11–23, gave the lessee, who received a 30-year tenancy, the right to make any constructions he chose, at his own expense, on a designated section of the property. At the end of the term, he was to remove the roof and woodwork, unless a prior agreement was made to the contrary.

48. See briefly Ehrenberg, *People of Aristophanes* 79–80, who cites Isaeus, *On the Estate of Astyphilos* 9.28, Xenophon, *Oeconomicus* 1.2–5 and 20.23; cf. Chap. V, note 37. To this list may be added Demosthenes, *Against Aphobos I* 27.58–59, where the orator gives instances of the doubling and even trebling of the estates of orphans, in contrast to the diminution of his own. The argument is highly dubious. What is most noteworthy about it is Demosthenes' assumption that the income from these estates was absolutely identical, in monetary terms, year in and year out. That assumption lies at the base of all his calculations and ultimately of the amount of his claim against his guardians, and it has given great difficulty to modern commentators because it is so obviously "uneconomic" in character. See, for example, Oertel, "Großindustrie" 236–42. The starting point for a reconsideration of this whole question must be, in my judgment, two articles by Gunnar Mickwitz, "Economic Rationalism" and "Betriebsführung."

49. See Chap. VII at notes 35–38.

50. Hitzig, *Pfandrecht* 38–40, in his enumeration of the sources of security obligations already noted, ranks lease third. This is a misleading classification, brought about by his combining *misthosis oikou*, in which hypothecation was important, with ordinary rental of land and houses, in which hypothecation was negligible. In Chap. IV, sect. 1, I have shown that the fact of rental was irrelevant, protection of orphans decisive, in the Athenian requirement of security for the estates of orphans administered by a lessee in place of the guardian.

51. Isaeus, *On the Estate of Aristarchos* 10.13 (cf. *On the Estate of Pyrrhos* 3.42,68). On the family-property link, see the brief but valuable statement in Jürgen Brake, *Wirtschaften und Charakter in der antiken Bildung* (Frankfurt 1935) 72–74; on property and the *epikleroi*, Louis Gernet, "Sur l'épiclérat," REG 34 (1921) 337–79, especially pp. 358–75. In the agricultural regions of modern Europe, the hypothec is often used in the division of an inheritance: one heir takes over the land and promises to pay the others their shares in cash or chattels. In the meantime, he hypothecates the land to the other heirs as security against possible failure on his part to pay them their shares; see Nussbaum, *Lehrbuch* 198–99. I know of no clearcut instance of such a practice in the Greek cities, though an occasional occurrence cannot be ruled out in principle. Isaeus, *On the Estate of Menekles* 2.27–29, is sometimes cited as a case of hypothecation between brothers holding an undivided estate, but that is a clear misinterpretation of the difficult text, as was demonstrated by Rabel, *Verfügungsbeschränkungen* 15–16; recently Paoli, "Ipoteca" 187–88, has revived the old view, but without sufficient ground. [Demosthenes], *Against Nikostratos* 53.10, is indecisive; see Rabel, *ibid.*; for other views of this text, see Weiss,

Privatrecht 334–35. Examples of the existence of "business" relationships among members of a family (loans at interest, etc.) will be found in Demosthenes, *Against Spudias* 41.8, and Lycurgus, *Against Leokrates* 23–24.

52. Most of the word τρα[πεζίτηι] is missing on the stone, but, like Ziebarth, I have been unable to find a patronymic with which to restore the lacuna.

53. The identifications can be found in IG and other editions of *horoi*.

54. I have not collected and classified the names; that study must await the new Attic prosopography.

55. See briefly Heichelheim, *Wirtschaftsgeschichte* I 357. The story in Xenophon, *Memorabilia* 2.7.2–12, describing at length the effort required for Socrates to persuade Aristarchos, impoverished by the Peloponnesian War, to borrow money with which to purchase the tools and raw materials so that his female relatives could support the family by their work, is a clear indication of the "non-productive mentality" of precisely that section of the population that owned adequate property for hypothecation and of the relative infrequency of this type of borrowing. There is no indication of legal security in the story, it should be noted.

56. See, for example, Lysias, *On the Property of Aristophanes* 19.22,25–26; Demosthenes, *Against Aphobos II* 28.17–18 (further details in *Against Meidias* 21.78–80); and generally [Demosthenes], *Against Polykles* (orat. 50). The speaker in [Demosthenes], *Against Boiotos II* 40.52, went into debt for 1,000 drachmas to meet the costs of his father's funeral, a sum to be compared with the 2,000 drachmas he and his father together had borrowed for a mining venture, one of the few genuinely productive loans, apart from bottomry, to be found in the entire literature. Aristophanes' *Clouds* is especially pertinent in this context. The rustic Strepsiades complains that his wife and even more his son are driving him to financial ruin by their extravagances. He makes specific reference (lines 21–31) to two debts, 1,200 and 300 drachmas borrowed from Pasias and Amynias respectively, incurred for the purchase of horses for his son (not for use on the farm, it must be underscored). The economic and legal problems raised by the play require thorough re-examination.

57. [Demosthenes], *Against Nikostratos* (orat. 53). For a summary of the facts and a discussion of the date and authenticity of the speech, see Paley-Sandys, ed., *Demosthenes* II li–lix.

58. On the nature of the *eranos*-loan, see chap. VII, section 4.

59. [Demosthenes], *Against Nikostratos* 53. 12–13. The verb for "hypothecate" used throughout is τίθημι. For the "loan" of the property to Nikostratos, Apollodoros uses κίχρημι. This text raises certain difficult legal problems which cannot be discussed here, notably in the seeming

contradiction between Apollodoros' offer to Nikostratos and his final sentence indicating that he himself hypothecated the building. A summary of the literature will be found in Weiss, *Privatrecht* 334–35; see more recently Paoli, "Ipoteca" 188–89.

60. [Demosthenes], *Against Timotheos* (orat. 49), dated by Blass, *Beredsamkeit* III 1, 522–23, in 362 B.C., but in 368/7 by Karl Klee, "Timotheos [3]," PWRE, 2nd ser., 6 (1937) 1323–29, at col. 1327. The authority for the statement that Apollodoros was the victor in the suit is Plutarch, *Demosthenes* 15.

61. The terminology of the oration is most interesting. Ἐνέχυρον is used three times as the generic word for security (§§ 2,53,61) and once to mean "pawn" (§ 52). Ὑποτίθημι is used for hypothecation except for the one reference to an *apotimema* in § 11 and one use of ὁρίζομαι (§ 61). Despite the fact that Pasion's loans were friendly and bore no interest, δανείζειν is used throughout.

62. Note the list of famous Athenians with whom Pasion is known to have had dealings in the first three decades of the fourth century B.C., in Schaefer, "Pasion" 2066. Schaefer's evaluation of Pasion's wealth and position shifts from "typical for his time" (col. 2064) to "unique" (col. 2068).

63. [Aristotle], *Problems* 29.2,950a28; cf. 29.6,950b28. On the ethic of deposits (with strong religious overtones), see the long story in Herodotus 6.86, supposedly told by Leotychidas, king of Sparta, when requesting the return of hostages from Athens; cf. also Konon, frag. 1.38 (Jacoby, FGH no. 26); Demokritos, frag. 265 (Diels). Note the proposals in Plato, *Laws* 742C, that no one should deposit money ὅτῳ μή τις πιστεύει and that interest-bearing loans be prohibited altogether. The same ethic underlies the encomium in Xenophon, *Agesilaos* 4.1–4.

64. See Chap. VII, sect. 4.

65. Hypereides, *Against Athenogenes* 5.4. I do not mean to imply that *eranoi* were never used to raise money for "business" purposes. But an examination of the examples given by Th. Reinach, "Eranos," *Dar.-Saglio* II, 1 (1892) 805–8, at p. 806, or by Lipsius, *Attisches Recht* II 731, proves that the productive *eranos*-loan was the exception.

66. The amount of the obligation in no. 27 is 420 drachmas. Below the figure someone subsequently inscribed, in smaller letters that are now difficult to read, the following numerals: ΔΔΓⱵⱵIIII⟨. It is tempting to suggest that the correct reading should be ΔΔΓⱵⱵⱵII⟨, for 29 drachmas and 2½ obols equal exactly 7 per cent of the principal. Only an examination of the stone can determine the merit of this suggestion.

67. *Horos* no. 132 has two dates, the one at the beginning, 305/4 B.C., indicating when the *horos* was set up, and another, 303/2, introducing a second phase of the transaction. Whatever the meaning of this difficult text may be, it deals with a dowry question and is therefore of no particular significance in the present context.

68. Demosthenes, *Against Pantainetos* 37.5: ἕν τινι ῥητῷ χρόνῳ.

69. The modern literature on Greek economics has been singularly indifferent to this problem of the duration of loans, apart from the obvious fact that bottomry loans were made for the duration of a voyage, hence a few months at most. Yet the question is important enough to deserve special study. In the present context, I am ignoring the legal problems of loans in which the creditor was given the use of the pledged property during the term of the obligation and of the possible right of a defaulting debtor to repossess his property by payment of the debt after default and forfeit had taken place. One of these two situations may lie at the root of the case of the twenty bedmakers who were included in Demosthenes' inheritance though presumably still the property of the debtor who had pledged them to Demosthenes senior (Demosthenes, *Against Aphobos I* 27.9,24–29, II 28.12).

70. The comment on public loans by Andreades, *Public Finance* 172, is equally pertinent to private loans: "Usually ... the payment of the loaned capital was to be made within five years, while at times even shorter limits are mentioned. The archaeologists have not sufficiently emphasized the consequences of this fact, which rendered the loans a very burdensome load for the states which were hard pressed at the expiration of the time limit and presumably formed one more reason for the infrequency of such loans." Cf. briefly on private, short-term loans, Oertel in Pöhlmann-Oertel, *Sozialismus* II 529–31. The material on interest rates in Billeter, *Zinsfuß*, Pt. I, Chap. IV, and Pt. II, Chap. I, is still very valuable.

71. See briefly Nußbaum, *Lehrbuch* 190–92, 263–65.

72. Aristophanes, *Ecclesiazusae* 753–55. Ehrenberg, *People of Aristophanes* 93, is therefore wrong — no doubt misled by a mistaken comparison with the Solonic situation — when he cites the number of *horoi* as evidence of the impoverishment of the small farmer in the fourth century B.C., as proof that "during the fourth century the small farmers ran more and more into debt, and were frequently forced to give up their farms." This error is commonly made, for example by Busolt, *Staatskunde* I 179, Jardé, *Céréales* 118–19, E. Kornemann, "Bauernstand," PWRE Supp. 4 (1924) 83–108, at col. 89.

73. Theophrastus, *Characters* 10.2. In this connection, the very small scale that characterized individual transactions in commerce and the crafts offers a most significant contrast to the amounts involved in real security; see the excellent summary statement by A. W. Gomme, *Essays in Greek History and Literature* (Oxford 1937) 48–52. Gomme further calls attention to the "isolated" nature of each transaction (p. 53): "There was no regular investing public.... There were no commercial banks, no discount houses, whose main business it would be to finance foreign trade; there was no *creation* of credit which is the foundation of modern trading methods."

Notes to Chapter VII

1. Aristotle, *Nicomachean Ethics* 8.9.4–5,1160a9. The final two sentences of the quotation are rejected by many editors as a later interpolation, but they have been retained by Susemihl.

2. See the material in Franz Poland, *Geschichte des griechischen Vereinswesens* (Leipzig 1909) 163–66, and the recent work of P. J. T. Endenburg, *Koinoonia, En Gemeenschap van Zaken bij de Grieken in den klassieken Tijd* (Amsterdam 1937). E. Kornemann, "Κοινόν," PWRE Supp. 4 (1924) 914–41, is useful on terminology, particularly §§ 1–2.

3. *Digest* 47.22.4: ἐὰν δὲ δῆμος ἢ φράτορες ἢ ἡρώων ὀργεῶνες ἢ γεννῆται ἢ σύσσιτοι ἢ ὁμόταφοι ἢ θιασῶται ἢ ἐπὶ λείαν οἰχόμενοι ἢ εἰς ἐμπορίαν, ὅ τι ἂν τούτων διαθῶνται πρὸς ἀλλήλους, κύριον εἶναι ἐὰν μὴ ἀπαγορεύσῃ δημόσια γράμματα. In the opening, the MSS read ἐὰν δὲ δῆμος ἢ φράτορες ἢ ἱερῶν ὀργίων ἢ ναῦται (or μηνυταί). I have followed the emendation proposed, on the basis of an earlier suggestion of Wilamowitz's, by Ferguson, "Orgeones" 64, note 1. Ferguson gives a full bibliography on this text.

4. See the cogent arguments for the use of the German *Vereinigung* rather than the customary *Verein* (and the Dutch equivalents) presented by Endenburg, *Koinoonia* 1–8.

5. The general statement with which I find myself in most complete agreement is that of Leopold Wenger, *Das Recht der Griechen und Römer* [*Die Kultur der Gegenwart* II, VII,1, *Allgemeine Rechtsgeschichte*, Heft 1 (Leipzig and Berlin 1914) 154–302] 208–11. Wenger writes, p. 209, "*Eine Auffassung, die das Vermögen des Vereins nicht loszutrennen vermag vom Vermögen der Mitglieder, liegt dem griechischen Denken viel näher als saubere Scheidung.*" Any future study of the whole question will have to begin with the elaborate terminological investigations made by Endenburg, *Koinoonia*, who gives a convenient survey of the literature on pp. 1–23. At present, the overwhelming majority of writers remains under the spell of modern notions.

It would be difficult, in this connection, to underestimate the harm done by Erich Ziebarth, *Das griechische Vereinswesen* (Leipzig 1896), a work which, despite its wealth of material and its mastery of the epigraphic sources, is unsound in theory and method; Ziebarth always saw in ancient Athens a replica of modern Hamburg. Even Franz Poland, whose monumental *Vereinswesen* offers a thorough and devastating critique of Ziebarth's book on every other aspect of the Greek associations, accepts the latter's discussion of the legal side as satisfactory. Yet in Ziebarth's 18-page chapter on law (pp. 166–83), he does not raise the question of juristic personality until five pages from the end, and then merely to assert its existence as a matter of fact, requiring no proof. A partial answer will be found in Max Radin, *The Legislation of the Greeks and Romans on Corporations* (New York 1909) Chaps. V–VI. Ziebarth's chapter has become the standard reference for all the casual and incidental remarks scattered through the literature of the past half-century, bolstered by M. San Nicolò, *Aegyptisches*

Vereinswesen zur Zeit der Ptolemäer und Römer [*Münchener Beiträge*
1 and 2 (Munich 1913–15)], an important study of Hellenistic law
which digresses repeatedly into the earlier law of the Greek cities.

A significant contribution to the subject that seems to have gone
unnoticed is Werner Kamps, "Les origines de la fondation cultuelle
dans la Grèce ancienne," AHDO 1 (1937) 145–79. Kamps showed that
the famous family-cult "foundations" of the third and second centuries
B.C. (Diomedon of Kos, Poseidonios of Halicarnassus, Epikteta of
Thera, etc.) reveal a groping towards the notion of juristic person, and
hence the absence of that conception in earlier times. He showed
further that the whole institution was geographically limited in pre-
Roman times; it did not spread to Athens and its sphere of influence.
(The significance of this discovery in the discussion of the so-called
unity of Greek law is apparent.) It was the failure of the Athenians to
develop the institution of the juristic person that explains the ambi-
guity of the legal provisions in the wills of the philosophers preserved
by Diogenes Laertius. This is seen most clearly in the wills of Theophrastus and Epicurus, 5.53 and 10.16–17 respectively, as was long ago
recognized by K. G. Bruns, "Die Testamente der griechischen Philo-
sophen," ZSS 1 (1880) 1–52, at pp. 31–33, 49, and R. Dareste, "Les
testaments des philosophes grecs," *Annuaire de l'Association pour
l'encouragement des études grecques en France* 16 (1882) 1–21, at pp.
11, 21.

6. See Poland, *Vereinswesen* 303–14; Ferguson, "Orgeones" 67–68.

7. IG II² 337, lines 38–45.

8. IG II² 1283, lines 4–6: ἐπειδὴ τοῦ δήμου τοῦ 'Αθηναίων δεδωκότος τοῖς
Θραιξὶ μόνοις τῶν ἄλλων ἐθνῶν τὴν ἔγκτησιν καὶ τὴν ἵδρυσιν τοῦ ἱεροῦ κτλ.
The date 261/0 is fixed by Pritchett and Meritt, *Chronology* xx. The
grant was probably made in the time of Pericles; see Ferguson, "Orgeones" 98, and the detailed analysis of the founding of the Bendis
cult in Athens in Ferguson, "Orgeonika," *Hesperia* Supp. 8 (1949)
130–63. IG II² 1361, dated after the middle of the fourth century B.C.,
is a fragment of a decree of the *orgeones* of Bendis; lines 8–12 deal with
the rental of a house they owned, hence they had ἔγκτησις by that
time.

9. Poland, *Vereinswesen* 312–13, gives the pertinent material. Emile
Szlechter, *Le contrat de société en Babylonie, en Grèce et à Rome* (Paris
1947) 108, makes the astounding statement, on the sole authority of
Guiraud, *Propriété foncière* 386, that "all societies formed in Athens
possessed 'Athenian nationality' without regard to the nationality of
their members." Guiraud offers as proof the Solonic law quoted above
in note 3, which is irrelevant since it grants associations freedom to
make any arrangements "unless forbidden by the laws" and the laws
forbade non-citizens to acquire real property. Guiraud's remaining
references are the wills of the third-century philosophers, Strato and
Lykon, preserved in Diogenes Laertius, *Lives of the Philosophers* 5.61–
64, 69–74, but I see nothing pertinent in either document. The correct

view is stated, *e.g.*, by Busolt, *Staatskunde* II 1169: "*Einer besonderen Erlaubnis zur Bildung eines Kultvereins bedurfte es nicht. Fremde, die ein Heiligtum bauen wollten, mußten sich lediglich deshalb an den Staat wenden, weil sie ohne besondere Willigung kein Grundeigentum erwerben durften.*"

10. Actually there is one duplication in these figures, for nos. 107 and 108, from Lemnos, appear on the same stone; both *horoi* mark debts to the *orgeones* associated with the temple of Herakles in the village of Kome. The stone was found in the temple precinct; see C. Fredrich, *Athen. Mitt.* 31 (1906) 251–52, and Ferguson, "Orgeones" 82. In his note to no. 109 (IG XII 8,21), Fredrich identifies the *orgeones* mentioned in that text with the group in nos. 107 and 108. His argument is that no. 109 was found in Mudri, which borders on Kome. In the absence of any textual identification of the *orgeones* of no. 109, no certain conclusion seems possible.

11. In one case, that of the *orgeones*, there is no word in Greek for the group as such; see Ferguson, "Orgeones" 61–62.

12. The Greek is οἱ μετά followed by the individual's name in the genitive. In Attic inscriptions and in the literature, this combination has a variety of meanings: "under the leadership of," "in cooperation with," "among," "under"; see briefly K. Meisterhans, *Grammatik der attischen Inschriften* (3rd ed. by Eduard Schwytzer, Berlin 1900) 218. I have deliberately avoided all these renditions and resorted to the equivocal "those with" because each of the possible translations indicates a different legal relationship. Only a full examination of all the pertinent material can determine whether the group was "under," "under the chairmanship of," or "in cooperation with" the "leader" named. At times there seems to be an interchangeable use of οἱ μετά and καί, the legal significance of which has not received adequate attention. In *Hesperia* 10 (1941) 14, no, 1, for example, there is repeated use of the formula, "Kichonides and the brothers," rather than "the brothers, those with Kichonides" (see the full text in Chap. VIII, note 13). Cf. the lease inscriptions, IG II² 1241 (with corrections by Wilhelm, "Pachturkunden" 200–3) and Πραγματεῖαι 'Ακαδ. 'Αθηνῶν 13, fasc. 2 (1948) 5–23. Note also that in the four Amorgian *horoi* in which women are involved, one (no. 9) uses the form, μετά κυρίου, whereas the other three link the woman and her *kyrios* by καί (nos. 8, 102, and 155).

13. Among the *horoi*, the exceptions are no. 8, already noted, which refers to the *eranos* and its head (not in the form οἱ μετά); no. 40, which uses the form, Λεωχάρει πληρωτεῖ καὶ συνερανισταῖς, a more explicit way of saying the same thing (see below at note 61); no. 109 with its unidentified *orgeones*; and nos. 44 and 71, which say merely "the eranists" without further identification. Poland, *Vereinswesen* 29, note 1, thought the absence of an individual's name in no. 44 was an oversight on the part of the stonecutter, but the subsequent discovery of no. 71 suggests that the explanation is probably to be found, here as in analogous situations, in the tendency to restrict the texts to a minimum, even at

the risk of much uncertainty. (To complete the list of possible exceptions, the difficulty in reading no. 43 should also be noted.) Even greater consistency in the formula, "the eranists, those with so-and-so," will be found in the lists of the so-called "freedmen's bowls" and in the Delphic manumission inscriptions; see the references in W. L. Westermann, "Two Studies in Athenian Manumission," JNES 5 (1946) 92–104, at p. 94, and sect. 4 below.

14. See Andreades, *Public Finance* 168–78, and the still valuable analysis in Kurt Riezler, *Über Finanzen und Monopole im alten Griechenland* (Berlin 1907) 56–66. Andreades points out, pp. 169,319–22, that the so-called borrowings from the treasures of Athena were in no sense loans but merely the expenditure of reserves. The most important new documents to be added to Andreades' material are the Boeotian inscriptions, SEG III 342, 356, and 359, on which consult, with caution, W. Schwahn, "Boiotische Stadtanleihen aus dem dritten Jahrhundert v. Chr.," *Hermes* 66 (1931) 337–46, and more generally Feyel, *Polybe* 247–50; and the inscription published in 1943 by Feyel, "Décret de Kopai sur un emprunt public," *Contribution* 148–55.

15. The texts are published as IG XII 7,66–70. All but the first are reprinted, with translation and commentary, as I J I xv. No. 67B is also reprinted as *Syll.* 955, with excellent notes by Hiller. On these inscriptions, which raise a variety of interesting historical, economic, and legal problems, see Eilhard Schlesinger, *Die griechische Asylie* (Gießen 1933) 18–28; J. Delamarre, "Les contrats de prêt d'Amorgos," RP 28 (1904) 81–102; Goldschmidt, "Inhaberurkunden" 360–79; Émil Szanto, "Anleihen griechischer Staaten," WS 7 (1885) 232–52, and 8 (1886) 1–36, reprinted in his *Abhandlungen* 11–73; Curt Wachsmuth, "Öffentlicher Credit in der hellenischen Welt während der Diadochenzeit," RhM 40 (1885) 283–303; and the references on certain details given by Ruppel, "Amorginische Städte" 317. W. W. Tarn, in J. B. Bury, ed., *The Hellenistic Age* (Cambridge, Eng., 1925) 108–12, gives a brilliant picture of the social background of the loans, but he misreads the economic implications (on which see Chap. VI, note 70).

16. IG XII 7,67B 42–44: ὑπέθετο δὲ Πραξικλῆς τά τ[ε κ]οινὰ τὰ τ[ῆ]ς πόλεως ἅπαντ[α κ]αὶ [τ]ὰ ἴδια τὰ 'Αρκεσινέων καὶ τῶν οἰκούν[τ]ων ἐν 'Αρκεσίνηι ὑπάρχ[οντα] ἔγγαια καὶ ὑπερπόντια. The executory clause is B57–76. Identical provisions, with insignificant differences in wording, appear in IG XII 7,69, lines 8–10,23–45; cf. the fragmentary line 67 A 24.

The editors of IJ, following Wachsmuth, translate ἔγγαια καὶ ὑπερπόντια as "*propriétés situées tant sur terre que sur mer*," in an attempt to strengthen the parallel between these agreements and the contract in [Demosthenes], *Against Lakritos* 35.12, where we find the expression, καὶ ἐγγείων καὶ ναυτικῶν. But ὑπερπόντια cannot be given the meaning "on sea." Tarn, in Bury, *Hellenistic Age* 110, tries to circumvent the difficulty when he says ὑπερπόντια is "overseas property, which here means ships and their cargoes, as Arcesine owned no property overseas." The text, however, refers to overseas holdings of individual inhabitants of the city, not of the *polis* itself. For a correct parallel, see Xenophon, *Symposium* 4.31: νῦν δ'ἐπειδὴ τῶν ὑπερορίων στέρομαι καὶ τὰ ἔγγεια (MSS: ἔγγαια) οὐ καρποῦμαι. The ὑπερπόντια of the inscription is perfectly analogous to Xenophon's ὑπερόρια; ; see Hiller, in *Syll.* 955, and Jan Korver, *De Terminologie van het Crediet-Wezen in het Grieksch* (Amsterdam 1934) 127.

17. Two inscriptions, neither of which has received adequate notice, indicate the existence of the practice of hypothecating private property for public purposes in other communities: IG XI 4,543 (Delos, early third century B.C.), reprinted with a translation by F. Durrbach, *Choix d'inscriptions de Délos* (only vol. 1 published, Paris 1921–22) no. 27; and IG XII Supp. 236 (Keos, fourth century B.C.), originally edited by E. Preuner, in *Athen. Mitt.* 49 (1924) 136–42. From the Amorgian loans, Thiel, "Retributies," concludes that the Greeks drew no sharp distinction between the public and private domains of the state, that all state property was *in commercio* (cf. Guiraud, *Propriété foncière* 350–51). His evidence is made up largely of the Amorgian text and the hopeless story in [Aristotle], *Oeconomica* 2.2.4,1347a4, of Hippias' confiscating the upper stories of private houses as a device to raise revenue. A sounder approach will be found in the brief analysis of K. Latte, "Kollektivbesitz und Staatsschatz im Griechenland," *Nachrichten d. Akad. d. Wiss. in Göttingen, Phil.-hist. Kl.* (1946/7) 64–75, at pp. 74–75. The summary of present knowledge on security for public loans in B. Laum, "Anleihen," PWRE Supp. 4 (1924) 23–31, at cols. 27–29, is confused and exaggerates the frequency of real security.

18. There is evidence of the "hypothecation" of future public revenues, in general or in particular, as security for a loan; see Aeschines, *Against Ktesiphon* 3.103–5; [Aristotle], *Oeconomica* 2.2.29,1351b6; AJP 56 (1935) 359–77, a pair of late fourth-century inscriptions from Kolophon, on which see the analysis, with complete bibliography, by A. Wilhelm, "Athen und Kolophon," *Anatolian Studies Presented to William Hepburn Buckler* (Manchester 1939) 345–68, at pp. 352–65; OGIS 46, lines 9–21, a third-century B.C. inscription from Halicarnassus. Though the word "hypothecate" may be used, as in the Kolophon and Halicarnassus documents, this type of transaction is in reality a budgeting device whereby certain revenues are earmarked in advance, rather than a true illustration of legal security. DGE 526 C 25–40 (Orchomenos, Boeotia) is frequently cited in this connection through a misunderstanding; what is involved is merely the grant by the city either of the right of pasturage or of tax exemption (see the material in Feyel, *Contribution* 151–52). The editors of IJ, I pp. 164–65, see "*des gages et des hypothèques*" securing the loan made to the city of Kalymna in the third century B.C. by two citizens of Kos, *Syll.* 953. They base their interpretation on lines B60–64 (lines 8–12 in the IJ edition): ... καὶ τᾶν φιαλᾶν καὶ τῶν ἀλσέων καὶ τᾶν πεμπτᾶν ἀφαιρεθεισᾶν τᾶν ἀποδοσίων ἆς φαντι ἀποδεδώκεν Καλύμνιοι.... The one-fifth is presumably a tax (see Wilhelm, "Athen und Kolophon" 361–62) and we therefore have here another example of this kind of budgeting procedure. Whether the *phialai* and *alse* were pledged or not is not discoverable from the inscription, but certainly there is nothing to suggest real

security. On the date of the inscription, see Wilhelm, in *Anzeiger Wien* 61 (1924) 137–39; on the meaning of ἀφαιρεθεισᾶν, see R. Feist *et al.*, "Zu den ptolemäischen Prozeßurkunden," APF 6 (1920) 348–60, at pp. 359–60. Finally, there is a story in Strabo 13.3.6 that the people of Kyme once offered their public stoas as security and lost them by default. This story deserves to be taken as seriously as its purpose, which was to illustrate the traditional stupidity of the Kymeans. Cf. the story, repeated by Athenaeus, *Deipnosophists* 11.508F, of Plato's disciple, Euaios of Lampsakos, who lent his native city money on the security of its Acropolis and attempted to become tyrant when he was unable to foreclose. SEG III 359 may indicate that the Boeotian city of Akraiphia hypothecated "the sacred land of Apollo" against a loan, as Schwahn, "Boiotische Stadtanleihen" 343–45, argues. Even if so, the creditor failed to take the security upon default and surrendered a large share of his claim instead.

19. IG XII 7,67B 44–52; cf. 69, lines 11–17.

20. The most complete collection of material will be found in Ernst Hoyer, *Die Verantwortlichkeit und Rechenschaftspflicht der Behörden in Griechenland* (Karlsbad 1928).

21. In the Athenian literature, see, for example, Isaeus, *On the Estate of Aristarchos* 10.17,20; [Demosthenes], *Against Euergos and Mnesibulos* 47.54, *Against Timotheos* 49.11–12, and virtually the whole of *Against Polykles* (orat. 50). In general on this question as related to the *horoi*, see Chap. VI, latter part of sect. 2.

22. Some of the pertinent material will be found in the ensuing pages. It is enough to cite [Demosthenes], *Against Boiotos II* 40.20–23.

23. The words *apographo* and *apographe* have a great variety of uses, all connected in one form or another with the preparation of a statement, inventory, or other document; see Schodorf, *Attische Gerichtssprache* 72–73, for uses among the orators; Crosby, "Laureion Mines" 200–1; and briefly, Lipsius, *Attisches Recht* II 300, note 8. One specific use was in the kind of procedure summarized in this inscription. I have chosen to render the word as "denounce" in the present context rather than "register" or "inscribe" because it is the formal denunciation as a way of initiating legal proceedings that was the essence, not the act of writing.

24. *Hesperia* 5 (1936) 393, no. 10, lines 117–49. My translation is based on that of the editor, B. D. Meritt, though I have preferred "surety" to "bond" as the rendition of ἐγγύη since the word "bond" in English brings up the image of a deed or other negotiable instrument deposited with the creditor, whereas the Greek surety was only personal. [Demosthenes], *Against Nikostratos* 53.27, says that the "laws order that the property be confiscated (of a man) who, having guaranteed (ἐγγυησάμενος) something due the *polis*, does not pay the surety." For a full discussion of the state and suretyship, with citation of all the then available sources, see Partsch, *Bürgschaftsrecht* 386–417. The

present inscription is important new evidence for Partsch's discussion,
pp. 178–91, of the legal position of the suretor vis-à-vis the creditor.

25. See Partsch, *Bürgschaftsrecht* 256–71, on the simultaneous use of
suretyship and hypothecation.

26. Of the four deme leases, all from the second half of the fourth century
B.C., in which the *eisphora* provision appears, the deme agrees to pay
the taxes in three: Aixone, IG II^2 2492; Peiraieus, IG II^2 2498;
Prasiai, IG II^2 2497. The tenant is held liable in the fourth, *Athen.
Mitt.* 49 (1924) 1–13, re-edited in large part by Wilhelm, "Pachturkunden" 189–200 (Teithras). The tenant is also liable in IG II^2 2496,
but there is uncertainty as to who is actually the landlord in this case.
On the problem of juristic personality, it should be noted that the
preferred phrasing is "the Aixoneans lease," "the demesmen shall pay
the *eisphora*," rather than "the deme leases." The Aixonean agreement
IG II^2 2492, lines 29–31, further grants the tenant a *dike blabes* against
any member of the deme who proposes a measure contrary to the
provisions of the lease during its 40-year term. The whole problem of
the legal status and activity of the demes and other subdivisions of the
state needs thorough study. Probably the best available summary is
still the brief account in Haussoullier, *Vie municipale* 97–100. The
question is ignored in V. Schoeffer, "Δῆμοι," PWRE 5 (1905) 1–131.
J. B. Edwards, *The Demesman in Attic Life* (diss. Johns Hopkins 1916),
makes no contribution.

27. *Hesperia* 5 (1936) 393, no. 10, lines 153–85. The editor, B. D. Meritt,
read lines 183–84 incorrectly as ἔδ[ωκε δ]ὲ ἐνεπίσκημμα τ[ὸ] φυλῆς εἶναι.
The proper restoration is ἔδ[οξε δ]έ, as was first noted by Margaret
Crosby in *Hesperia* 10 (1941) 23. Because of the error, Meritt went
astray in the translation of the final lines and in the analysis of the
facts and procedure.

28. The most complete account of the *apographe* procedure is in Lipsius,
Attisches Recht II 299–308. When he wrote, the most important source
material was to be found in [Lysias], *For the Soldier* (orat. 9), Lysias,
Δημοσίων ἀδικημάτων (orat. 17), and *On the Property of Aristophanes*
(orat. 19); Demosthenes, *Against Aphobos II* 28.1–4; [Demosthenes],
Against Boiotos II 40.20–23, *Against Timotheos* 49.45–47, and *Against
Nikostratos* (orat. 53); and, in the naval records, the "cases" of
Kephisodoros and Sopolis, IG II^2 1631, lines 351–403 (on which see
IJ II pp. 150–54); of Stesileides, *ibid.*, lines 430–41; and of Demonikos
(during the years 334/3 to 323/2 B.C.), IG II^2 1623, lines 218–22; 1628,
lines 620–41; 1629, lines 1098–1132; and 1631, lines 288–325. Since
Lipsius wrote, the Agora excavations have provided important new
material, of which the text we are discussing and, even more so,
Hesperia 10 (1941) 14, no. 1, are the most valuable; on the latter, see
Chap. VIII at notes 13–19. Mention should also be made of the fragmentary inscription, *Hesperia* 4 (1935) 565, no. 41. Because of its
importance for the still uncertain chronology of the years 285–75 B.C.,
the latter has been repeatedly studied, each time with new restorations.

and a new interpretation of the contents. See B. D. Meritt in *Hesperia* 7 (1938) 107–8; W. B. Dinsmoor, *The Athenian Archon List in the Light of Recent Discoveries* (New York 1939) 52–53; Pritchett and Meritt, *Chronology* 46, 88–91.

29. [Demosthenes], *Against Timotheos* 49.45–47.

30. Ziebarth, *Vereinswesen* 174–76, who of course could not know this text, tried to argue, against Mitteis, *Reichsrecht* 417, that Attic *Vereine* had a sort of "police power" over their members, including the right to collect fines and penalties by direct execution, without resort to court proceedings. His argument rests on IG II² 1273 (an honorary decree of the *thiasos* of the Great Mother, 281/0 B.C.), lines 24–26: ἡ δ'εἴσπραξις ἔστω τ[ο]ῖς θιασώταις καθάπερ καὶ τἄλλα ὀφειλήματα; and IG II² 1328 (a decree of two groups of *orgeones* of the Great Mother, c. 183/2 B.C.), lines 13–14: [κα]ὶ εἰσπραττ[όν]των τρόπωι ὅτωι ἂν [δύνωνται]. These clauses Ziebarth equates, quite erroneously, with the familiar executory clause found in the bottomry contract in [Demosthenes], *Against Lakritos* 35.12: ἔστω ἡ πρᾶξις τοῖς δανείσασι καθάπερ δίκην ὠφληκότων καὶ ὑπερημέρων ὄντων, and elsewhere; on which see Partsch, *Bürgschaftsrecht* 219–28; Mitteis, *Reichsrecht* 404–9; Goldschmidt, "Inhaberurkunde" 360–79.

An exact parallel that Ziebarth overlooked is the decree cited in [Demosthenes], *Against Euergos and Mnesibulos* 47.33, authorizing a trierarch whose predecessor failed to turn over the ship's equipment, as he put it, εἰσπράττεσθαι τρόπῳ ᾧ ἂν δυνώμεθα. What this means is clearly revealed in the oration. The new trierarch may personally seize sufficient property belonging to the alleged offender as a guaranty that the debt will be paid, but not in satisfaction of his claim. A late fifth-century inscription has been found that quite certainly is a fragment of an identical decree; *Hesperia* 4 (1935) 5, no. 1, reprinted as SEG X 142. The editor, James H. Oliver, correctly draws the distinction (on p. 19, note 1) between the provision in this text and the true executory clause. This text reveals the same distinction which German law indicates by the words *Pfändungspfand* and *Vertragspfand*, on which see Hitzig, *Pfandrecht* 99–104 (a discussion which, incidentally, reveals how little we know about the former).

31. The denouncer could, of course, surrender his three fourths, either to the state, as in [Demosthenes], *Against Nikostratos* 53.2, or to the unfortunate debtor whose property had been confiscated, as in IG II² 1631, lines 365–68. See further Chap. VIII at notes 13–19. For an old, but still useful, collection of materials on the Greek practise of rewarding informants, see E. Ziebarth, "Popularklagen mit Delatorenprämien nach griechischem Recht," *Hermes* 32 (1897) 609–28.

32. For the deme site, see W. Kolbe, PWRE 7 (1912) 2226–27, or the map in Gomme, *Population*.

33. IG II² 1183, lines 27–30: ἐὰν δέ τ[ινι δέ]ει ἀργύριον, δανείζειν τοὺς ἱερέα[ς] ἀξιοχρείωι ἐπ[ὶ χωρίω]ι ἢ οἰκίαι ἢ συνοικίαι καὶ ὅρον ἐφ[ισ]τάναι, οὗ ἂν ἔι [θεοῦ πα]ραγράφοντα ὁ{υ}του ἂν ἔι τὸ ἀργύριο[ν]. A lost oration

of Isaeus dealt with a dispute over land hypothecated to a deme; see Dionysius, *On the Orations of Isaeus* 10.

34. On this point and generally on the "legal personality" of Greek gods, see Weiss, *Privatrecht* 153–60. To his references add IG XII Supp. 533 (SEG III 760), a brief but important early third-century B.C. inscription from Dystos in Euboea with regard to the sale or hypothecation to a third party of property belonging to a debtor of "the gods," and on the inscription, Weiss, "Dystos," whose analysis corrects the basic misconceptions of the original editor, Ziebarth, "Dystos," as Ziebarth acknowledged when preparing the edition for IG XII Supp; and the Attic inscription, SEG X 210, discussed below in notes 39 and 43.

35. See IG II² 2496, lines 20–22; IG II² 1168, with corrections by Wilhelm, "Pachturkunden" 205 (a tribal decree, probably of the third century B.C.); and the late fourth-century fragment, IG II² 2495. The latter may have emanated from the state itself; cf. IG I² 94, lines 23–25 (decree regarding the leasing of the sanctuary of Kodros, Neleus, and Basile, 418/7 B.C.; for the most recent bibliography, see SEG X 103): τὸν δὲ μισθοσάμενον τὸ τεμένος καὶ ὁπόσο ἄν μισθόσεται ἀντενγραφσάτο ὁ βασιλεὺς ἐς τὸν τοῖχον καὶ τὸς ἐγγυετὰς κατὰ τὸν νόμον ὅσπερ κεῖται τὸν τεμενὸν; IG II² 1590, a fragmentary roster of the leases of houses belonging to Athena Polias (343/2 B.C.); IG II² 1591, a similar list (see J. Sundwall, in *Athen. Mitt.* 34 [1909] 65–66); or IG II² 1590a (early fourth century B.C.), a list of leases by the state of holdings in Salamis, according to A. Wilhelm in *Anzeiger Wien* 64 (1927) 212–22. For a suretyship in Amorgian leases, see the fourth-century B.C. rules, *Syll.* 963, §§ 1,3,9–10, with commentaries by J. Delamarre, "Location du domaine sacré de Zeus Téménitès (Amorgos)," RP 25 (1901) 165–88, and Heinrich Lattermann, "Zu IG XII 7,62," *Athen. Mitt.* 34 (1909) 369–73. On Delos, see Kent, "Temple Estates" 274–82, and the literature he cites. On suretyship and the rental of public lands, see Partsch, *Bürgschaftsrecht* 396–410.

36. IG II² 2492 (deme Aixone, 346/5 B.C.), lines 7–9: εἶναι ἐνεχυρασίαν Αἰξωνεῦσιν καὶ ἐκ τῶν ὡραίων τῶν ἐκ τοῦ χωρίου καὶ ἐκ τῶν ἄλλων ἁπάντων τοῦ μὴ ἀποδιδόντος; on which see Weiss, *Privatrecht* 481–82, and the references he gives.

37. IG II² 2498, lines 3–6: καθιστάναι ἀποτίμημα τῆς μ[ι]σθώσεως ἀξιόχρεων. Cf. IG II² 2494 (a difficult fragment, found in Sunion, of the lease of the precinct of Apollo Lykios, corrected by Wilhelm, "Pachturkunden" 205), lines 7–8: [– – ἀποτίμ]ημα δὲ καταστήσει [τῆς μισθώσεως ἀξιόχρεων].

38. See Chap. III, note 5. The surety clause in IG II² 2498 creates added complications. It reads (grammatically dependent on the word καθιστάναι): ἐγγυ⟨η⟩τὴ[ν] ἀποδιδόμενον τὰ ἑαυτοῦ τῆς μισθώσεως. The editors of IJ translate, at I 237, *"fourniront une caution qui engagera ses biens,"* and explain the provision as requiring the suretor to put up his property as security by *prasis epi lysei* for the duration of the agreement (p. 270). They have been followed by Partsch, *Bürgschafts-*

recht 259–61, who narrows the obligation down to *prasis epi lysei* of a comparably small thing, perhaps even a movable. Though the use of the unqualified verb *apodidomi* to describe a *prasis epi lysei* can now be documented (see Chap. VIII, note 16), neither explanation is tenable. They rest on a misunderstanding of both *apotimema* and *prasis epi lysei* and they fail completely to explain why a property guaranty should be required of the principal debtor for larger sums, but of a suretor for smaller, virtually infinitesimal amounts. Above all, they fail to explain the absence of the word *apotimema* with reference to the suretor's burden, to which it would be especially appropriate if Partsch were right. The correct interpretation must be that of Hitzig, *Pfandrecht* 39, that the suretor shall be prepared to make good the tenant's default out of his own property. See also Lipsius, *Attisches Recht* II 756, note 297, followed by Kirchner in IG (who exaggerates the obligation by rendering τὰ ἑαυτοῦ as *omnia sua*). It should be noted that hypothecation was perhaps somewhat more common outside Athens in the leasing of public land; see the material in IJ I 267–70.

39. IG II² 1172 (400 B.C. or a trifle earlier), line 10: [μ]ισθώσεων ΗΔΔΑⱵ-ⱵⱵⱵIⱵIС. This inscription has evoked widespread disagreement. The first nine lines consist of sums, totaling over 22,000 drachmas, each allocated to a specific official or expenditure. Then comes the line just quoted, followed by a decree laying down rules for making loans and for disbursing the receipts. Emil Szanto, *Untersuchungen über das attische Bürgerrecht* (Wien 1881) 39–42, argued that the 22,000 drachmas represented funds on hand, the income from which (*i.e.*, interest on loans) was being allocated. He was followed, with modifications, by Haussoullier, *Vie municipale* 63–64, 75–76. Schoeffer, "Δῆμοι" 19–20, and more recently and more elaborately, Margherita Guarducci, "Intorno ad una iscrizione del demo attico di Plotheia," *Historia* 9 (1935) 205–22, at pp. 207–10, have argued that the figure must represent expenditures, since the income alone would have been too small to meet their idea of the deme's needs. On the analysis alone, Szanto and Haussoullier have much the better of the debate. Strong confirmation has recently been provided by the mid-fifth-century account of the temple of Nemesis of the deme Rhamnus, SEG X 210. Rhamnus was considerably more populated than Plotheia, yet its total cash holding during a period of five or more years, some decades earlier than the Plotheia account, ranged from 48,723 1/2 to 56,606 2/3 drachmas. Furthermore, the inscription suggests that about three fourths of the money was kept as a reserve all the time.

Guarducci also argues, admittedly without precedent, that the figure of 134 drachmas and 2½ obols on the Plotheia record is too small an income from rents in the face of the supposed financial needs of the deme, and that the amount indicates expenditure on rental, whatever that could mean. That this is untenable logically and linguistically was indicated by V. Arangio-Ruiz, "Epigrafia giuridica greca e romana I," SD 2 (1936) 429–520, at p. 451, note 14. Arangio-Ruiz himself offers the possibility that the reference is not to rental from deme-owned land but to interest in the form of rent from property put up as security by debtors in a *prasis epi lysei*. Though there is precedent for that use of the word the proposal seems quite gratuitous, especially in view of the expression, ἀπὸ δὲ τὸ τόκο [τε κ]αὶ τῶμ μισθώσεων, in lines 22–23 of the inscription. As a final point, it should be noted that the Plotheia inscription dates in the final years or immediately after the Peloponnesian War and no doubt reflects an extraordinary situation in the operations of the deme, as both Haussoullier and Guarducci agree.

40. The Peiraieus was an exceptional deme in every respect. Hence its leasing out of its theater about 360 B.C. for 3,300 drachmas (IG II² 1176) is irrelevant to the present discussion.

41. See generally Haussoullier, *Vie municipale*, Chap. 2.

42. IG II² 1172, lines 20–22: ὃς ἄ[ν πείθ]ηι τὸς δανείζοντας ἄρχοντα[ς τιμή]-ματι ἢ ἐγγυητῆι. The reconstruction I consider certain. On the use of *timema* in place of *apotimema*, see Chap. IV, note 51.

43. There remains the Rhamnus account, SEG X 210, already noted. The entry includes for the first year κεφά⟨λ⟩αιον τὸ παρὰ τοῖσι τὰς διακοσίας δραχμὰς ὀφέλοσι 37,000 Ⱶ, and the same reference is made for the third and fifth years, in the latter simply by the word διακοσιοδράχμων, again with the total of 37,000. In the fourth and fifth years, τριακοσιοδράχμων appears with totals of 13,500 and 14,400, respectively. The original editor, Ph. A. Stavropoulos, followed in the "Bulletin épigraphique," REG 51 (1938) 430, says the reference is to 200- and 300-drachma loans. Though I have no alternative to offer, I cannot accept that interpretation, first because it would require 185 debtors at 200 drachmas and 45 or 48 at 300, fantastic numbers, second because of the irregularity with which the terms appear in the various years, third because the total of the 200's is invariably the same. Our knowledge of deme officials is too scanty to permit us to tell from the five names, two of whom are called "demarch" and three "archon," whether the five years are consecutive or not.

44. Victor Ehrenberg, *Der griechische und der hellenistische Staat* (Leipzig and Berlin 1932) 6.

45. On this point as on all matters of structure, organization, and social and religious functioning of Athenian cult bodies, the fundamental study is now Ferguson, "Orgeones," with important supplementary studies in his "Orgeonika." Of the older literature, Poland, *Vereinswesen*, remains indispensable. The legal distinction between the state and all other groupings, including subdivisions of the state, is too often ignored, as, for example, when the category "sacral property" is created, as in the still regularly cited chapters of Guiraud, *Propriété foncière*: "De la propriété sacrée" (pp. 362–81) and "Propriétés des associations" (pp. 382–88). Some "sacral property" belonged to the state, the rest to groups operating as private-law subjects, and the distinction between the two was of great significance, for example in the field of execution which we have examined in sect. 2. As an illustration of the confusion that results from this initial error, see the

sections on Greece in von Bolla, "Pacht." Even Latte, *Heiliges Recht* 51–54, fails to see the distinction clearly, despite his stress (p. 39; cf. p. 51, note 7; 54, note 13) on the point, *"Es ist ein Verdienst des attischen Rechts, mit einer bei ihm auch sonst wahrnehmbaren Abneigung gegen sakrale Bindung die erforderliche Umbildung mit Entschiedenheit durchgeführt zu haben."*

46. IG II² 1289, lines 4–6: τὰ μὲν κτήματ[α εἶναι τῆς] θεοῦ καὶ μηθενὶ ἐξεῖναι μήτ' [ἀποδόσθαι] μήτε ὑποθεῖναι; lines 10–12: μηθένα ὀ[ρ]γ[εῶνα τῶν κτη]μάτων τῶν ἑαυτῆς μηδ[ὲν ἀποδίδοσθαι μη]δὲ μισθούσθαι. It is unfortunate that the word ἀποδίδωμι has been restored both times without a single letter remaining on the stone. We cannot be at all sure that the question of outright alienation of the land was ever suggested. Hence this text need not be treated as an exception to the practice already discussed in Chap. VI, at notes 4–7, of not mentioning hypothecation explicitly when alienation is involved. On the inscription generally, see Ferguson, "Orgeones" 84–86.

47. IG II² 2631 and 2632, almost certainly prepared by the same stonecutter according to Kirchner in IG and G. Klaffenbach, in *Athen.Mitt.* 51 (1926) 34: ὅρος χωρίου κοινοῦ Εἰκαδείων· μὴ συμβάλλειν εἰς τοῦτο τὸ χωρίον μηθένα μηθέν. Poland, *Vereinswesen* 484, note 3, following Larfeld, translates quite differently: "No one is to throw anything (*i.e.*, refuse) whatsoever on this land." That can hardly be right. Prohibitions against the use of public and sacral property as dumping-grounds are not uncommon in the inscriptions, but some other verb is always used, to my knowledge, as in the decree of the agoranomoi of 320 B.C., IG II² 380, lines 37–40: μὴ ἐξεῖναι [μηδενὶ μήτε] χοῦν κα[ταβά]λλειν μήτε ἄλλ[ο μηδὲν μήτε] κοπρῶ[να....ἐ]ν τῆι ἀγορᾶι κτλ. The verb συμβάλλειν is frequently difficult to render when it appears in a brief or equivocal context. Legally and economically, it has a wide variety of connotations, all stemming from the root-idea of "transacting together" or "creating an obligation together." When followed by the preposition *eis* with the accusative, it often means "to lend on something (as security)"; see Demosthenes, *Against Aphobos I* 27.27, and other references in Liddell-and-Scott (*s.v.* συμβάλλω and συμβόλαιον). That is the meaning that seems most probable here; see also Ziebarth, *Vereinswesen* 159. A detailed study of the uses of *symballein* is badly needed; for brief analyses, see Korver, *Terminologie* 93–94; K. Latte, "Symbolaion [1]," PWRE, 2 ser., 4 (1932) 1085–87; G. Beseler, "Συμβόλαιον," ZSS 50 (1930) 441–42. (For the translation of *koinon* as "fraternity" in this instance, see Poland, *Vereinswesen* 64.)

48. IG II² 1258, on which see Ziebarth, *Vereinswesen* 182. Paoli, "Ipoteca" 189, uses the Eikadeis inscriptions (only II² 2631 was available at the time he wrote, so that he was unable to see the implications in the existence of the pair) in a curious way in his discussion of a claimant's right to prevent sale or hypothecation of property by its owner. He argues, without foundation as we have seen, that the *horoi* served automatically to block further transactions involving land they marked, and hence that the warning added by the Eikadeis was quite

unnecessary. Paoli obviously overlooked the fact that not all *horoi* containing special information were necessarily markers of legal encumbrance. The two we are discussing were boundary-stones and nothing else. The fraternity used them for public announcement, to be sure, but in the form of a prohibition against future hypothecation that had nothing whatever to do with the present status of the property. For a decisive parallel, see the fifth-century bronze tablet from Sikyon, SEG XI 244. Within the context of Paoli's thesis regarding the transfer of possession to the creditor before any default, this oversight on his part seriously weakens his argument.

49. I have already alluded briefly above, note 5, to the absence of the trust idea in Athens. In the second of two inscriptions dealing with the *genos* of the Salaminioi, *Hesperia* 7 (1938) 1–74, we find the phrase, where a division of the property is involved, εἶναι ἀρχαῖο Σαλαμινίων (lines 25–26, 39–40). This is Ferguson's reading, which he explains with considerable hesitation, p. 72, as follows: "I assume that it is an archaic spelling preserved as a business, perhaps legal, expression, and thought of as a neuter adjective. The word is used to denote a particular kind of ownership; otherwise it would be unnecessary. What ἀρχαῖο adds to plain ownership is, doubtless, the limitation of inalienability." Admittedly there is no precedent either for the reading or for the interpretation. The riddle disappears, and the suggestion of inalienability along with it, if we read Ἀρχαιοσαλαμινίοι as one word, as proposed by G. Daux, REG 54 (1931) 220–22, and M. Guarducci, "L'origine e le vicende del γένος attico dei Salaminii," RFC, n.s. 26 (1948) 223–43, at pp. 235–37 (they differ in turn on the interpretation).

50. In no. 43, the word *thiasotai* actually appears on the stone, whereas no. 41 has the wording, both times, φράτερσι τοῖς μετά followed by a proper name. A. von Premerstein, "Phratern-Verbände auf einem attischen Hypothekenstein," *Athen. Mitt.* 35 (1910) 103–17, at pp. 107–9, 115, suggested that the absence of the phratry's name and the use of the individual's name in no. 41 indicate that the creditor was not the phratry itself but an autonomous cult-group within the phratry, a *thiasos*; see also briefly Ferguson, "Orgeones" 67–68. Premerstein also suggested that the presidency of a *thiasos* was probably a lifetime post because the naming of an annually rotating chairman in a legal document would lead to grave difficulties. The entire question of the legal implications of such terminology in inscriptions emanating from associations needs study, as indicated above, note 7.

51. For a further discussion of the "surplus" problem and of multiple creditors generally, see Chap. VIII.

52. It is worth noting that in his exhaustive survey, Poland, *Vereinswesen* 487, note 10, found but one reference to an association's purchasing property, and that in the first century after Christ.

53. See Ziebarth, *Vereinswesen* 157–59, for example, who vacillates between a fundamentally erroneous notion of the economic activities of

the societies and a realization that the evidence indicates that they rarely had money available for loans. In fact, indisputable examples of loans by associations virtually disappear if we eliminate the so-called "family foundations" of the Hellenistic age, none of them Athenian, and the *eranoi* (which are discussed at length in the following section). Ferguson goes even further than Ziebarth, at least in language, and speaks of "investments" in "mortgages"; see, *e.g.*, "Orgeones" 78,92.

54. *Hesperia* 11 (1942) 282, No. 55. The inscription makes no reference to security in any form. For the financial implications drawn in my text, see Ferguson, "Orgeones" 76–79. The two groups who held claims against the confiscated house recorded in *Hesperia* 10 (1941) 14, no. 1, it may be noted, were owed only 100 and 24 drachmas respectively; see the text in Chap. VIII at note 13. There is no indication of the reason for the debts.

55. See the overwhelming mass of data in Poland, *Vereinswesen*, Chap. 5; cf. A. Stöckle, "Berufsvereine," PWRE Supp. 4 (1924) 155–211, especially cols. 156–57, 198.

56. For an example of such a clearly "fictitious" hypothecation without the sacral element, see Isocrates, *Against Euthynus* 21.2, discussed in Chap. II at note 13. Latte, *Heiliges Recht* 100, cites Isaeus, *On the Estate of Nikostratos* 4.9, and Aeschines, *Against Ktesiphon* 3.21, as instances of dedications in which the god was *"nur Treuhänder, dessen Eigentumsrecht den tatsächlichen Besitzer schützt."* (He also mentions *horos* no. 155, without explanation, but I fail to see why.) An analogous fiction is the use of sale or dedication to a god as the legal cloak for manumission of a slave; see W. L. Westermann, "The Freedmen and the Slaves of God," *Proceedings of the Amer. Philosophical Soc.* 92 (1948) 55–64.

The evidence of the *horoi* is added confirmation that, unlike the Roman *collegia*, Greek associations served no humanitarian or benevolent functions; see Ferguson, "Orgeones" 110–11, and the excellent brief summary in W. W. Tarn, *Hellenistic Civilisation* (2 ed., London 1930) 86–88. In general, the virtually complete silence in the literary material cannot be ignored. References to the importance of *eranoi* as sources of financial assistance are frequent, to cult bodies of any kind in an economic context practically non-existent. The one exception that comes to mind is the miserably preserved little speech appearing as no. 8 in the Lysianic corpus, under the title πρὸς τοὺς συνουσιαστάς (*Against the Co-Associates*). There is agreement among scholars that the speech was not written by Lysias but that it is an authentic document; see Blass, *Beredsamkeit* I 640–44, who suggests a late fourth-century date; Angela Darkow, *The Spurious Speeches in the Lysianic Corpus* (diss. Bryn Mawr 1917) 35–41; L. Gernet and M. Bizos, ed. of Lysias I (2 vols. Paris 1924–6) 121–23. Not even the character of the group under attack is clear, for the speaker uses none of the standard titles, but that it centered around some cult is certain (cf. Aristotle, *Nicomachean Ethics* 8.9.5,1160a20: θυσίας ἕνεκα καὶ συνουσίας). The dispute began with the pledge of a horse as security for a loan and became increasingly virulent when the horse died and legal action followed. The society was involved because some of its members helped, informally and unofficially, to negotiate the loan and then took the opponent's side in the legal altercation. At no time did the society participate as a party and neither the group nor its members were liable to court action. All the speaker could do in retaliation was resign and he did so with a bitter speech, which we have. (The key passage for our purpose is §§ 10–12.) The oration in its present form raises many difficulties, but one point stands out clearly — this particular group lent no money. And it is the one major literary text that is pertinent.

57. Eranists also appear in nos. 112–14, analysis of which must be postponed until later in this section because these *horoi* say "sold" without the qualifying *epi lysei*.

58. For a translation of this text, see Chap. II at note 65.

59. The basic study of the *eranoi* was made by Reinach, "Eranos," who first drew the proper distinction among the three meanings; he has been followed closely by Lipsius, *Attisches Recht* II 729–35. Erich Ziebarth, "Ἔρανος," PWRE 6 (1909) 328–30, marks a considerable step backwards. Somehow Ziebarth could never differentiate properly between the *eranos*-loan and the *eranos*-club, and this failure is closely linked with his persistent efforts to people the Greek cities with *Wirtschaftsvereine*.

60. The material is assembled in Poland, *Vereinswesen* 28–33.

61. See Demosthenes, *Against Meidias* 21.185, *Against Aristogeiton I* 25.21 (the basis for Harpocration, *s.v.* πληρωτής), or Hypereides, *Against Athenogenes* 5.7.

62. For the various, mutually contradictory analyses, see the notes by Delamarre to IG XII 7,58 and by Ziebarth to *Syll.* 1188; IJ I pp. 117–19, 136; Partsch, *Bürgschaftsrecht* 318–21; Lipsius, *Attisches Recht* II 733, note 209; San Nicolò, *Aegyptisches Vereinswesen* I 215–17; and the additional bibliography cited in these works. There is no need to enter into a lengthy discussion here since most of the commentaries are concerned primarily with the suretyship and the legal relationship between Xenokles and Aristagoras that ensued, a problem of no concern in the present context. On the matter of the nature of the two *eranoi* mentioned, no one can offer direct evidence apart from the text itself; my view will be apparent from my suggested translation and discussion. Two points regarding the translation require comment. On the "recorded pledges" (ἐπικύρβια ἐνέχυρα), see Chap. II, note 81. Virtually all commentators have assumed that the συνέλεξεν of line 13 indicates an *eranos*-loan which Aristagoras collected himself. But this is not the natural implication in the use of the active, and, since *eranoi* were not infrequently collected on behalf of others, the latter interpretation is preferable here.

63. Poland, *Vereinswesen* 354, note 2, and Lipsius, *Attisches Recht* 731, note 204, draw a sharp terminological distinction between an ἐρανάρχης as the collector of an *eranos*-loan and an ἀρχέρανος (or ἀρχερανιστής) as the head of an *eranos*-club. If they are right, then my analysis must give way to their view, the prevailing one I must note, that this *horos* names both kinds of *eranos*. Against their position I would argue, first, that it assumes a precision in terminology which the Greeks never demonstrated; second, that the word ἐρανάρχης is a late one, as Harpocration, *s.v.* πληρωτής, clearly implies, the first known use being in BGU IV 1133 (19 B.C.); and third, that we are not sufficiently informed about the mechanics of the *eranos*-loans to draw terminological distinctions too finely in any case.

64. It should be noted that those scholars who use the argument based on the appearance of the collective noun *eranos* as proof that *horos* no. 8 mentions a society, must, if they would be consistent, draw the further conclusion that all the other *horoi* do not refer to clubs or *Vereine*.

65. Reinach, "Eranos" 807, observed that we know nothing about the legal forms in which *eranos*-loans were made. In the absence of concrete evidence, he added, we may presume that there were written agreements as with ordinary loans. The evidence of the *horoi* argues the opposite; see in general Chap. II, sect. 3.

66. See Partsch, *Bürgschaftsrecht* 317–18, for illustrations.

67. When San Nicolò, *Aegyptisches Vereinswesen* I 214, says that *eranoi* were protected by suretyship or hypothecation, as if that were the rule, he is surely confusing the exception with the basic pattern. Ziebarth, "Ἔρανος" 329, on the other hand, stresses the rarity of hypothecation, but he exaggerates it by simply ignoring the *horoi*.

68. The material is presented in Chap. VIII, note 16.

69. See note 52 above.

70. It is of some interest to see what modern editors have done with these texts. Kirchner published the two which appear in IG II² (nos. 112 and 113) under the rubric, *Termini fundis emptis appositi* (along with nos. 174 and 176, which, as indicated in Chap. VI, note 23, had nothing to do with either sale or security). He has been followed by A. E. Raubitschek, the editor of no. 114. Ziebarth, who originally edited no. 113 in "Neue Hypothekeninschriften" 668, no. 15, suggested sale with some hesitation. The editors of IJ, who knew only no. 112, were inclined to sale but also put forth the suggestion of *prasis epi lysei* (I p. 126). Now Pringsheim, *Sale* 165, has come forward with the ingenious explanation that "the purchaser had already paid the price and fulfilled other requirements for the transfer of land, but had left possession to the vendor." But he presents no evidence, nor reasons why purchasers of land and houses should have left possession to the vendors. His own Chap. II in Pt. III, entitled "Contracts for Cash Payment with Deferred Delivery," cites only papyri and Plautus, *Asinaria* 453.

Horos no. 115 reads πεπραμένου παντός, followed by the name of an individual, not an *eranos*. The two points on which this text, from Lemnos, differs from the three Attic *horoi* do not affect the general conclusion, in my judgment. In the absence of additional information, it would be useless to speculate on the reasons for including the word παντός, which could have been as necessary or unnecessary, as the case may be, in hypothecation as in sale. The word "all" (or "in full") also appears in nos. 102, 131, and 156. In those *horoi* the reason for its insertion is more apparent because the texts are considerably more detailed. They do not throw light on παντός in no. 115 but they do indicate that it is not unprecedented and that its use does not compel us to assume that the transaction was sale rather than security.

71. The lists are published in IG II² 1553-78. Reference to the bowls is also made in the treasurers' accounts of 320/19 B.C. and of *c.* 314/3 (IG II² 1469, lines 5–6,15, and II² 1480, line 9, respectively). The fact that all the evidence is crowded within a time span of two decades or less (a few years before and after the death of Alexander the Great), suggests that the whole procedure was not a normal one in Athens but was created to meet peculiar conditions of the moment. The most recent discussion of the bowls is Westermann, "Two Studies" 94–99, which is limited to certain legal aspects, particularly their connection with *paramone* agreements in manumission. Economic and demographic analyses of the same material will be found in M. N. Tod, "Some Unpublished 'Catalogi Paterarum Argentearum,'" BSA 8 (1901/2) 197–230; Gomme, *Population* 41–43; and Westermann, "Sklaverei" 912–13.

72. The *eranos* references will be found in IG II² 1553.7–10,20–23; 1556 B27–29; 1557 B105–7; 1558 A37–43; 1559 A II 26–31; 1566 A27–29; 1568 B18–23; 1569 A III 18–21; 1570.24–26,57–62,82–84; 1571.8–13; and 1572.8–11.

73. This view has been stated most unequivocally by Ziebarth, *Vereinswesen* 159, whose proof is limited to assertion. In reply, Poland, *Vereinswesen* 28–29, argued that the whole picture of Greek societies leaves little room for slave ownership. Ziebarth held his ground. In his article, "Ἔρανος," in PWRE he completely ignored these texts and in his review, PhW 48 (1928) 740–41, of the fascicle of IG II² containing the lists, he noted the support he had received from San Nicolò, *Aegyptisches Vereinswesen* II 114. San Nicolò, however, contributed nothing to the discussion, merely stating his agreement with Ziebarth. Their view is also shared by Kahrstedt, *Staatsgebiet* 306 and 308, who, in his characteristic fashion, pronounces these *eranoi* to be *Vereine* as a matter of simple fact, without reference to any possible disagreement or to the earlier literature. He then proceeds to entangle himself in a hopeless legal confusion as he seeks to interpret the juristic aspects of the form, "Nikodemos and *koinon*."

74. IG II² 1559 A II 26–31 and 1558 A 37–43, respectively. A Chairippos son of Chairedemos also appears in two other entries, IG II² 1568

B18–23 (the patronymic is certain in one case, less so in the other), both times followed by "and *koinon* of eranists." Though the demotic is lost in both entries, it is probable that we have here an instance of one man who had manumitted three slaves, each time in conjunction with an *eranos*.

75. The speech is no. 59 in the Demosthenic corpus. On the date, see Blass, *Beredsamkeit* III 1, 536.

76. [Demosthenes], *Against Neaira* 59.29–32.

77. *Ibid.* 59.31: ἔρανον εἰς τὴν ἐλευθερίαν συλλέγουσα.

78. No full study of the *eranos*-loans in manumissions is available. A very brief summary of the Delphic material will be found in Westermann, "Two Studies" 94, based on a longer study as yet unpublished, which he has kindly permitted me to examine. Westermann cites the following references to *eranoi* in the Delphic manumission inscriptions: SGDI 1754, 1772, 1791, 1804, 1878, 1909, and 2317. Another illustration, from Chaironea, is IG VII 3376.

79. [Antiphon], *Tetralogy* I β 12. Cf. the metaphoric references to *eranoi* in Demosthenes, *Against Meidias* 21.101,184–85.

80. [Aristotle], *Problems* 29.2,950a28; see Chap. VI at note 63.

81. Plato, *Laws* 915E. Egon Weiss, "Platons Rechtsphilosophie in ihren Beziehungen zur Gegenwart," *Arch. f. Rechts- und Wirtschaftsphilosophie* 20 (1926/27) 355–68, at p. 357, writes that with this proposal and his law prohibiting credit sales Plato "*hinter seiner eigenen Zeit zurückbleibt*" and sought to block the road to social and legal progress. The economics and ethics of both Plato's thinking and the realities of fourth-century Greek society are too complex for so simple a view of progress; see the approach suggested by S. Lauffer, "Die platonische Agrarwirtschaft," *Vierteljahrschrift* 29 (1936) 233–69. In the nineteenth century, no less a legal authority than Joseph Story could write that gratuitous loans "have furnished very little occasion for the interposition of judicial tribunals, for reasons equally honorable to the parties and to the liberal spirit of polished society" (quoted by N. S. Marsh, "The Liability of the Gratuitous Transferor: A Comparative Study, " LQR 66 [1950] 39–61, at p. 39, note 2).

82. Theophrastus, *Characters* 23.6.

83. Though I would place little stress on the fact, it should be indicated that in none of the *eranos*-stones is a workshop put up as security. Reinach, "Eranos" 805, had already noted that in the literary materials, *eranos*-loans always involve large sums. But when he adds, p. 806, that the *eranos* was sometimes used to raise capital for business purposes, comparable to the modern *commandite* except that the "*éranistes n'ont droit ni à l'intérêt de leurs avances ni à une part des bénéfices*," he gives us *Hamlet* without the Prince of Denmark. It has already been indicated that stress on the non-productive character of the *eranoi*

need not deny their occasional use for "business" purposes. In late Hellenistic and Roman times, the *eranos* seems to have undergone a fundamental change in the direction of interest-bearing, even usurious, lending, as evidenced by the word ἐρανέμπολος known from the lexicographers. Whatever the change was, however, it cannot be traced until well after the time limits set for this discussion; some of the material will be found in San Nicolò, *Aegyptisches Vereinswesen* I 212–25.

84. Theophrastus, *Characters* 22.9; cf. Menander, *Adelphoi*, frag. 4 (Kock), where the word *eranos* does not appear. The relatively large number of references to *eranos* in the *Characters* is itself significant; other instances are 1.5; 15.7; 17.9; and 23.6.

85. Cf. Aristophanes, *Acharnians* 614–17. When Max Weber, *Agrarverhältnisse* 146, properly stressing the fundamental economic implications inherent in the prevalence of the *eranos*, attributes the institution to the *"urwüchsigen Bauern- und Kleinbürger-Ethik, welche 'unter Brüdern' unentgeltliches Leihen fordert,"* he seems to be neglecting one side of the practice as it appears in the fully developed *polis*. What he says fits Aristophanes' peasants, but not the wealthy debtors of the *horoi*, at least not without further qualification.

Notes to Chapter VIII

1. See note 7 below on ὅσωι πλείονος ἄξιον in Demosthenes, *Against Onetor II* 31.6. The verb for "to put up as security" is missing from the opening portion of *horos* no. 146, but the omission is quite certainly meaningless in the light of no. 147. No. 146 was a key document in the attempt of Pappulias, Ἀσφάλεια, to disprove, in part, the view generally accepted since Hitzig that Greek law normally took no cognizance of the possibility that hypothecated property might have had a greater value than the amount of the debt. When Pappulias wrote, *horos* no. 147 was unknown. He seized on the absence of the verb in the one *horos* available to him which specifically mentioned a surplus that was in turn hypothecated (pp. 158–59). The recent discovery of no. 147 cuts the ground out from under his argument.

2. *Horos* no. 32 has been endlessly debated; see the bibliography in Weiss, *Privatrecht* 340, note 313. A translation of the text appears in Chap. II at note 64.

3. Note should also be taken of no. 18 naming suretors, on which see Chap. VII at note 25; no. 114, the purpose of which is uncertain (see Chap. VII at notes 68–70); and no. 166, one of the fragmentary stones not included in the Tables. Most of the *horoi* marking pupillary *apotimema* obligations indicate that two or more orphans were the potential beneficiaries of the security transaction. But that was a special situation that has nothing to do with the problem under dis-

cussion. The estate was undivided and therefore treated as a single unit administered by a guardian. The number of heirs made no difference until at least one of them had attained his majority and at that point the lease of the estate terminated and the security offered by the lessee was either defaulted or withdrawn. The two or three "double" *horoi* discussed in Chap. II, end of sect. 2, have been ignored in the present context.

4. [Demosthenes], *Against Phainippos* 42.28–29. There are problems connected with the reading in the first sentence, in which Bekker's emendation of τάλαντον ἐνοφέιλειν for the τάλαντον ἐν ὀφείλειν of the better manuscripts and the τάλαντον ὀφείλειν of the inferior has been accepted by modern editors. The exact translation of ἐνοφείλειν is not always certain and the implication underlying Bekker's suggestion, that all these debts were secured by Phainippos' estate, is in my judgment far from certain. A solution of these questions is unnecessary in the present discussion.

5. Note the seemingly inextricable confusion as to creditor-debtor relations in Demosthenes, *Against Zenothemis* (orat. 32). For the various explanations that have been offered on the latter, see Arnold C. Cosman, *Demosthenes' Rede tegen Zenothemis (Oratie XXXII) mit Inleiding en Commentaar* (Leiden 1939). In [Demosthenes], *Against Dionysodoros* 56.6, we are told explicitly that, though there were two co-lenders, only one was named in the written agreement.

6. IG II² 2492.

7. The two *horoi* (nos. 146 and 147) involving an *apotimema* with the phrase "by whatever it is worth more" do not constitute an exception. As we have seen in Chap. IV, the procedure in the *apotimema* was a redefinition of the property. The part excluded from the evaluated portion remains clear and unencumbered property, as if no security obligation existed at all. In Demosthenes' dispute with Onetor, which involved the question of the latter's prior right based on a dotal *apotimema* (see briefly Chap. II at note 37), the law on the matter comes out very clearly. Onetor, according to Demosthenes (*Against Onetor II* 31.6), had argued that he "is not depriving me (*i.e.*, Demosthenes) by whatever is worth more than one talent." But this defense is sheer impudence, the orator continues, for Onetor himself had "evaluated it (the property) as not worth more (than one talent)." (σκέψασθε τοίνυν τὴν ἀναίδειαν, ὃς γ'ἐν ὑμῖν ἐτόλμησεν εἰπεῖν, ὡς οὐκ ἀποστερεῖ μ' ὅσῳ πλείονος ἄξιόν ἐστι ταλάντου, καὶ ταῦτ' αὐτὸς τιμήσας οὐκ ἄξιον εἶναι πλείονος.) On this point, therefore, the two men were disputing the facts, not the law; see Paoli, "Ipoteca" 182–83. Was the property in fact worth more than one talent? That was the point at issue; not, if the property is worth more, does Onetor's claim exclude Demosthenes from the remainder of the property. On the surplus, they were agreed, Demosthenes had full freedom of action.

The persistence of the clumsy phrase, ὅσῳ πλείονος ἄξιον, is itself significant. In time, the Greeks began to use the word ὑπεροχή, though infrequently, and the three earliest uses known in Greek sources in this context, according to Manigk, "Hyperocha" 295, are: *Syll.* 364, Ephesus, early third century B.C. (see note 20 below); *Syll.* 976, Samos, early second century B.C.; and IG XII 7,515, Amorgos, end of the second century B.C. Its failure to displace ὅσῳ πλείονος ἄξιον is a clear sign that pure substitution remained the overwhelmingly prevalent form of security.

8. It has already been indicated that Pappulias, 'Ασφάλεια, virtually alone among modern scholars has tried to uphold the notion that collateral security (on which see the end of this chapter) was already known at the time of the Attic orators. For a rather detailed criticism of Pappulias' arguments, see Raape, *Verfall* 1–48, a difficult work to use because Raape engages in little general discussion but limits himself to a reply to Pappulias text by text. Furthermore, Raape treats bottomry and real security as if they were identical in all respects and he carries his analysis well into Roman times without proper concern for possible changes in Greek society in general or in the institution of security in particular.

9. If the suggestion offered in Chap. VII, at note 56, that the debts to such groups as phratries may have been fictitious, is correct, then the idea of five ranking claims is weakened still further.

10. On the name sequence, cf. the lease of the theater belonging to the deme Peiraieus, IG II² 1176, lines 21–24, in which the four lessees are responsible for unequal shares of the rental, listed on the stone in the following order: 600 drachmas, 1,100, 500, 1,100. The lack of organic connection has been correctly noted, on the basis of *horos* no. 146, by Ferguson, "Orgeones" 70, note 11, in criticism of Bruck and Guarducci. But Ferguson himself, in "Laws of Demetrius" 266–67, makes much of the sequence of amounts on the same stone; see Appendix II.

11. It is sufficient to cite Parmenon and the unnamed speaker in [Demosthenes], *Against Apaturios* (orat. 33), or Euergos and Nikobulos in Demosthenes, *Against Pantainetos* (orat. 37). Guardianship and agency, of course, are irrelevant to the problem.

12. The best summary is still Rabel, *Verfügungsbeschränkungen*, Chap. I, the dominant note of which is complete agnosticism. For a somewhat later summary, with full bibliography, see Weiss, *Privatrecht* 330–41. The most recent work, Paoli, "Ipoteca," is largely vitiated by his erroneous conception of the possession of the encumbered property.

13. *Hesperia* 10 (1941) 14, no. 1. The analysis of this inscription that follows will appear in somewhat more extended form in an article in the forthcoming *Studi in onore di Vincenzo Arangio-Ruiz*. Several problems of translation and some details not directly relevant to the present discussion are examined in the article and not repeated here. The Greek text reads as follows: ' Ἐπὶ Πολυζήλο ἄρχοντος πωληταί / (names follow) ⁶τάδε ἀπέδοντο παραλαβόν/τες παρα τῶν ἕνδεκα Φαίακος ' Αφιδναίο καὶ συναρ/ χόντων· Μονιχιῶνος δεκάτηι ἱσταμένο, Θεόμνηστ/ος Δεισιθέο ' Ιωνίδης ἀπέγραψεν

Θεοσέβος τοῦ Θε/¹⁰οφίλο Ξυπεταιόνος οἰκίαν ᾽Αλωπεκῆσιν δημοσία/ν εἶναι (boundaries), ¹³ἁλόντος Θεοσέβος ἱεροσυλίας καὶ οὐχ ὑπομ/είναντος τὴν κρίσιν ὅσωι πλείονος ἀξία ἢ ὑπόκε/¹⁵ιται Σμικύθωι Τειθρασίωι: ΗΙ↑ δραχμῶν, (witnesses). ¹⁶Κιχωνί/δης Διογείτονος Γαργήτ(τιος) καὶ κοινὸν φρατέρων Με/δοντιδῶν ἐνεπησκήψατο ἐνοφείλεσθαι ἑαυτῶι κ/αὶ τοῖς φράτερσιν ἐν τῆι οἰκίαι τῆι ᾽Αλωπεκῆσι Η δ/²⁰ραχμάς, ἢν ἀπέγραψεν Θεόμνηστος ᾽Ιωνί(δης) Θεοσέβος/ εἶναι Ξυπετα(ιόνος) (bounderies repeated), ²³ἀποδομένο ἐμο⟨ὶ⟩ καὶ τοῖς φράτερσιν τὴ/ν οἰκίαν ταύτην Θεοφίλου Ξυπε(ταιόνος) τὸ πατρὸς τοῦ Θεο /²⁵σέβος. ἔδοξεν ἐνοφείλεσθαι. ῎Ισαρχος Φίλωνος Ξυπ/εται(όνος): ἀμφισβητεῖ ἐνοφείλεσθαι ἑαυτῶι ἐν τῆι οἰ/κίαι τῆι ᾽Αλωπεκῆσι ἢν ἀπέγραψεν Θεόμνεστος Δε/ισιθέο ᾽Ιωνίδης, θάψαντος ἐμὸ Θεόφιλον ὃ ἦν ἡ οἰκ/ία καὶ τὴν γυναῖκα τὴν Θεοφίλο ΔΔΔ: δραχμάς. ἔδοξ /³⁰εν ἐνοφείλεσθαι. Αἰσχίνης Μελιτε(ὺς) καὶ κοινὸν ὀ/ργεώνων ἐνεπεσκήψαντο ἐν τῆι οἰκίαι ἢν ἀπέγραψ/εν Θεόμνηστος ᾽Ιωνίδης ἐνοφείλεσθαι ἑαυτοῖς: / ΔΔΗΗΗ δραχμάς, πριαμένων ἡμῶν τὴν οἰκίαν ταύτ/ην παρὰ Θεοφίλου τοῦτο τοῦ ἀργυρίο ἐπὶ λύσει. ἐδ /³⁵οξεν ἐνοφείλεσθαι. ὠνητής· Λυσανίας Παλαθίωνο/ς Λακι(άδης) Γ Ρ ΔΔΓ· τοῦτο τὴν προκαταβολὴν τὸ πέμπτον / μέρος ἔχει ἡ πόλις καὶ τὰ ἐπώνια καὶ τὰ κηρύκεια / καὶ Σμίκυθος Τειθράσιος τὰς πεντήκοντα καὶ ἑκ/ατὸν ἀθρόον κατὰ τὴν ἀπογραφήν.

14. On the translation of *apographo* as "denounce," see Chap. VII, note 23.

15. On the phrase ὅσωι ᾽πλείονος ἀξία in line 14, see notes 1 and 7 above.

16. The context demands that the word ἀποδομένο in line 23 be translated "having put up as security by *prasis epi lysei.*" (᾽Απέδοντο in line 6 simply means "sold," of course.) The omission of the words *epi lysei* may be no more than a stonecutter's error. It is more probable, however, that ἀποδομένο· alone appeared in the document from which the inscription was copied. We have the authority of Pollux, *Onomasticon* 8.142, that Hypereides, in an oration against Charitas (frag. 193 Blass), ἔφη ἀποδόμενος ἀντὶ τοῦ ὑποθείς; cf. Chap. III, note 11. For the possibility that πεπραμένος standing alone in *horoi* nos. 112–115 signified *prasis epi lysei,* see Chap. VII at notes 72–74; cf. Chap. III, note 51, on Isaeus, *On the Estate of Dikaiogenes* 5.21. Elsewhere, ἀποδίδωμι appears in place of πιπράσκω with ἐπὶ λύσει only once, in *horos* no. 102, an Amorgian stone.

17. The contract-clause in the bottomry agreement, [Demosthenes], *Against Lakritos* 35.11–12, deals with a ship and cargo, not with realty. There, it is worth noting, the agreement protects the creditors against the possibility that the security may not be worth as much as the loan, but it makes no provision in favor of the debtor if a surplus should eventuate.

18. The debt arising from payment of burial costs has been excluded because it lacks the element of hypothecation and is more like the Anglo-American lien.

19. Aristotle, *Constitution of the Athenians* 47.3.

20. The only reference to a law is in Demosthenes, *Against Spudias* 41.7, and that provision, as I have suggested in Chap. IV, end of sect. 2,

deals with the special and limited problem of the evaluation fixed in an *apotimema*. Indirect corroboration of the absence of general legislation comes from the fact that there is no trace in the sources of a single procedural action especially designed for use in legal controversies arising from hypothecation. The normal remedies for the protection of property rights were used. The most comprehensive lists of actions are to be found in Aristotle, *Constitution of the Athenians* 56–59, and in the eighth book of the *Onomasticon* of Julius Pollux (second century after Christ). Neither list is complete, but the absence of a single action assigned specifically to cases arising from hypothecation is no accident. See Hitzig, *Pfandrecht* 138–42, on this matter generally, with an important qualification by Pringsheim, *Sale* 50. E. Ziebarth, "Beiträge zum griechischen Recht I. Die Stiftung nach griechischem Recht," ZVR 16 (1903) 249–315, at p. 268, note 14, charges Hitzig with having overlooked CIG 3641b, lines 24–27, a second-century B.C. Lampsakos inscription (new readings in SEG IV 668). But the νόμος περὶ τῶν παρανόμως ἐνεχυρασάντων of Lampsakos dealt with illegal execution on property (for which there are many parallels), not with hypothecation.

The one body of statutory law on hypothecation for which we have firm evidence from a Greek city existed in Ephesos, part of it embedded in the debt-moratorium decree of the first decade of the third century B.C., *Syll.* 364, as has been demonstrated by Partsch, *Bürgschaftsrecht* 261–67. (Translations of the inscription, in French and German, respectively, are available in IJ I v and Hermann-Thalheim, *Rechtsalterthümer* 152–68.) Until Heberdey announced in 1912 that re-examination of the stone revealed its early third-century date, the inscription had been assigned either to the period of the Mithradatic Wars in the first century B.C. or to the preceding century. All discussions of the inscription prior to its publication with the correct date and a revised commentary in the 3rd ed. of *Syll.* (1915) are colored by this 200-year error (and some later ones as well, such as Pringsheim, *Sale* 164, and Paoli, "Ipoteca" 148, 162–63, both of whom give the correct *Syll.* citation and a now rejected date, Paoli even using the date 85 B.C. as an essential part of his argument at one point).

21. An important contribution towards giving proper perspective to secondary security obligations was made long ago by Th. Reinach, in REG 22 (1909) 242, note 1, when he noted, writing about IG XII 7,515, that the word ἐπιδανείζειν, rare as it is in the sources, need not always mean "to lend money on property already mortgaged" (the sole definition given by Liddell-and-Scott) but may mean simply δανείζειν ἐπί, "to lend on." Reinach's note seems to have been overlooked, but it has now been revived by Korver, *Terminologie* 131–35. Reference should also be made here to the implication in the deletion on some *horoi* of part of the amount; see the analysis of *horos* no. 154 in Chap. II at note 51, and cf. Weiss, *Untersuchungen* I 23–24.

22. The law is cited, in almost identical wording each time, in [Demosthenes] *Against Phainippos* 42.12, *Against Euergos and Mnesibulos*

47.77, *Against Dionysodoros* 56.2, and Hypereides, *Against Athenogenes* 5.13. All four citations date in the middle or second half of the fourth century B.C., but that is not of great moment, for a reading of the earlier orations leaves little doubt that the principle, if not its statutory embodiment, was much older. The broad range of contexts in which the law is called upon is notable: taxation and property exchange, judgment debt, bottomry, and the sale of slaves (accompanied by a transfer of debts). For all the texts pertaining to this law and a detailed discussion, see Pringsheim, *Sale* 34–43. Pringsheim makes an ingenious attempt to demonstrate that "the rule applied only to witnessed ὁμολογίαι," and hence that it does not disturb his thesis that the Athenians never developed the consensual contract. I do not find the argument convincing, and Pringsheim himself later introduces an element of doubt when he writes, p. 46, note 1, with reference to Hypereides, *Against Athenogenes* 5.8: "The absence of witnesses... did not invalidate the contract.... So it seems that at this time other forms could replace witnesses, at least if slaves were sold."

23. Generally on practice as a source of law, see Weiss, *Privatrecht* 25–28. Cf. note 33 below. Werner Kamps, "Affaire de fraude," following a suggestion of Bruck's, has demonstrated that special agreements regarding the distribution of family property often lie concealed behind the facts in a case as presented by the orators. His study of one particular illustration deserves to be followed by intensive re-examination of the orations dealing with inheritance and family property.

24. Wigmore, "Pledge-Idea" X 332 (stated in connection with his discussion of late medieval Germanic law).

25. Thornbrough *v.* Baker (1676), 1 Ch.Ca. 284. On the historic significance of this case in the evolution of the mortgage, see Turner, *Equity of Redemption*, Chap. III. Note the parallel quotations from later cases given by Turner on pp. 66, 69, and 83.

26. For an excellent introduction to this subject, see Nussbaum, *Lehrbuch* 209–19.

27. See the detailed discussion of the case in Chap. III, sect. 2.

28. Note the significance of Lysias, Δημοσίων ἀδικημάτων 17.6–7, on this point. In the bottomry contract, [Demosthenes], *Against Lakritos* 35.12, express provision is made for the sale of the ship and cargo in case of default. (Cf. 33.12 and the provisions, nearly two centuries later, in *Syll.* 672, lines 67–72, a Delphic inscription of 160/59 B.C.; the best edition is in G. Daux, *Delphes au IIe et au Ire siècle* [Paris 1936] 686–98. In the latter, as in the Lakritos agreement, provision is made for failure of the sale to produce enough, none for a surplus [see note 17 above].) This clause is significant on two counts. The very fact that it is stated explicitly suggests that it was not the regular, certainly not the legally required, practice. Whether this is so or not, however, this is the contract already noted which gives the creditor further action if the sale does not produce the full amount of money owed. There could be

no clearer indication that the sale of the security is a necessary condition of a collateral guaranty. On sale in present-day security law, see, e.g., *Restatement: Security* §§ 48–58.

29. On the meaning of "workshops" here, see Chap. V at notes 90–93.

30. Demosthenes, *Against Aphobos I* 27.9. "Hypothecated for forty minas" is τεττάρακοντα μνῶν ὑποκειμένους in the Greek. Schwahn, *Demosthenes gegen Aphobos* 15–18, insisted on slight modifications in the text, chiefly in punctuation, in order to obtain a different formulation of the value of the slaves. The purpose of the change was to further Schwahn's general economic analysis, on which see Chap. V, notes 89 and 92.

31. See Westermann, "Sklaverei" 915. As an indication of how hopeless the details in this case are, note that in *Against Aphobos II* 28.12, Demosthenes casually refers to "the other things" received along with the slaves for the 40-mina debt. Since there were other things, the disparity between the actual value of the slaves and the debt for which they were substituted was even greater.

32. An interesting contrast in attitude is offered by David Hume, perhaps the first modern student of ancient aconomic and demographic problems. When Hume was collecting material on ancient slave populations, he made the following entry in his notebooks: "Timarchus is spoken of by Aeschines as a rich man for possessing 20 Slaves; Demosthenes' Father had thirty." (See E. C. Mossner, ed., "Hume's Early Memoranda, 1729–1740," *Journal of the History of Ideas* 9 [1948] 492–518, at p. 517.) Hume ignored the 20 bedmakers, not through ignorance or carelessness, I am confident, but because according to the notions of his eighteenth-century mercantile world, Demosthenes senior did not "have" the bedmakers since they were in his possession only as security.

33. Manigk, "Hyperocha" 311, writes: "*Hiernach entschied über das Schicksal der hyperocha immer die konkrete Abrede, der als gemeines Recht nur das Verfallsprinzip zugrunde lag*" through the third century after Christ. With this emphasis on the role of agreements as the source of departures from the pattern I am in full agreement, though I think the exceptions were less frequent in practice than Manigk seems to suggest.

34. For example, Rabel, *Verfügungsbeschränkungen* 19–20; cf. Paoli, "Ipoteca" 194. Rabel apparently believes (p. 17) that a body of statutory law on hypothecation existed in fourth-century Athens.

35. In explaining the gradual obsolescence of the Roman *fiducia* and the contrasting vigor of the English mortgage, Hazeltine, "*Fiducia* and Mortgage" lxii-lxiii, writes: "The historical causes of the different fates of two securities, which bear several outward resemblances, are partly legal and partly social and economic." *Fiducia* had to give way to *hypotheca* because the former was not only "tied to antique modes of

conveyance, but it was also fettered by other archaic features which failed to express the true intention of the parties." But in England, it was chancery, "with its elaborate system of equitable rights, which enabled the mortgage to persist and flourish in modern times. In the hands of chancery the legal technicalities of the medieval mortgage ... were made subservient to the spirit of equity."

LIST OF ABBREVIATIONS

AG — *Archivio giuridico*
AHDO — *Archives d'histoire du droit oriental*
AJA — *American Journal of Archaeology*
AJP — *American Journal of Philology*
Anecdota Bekker — I. Bekker, ed., *Anecdota Graeca* (3 vols., Berlin 1814–21)
Annuario — R. Scuola Archaeologica italiana di Atene, *Annuario*
Anzeiger Wien — Akademie der Wissenschaften, Wien, Philosophisch-historische Klasse, *Anzeiger*
APF — *Archiv für Papyrusforschung und verwandte Gebiete*
Arch. Anz. — Archaeologisches Institut des Deutschen Reichs, *Jahrbuch*: *Archaeologischer Anzeiger*
Athen. Mitt. — Archaeologisches Institut des Deutschen Reichs, Athenische Zweiganstalt, *Mitteilungen*

BCH — *Bulletin de correspondance hellénique*
Bibl.Éc.fr. — *Bibliothèque des Écoles françaises d'Athènes et de Rome*
Bibl.Éc.HE — Paris. École des hautes études, *Bibliothèque*
BGU — *Aegyptische Urkunden aus den Königlichen Museen zu Berlin: Griechische Urkunden* (Berlin 1892 –)
BIDR — Università di Roma, Istituto di diritto romano, *Bulletino*
BSA — British School at Athens, *Annual*

CIG — *Corpus Inscriptionum Graecarum* (Berlin 1828–77)
CP — *Classical Philology*
CR — *Classical Review*

Dar.-Saglio — Ch. Daremberg and E. Saglio, ed., *Dictionnaire des antiquités grecques et romaines...* (5 vols. in 9, Paris 1877–1919)
Δελτ. — ’Αρχαιολογικὸν Δελτίον
DGE — E. Schwyzer, ed., *Dialectorum graecarum exempla epigraphica potiora* (Leipzig 1923)

EnSS — *Encyclopaedia of the Social Sciences* (New York 1930–35)

FGH — F. Jacoby, ed., *Fragmente der griechischen Historiker* (1923–)

GGA — *Göttingische gelehrte Anzeigen*

HWB — Handwörterbuch

IC — M. Guarducci, ed., *Inscriptiones Creticae* (Rome 1935–   )
IG — *Inscriptiones Graecae* (Berlin 1877–   )
IJ — R. Dareste, B. Haussoullier, and Th. Reinach, *Recueil des inscriptions juridiques grecques* (2 vols., Paris 1891–1904)

Jahreshefte — Oesterreichisches archäologisches Institut in Wien, *Jahreshefte*
Jahrbücher KP — *Jahrbücher für klassische Philologie*
JEBH — *Journal of Economic and Business History*
JJP — *Journal of Juristic Papyrology*
JNES — *Journal of Near Eastern Studies*

KVJ — *Kritische Vierteljahresschrift für Gesetzgebung und Rechtswissenschaft*

Liddell-and-Scott — H. G. Liddell and R. Scott, *Greek-English Lexicon*, rev. ed. by H. S. Jones and R. McKenzie (2 vols., Oxford 1940)
LQR — *Law Quarterly Review*

M — C. Michel, *Recueil des inscriptions grecques* (Paris 1896–1912)
MB — *Musée belge*
Milet — T. Wiegand *et al.*, *Milet. Ergebnisse der Ausgrabungen seit 1899* (Berlin 1906–   )
Münchener Beiträge — *Münchener Beiträge zur Papyrusforschung und antiken Rechtsgeschichte*

OGIS — W. Dittenberger, ed., *Orientis Graeci inscriptiones selectae* (2 vols., Leipzig 1903–5)

P. A.-M. Desrousseaux — P. Jouguet, "Quittance de prêt en forme de contrat à six témoins datant de l'an 7 de Ptolemée Aulète," *Mélanges offerts à A.-M. Desrousseaux...* (Paris 1937) 229–38
P. Fay. — B. P. Grenfell *et al.*, ed., *Fayûm Towns and Their Papyri* (London 1900)
PhW — *Berliner philologische Wochenschrift*
P.Oxy. — B. P. Grenfell *et al.*, ed., *Oxyrhynchus Papyri* (London 1898–)
PWRE — Georg Wissowa, W. Kroll, *et al.*, ed., *Paulys Real-Enzyklopädie der klassischen Altertumswissenschaft* (Stuttgart 1894–)

RB — *Revue belge de philologie et d'histoire*
REG — *Revue des études grecques*
RFC — *Rivista di filologia e d'istruzione classica*
RhM — *Rheinisches Museum für Philologie*

RIDA — *Revue internationale des droits de l'antiquité*
RP — *Revue de philologie, de littérature et d'histoire anciennes*

SD — *Studia et documenta historiae et iuris*
SEG — *Supplementum epigraphicum graecum* (Leiden 1923–)
SIFC — *Studi italiani di filologia classica*
Sitz. — *Sitzungsberichte* (followed by the name of the city in which the Academy is located; the Philologisch-historische Klasse is always meant if the Academy is so divided)
Syll. — W. Dittenberger, ed., *Sylloge inscriptionum graecarum*, 3rd ed. by F. Hiller von Gaertringen (4 vols., Leipzig 1915–24)

TAPA — American Philological Association, *Transactions*

Vierteljahrschrift — *Vierteljahrschrift für Sozial- und Wirtschaftsgeschichte*

WS — *Wiener Studien*

ZSS — *Zeitschrift der Savigny-Stiftung für Rechtsgeschichte, Romanistische Abteilung*
ZVR — *Zeitschrift für vergleichende Rechtswissenschaft*

BIBLIOGRAPHY

(The following list is not intended to be complete. It is rather a list of books and articles cited several times by short title. The few reviews included appear immediately following the books to which they pertain.)

Accame, Silvio, *La lega ateniese del secolo IV A.C.* [*Studi pubblicati dal R. Istituto italiano per la storia antica* 2 (Rome 1941)].

American Law Institute, *Restatement of the Law of Security* (St. Paul 1941).

Andreades, A., *A History of Greek Public Finance*, transl. by C. N. Brown (only vol. I published, Cambridge, Mass., 1933).

Arangio-Ruiz, V., and Olivieri, A., ed., *Inscriptiones Graecae Siciliae et infimae Italiae ad ius pertinentes* (Milan 1925).

———— review by O. Gradenwitz, ZSS 47 (1927) 493–97.

———— review by K. Latte, *Gnomon* 3 (1927) 370–79.

Ardaillon, E., *Les mines du Laurion dans l'antiquité* [*Bibl.Éc.fr.* 77 (Paris 1897)].

Beauchet, L., *Histoire du droit privé de la République athénienne* (2 vols. in 4, Paris 1897).

Billeter, G., *Geschichte des Zinsfußes im griechisch-römischen Altertum bis auf Justinian* (Leipzig 1898).

Blass, F., *Die attische Beredsamkeit* (2 ed., 3 vols. in 4, Leipzig 1887–98).

Bolla, Sibylle von, "Pacht," PWRE 18,4 (1949) 2439–83.

Bruck, E. F., *Die Schenkung auf den Todesfall im griechischen und römischen Recht* [*Studien zur Erläuterung des bürgerlichen Rechts* 31 (only vol. I published, Breslau 1909)].

Burgkhardt, R., *De causa orationis adversus Spudiam Demosthenicae (XLI)* (diss. Leipzig 1908).

Busolt, Georg, *Griechische Staatskunde* (2 vols., vol. 2 ed. by H. Swoboda, Munich 1920–26).

Calhoun, G. M., *The Business Life of Ancient Athens* (Chicago 1926).

Clerc, M., *Les métèques athéniens* [*Bibl.Éc.fr.* 64 (Paris 1893)].

Crosby, Margaret, "The Leases of the Laureion Mines," *Hesperia* 19 (1950) 189–312.

Dow, S., and Travis, A. H., "Demetrios of Phaleron and His Lawgiving," *Hesperia* 12 (1943) 144–65.

Ehrenberg, V., *The People of Aristophanes. A Sociology of Old Attic Comedy* (2 ed., Cambridge, Mass., 1951).

Endenburg, P. J. T., *Koinoonia, En Gemeenschap van Zaken bij de Grieken in den klassieken Tijd* (Amsterdam 1937).

Erdmann, W., *Die Ehe im alten Griechenland* [*Münchener Beiträge* 20 (Munich 1934)].

Ferguson, W. S., "The Attic Orgeones," *Harvard Theological Review* 37 (1944) 61–140.

————, *Hellenistic Athens* (London 1911).

————, "The Laws of Demetrius of Phalerum and Their Guardians," *Klio* 11 (1911) 265–76.

————, "Orgeonika," *Hesperia* Supp. 8 (1949) 130–63.

Feyel, M., *Contribution à l'épigraphie béotienne* [*Publ. de la Fac. des Lettres de l'Univ. de Strasbourg* 95 (Paris 1943)].

————, *Polybe et l'histoire de Béotie au IIIe siècle avant notre ère* [*Bibl. Éc.fr.* 152 (Paris 1942)].

Gernet, L., "Sur les actions commerciales en droit athénien," *REG* 51 (1938) 1–44.

Glotz, G., *Le travail dans la Grèce ancienne* (Paris 1920).

Goldschmidt, L., "Inhaber-, Order- und exekutorische Urkunden im classischen Alterthum," *ZSS* 10 (1889) 352–96.

Gomme, A. W., *The Population of Athens in the Fifth and Fourth Centuries B.C.* (Oxford 1933).

Guenter, E., *Die Sicherungsübereignung im griechischen Rechte* (diss. Königsberg 1914).

Guiraud, Paul, *La propriété foncière en Grèce jusqu'à la conquête romaine* (Paris 1893).

Haussoullier, B., *La vie municipale en Attique* [*Bibl.Éc.fr.* 38 (Paris 1884)].

Hazeltine, H. D., "The Roman *fiducia cum creditore* and the English Mortgage. A Comparison, with Special Reference to the Right of Redemption" [General Preface to Turner, *Equity of Redemption*].

Heichelheim, F. M., *Wirtschaftsgeschichte des Altertums* (2 vols., Leiden 1938).

Hellebrand, W., "'Ωνή," *PWRE* 18 (1939) 417–37.

Hermann, K. F., *Lehrbuch der griechischen Rechtsalterthümer* (4 ed., by Th. Thalheim, Freiburg and Tübingen 1895).

Hitzig, H. F., *Das griechische Pfandrecht* (Munich 1895)

Jardé, A., *Les céréales dans l'antiquité grecque* [only vol. 1 published, *Bibl.Éc.fr.* 130 (Paris 1925)].

Kahrstedt, U., *Studien zum öffentlichen Recht Athens* I. *Staatsgebiet und Staatsangehörige in Athen* (Stuttgart and Berlin 1934).

Kamps, W:, "Une affaire de fraude successorale à Athènes," *Annuaire de l'Inst. de phil. et d'histoire orientales et slaves* 6 (1938) 15–27.

Kaser, M., "Der altgriechische Eigentumsschutz," ZSS 64 (1944) 134–205.

Kent, J. H., "The Temple Estates of Delos, Rheneia, and Mykonos," *Hesperia* 17 (1948) 243–338.

Korver, Jan, *De Terminologie van het Crediet-Wezen in het Grieksch* (Amsterdam 1934).

Latte, K., *Heiliges Recht* (Tübingen 1920).

Lipsius, J. H., *Das attische Recht und Rechtsverfahren* (3 vols., Leipzig 1905–15).

Maitland, F. W., *Equity*, rev. ed. by John Brunyate (Cambridge, Eng., 1947).

Manigk, A., "Hyperocha," PWRE 9 (1916) 292–321.

Mickwitz, G., "Economic Rationalism in Graeco-Roman Agriculture," *English Historical Review* 52 (1937) 577–89.

————, "Zum Problem der Betriebsführung in der antiken Wirtschaft," *Vierteljahrschrift* 32 (1939) 1–25.

Mitteis, L., *Reichsrecht und Volksrecht* (Leipzig 1891).

Münscher, K., translation of Isaeus, ZVR 37 (1919) 32–328.

Nussbaum, A., *Lehrbuch des deutschen Hypothekenwesens nebst einer Einführung in das allgemeine Grundbuchrecht* (2 ed., Tübingen 1921).

Oertel, F., "Zur Frage der attischen Großindustrie," RhM 79 (1930) 230–52.

Paley, F. A., and Sandys, J. E., ed., *Select Private Orations of Demosthenes* (3 ed., 2 vols., Cambridge, Eng., 1896–98).

Paoli, U. E., "La 'datio in solutum' nel diritto attico," SIFC 10 (1933) 181–212.

————, "Ipoteca e ἀποτίμημα nel diritto attico," *Studi di diritto attico* (Florence 1930) 141–94.

————, review by V. Arangio-Ruiz, AG 107 (1932) 246–51.

————, review by G. LaPira, BIDR 41 (1933) 305–20.

————, "Sul diritto pignoratizio attico," AG 108 (1932) 161–78.

Pappulias, D. P., Ἡ ἐμπράγματος ἀσφάλεια κατὰ τὸ ἑλληνικὸν καὶτὸ ῥωμαϊκὸν δίκαιον (only vol. 1 published, Leipzig 1909).

Partsch, J., *Griechisches Bürgschaftsrecht* (only vol. 1 published, Leipzig and Berlin 1909).

Pöhlmann, R., *Geschichte der sozialen Frage und des Sozialismus in der antiken Welt* (2 vols., 3 ed. by F. Oertel, Munich 1925).

Poland, Franz, *Geschichte des griechischen Vereinswesens* (Leipzig 1909).

Premerstein, A. von, "Phratern-Verbände auf einem attischen Hypothekenstein," *Athen.Mitt.* 35 (1910) 103–17.

Pringsheim, Fritz, *The Greek Law of Sale* (Weimar 1950).

————, *Der Kauf mit fremdem Geld* (Leipzig 1916).

Pritchett, W. K., and Meritt, B. D., *The Chronology of Hellenistic Athens* (Cambridge, Mass., 1940).

Raape, Leo, *Der Verfall des griechischen Pfandes, besonders des griechisch-ägyptischen* (Halle 1912).

Rabel, E., "Nachgeformte Rechtsgeschäfte," ZSS 27 (1906) 290–335; 28 (1907) 311–79.

————, *Die Verfügungsbeschränkungen des Verpfänders, besonders in den Papyri* (Leipzig 1909).

Reinach, T., "Eranos," *Dar.-Saglio* II,1 (1892) 805–8.

Rostovtzeff, M., *The Social & Economic History of the Hellenistic World* (3 vols., Oxford 1941).

Ruppel, W., "Zur Verfassung und Verwaltung der amorginischen Städte," *Klio* 21 (1927) 313–39.

Salin, E., "Der 'Sozialismus' in Hellas," *Bilder und Studien aus drei Jahrtausenden (Gothein Festgabe)* (Munich and Leipzig 1923) 15–59.

San Nicolò, M., *Aegyptisches Vereinswesen zur Zeit der Ptolemäer und Römer* [*Münchener Beiträge* 1–2 (Munich 1913–15)].

Schodorf, K., *Beiträge zur genaueren Kenntnis der attischen Gerichtssprache aus den zehn Rednern* (Würzburg 1904).

Schulthess, O., "Μίσθωσις," PWRE 15 (1932) 2095–2129.

————, "Συνθήκη," PWRE Supp. 6 (1935) 1158–68.

————, *Vormundschaft nach attischem Recht* (Freiburg 1886).

Schwahn, W., *Demosthenes gegen Aphobos. Ein Beitrag zur Geschichte der griechischen Wirtschaft* (Leipzig and Berlin 1929).

Simonetos, G., "Das Verhältnis von Kauf und Übereignung im altgriechischen Recht," *Festschrift Paul Koschaker* 3 (3 vols., Weimar 1939) 172–98.

Szanto, E., "Hypothek und Scheinkauf im griechischen Rechte," WS 9 (1897) 279–96, as republished in his *Ausgewählte Abhandlungen* (Tübingen 1906) 74–92.

Taubenschlag, Raphael, *The Law of Greco-Roman Egypt in the Light of the Papyri, 332 B.C.–640 A.D.* (2 vols., New York and Warsaw, 1944–49).

Thalheim, T., "Ὅροι," PWRE 8 (1913) 2414–16.

20*

Thiel, J. H., "Iets over retributies en burenrecht in de Grieksche Oudheid," *Tijdschrift voor Rechtsgeschiedenis* 6 (1925) 222–35.
Turner, R. W., *The Equity of Redemption. Its Nature, History and Connection with Equitable Estates Generally* (Cambridge, Eng., 1931).

Wade-Gery, H. T., "Horos," *Mélanges Gustav Glotz* 2 (2 vols., Paris 1932)
877–87.
Weber, Max, "Agrarverhältnisse im Altertum," *HWB der Staatswissen-
schaften* 1 (3 ed., Jena 1909) 52–188, as republished in his *Gesam-
melte Aufsätze zur Sozial- und Wirtschaftsgeschichte* (Tübingen 1924)
1–288.
Weiss, Egon, *Griechisches Privatrecht* (only vol. 1 published, Leipzig 1923).
————, *Pfandrechtliche Untersuchungen* (2 vols., Weimar 1909–10).
————, "Tempelinschrift aus Dystos über Haftungsübernahme," *By-
zantinische Zeitschrift* 30 (1929/30) 638–40.
Westermann, W. L., "Sklaverei," PWRE Supp. 6 (1935) 894–1068.
————, "Two Studies in Athenian Manumission," JNES 5 (1946)
92–104.
Wigmore, J. H., "The Pledge-Idea: A Study in Comparative Legal
Ideas," *Harvard Law Review* 10 (1896/7) 321–50, 389–417; 11
(1897/8) 18–39.
Wilamowitz-Moellendorf, U., "Demotika der attischen Metoeken," *Her-
mes* 22 (1887) 107–28, 211–59.
Wilhelm, A., "Attische Pachturkunden," APF 11 (1935) 189–217.
Wolff, H. J., "Marriage Law and Family Organization in Ancient
Athens," *Traditio* 2 (1944) 43–95.
Woodhouse, W. J., *Solon the Liberator. A Study of the Agrarian Problem
in Attika in the Seventh Century* (London 1937).
Wyse, W., *The Speeches of Isaeus* (Cambridge, Eng., 1904).

Ziebarth, E., "Ἔρανος," PWRE 6 (1909) 328–30.
————, *Das griechische Vereinswesen* (Leipzig 1896).
————, "Hypothekinschrift aus Dystos," *Philologus* 83 (1928) 204–7.
————, "Neue attische Hypothekeninschriften," *Sitz. Berlin* (1897)
664–75.

INDEX OF SOURCES

(Page references are given solely to the notes unless a work
receives extended discussion in the text.)

LITERARY TEXTS

INSCRIPTIONS

A. *Horoi*

(The *horoi* in Appendix III are not included)

B. Other Inscriptions

PAPYRI AND PARCHMENT

LEXICA

LATIN WORKS

INDEX OF GREEK WORDS

GENERAL INDEX

(Page references are not given to the notes unless the discussion includes topics not taken up in the text on the particular page indicated).

GREEK HISTORY

AN ARNO PRESS COLLECTION

Aeschinis. **Aeschinis Orationes.** E Codicibus Partim Nunc Primum Excussis, Edidit Scholia ex Parte Inedita, Adiecit Ferdinandus Schultz. 1865.

Athenian Studies; Presented to William Scott Ferguson (*Harvard Studies in Classical Philology,* Supplement Vol. I). 1940.

Austin, R[eginald] P. **The Stoichedon Style in Greek Inscriptions.** 1938.

Berve, Helmut. **Das Alexanderreich:** Auf Prosopographischer Grundlage. Ersterband: Darstellung; Zweiterband: Prosopoghaphie. 1926. 2 volumes in one.

Croiset, Maurice. **Aristophanes and the Political Parties at Athens.** Translated by James Loeb. 1909.

Day, John. **An Economic History of Athens Under Roman Domination.** 1942.

Demosthenes. **Demosthenes,** Volumina VIII et IX: Scholia Graeca ex Codicibus Aucta et Emendata, ex recensione Gulielmi Dindorfii. 2 volumes. 1851.

Ehrenberg, Victor. **Aspects of the Ancient World:** Essays and Reviews. 1946.

Finley, Moses I. **Studies in Land and Credit in Ancient Athens, 500-200 B.C.:** The Horos Inscriptions. 1952.

Glotz, Gustave. **La Solidarité de la Famille dans le Droit Criminel en Grèce.** 1904.

Graindor, Paul, **Athènes Sous Hadrien.** 1934.

Grosmann, Gustav. **Politische Schlagwörter aus der Zeit des Peloponnesischen Krieges.** 1950.

Henderson, Bernard W. **The Great War Between Athens and Sparta.** 1927.

Herodotus. **Herodotus: The Fourth, Fifth, and Sixth Books.** With Introduction, Notes, Appendices, Indices, Maps by Reginald Walter Macan. 1895. 2 volumes in one.

Herodotus. **Herodotus: The Seventh, Eighth, and Ninth Books.** With Introduction, Text, Apparatus, Commentary, Appendices, Indices, Maps by Reginald Walter Macan. 1908. 3 volumes in two.

Jacoby, Felix. **Apollodors Chronik.** Eine Sammlung der Fragmente (*Philologische Untersuchungen*, Herausgegeben von A. Kiessling und U. v. Wilamowitz-Moellendorff. Sechzehntes Heft). 1902.

Jacoby, Felix. **Atthis:** The Local Chronicles of Ancient Athens. 1949.

Ledl, Artur. **Studien zur Alteren Athenischen Verfassungsgeschichte.** 1914.

Lesky, Albin. **Thalatta:** Der Weg der Griechen Zum Meer. 1947.

Ollier, Francois. **Le Mirage Spartiate.** Etude sur l'idéalisation de Sparte dans l'antiquité Greque de l'origine Jusqu'aux Cyniques and Etude sur l'idéalisation de Sparte dans l'antiquité Greque du Début de l'école Cynique Jusqu'à la Fin de la Cité. 1933/1934. 2 volumes in one.

Ryffel, Heinrich. ΜΕΤΑΒΟΛΗ ΠΟΛΙΤΕΙΩΝ Der Wandel der Staatsverfassungen (*Noctes Romanae.* Forschungen Uber die Kultur der Antike, Herausgegeben von Walter Wili, #2). 1949.

Thucydides. **Scholia in Thucydidem:** Ad Optimos Codices Collata, edidit Carolus Hude. 1927.

Toepffer, Iohannes. **Attische Genealogie.** 1889.

Tscherikower, V. **Die Hellenistischen Städtegründungen von Alexander dem Grossen bis auf die Römerzeit** (*Philologus*, Zeitschrift fur das Klassische Alterum, Herausgegeben von Albert Rehm. Supplementband XIX, Heft 1). 1927.

West, Allen Brown. **The History of the Chalcidic League** (*Bulletin of the University of Wisconsin*, No. 969, History Series, Vol. 4, No. 2). 1918.

Woodhouse, William J. **Aetolia:** Its Geography, Topography, and Antiquities. 1897.

Wüst, Fritz R. **Philipp II. von Makedonien und Griechenland in den Jahren von 346 bis 338** (*Münchener Historische Abhandlungen.* Erste Reihe: Allgemeine und Politische Geschichte, Herausgegeben von H. Günter, A. O. Meyer und K. A. v. Müller. 14, Heft). 1938.